1963

FIVE HUNDRED DAYS

1963

FIVE HUNDRED DAYS

—

History as Melodrama

John Lawton

Hodder & Stoughton
LONDON SYDNEY AUCKLAND

BRITISH LIBRARY CATALOGUING-IN-PUBLICATION DATA

Lawton, John
   1963: five hundred days: History as melodrama.
   I. Title
   909.82

   ISBN 0-340-50846-9

Published by Hodder and Stoughton,
a division of Hodder and Stoughton Ltd,
Mill Road, Dunton Green, Sevenoaks, Kent TN13 2YA.
Editorial Office: 47 Bedford Square, London WC1B 3DP.

Photoset by E.P.L. BookSet, Norwood, London.

Printed in Great Britain by
Mackays of Chatham PLC, Chatham, Kent.

for
David Rappaport
1951-1990

CONTENTS

"Auch die Kultur, die alle Welt bedekt,
hat auf den Teufel Sich erstrecht."
                    Goethe, *Faust*

INTRODUCTION

This is a book about a generation, as loosely defined as the year 1963 itself – loosely because the parts of a generation run at different speeds, politics runs a long way behind the arts and the front runners in politics will be ten or fifteen years older than that generation born largely between 1937 and 1947, which is most of my subject. I was in 1963 a watcher from the remotest sidelines. I took no part in anything I describe, and I hasten to add that this is not my generation, in the hope that such a disclaimer will keep me well clear of hagiography.

The year is loosely defined because in any sense other than one of strict chronology a year is no neater of definition than a decade. Who, after all, includes 1960, 1961 or 1962 in the cultural notion of 'the Sixties'? This book, therefore, concerns itself perversely with a 1963 that began on September 12th, 1962 and ended on February 7th, 1964. That is, between the arrest of John Vassall and the arrival of the Beatles in the USA – 514 days to be precise, but since precision looks a mess on a book jacket 500 it will have to be – five hundred days in which Britain saw certain old ways and forms fall apart and new ones arise, that enabled the British to seize centre stage in popular culture for the first time since the war.

As much as is possible I've gone back to first sources, and to first reactions, to the newspapers, documentaries and, where available, diaries of the day. What follows is partly oral history – if an interview was any good I tried to let it tell its story with little intervention from me. If the choice of interviewees looks idiosyncratic, there may be good reasons for this. I wanted to talk to those members of the loose 1937-47 generation who had been the shakers and movers in 1963. In some cases this was impossible – the Kennedys are dead, Lennon is dead. Among those who survive there are those who have no wish to say any more than they have already done about events that took place nearly thirty years ago – among whom I'd class Sean Connery and Paul McCartney. There are people who would only be interviewed off the record. There are also people I approached who said no. And there are also people whom, it could

1

be argued, I would have done well to approach, but whose previous interviews led me to the opposite conclusion. But finally the choice of who I did talk to was mine, and it has to be said that I stand by the idiosyncrasy – if Robert Kennedy were alive, if Martin Luther King were alive, I would still have chosen John Lewis as the person to talk to about the events of August 28th, if Lennon were alive, I'd still want Billy Kinsley's point of view on record next to Lennon's, and if Peter Cook had proved unavailable at the outset I might seriously have asked myself whether it was possible to write the book at all.

In most cases the central events presented themselves as the actions of a single day. The March on Washington, on August 28th, the Beatles' appearance at the London Palladium on November 5th, Wilson's White Heat speech on October 2nd, for example. With the first I worked up to the event, with the latter two around them. This entails some context setting. I cannot, after all, see any point to a history that emerges rootless, and one point of the book is to show that 1963 was a radical year in that Britain broke with the past. That said, it isn't a book wholly about Britain. The question I set out to answer was 'what in 1963 contained the making of the sixties?' – and that cannot be answered except with reference to the USA. If only in the repeated appearance of the Kennedys, the USA is a running thread, and, since the sixties foundered on the rock of Vietnam, it is inevitably the book's conclusion. Nor can I see any point to a history that presents the world of the past as unified, if only by a single tone of voice – what I've written might seem to veer between the deadly serious and the flip, the linear and the mosaic and I've no apology to make for that. I can only state that the subtitle was added after I'd read what I'd written, and reflects a conclusion rather than an intention.

A common, corny opening for works of recent history is to refer to 'a world we have lost' and then to dribble down into nostalgia – the world as it was in 1962 is not a world we lost, it's one we threw away.

CHAPTER ONE

CAT AMONG THE PYGMIES

On September 12th, 1962 a minor Admiralty civil servant was arrested by Special Branch detectives on suspicion of spying for the Soviet Union. His name was William John Christopher Vassall, and the consequences of his confession and trial rumbled on for more than a year, creating an antagonism between the press and the then Prime Minister, Harold Macmillan, that shadowed the last months of his government (eventually destroying the credibility of his chosen successor) and set much of the 'tone' for 1963 – a tone of moral reprimand and hypocrisy, of liberation and prurience.

Vassall had been working for the Russians since 1955. Posted to Moscow as a clerk in the Naval Intelligence section of the embassy the year before, he had proved an easy target for recruitment. John Vassall was a homosexual. In 1962, despite the recommendations of the Wolfenden report, homosexuality was still illegal – it was variously held to be perverted, pathological, ungodly and criminal, and the English, failing to appreciate the partiality of the French term, *le vice anglais*, were particularly strident on the matter. As Vassall himself wrote: "It is a secret world, a kind of masonic society to protect one against mankind because they can be so cruel – especially in the Anglo-Saxon world."[1]

It was probably this combination of fear and loneliness that identified Vassall to the Russians as a homosexual and hence as a likely subject for blackmail. They exploited his loneliness through their plant inside the embassy – a Polish clerk in the administrative section, named Sigmund Mikhailski – who offered 'friendship', and then played on his fear by a tactic grotesquely nicknamed 'son et lumière'. Mikhailski's friendship led Vassall into the social life outside the embassy. He made more friends among the Russians, he attended their parties, and one night in March 1955 he went with a small group to a Moscow flat where a man in the uniform of a military officer (Vassall is no more precise than this) waited to meet him. Left alone in the bedroom Vassall and the Russian officer made love. When the lights went up, his 'friends' told him to get dressed and showed him photographs they had taken of him at a party. He was naked and twirled a pair of underpants from one finger. He had no recollection of doing anything like this, and it began to dawn on him that at some point he must have been drugged. The worst was still to come. They then produced photographs of Vassall and the officer, showing them engaged in oral and anal sex, and Vassall knew he was trapped: "I was told that I had committed a grave offence under Soviet law and that I was in serious trouble with the state."[2]

And he would not be allowed to leave the Soviet Union if he told his superiors at the embassy, although this could scarcely have been uppermost in Vassall's mind, since he would hardly have expected a sympathetic response from the British, who were still recoiling from the defection of Guy Burgess, also a homosexual – nor was it what the Russians had in mind. What they wanted was a spy in England.

After Vassall's return home in June 1956 he passed photographs of Admiralty documents back to the Russians via his contact, 'Gregory', until his arrest. In 1959 Vassall was promoted to become Assistant Private Secretary to the Civil Lord of the Admiralty, Thomas Galbraith, MP for the Glasgow constituency of Hillhead, son and heir of Lord Strathclyde – and at the end of that year he transferred to the Military Branch of the Admiralty, where he was still employed at the time of his arrest.

As APS to the Civil Lord, Vassall received a salary of about £700 per annum. His work for the Russians roughly doubled this, and, however reluctant a spy, he proved a willing and conspicuous consumer. His contact urged on him that it would be very convenient if he lived alone, and Vassall, after considering the delights of St John's Wood, took a flat in Dolphin Square, Pimlico in the autumn of 1958. At an annual cost of about £500, it was clearly beyond his means, and this obvious fact seems to have aroused no curiosity at the Admiralty, even though they had, by this time, cottoned on to Mikhailski and might therefore have been expected to scrutinise those former embassy employees known to have associated with him. They might also have been suspicious of Vassall's holidays. In 1959 he holidayed in Capri and Egypt at a time when most people still went to Clacton or Bognor. If that was not enough, they might have noticed the frequency with which Vassall changed his suits. The day after his trial the *Daily Mail* estimated the contents of Vassall's wardrobe as "nineteen suits, one hundred ties, twelve pairs of shoes, three dozen shirts", and for good measure added that he was known to dine regularly at Simpson's.[3] In his oblique way Vassall illustrated one of the political maxims of the late nineteen-fifties – he'd never had it so good.

4

In the Summer of 1962 the Security Service was forced to act. Soviet defector Anatoli Golnitsin told them what should have been obvious – there was a spy in the Admiralty. Once they looked, Vassall's lifestyle betrayed him and his arrest was inevitable. From the beginning Vassall had no other intention but to confess, but he does seem to have entertained the illusion that once he'd done this he would somehow miraculously be spared prosecution – the inconceivable innocence of the victim. Whilst he awaited trial two far-reaching disclosures took place. A search of the Dolphin Square flat revealed not only film of secret Navy documents, but a collection of private letters and postcards. Somehow these fell into the hands of the *Sunday Pictorial*, which offered Vassall a sum variously estimated at between £5000 and £7000 for his 'own story'. And at some point Vassall let it be known to a fellow prisoner he had written to a high Admiralty official before his selection for the service, which might imply that someone had 'sponsored' Vassall. Once the story got out it was quickly inflated into the notion that there were other, vulnerable, homosexuals within the Civil Service, some of them in very senior positions. Both of these factors became contentious as soon as the trial ended on October 22nd. The serialisation of Vassall's 'story' duly began in the *Sunday Pictorial* on October 28th (Vassall had accepted the *Pictorial*, in preference to the *News of the World*, and did so on the grounds that he was ineligible for legal aid, and without the money would find it impossible to afford the services of a 'top counsel'), and on the following Sunday contained the allegation of homosexuals in high places. This became a much repeated item in the press generally, and there began a wave of rumour and innuendo about cover-ups and revelations yet to come. The *Daily Express* even suggested that the First Lord of the Admiralty had been warned of the presence of a spy as long ago as the summer of 1961, during the Portland spy case. Macmillan appointed a committee of enquiry, under Sir Charles Cunningham, the Permanent Secretary to the Home Office. This, since it was a civil servant enquiring into misdemeanours within the civil service, satisfied none of the critics and within a week of Cunningham's appointment rumours were rife that Labour would call for the resignations of both the First Lord (Lord Carrington) and the former Civil Lord, Galbraith, now Under-Secretary of State at the Scottish Office. Galbraith had been quoted in the *Mail* as saying of Vassall "he seemed to have a screw loose", but that he was "a decent enough chap".[4]

In its tabloid wisdom the *Sunday Pictorial*[5] had seen fit to send copies of the Vassall letters to the government (quite why they should think they did not already possess them, I can only guess) and to the deputy leader of the Opposition, George Brown. Brown took the earliest opportunity to raise the matter in the Commons. At the end of the debate on the Queen's speech (Parliament having only just returned from its summer recess and the round of party conferences) Brown spoke up saying, "We cannot leave the Vassall case where it is," and announcing that he had seen letters which indicated "a degree of ministerial responsibility that goes far beyond the ordinary business of a Minister". The vagueness of this would be only partially clarified by the events of the next day (November 6th) when the Shadow Cabinet met to discuss the issue of the Vassall letters. They revealed, it was claimed, good relationships between Vassall and high Admiralty officials. There was also a holiday postcard from someone described only as a leading figure, a term which did nothing to conceal the identity of Galbraith. The pressure for a stronger enquiry was mounting, and Brown took the opportunity to remind Macmillan that he had tried to raise the matter privately with him and had been brushed aside. He would have no choice now but to go public and surprise no one by naming the leading figure involved. Macmillan responded by saying he would broaden the enquiry's base by at least consulting the high court judge, Lord Radcliffe, who had reviewed security after the Portland and Blake spy cases,[6] and by authorising publication of the letters in question.

In another age this might have been an end to the matter. Half a dozen letters from Galbraith showed him behaving with courtesy towards a junior, and maintaining a sense of distance and formality. All the letters begin either 'Dear Vassall' or 'My Dear Vassall' and are signed 'Yours Sincerely T. G. D. Galbraith'. The holiday postcard ends simply with the initials T. G. D. G. Nothing in this trivial correspondence revealed any impropriety in the relationship between Vassall and Galbraith, nor did it bear out the claims of George Brown on the issue of 'ministerial responsibility'. Any attempt to infer a closer relationship between Vassall and Galbraith would be pure hype – but then both the press and the Labour Party were hyping. The *Mail* made much of Vassall's enquiry as to his prospects of a job at Downing Street, but Galbraith's response had been simply to tell him he was wasting his time.

Macmillan announced to the house that he was releasing an interim report by the Cunningham Committee in order to avoid a situation in which " . . . perhaps six weeks or two months of the committee's work would have gone by with these terrible imputations made and no method of repudiating them."

6

Yet on the same day Galbraith handed his resignation to Macmillan, and Macmillan accepted. It was an astonishing move on the part of both minister and leader. The Cunningham Committee had not yet reported in full (and even in its interim form exonerated Galbraith completely), and this action only deepened the crisis. Now Conservative voices were added to the Commons clamour for a stronger, more authoritative enquiry. Dame Irene Ward spoke from the Tory back benches to say that she regretted that Galbraith had felt it necessary to resign, but also regretted that Macmillan had accepted. Rumour spiralled from speculation on the 'familiarity' between Vassall and Galbraith to suggestions that they had been planning a holiday together, to the height of the fantastic as Macmillan himself recorded in his memoirs: "A journalist actually informed a Conservative MP that Mr Galbraith and Vassall had planned to escape to Russia."[7]

Meanwhile the continuing serial of Vassall's 'memoirs' can only have fuelled the flames. On November 11th he wrote that his time as private secretary to Galbraith had been "the most pleasant period I had in my job". With a faint touch of snobbery he plays up his acquaintance with Galbraith and his wife, recalling how much he enjoyed the trips to Galbraith's house in Scotland, when he had delivered ministerial papers, and makes mention of a visit by Mr and Mrs Galbraith to the flat in Dolphin Square. It seems highly improbable that Vassall himself wrote these memoirs, in any other sense than that he supplied the material, and the obvious assumption is that the particular emphases of the serialisation are those the newspaper wished to create.

Macmillan now had plenty of cause to regret that he had not instituted a full tribunal sooner, and forty-eight hours later it was announced that Lord Radcliffe would head a formal tribunal. The following day in the Commons saw the Prime Minister in a mood of bitter indignation and near-paranoia about the activities of the press. He justified the tribunal not on the grounds of security, but in order to deal with the flurry of innuendo. Only a tribunal could restore public confidence, he declared, and the proof would be guilt – whether it be guilt of the government and Civil Service or of "those who pose as protectors of the public . . . [whilst] trying to destroy private reputations from motives of either spite or gain." With this clear target in mind the tribunal would be armed with unprecedented power to subpoena, to question on oath, to punish contempt and to punish perjury. He lashed out at the newspapers . . . "Fleet Street has generated an atmosphere around the Vassall case worthy of Titus Oates or Senator McCarthy" . . . "a dark cloud of suspicion and innuendo" . . . and at the deputy leader of the Opposition whose claims he rightly dismissed as equally nebulous . . . "obscure and not to have any meaning." He singled out the *Sunday Pictorial* for a particularly sarcastic crack. Doubtless they had published Vassall's story not from any motives of profit but out of "a deep sense of public duty".

His attack on Brown, despite the fact that Gaitskell himself had been disturbed by the vigour of his deputy's persistence, continued to rebound on him, and winding up for the Opposition Patrick Gordon Walker said that the Prime Minister had "come perilously near to alleging that Mr Brown had been at the bottom of a sort of rolling up of rumour". In answer to a final question from Gordon-Walker as to whether journalists would be compelled to reveal their sources to the Radcliffe tribunal, the Attorney-General Sir John Hobson said that that would be a matter for the tribunal – an answer that gave no hint of what was to come.

Brown appeared on television the same night and, despite the truth of Macmillan's criticism, told the nation (or whatever portion of it listened to him) that the government was sidestepping the issue by trying to shift it all onto him – a view in which he was supported by the *New Statesman* of November 16th: "He [Macmillan] behaved in the Commons last Wednesday as if he conceived the function of the tribunal not so much as to indict culpable officials, as to place Mr Brown and certain popular newspapers in the dock."

The *Statesman*'s anonymous author ended his piece with a prophetic warning to the members of the tribunal "to avoid the Prime Minister's political trap".[8] Macmillan himself seemed to be experiencing moods of paranoia tinged with complacency, and complacency shot through with paranoia, as he recorded in his diary: "In a curious way, I may have gained by this incident, as it has helped to re-establish my ascendancy over the House of Commons."[9]

I cannot help wondering if his grip on reality had slipped completely. There is something of cloud-cuckoo-land in the next chapter of this curious saga.

On the same Wednesday evening that Macmillan had addressed the Commons, the Granada TV programme *What The Papers Say* had been hosted by Bernard Levin, the *Daily Mail* theatre critic, and, since the week's news had been preoccupied with the Vassall case, it was naturally mentioned in his commentary. By the Friday of that week it had been inflated into an issue of sufficient importance to be discussed in the House of Commons. Had Mr Levin been in breach of the sub judice rules governing press reports which the announcement of the Radcliffe tribunal carried with it? From what moment precisely had the matter been sub judice? It was decided that the Vassall case had been sub judice since ten o'clock on the Wednesday evening. Levin's broadcast had begun at five to eleven. The Speaker subsequently requested a copy of the text of *What The Papers Say*, and twenty-four hours to consider whether, by a margin of fifty-five minutes, Levin had broken the rules. At this point it must have been clear to many people that the Prime Minister's exaggerated fear of the press had been passed on to other members of his party.

Many, many weeks would pass before the Radcliffe tribunal reported (Vassall himself was still being questioned as late as February 1963), but on March 7th, 1963 Macmillan's resentment of the press treatment of his ministers finally found its target. Questioned by the tribunal as to the sources of their stories, Brendan Mulholland of the *Daily Mail* and Reginald Foster of the *Daily Sketch* refused to answer and were imprisoned for contempt, receiving six months and three months respectively. Bernard Levin himself wrote of the hearings: "The press witnesses cut, almost without exception, a poor figure, as, one after the other, they turned out to have got most of what they printed by taking previously printed articles and repeating them with embellishments."[10]

Mulholland had declined to name his source for a story stating that Vassall's colleagues had nicknamed him Auntie, and similarly would not say who had told him that a typist at the Admiralty had noticed Vassall's elevated standard of living and had expressed the view, beforehand, that no one could live in such a manner "honestly" and hence had formed the view that Vassall had somehow avoided a full vetting. Foster had guarded his source on the story of Vassall buying women's clothing in West End shops. Once the detail is known it all looks to be a fuss about nothing, but great principles were at issue. The jailing of a journalist for contempt in this way was almost without precedent – the only other case being as long ago as 1888, when a forged letter, purporting to be from the Irish leader Charles Parnell, appeared in *The Times*.

What followed was a predictable display of solidarity in outrage – something which Macmillan never understood – in which all major papers virtually declared war on the Prime Minister . . .

The *Daily Mail* warned that "a formidable attack may soon be mounted on the right of free speech" and ended a leader on the now familiar note of "the price of liberty is eternal vigilance."

The *Guardian* (more level-headed than most on this matter) stressed that secrecy was not so much a right as a duty "except when the interests of society demand disclosure", but then added that it was for the journalist to judge such interests for himself.

The *Daily Sketch*: "Such is the path to dictatorship."[11]

The Times rose to the eloquence of: "The techniques of power, of political manipulation, of the predatoriness of officialdom become even more insidiously efficient."

Mulholland himself, certain of his cause, evoked a catch-all populism: "The milkman, the grocer, the man who services my car, and the local vicar all understand and agree. Even my mother-in-law agrees."

And in the *Daily Mirror* Cassandra wailed that the government had managed to jail two journalists, but "only one pervert spy".

As one who heard their words as well as reading them put it: "The extravagant bitterness and self-dramatisation of many journalists knew no bounds. The breach between Mr Macmillan and much of the popular press was complete; and the 'revenge' they were so eagerly looking for was already close at hand."[12]

In parliament the initiative seems to have slipped from the front benches to the back. The new Labour leader, Harold Wilson (Hugh Gaitskell had died in January 1963), preferred to wait for the Radcliffe Report, saying that he would change the law when he became Prime Minister, and in the absence of any firm lead from the top George Thomson, Manny Shinwell, Dingle Foot, Tom Driberg, Sir George Benson, George Darling, Marcus Lipton and Dick Taverne all put their names to a motion calling for the sentences to be remitted. Desmond Clough had been sentenced for his refusal to name his source before either Foster or Mulholland, but had had the term remitted, so there was ample precedent. Eventually the Vassall case and the sentencing of the two journalists was debated, without the desired result, on March 21st. But now there were bigger fish. George Wigg and Barbara Castle took the occasion at the end of the debate to ask the Home Secretary, Henry Brooke, to deny rumours concerning Christine Keeler and a "member of the Government front bench", or to set up a select committee to investigate the affair. Revenge was indeed close at hand.

By a wonderfully, perhaps carefully timed coincidence the Foreign Office chose March 7th to reveal that one Ivor Rowsell had been brought back from the Moscow embassy, after he had reported a blackmail attempt by Russian agents. A spokesman said, "Mr Rowsell was put in a position whence the Russians thought they might be able to intimidate him. It has happened before." Of course it had, but what had the FO learnt from their recent experiences? They had introduced a rule that any member of the staff having associations with a member of the *opposite* sex would be sent home at twenty-four hours' notice.

It remains to be asked why so many of the principal players in this drama of the absurd behaved so oddly. Macmillan's acceptance of Galbraith's resignation was a foolish error of judgment. That Galbraith offered to resign was hardly surprising – it is, after all, typical of his class to defend their impugned honour in this ostrich-like way. In his memoirs Macmillan records that he was reluctant to let Galbraith resign, but adds that Galbraith had been insistent and had wanted the necessary freedom from office to sue those who had libelled him – yet Galbraith sued no one. Throughout, Macmillan's attitude to the press had been one of incredulous naivety. To have instituted a tribunal might satisfy the demands of the Opposition, but the wide-ranging powers he gave to that tribunal only made him more enemies – and he learnt late in his career not only how inventive the newspapers could be in their taste for fiction, but also how persistent and vindictive.

The role of George Brown is odder still. True, he had been a thorn in Macmillan's side at the time of the enquiry into the Portland case, and this alone would explain why the *Sunday Pictorial* had singled him out as the recipient of their package of letters – but it doesn't explain why he made so much out of something so transparently innocent. A look at the calendar is helpful at this point – on the last day of October 1962, the first day of the new parliament, Harold Wilson announced his candidature for the deputy leadership of the Labour Party – the election would be on the November 8th. Wilson commanded a sizeable share of the vote and there was talk within the party of a large body of abstainers. Could Brown be certain of winning? Wilson had managed eighty-odd votes against Gaitskell himself in 1960. During the party conference at Brighton earlier in October Brown had taken several opportunities either to distance himself from Gaitskell or to reinforce the image of his own independence. He had openly criticised Gaitskell for his opposition to the Common Market and had attempted to push through a measure aimed at tightening the proscription rules on party membership. He had even come close, in his own terms, to heresy when he cited the example of Bevan (his left-wing predecessor as deputy leader, who had died in 1960) as support for his case that the leader and the deputy need not always agree. If he was this concerned about campaigning for his own image, since it governed his prospects in the imminent election, it must have seemed to him like a ready-made platform when the *Sunday Pictorial* handed him the Galbraith letters, with which he tried to make parliamentary hay at the end of the Queen's speech debate only two days before the deputy-leadership vote.[13] Reflecting on his punitive eighteen-year sentence,[14] and bemoaning his fate, Vassall described himself as "a pygmy among spies". Brown and the British press had been playing cat among the pygmies for a month.

Lastly – why, when John Vassall was alleged to have implied the existence of a number of potentially vulnerable homosexuals in high places, did no one ask (in public at least) how he knew this? Why was this allegation received so credulously? It is hardly likely that his position as an executive grade civil servant could have given him a ready introduction to the private lives of his lords and masters. Yet he found plenty of people willing to believe that the 'masonic society' was more than a metaphor – more the cornerstone of a network homosexual conspiracy against the Anglo-Saxon way of life. This willing suspension of disbelief stemmed less from any deep rooted fear that the Soviet Union had the British Civil Service stitched up, rather than that homosexuals had. The *News of the World* was not untypical in its queerbashing when it wrote of Vassall that he was sick – a stock in trade prejudice of the times – and added "men like Vassall don't want to be cured".[15]

In many ways this shabby affair coloured the waning moon of Macmillan's government. In 1963 another sex scandal would be debated by politicians who, with their eyes fixed firmly on their party image, used a moral issue to disguise a matter of national security and a matter of national security to disguise a moral issue. The press, whilst more cautious both of libel and contempt, would indulge in a year-long binge of salaciousness and prurience, and would have their revenge in spades. There is truth in Larkin's rueful assertion that sex began in 1963. Until it was displaced by assassination, sex was the topic of the year – and I would not be at all surprised to find that the Chinese calendar records 1963 as the Year of the Prurient Toad.

If the Vassall case was a victory for the Establishment – over the press and the Opposition, if not over any issue that might be represented by Vassall and his freedom of sexual preference – then it was a pyrrhic victory, and their last victory. In wider terms the case of John Vassall pointed up the necessity for reform of our antiquated law against homosexuality, but at the same time it can hardly have advanced the cause. As background to all this, the last week of October had seen the world on the edge as Kennedy and Khrushchev bluffed and double-bluffed each other in the Atlantic over Cuba and the ship-loads of missiles the Soviet Union was installing there. It is the one time I can recall when you could meet people who seriously thought the world was about to end. Far from claiming this as a distraction, the Prime Minister recorded that he felt the Cuban Missile Crisis, "so strangely is the human brain constituted",[16] to be the lesser worry. Once the waters had calmed, the Americans found that once again they had good reason to distrust the security of their closest ally, and that they could add the name of Vassall to the long list of Fuchs, Burgess, Maclean, Kroger, Lonsdale and Blake. While Kennedy and Khrushchev had been playing brinkmanship, Macmillan and Brown had been extracting sunbeams from cucumbers.

§

Early on in the debate the Minister of Aviation, former Chancellor Peter Thorneycroft, had fielded a question, as to why no one had spotted Vassall's conspicuous consumption, with a joke that was worthy of Macmillan himself on any other matter. "How many of us are living beyond our incomes?" he quipped, doubtless to the amusement of his own backbenchers. For once a chancellor spoke for the nation.

CHAPTER TWO

THAT CRIPPS FEELING[1]

"Indeed let's be frank about it; *some* of our people have never
had it so good."   Harold Macmillan, July 20th, 1957[2]

"Workington's slums are as horrifying as any in the country . . .
The children wear shoes, which they might not have done thirty
years ago: but their parents hardly know what affluence means."
                    Henry Fairlie, *Sunday Times*, January 24th, 1963

It will sound strange if I say that 1963 marked the break with the
nineteen-thirties, but in image and to a significant degree in
economics there is a greater similarity between the nineteen-fifties
and the thirties than there is between the fifties and the sixties. In
the first weeks of 1963, in the article quoted above, Henry Fairlie
recorded a great British anachronism, the North-South divide: the
rise in unemployment, the increase in factory closures and short
time working, he saw as recurring signs of the widening cracks in the
affluent society. Between the thirties and the fifties is the major
interruption of the Second World War, around which British political history loses continuity, but out of which grew the social policy
and the legislation that shaped the Britain of the forties, fifties and
sixties – shaped Britain in fact until roughly 1984, when on an
electoral crest born out of tactics that would not have disgraced a
mediaeval war lord, the government abandoned social policy
altogether. Throughout, post-war social policy looked back fearfully
on the hardships of the thirties, and carried with it the aspirations of
a nation and the support of all the main political parties. There was,
however, considerable diversity in the way its success was
measured, and familiar phrases, ideas and figures need scrutiny if
the Britain that existed in 1963, the Britain that was changed by the
events described in this book, is to be 'seen'. Chief amongst these
are Macmillan's assertion that we had never had it so good, the
notions of austerity and affluence and that much repeated crypto-
generic 'The Establishment'.

§

The surprising thing about the change of power from Labour to Conservative in 1951 is the continuity. If there had been serious fears amongst socialists that the welfare state would be dismantled, they must within a year or so have been transmuted into electoral apprehension at what the Conservatives seemed to be achieving while leaving the Labour creation intact.

The ending of the war, far from allowing a relaxation of wartime controls, had first perpetuated them and then increased them. To many socialists the directed wartime economy, and the controls on production and consumption that were its tools, was the exemplar of any civil economy, and it's arguable that the continuing hardships of the post-war years were less resented than tolerated by a great number of people, as milestones on the road to Jerusalem – but hardships they were nonetheless. The persistence of rationing and the unavailability of manufactured household goods led to the era being dubbed the Age of Austerity, and over it presided the man who had been Chancellor of the Exchequer since 1947, Sir Stafford Cripps. Cripps was a gaunt, deeply religious vegetarian – an apt symbol, a physical embodiment, of the austerity with which his name is forever linked. While relaxing controls on production, prices, imports and exports, he left rationing intact (the price to be paid in a massive export drive)[3] and as the ration card clung on until 1954 it served as a grim reminder that the British still lived under Cripps' shadow.

In the years between 1951 and 1963 several interludes were acclaimed as 'booms', periods of unprecedented affluence when the previously scarce consumer goods became available at the same time as the means of paying for them, but it is against a background of deprivation that they should be viewed. It's been argued many times that the rejection of Labour in 1951, after six years of government, was a response to too many years of such deprivation – this may well be the case, even though more people voted Labour in the 1951 election than at any time before or since. Whoever was in power between 1951 and 1955, it was time for the brakes to come off, to reap the benefits of Cripps' planned economy and of a general upsurge in world trade. It happens that it was the Conservatives, who experienced four years of sustained economic growth. By 1955 R. A. Butler was able to reassure the nation that he fully expected the standard of living to double in twenty years – a figure he cautiously revised to twenty-five, not long afterwards. And by 1957 Harold Macmillan could boast to an audience in Bedford that

15

we had never had it so good, or, more precisely, that *some of us* had never had it so good, quite possibly the most famous catchphrase in British politics since Churchill's Iron Curtain.[4] In this boast he's received a lot of critical support from historians.

"Only four years after the end of food rationing, it was beginning to dawn on people that they had embarked on the greatest spending spree in their history."[5]

" . . . stimulated by the new goad of commercial television, refrigerators, washing machines, lawnmowers, as well as television sets, had come into millions of homes for the first time . . . the austerity of the post war years had ended with a sudden spree, and the Labour Party was still stuck with the image of ration books and shortages."[6]

Booker and Sampson are writing of 1958 and 1959 respectively. There's something inescapably glib about the lists of hardware, and the repetition (such words as 'spree' crop up time and again in the histories of the period), that makes me sceptical about reading standards of living in hunks of processed metal and sheets of statistics: and there's too much in my own memory that doesn't fit. At its corniest and most Pennine – what use a lawnmower in a back yard? It seems a curious choice as though the author was stuck for a consumer durable at this point, and, the word vacuum-cleaner not springing readily to mind, had stuck a pin in a catalogue. However fridges and televisions (along with cars) are the luxuries that are usually taken as basics in calculations of this kind, and in a statistical playoff for the definition of never-so-good the 70% of homes that had a television set by 1961 must be weighed against the fifteen million people who lived without a bathroom or the six million people who still had access only to a shared lavatory by 1963, in what were undoubtedly some of the same homes into which some thirteen million television sets had been installed. In this is the necessary contrast – the juxtaposition of the hardware of the new affluence with the structural neglect of a country that was being run without planning, the juxtaposition of the immediate benefits of the fifties with the same problems and conditions that had faced the thirties. The one eye of the little god twinkling brightly in the squalor.

In the early sixties Penguin Books produced a series of specials under the heading Britain in the Sixties – among which was Geoffrey Moorhouse's *The Other England*, in which he argued the case that the view of England as divided North to South was better expressed, culturally and economically, as the Golden Circle (around London) versus the rest. The book was researched over

1963 and early 1964. In his book are many images of the country that would scarcely seem out of place (TV sets permitting) in any of the preceding three decades. He describes a family in Openshaw, Lancs – they live in a four-room terrace house, without an indoor lavatory, bath or running hot water. The house is damp and costs 17/– per week in rent. Before the 1957 Rent Act it had cost 9/–. The man of the house earns £16 per week, which Moorhouse admits isn't bad, but the family cannot afford to buy a house of their own. I do not think this is an example by exception. As recently as the late fifties the houses on the opposite side of the street in the town where I lived not only lacked baths or indoor lavatories, but also electricity. The gas refrigerator exists, a scientific mystery (as though Concorde were propelled by a large rubber band), but the gas television? Those houses, I was told as a child, had been 'condemned', which I now understand to mean that under the 1955 slum clearance scheme they had been scheduled for demolition (they're still there today, damp-proofed and sporting neo-Georgian windows), but while they awaited the iron ball and the bulldozer they continued to be lived in, unaltered. The inhabitants of such houses could scarcely have been among the 'some of us' who were filling up our crumbling homes with the new hardware if they'd wanted to – and they surely did.

Anthony Sampson offers the statistics of debt – in eighteen months over 1958 and 1959 hire purchase debts shot up by £300 million. This represents a peak in the 'never-never' – overall hire purchase debt rose by some £500 million while the Conservatives were in office, and the encouragement or restraint of such purchases became alternately an electoral bribe and a Treasury headache. The ostensible greater wealth of the working classes was in fact simply greater debt. Mr Macmillan himself was not deluded by the mirage of money – what he said, more fully, was:

"Indeed let's be frank about it; *most* of our people have never had it so good. Go around the country, go to the industrial towns, go to the farms, and you will see a state of prosperity such as we have never had in my lifetime – nor indeed ever in the history of this country. What is beginning to worry some of us is 'Is it too good to be true?' or perhaps I should say 'Is it too good to last?'"[7]

Which is tougher and more speculative than quotation usually allows, but Macmillan himself used it repeatedly, thereafter, in its lesser form.

1955 is the paradigm of manipulative 'consumer engineering'. With rising inflation, after the four fat years, Butler introduced a February mini-budget that imposed restrictions on hire purchase

17

borrowing. In April he made cuts in both purchase and income tax, thereby increasing public spending power by some £135,000,000. In May there was a general election. In July, inflation once more rising and reserves diminishing, hire purchase restrictions were greatly increased – the deposit necessary more than doubling – and ceilings were placed on industrial investment programmes and bank overdrafts. In October finding himself faced with roaring inflation and a run on the pound he introduced an 'emergency' budget, largely undoing the April reforms. The following year saw Britain apply for an IMF loan for the first time. Thus was Stop/Go born, and the pattern of Treasury management established for the rest of the Tory era. 1957, 1958, 1960 and 1961 all saw two budgets a year, with credit restrictions yoyoing, culminating in a second IMF loan and the introduction, in the second 1961 budget, of a completely unworkable pay pause – a sorry attempt at an incomes policy that is linked forever to the name of Selwyn Lloyd, as austerity is to Cripps. The result was a wave of strikes – industrial unrest was, by 1963, a major issue. In the middle of all this came the 1959 budget with its crude electioneering – 9d off income tax, and 2d off the price of a pint of beer. In a phrase he might have used himself, Macmillan had 'rolled out the barrel'.

Samuel Brittan, in the standard work on the subject, *The Treasury Under The Tories*,[8] refers to this, reluctantly, as the Macmillan cycle, and to the management of the economy as 'pavlovian' – reacting to the economic danger of a run on the pound, and the electoral danger of half a million unemployed. The Conservatives had come to power pledged to make the economy work without controls or punitive taxation (which was never as high as Labour's basic 50%, but also didn't drop below 40% until 1960) – for four years this showed every sign of working, but thereafter investment, and hence the infrastructure of both industry and society, suffered; and from 1955 onwards the policy became Stop/Go in an effort not so much to stabilise as to prolong office – which is the same as saying that the Conservatives, after 1955, had no policy at all.

If nothing else, Stop/Go deterred the kind of long term investment the country needed to restore its basic resources. Our gross national product rose by 40% under the Conservatives – but France put hers up by 100% and West Germany by 250% between 1951 and 1964.[9] By the time Mr Macmillan left office in 1963 (National Productivity Year) unemployment was at 900,000, our balance of payments deficit was heading for £400 million, and the fabric of society was visibly crumbling. This was nowhere more apparent than in the matter of housing.

In 1945 with half a million houses destroyed and a further three and a half million bomb-damaged there was a pressing need for a new building programme. It was an area in which no party succeeded. Macmillan, as Churchill's Housing Minister in the early fifties, achieved a target of 300,000 new houses a year, a figure that could not be sustained. In 1963 major cities like Birmingham and Manchester could still offer estimates of their own slums (albeit using no common definition) at 70,000 and 80,000 respectively, with seven hundred houses a year being abandoned as uninhabitable in Manchester. And of course it did nothing for the hidden problem of the homeless. By the Autumn of 1962 Macmillan's own Housing Minister was Keith Joseph, who found himself faced with the same challenge that had faced his leader twelve years before and had to make similar pledges and excuses, referring to "the huge problem of *obsolescence* and the shortage of land", when speaking of the four and a half thousand homeless families in London.

There was little notion of restoration at this time, no notion of an ecology of housing. What was condemned thirty years before might by 1980 be marketed as 'an artisan's dwelling'. Throughout my childhood my hometown (which was never bombed during the war) was pitted with houses that were abandoned or falling down around the families that still inhabited them, and I can recall a whole row of Victorian cottages that had holes under rotting front doors that would have admitted rats the size of a Jack Russell. I've no reason to think that the housing neglect in my town was the worst Britain had to show.

Such structural neglect created, in the Britain of 1963, an emphatic contrast between the immediacy of consumption and the failure of any longer term social strategy. There's more to this than just a puritanical whinge about the corrupt new materialism, although there was certainly a lot of that at the time; it was, crudely, jam today at the expense of bread tomorrow, and the twenty-five years that have elapsed since have seen no shortage of critics willing to cite chapter and verse on this contrast, and to lament the fact that Britain had cars aplenty without the new roads to put them on, an advertising culture that could flog aspirin by the ton but not build hospitals, a boom in property but not in housebuilding, a rail service that was being deliberately wrecked and schools that were bursting at the seams with the post-war baby boom. Britain at this time was a classic example of what J. K. Galbraith termed 'private wealth and public squalor'.

Macmillan himself is unwilling in his memoirs to confer the title of 'boom' on this era, preferring the more cautious 'equilibrium' and referring to the extremes of the hardships of unemployment and the 'debilitating ease of boom'. Yet, after his victory in the 1959 election he did not lack temerity in declaring the class war obsolete. The opposite point of view persisted. From 1962 to 1964 the *New Left Review* collected a series of articles simply entitled *Work*, amongst which is a statement by a factory worker on the land of contrasts, on the never-never land that was Britain in 1963:

"Everyone keeps telling us we are better off these days than we were in the nineteen thirties. Of course we are not. It looks as though we are because everyone's got things on tick. Take all the things off us that we have on tick and we would be worse off than we were in the nineteen thirties. The rich still get richer and the poor still stay poor. All this H.P. is a trick to make you think you are rich or well off. You own nothing. Not that you want to, but at the same time you are being told in a thousand ways that to own something is the only thing in life."[10]

Under the long reign of Conservative government the standard of living rose by 50%, and rises in wages kept ahead of rises in prices. In the most immediate terms the working class was better off. Against this must be set the 183% rise in the value of shares over the same period, and the fact that 80% of those shares were still owned by 1% of the population. Throughout, the working class 'slice of the national cake' remained at 42%.[11]

The same factory worker who summed up the never-never for the *NLR* also said, presumably not long after the 1964 election: "The people I work with . . . most of them are unaware that they deserve more from life than they get. 'Never had it so good' has come to mean 'couldn't have it any better.'"

It reads like a bitter summation of the era just departed, the last word on a famous phrase – a phrase that had worn so shabby that Labour even dropped a counter-slogan – Everyone will have it good under Labour – early in 1964 after a short run in the newspapers, on the advice of Tony Benn. It wasn't worth the risk of association, even in contradiction.

§

The modern, that is the post-war, usage of the term Establishment is accredited to Henry Fairlie (with whose words I opened this chapter) in the *Spectator* in September 1955, when he wrote of Burgess and Maclean that they had been shielded by "The Establishment".[12] A few years later Fairlie was a contributor to a 'symposium' on the subject edited by Hugh Thomas. Thomas offered some definitions of the term. The Establishment is "the English Constitution and the group of institutions and outlying agencies built around it for its protection."[13] Any the wiser? Nor will you be when I tell you that the term derives from the 'Establishment of the Church of England' which itself is "no more than the senior common room of that greater Establishment institution the public school".[14] Ah, the Tory party on its knees again? But . . . Fairlie himself adds to the confusion with . . . "the whole point about The Establishment is that it represents no interests"[15] . . . and we're back to square one wondering what it means. Yet it's solid enough. A touchstone of national feeling at any point between 1956 and 1966 is the sense of 'them': at their most powerful and anonymous the Establishment are 'them'. Sampson's colossal survey of the Britain of 1962 is peppered with quotations from various sections of society, ascribing cause, blame or power to 'them'. To the Trades Unions it's any other power bloc, to the frustrated scientist it's the national bias in favour of the arts. To the average person, therefore, it would seem to be whatever power is not vested in themselves – any power or interest outside that is capable of shaping and controlling their lives. Even the Prime Minister saw fit to comment on this, as Anthony Sampson recorded in his study of Macmillan:

"Macmillan talks wittily about the popular misconception of 'The Establishment'; how the press and the public are still obsessed by 'they', as something separate from themselves; how people still regard the foreign office or the banks as if they were run by a few noble families; and how gossip columns disclose a world of dukes and butlers, like drawing room comedies."[16]

For the record Macmillan's cabinet on the eve of 1963 contained six old Etonians, a marquess, four earls and a duke – he himself was the son-in-law of the late Duke of Devonshire, and two of his cabinet were sons-in-law of Churchill, the last commoner to be offered a dukedom. This could, and undoubtedly did, seem oppressive, as though England itself were a dinosaur and its government merely a collection of fossils. With this in mind Thomas called for the sweeping away of the Establishment and declared it to be nothing more than the museum of our former glories – and in this is the germ of a definition. Might the Establishment be those institutions, that system of order which served and maintained the empire we no longer possessed? An empire Macmillan had been too often accused of jettisoning in the search for a new international role for Britain? There are plenty of people alive today who can

21

recall how their schoolteachers used to point to the red bits on the map, and I'll add my voice – I too remember this piece of nonsense, and how hard a death the notion of empire died, and the cultural miasma that survived it. It cannot be but that it was kicked before it went down. In 1963 the sense of the Establishment was readily summed up as 'them', and whatever function 'them' had served had now, by and large, come down to one of obstruction. Obstruction not only against 'our' interests, but against their own. The Establishment that was still there to be kicked seven years after *Look Back In Anger* may not have been institutionally the same one it had been in 1956, but the sense of pervasive, obstructive tradition, the awareness of 'them' remains. The best summing up of this I have found comes from Peter Lewis's *The Fifties*:

"The point of the Establishment is that it continues to look after itself whatever party is in power . . . not so much a power bloc . . . as a ruling class mentality, a set of assumptions, objectives and opinions about English society and who should press the buttons that operate it . . . The vital lubricant of the Establishment is personal intimacy, the word in the ear or over the telephone, over lunch or a drink in the club."[17]

When Hugh Thomas called for the abolition of the Establishment any question as to what should replace it was easily answered with one of the most contentious terms of recent British history – a meritocracy. It would have been defined rather simply as the maximisation of the native resources and talents of the nation – the very talents obstructed by established tradition. I have first hand experience of this. Any child of the baby boom has. It's bigger nonsense than 'the red bits on the map' and almost as pernicious. At its most basic it meant the grading of children into can and can't, and the logical promise extended that this in due course would be rendered into have and have not. I was part of a generation that was constantly being bludgeoned by mindless aphorism ('Don't let your right hand know what your left hand's doing' or 'A bad workman always blames his tools') and ruthless segregation (a make or break exam at the age of eleven) into believing that we would inherit the earth. After all we 'had the benefit of an education that your parents lacked' (the war cry of the old socialists) as we were shoved fifty at a time into classrooms designed to hold half that number. We were the beneficiaries of a welfare state, as we were asked if any of us had spare trousers to lend so that the poorest among us might be able to attend school fully clothed. We were classified in terms of potential occupations at every turn – the thickest among us receiving the comfort of constant reassurance that he would 'end up a dustman'.

Meritocracy was meant to be a way of tapping resources, of reject-ing the limitations of class on ability and opportunity. It was in our interest and it was in the national interest – the war had proved this, as the Labour Party still tell us to this day in their advertisements. In practice it was a pavlovian system of reward and punishment, a flexible reinforcement of class division and class hatred, in which the deserving prospered and the rest were rubbished. The logic behind all this is only too familiar – harking back once more to pre-war hardships, it amounted to a reasonable belief that consensus politics would continue and a wholly unreasonable, almost blind faith in the transforming power of technology. The hovercraft, if not the hula hoop and the electric mangle, would lift us out of the gutter. If this sounds unduly short on gratitude, then I invoke the paradigm of all risen beasts: "You taught me language; and my profit on it is, I know how to curse."

A meritocracy, sooner or later, becomes the Establishment's new skin (a modern cliché is to point out that Osborne, Amis and Anderson are today the crustiest of old fogeys, less of one to suggest that Mick Jagger probably is too) – in 1963 this was not the percep-tion. In 1963, as in 1956, it was possible to think that we were on the verge of a change, a liberation that might be drastic or even final.

§

Put crudely the seven years between Suez and the Beatles is also the time when both sociology (that most spurious of sciences) and fiction discovered the working class. Not that the bear dances well but rather that it dances at all. John Braine's first novel *Room at the Top* was published in 1957 and quickly established itself as an archetype. Joe Lampton, milltown boy from Dufton, ruthlessly uses sex as his route to the good life of the envied 'thousand a year man', in Warley, West Riding. Lampton is the fifties social climber – a pattern critically discerned as central to the literature of the time – Osborne's Jimmy Porter has, after all, married the colonel's daughter. It's part of a new social mobility – hence social disruption – recognised in such works as *The Uses of Literacy* and *Education and the Working Class* (both still in print, if only for the benefit of teacher training colleges) which picked up on the self-destructive dilemma of the 'scholarship boy' – a theme which did not have its last, fruitful flowering until twenty-five-year-old Melvyn Bragg pub-lished his first novel, *For Want of a Nail*, in 1965. I suspect that it is out of this perception that the frequent use of the word 'classless' arose to cover anything in the arts that might deal with the North of

England or the East End of London. However discerning its initial use it soon degenerated into a cliché that served only to disguise the perpetual retrenchment of class lines. *Room at the Top* is a misleading example. It was begun as long ago as 1952 and reflects the immediately post-war period more than the middle fifties. By the late fifties you'll look hard for the sense of an open, mobile society in fiction. The hero of Stan Barstow's 1962 novel, *A Kind of Loving*, bears little resemblance to Lampton. The pattern of his life and the limitation of his ambition are narrowly working class, even if his cultural concerns are not. He thinks not of the rewards of Macmillan's meritocracy but simply of getting by. He works as a draughtsman and when he marries (like Lampton, because he 'has to') he lives with his mother-in law and begins the withering process of 'saving up for a place of our own'. Plain working class (his) meets pretentious working class (hers), but any criticism in terms of classlessness and 'newly opened horizons' is meaningless. When a Barstow hero thinks in terms of the gains of the new affluence he does so in the most basic terms, which by their very fastidiousness reveal how little they touch the core of working life. In Barstow's 1960 story *The Human Element*, the pride of Harry West's life are his motorbike, his transistor radio and his shoes. He's a skilled worker – an engineering fitter – whose horizons are bounded by the factory and his digs. At the end of the story the shoes and the radio are ruined:

"Just now I can't get over the shoes. I've had plenty of enjoyment out of the radio, but I've only worn the shoes today. A new pair of shoes like that; ruined first time on. A smashing pair of shoes, and they're done. It doesn't bear thinking about."[18]

Never had it so good? The way Harry overvalues a pair of winklepickers doesn't seem much different from the exaggerated values of rationing and emphasises the deprivation more than the acquisition. More of a damp squib than a boom.

What's emphatic in the fiction of the late-fifties is the persistence of old working ways, the numbing routines of earning a living. The illusion of affluence is noted, and registered in the wage packets of its heroes, but the price of labour – so wonderfully absent from Macmillan's vision of a giveaway society – is as obvious as the benefits. The best catalogue of this – of hours traded, pounds spent, and consumer durables run up on the slate – is Alan Sillitoe's *Saturday Night and Sunday Morning*, published in 1958.

Its hero is Arthur Seaton, almost twenty-one, ex-serviceman, piece-worker at a bicycle factory in Nottingham, high earner, high spender, owner of a wardrobe full of suits and silk shirts, accomplished liar, champion boozer, cuckolder of his workmates and all-round flash bastard. It would be easy and unanalytic to say he too has 'never had it so good', but he's only too aware of that himself. Cleverer than most of his friends and family, one of his diversions is to invent outlandish visions of the future under the new technology, which he constantly backs up with claims that he's "read it in the paper". It becomes a running satire on the prosperity and prospects of Macmillan's new England. A mockery of 'where's it all leading to?' from a man who doesn't believe a word Macmillan says. Yet the backward glance is one that Prime Minister and lathe operator share. Macmillan had, throughout his premiership (and it figures constantly in his memoirs) the memory of the depression in his constituency of Stockton as the touchstone in his approach to the issue of unemployment. In the thirties it had led to him being a Tory rebel (hardly the same thing as a wet), an advocate of the planned economy, and for a while he even took this as far as a call for nationalisation. Arthur Seaton, child of the depression and the war, uses that backward glance to undercut anything positive that might emerge in his thoughts on the new affluence. If he gives with one hand he takes with the other:

"The old man was happy at last, anyway, and he deserved to be happy, after all the years before the war on the dole, five kids and the big miserying that went with no money and no way of getting any. And now he had a sit down job at the factory, all the Woodbines he could smoke, money for a pint if he wanted one, though he didn't as a rule drink, a holiday somewhere, a jaunt on the firm's trip to Blackpool, and a television to look into at home."[19]

It's roughly the same list of electioneer's hardware that peppers the economic and political histories, but Sillitoe leaves the reader in no doubt about the slog of acquisition. Hard bought is hard fought.

"Born drunk and married blind, misbegotten into a strange and crazy world, dragged up through the dole and into the war with a gas mask on your clock, and the sirens rattling into you every night while you rot with scabies in an air raid shelter. Slung into khaki at eighteen, and when they let you out, you sweat again in a factory, grabbing for an extra pint, doing women at the weekend and getting to know whose husbands are on the nightshift, working with rotten guts and an aching spine, and nothing for it but money to drag you back there every Monday morning."[20]

This is Seaton's answer to 'you've never had it so good' – two fingers waving at the affluent society – to take all that's on offer with the utmost contempt, and never say that it's enough. It's changed the quality of life without touching the structure or rearranging the

25

lines of battle. Lawnmowers for the cobbled yard, fridges among the flaking plaster and televisions tossed out as voters' perks. Five years later Geoffrey Moorhouse, in *The Other England*, recorded the lives of Birmingham car workers: "They spend their days doing a repetitive job alongside a conveyor belt, the most deadly dull thing imaginable. Their wages are high because they work ridiculous extra stints in overtime. When they get home, some of them say, they are fit for nothing but flopping down in front of the television set or a supine contemplation of their other riches."[21]

The cat and dog warfare perceived by Sillitoe, Moorhouse records in no milder terms: "What is beyond question is that here, where by the highest standards something resembling a rich society has been established, society is at war with itself."[22]

It isn't simply a matter of trades and demarcation disputes – or even of a dissatisfaction born of greed – neither the novelist nor the social historian perceives the matter so tritely. It's living in a nation dressed up in the fripperies of a hire purchase boom, while the substructure of society crumbles into dust, a nation of wage slaves, a nation that cannot house its homeless or build a single hospital[23] – Nero, if no longer fiddling, shoots grouse.

Like most of the northern novels of the period *Saturday Night and Sunday Morning* was filmed. John Schlesinger made *A Kind of Loving*, Lindsay Anderson *This Sporting Life*, Jack Clayton *Room at the Top* (all within a couple of years of the books' publication) and Karel Reisz directed *Saturday Night and Sunday Morning* for Woodfall Films – the company set up by Tony Richardson, Oscar Lewenstein and John Osborne in 1958. Francis Wyndham wrote in *Queen* that by making a film about working class life as it is today the British cinema had "really grown up at last". Twenty-five years later neither the film nor that review stands up well. Albert Finney gives the part of Arthur all the necessary guts but plays it throughout in his natural Salford accent, and is supported by a stock cast of British northerns. It looks like nothing so much as a latter day Ealing comedy without the jokes.

Private Eye summed up the new movement in the cinema with a spoof entitled "How We Made A Taste of Living": the director's account of the new realism gets no further than a pub in Soho which is on the outer limit of his establishment geography of Britain. Nothing could be quite such a pristine demonstration of Moorhouse's notion of The Other England, that vast tract of wode-plastered wasteland outside the golden circle around the capital, than this travesty of Sillitoe's Nottingham. The film lost the book's locality, the care with which Sillitoe had caught the patterns of speech, and a great deal of its individuality in an amorphous, ignorant notion of the North of England as being 'somewhere out there, and it didn't really matter if film-makers didn't get it right because no-one in Wardour Street would spot the difference.'

In 1963, with an equally daring sense of the appropriate, Macmillan appointed the Viscount Hailsham to be Minister with special responsibility for the North-East. He was already Minister of Science and the British negotiator in the Test Ban talks. The north, like the working class, was still 'somewhere out there'.

§

At almost the same time as *Look Back in Anger* opened, rock'n'roll arrived in Britain. It aimed itself at, and spoke for, a different age group from the new drama, but in its way it expressed some of the same dissatisfactions. The teenager, like the Northerner, the Cockney, the poor, was unfranchised on the Establishment map of Britain. And since the term teenager itself was probably unheard before 1956, he or she wasn't even 'out there somewhere'. Unlike the drama rock'n'roll was uniquely, but not wholly, American, and despite the efforts of British music would stay that way for another seven years. It's a vital development in the shaping of the Beatles, the Rolling Stones and their audience.

Elvis Presley entered the British charts in the May of 1956 with *Heartbreak Hotel*. What Elvis looked like, sounded like and performed like are too well-known ever to need description. What matters is that American popular music had at last found that elusive creature, the white boy who sounded black.[24] In consequence the British search began for an even more peculiar hybrid, the white British boy who sounded and looked enough like the American to pass for the real thing. (That the real thing was already in action in the USA and had been recording since 1952 under the name of Little Richard was neither here nor there, and would only be *here* when, after some pressure from his British fans, Little Richard's records were released in the UK at the end of the year.) Much has been written about the new spending power of the teenager, compared to earlier generations, and about the commercial satisfaction of this market – little attention has been paid to the cultural concerns of the newly economically enfranchised teenager, but of that more later – and the terms seem exact for the moment. The British music business, having noticed the effect of Haley and Elvis, saw its market changing and opening up. Some impresarios lacked foresight and dismissed rock as ephemeral, as simply the latest in a long series of dance crazes, others recognised that it had its own separate market, and whatever its associations and origins was distinctly itself.

The white boy was found – by name Tommy Hicks, by stage-name Tommy Steele. In seeking the British rock star, British promoters were in pursuit of a snark – when discovered one or the other might well just disappear – and were looking for an image (not necessarily a sound) to fit what was discerned as a ready-made market, whether the real demands of that market force were perceived or not. Colin MacInnes described Steele as 'puckish'. He was, and still is, lively, good looking and possessed of a cheeky grin that has immediate charm. An unlikely rock hero? Probably, but what his managers, Larry Parnes and John Kennedy, offered the British teenager wasn't the rawness of Presley but the identification within a generation – a teenager's teenager – tinged with the merest smattering of the Elvis sexuality and the James Dean rebelliousness – some of the photographs of Steele show him playing the part, looking mysterious, surly and unconvincing. That they should find this combination in a wholesome every-mother's-son should not be surprising, any more so than that all his songs were instantly forgettable or that within a year or so of his first single hitting the charts (*Rock With The Caveman*, October 1956) he should be appearing in panto in Liverpool (he was surely born to play Buttons?). It's part and parcel of the same process. With Kennedy's skilful promotion Tommy Steele was for about eighteen months the darling of British rock fans, and was duly rejected by the mums and dads as surely as if he'd been the teen rebel he might have pretended to be. My father remarked that he doubted Steele could write his own name and even before he'd appeared in *Half a Sixpence*, my mother remarked on 'what a nice boy he'd turned out to be'. And within that is the span not of Tommy Steele (whose intelligence and traditional show-biz talent have been proved time after time in the last thirty years) but of the pop business. The snark was a boojum, you see.

When Steele 'disappeared' others quickly enough were found to take his place – Parnes and Kennedy soon developed a stable of talent with increasingly outlandish names – Vince Eager, Marty Wilde, Duffy Power, Dickie Pride, Johnny Gentle and Wee Willie Harris, he of the shocking pink hair. But it would be wrong to suggest that the power in popular music rested with management. On the whole they were more forward looking than the real powers, the big four record companies (Pye, EMI, Philips and Decca) and their A (Artistes) & R (Repertoire) men. If I stress that the development of popular music in Britain was held back by the role of adults in a youth culture they did not understand, I'm not simply arguing that the business of business gets in the way of the business of music, but that it failed even in its own terms to see how the market lay and to offer what it wanted and what it might be prepared to pay for. In 1956 few A&R men had the ear for the new music, no record company could see the room for originality in British recording or perceive the performers as anything more than packages: it took two years for this situation to change, and a further five before the young voice broke through the old ways. In 1956 British rock had neither the recording capability nor the venues (dance halls rather than clubs still dominated the circuit) to succeed as anything but a pale imitation of America. It would remain a hybrid of what pop had been before and what promotion could now develop along bowdlerised American lines, and this was nowhere more obvious than in the way television chose to handle the new monster. If the fans had rocked in the cinema aisles to Bill Haley, swooned over Elvis and screamed for Tommy Steele, on television Brown Owl and Akela would always be on hand to mete out wholesome common sense and see that everyone had a jolly good time.

From the beginning of television's post-war revival there had been a black hour between six and seven in the evening when nothing was shown. Since all broadcasting ceased promptly at ten-thirty, and the BBC bothered to list what was on only in the final four pages of the *Radio Times* (paper itself was still rationed at that time), it would look as though the broadcasters themselves did not take the new medium seriously, or worse still, and truer, that they took it seriously enough to be in awe of its power and rationed it. The black hour was nicknamed the toddlers' truce, and this represented the touching belief that parents put the children to bed between six and seven free from the attentions of the one-eyed idol. This wonderfully middle-class sense of gentility (a touch of the pre-war nursery) might have persisted longer but ITV, after a poor start in 1955, had begun to command an audience. Weekdays a new, topical magazine programme, *Tonight*, would fill the space and on Saturdays . . . ? On Saturdays the *6.5 Special* would go over the points. The BBC was to get its first youth programme for those past watching Andy Pandy – or that's the way it seemed. The *6.5 Special* began in February 1957, produced by Jack Good and Josephine Douglas and presented by Douglas herself and Pete Murray, with help from Freddie Mills, the former World Light-Heavyweight boxing champion. The choice of all three shows the perspective. A BBC staff producer, a rather bad actor turned DJ and a personality. In his

29

day Mills was as popular as Henry Cooper for much the same reasons, but who today would offer Henry Cooper a pop programme? In 1957 it marked the formula of pop on TV that Mills could be offered such a job. The *6.5 Special* aimed not at the teenagers but at that mythical creature, beloved of advertisers and programme planners, the family audience, and this conditioned the presentation and the content – a mixture of musical styles and a magazine-like mixture of pop and comedy. One ludicrous moment from the programme has stuck in my memory for thirty years. The question was raised by the presenters . . . how did rock'n'roll get its name? Cue sketch of a pair of mediaeval knights jousting in armour. Each loses his lance in the course of combat. Enter some fool to save the day, arming one with a stick of french bread and the other with an oversize rod of Blackpool rock. All participants now proceed to jive . . . the rest is not history. A good time was (probably) had by all.

It's arguable in defence of such a rag-bag approach that the BBC had few native rockers to pick their line-up from, but it's the pattern of avuncular supervision that matters as much as the mixture of styles – with few exceptions it determined the presentation of rock and pop on television until the mid-sixties, until the newly redundant pirate DJs were snapped up in 1967. The gap between those who made and listened to the music and those who fronted it was a generation wide. The image of rock and pop on television was at odds with its sound and at odds with its content. It was all too clean cut, too middle-aged and too headmasterly – all suggesting that the wildness, sexuality and energy that lurked so near the surface of rock'n'roll was either safely contained or might really not be as 'bad' as it seemed, when, in fact, the overwhelming teenage fantasy was that it should be.

At about the same time that *6.5 Special* chugged out for the last time, Huw Wheldon would habitually sign off his programme of child flautists and cellists with an assurance to the young viewer that it was indeed '*All Your Own*'. Rock in Britain in the late fifties and early sixties wasn't.

What, then, was? What in the teen culture was distinctly itself? What was shaping it, other than regret at being thrown out of the youth club for turning up the volume on the auto-changing, 78 rpm playing, mother of all hi-fis, the Dansette? That it was based on sexuality is obvious, but only a part of the picture – the sexual element was less a statement than a question, the question being centred on the confusions and frustrations of the time, of being a teenager[25] – whereas before there had simply been small adults.

The difference being that the economic enfranchisement of people still in their teens (whatever the gap between the USA and Britain at this time) held out the possibility that for the first time they might create their own culture – a culture inevitably inarticulate and frustrated, simply because the old code persisted across the new money and the new idea. Rock critic Peter Brookesmith sums up the 'meaning' of Elvis for the American teenager: "He made explicit their latent frustration at the bloodless hypocrisies and rigid conformities of white middle-class America."[26]

Accurate, but it travels less well than Cynthia Rose's: "It was an insecure era, huddling under the shadow of the Bomb . . . a pervading sense of emptiness and unease."[27]

Which statement, although made by an American about America, could equally describe Britain. Within the overt sexuality lay real tensions, which, as the music moved on from the primal squeal of *Tutti Frutti*, became the subjects of rock'n'roll.

"The sexuality of pure rock'n'roll was, like all eroticism, an excitement aroused through conflict and tensions. Many of these tensions were merely a case of the sound colliding with the psyche of the era – symbolising rebellion in conflict with authority, tradition with novelty, 'good taste' with vulgarity, 'respect' with abandon."[28]

Emptiness and unease – they seem to me to be consequences not simply of the global insecurity of the time but also of a fixation on the recent past that dominated British society – a society that had shaken off neither the thirties nor the war, and was still dodging all the lesser bombs (in the output of the cinema at least) while living under the shadow of the big one. It seemed that there was no place in such a backward looking society for the young. The young exist in the margins simply because they're young, and perhaps in previous generations there had been little recourse but to bide their time resentfully. In the fifties, perhaps for the first time, there was more to do than wait. However slight the new affluence, it was enabling the teenagers to shape those social and cultural margins around their own concerns – and it was from this that the Beatles and a dozen other bands that broke through in 1963, arose.

The touchstone is still the 1955 film *Rebel Without a Cause*. Billed as being about 'today's juvenile violence', in fact through the muttering and mumbling accusations of James Dean it is an intensely moral story, questioning the morality of the fathers who can provide all the hardware of new American consumerism but cannot make an honest, decent or sensible decision. If the hardware seemed elusively un-English, the tensions were not, nor was the film's

31

expression of the conflicting demands of home, school and sex. The new freedom to look around was also the freedom to be dissatisfied with what was found.

If the British teenager was not to drive his own car to high school (or someone else's over a cliff) what was he to make of the space left to him? What was coffee bar culture like? The sociologists came up with different, if equally urgent responses. Richard Hoggart saw teenage life as synthetic, pseudo-American, and hence not sustainable or sustaining:

"Compared even with the pub around the corner, this is all a peculiarly thin and pallid form of dissipation, a sort of spiritual dry-rot amid the odour of boiled milk. Many of the customers – their clothes, their hair-style, their facial expressions all indicate – are living to a large extent in a myth world compounded of a few simple elements which they take to be those of American life . . . they have no aim, no ambition, no protection, no belief."[29]

T. R. Fyvel has more generosity of spirit and more perception:

"To the refined middle-class ear, the raucous sound of an infernal machine blaring out something like *Jailhouse Rock* at deafening volume in a small, confined space, i.e. a small café crowded with overdressed teddy boys and their girlfriends, may seem like a good idea of hell. And yet, and yet . . . talking to those in touch with these young people, I have always felt that there is a good deal to be said for the jukebox. First of all it has made the café a place to which girls can come on their own. The music provides justification; they can sit and nod their head to the rhythms as they sip their coffee without appearing too obviously to be waiting to be picked up. Conversely the juke-box enables the boys to express their personalities at 6d a time through the individual choice of records . . . For many youngsters the most vivid link with contemporary culture is through the lyrics of 'pop' music. The juke-box café, especially if featuring the top twenty, fits with this emotional attitude."[30]

As a teenager Billy Morton (born 1938), a grammar school boy at the Liverpool Institute, was a regular at coffee bars in the fifties and early sixties, and offers an aspect of the picture not hinted at by the sociologists – the juke box doesn't come into it: "Allan Williams had a coffee bar called the Jacaranda . . . there were three or four [like it] – there was one that used to be open until really late, and it wasn't licensed. And you drank instant coffee – not even espresso. And you'd just *talk*. It was *like-minded people* . . . There was that sort of coffee bar where you'd go late at night. Then there were espresso bars, frequented by sixth formers . . . you'd always carry something around like *An Introduction to Mathematical Philosophy* by Bertrand Russell. I carried that around for about three months – I read it too."[31]

Among the other late nighters, among the like-minded people, at Allan Williams' Jacaranda that Billy Morton rubbed shoulders with were John Lennon and Paul McCartney.

Out of this Cliff Richard emerged as our first and most enduring pop superstar. He began as Tommy Steele did, as an imitation Elvis, but at his best recorded original material, which, if still part of the Tin Pan Alley machine, might arguably be termed the voice of British rock in 1960. His chief rival of the late fifties offered more but fared less well. Billy Fury was Liverpool's first rock star, and under better conditions might have been the first Mersey singer-songwriter too. At the age of eighteen (a contemporary and schoolmate of George Harrison) he talked his way into Marty Wilde's dressing room at a Liverpool concert to sing him some of his own songs. The effort wasn't wasted. He became the youngest member of the Parnes stable and began to record on Decca. The first 10-inch LP features several of his own compositions, but when his career failed to take off he was made to record cover versions of American hits (something Cliff managed to avoid). At this he excelled, but I can't help wondering what might have happened if Fury had been allowed to go his own way. Might there have been a real teenage voice in rock'n'roll, alongside the outpourings of Tin Pan Alley and the imitation of, as the only homage to, America? It points up once again how the music business failed to encourage or to generate an originality in British music. In music as in so many other respects we were still the poor relation.

George Melly wrote that the "teenage thing was initially the work of the teenagers themselves",[32] that Elvis, Haley and eventually Steele were the teenager's own choices. It could also be argued that once the 'thing' itself had arisen it was taken over with a cynical disregard for the music or the performer. Terry Dene was a one-hit wonder ill equipped to cope with his share of instant fame. By the time he received his call up for National Service, his personality and 'career' were in tatters, and the army discharged him as unfit for duty after only a couple of weeks. Giles caught the spirit of the times, as ever, in a cartoon in the *Daily Express*. A newspaper seller stands yelling his wares on a dim suburban station – the poster in the wire cage announces the serialisation of Terry Dene's army memoirs.

§

"From one day to the next, the basement fell silent. The age of the radio was over, no longer was the house filled with the roar of sound – music and voices . . . The great table, which had been the centre of the room, had been pushed to one side, to make room for a half circle of chairs used for the television . . . Flo no longer cooked two meals an evening, but food that could be eaten off people's knees as they watched."[33]

This is how Doris Lessing recorded the coming of television to a large house in the East End of London where she lodged about 1950. Television annihilates the almost communal way of life which she has shared, and chronicled, as a newcomer to England, over the previous two hundred pages. Well into the nineteen-sixties there were people who resisted television with phrases like "wouldn't have it in the house", but they were more often resistances based on a sense of the debasement of high culture and the 'art of conversation' than on any sense of the destruction of community or popular culture, and they were few in number. Many years would pass before you could enter a house that owned a television and find it switched off during broadcasting hours. Television quickly became a national obsession, capable of conferring uneasy stardom on the unlikely (Gilbert Harding, Sir Mortimer Wheeler) and of making household names of the more likely (Hughie Greene, Benny Hill). Without checking I think I can safely assert that by 1963 the TV set was the most hire purchased item in the land, ahead of the fridge, and miles ahead of the lawnmower. Nor was it cheap – in the mid-fifties the average table-top set cost around seventy guineas, and those that stood like squat coffins in the corner as much as one hundred and thirty guineas. That it changed our way of life, very much in the way Doris Lessing indicates, goes almost without the saying. It reshaped our lives and our culture as well as our living rooms, and if I suggest that the social life of the British was not always conducted sitting in a semi-circle and offer to speculate on the transition, it's another book in itself.

BBC television, like radio, was still charged with the trusteeship of 'the national interest', until the coming of independent television in 1955. ITV was instructed to do nothing more grand than avoid giving offence, and inevitably there was much opposition to its breaking of the BBC's monopoly, loudly voiced fears of a decline in standards and a questioning of the role and effect of advertising that cut across party political boundaries.[34] With this in mind the first issue of the *TV Times* resorted to a pacifying editorial – something I doubt it has felt the need of since. On September 22nd, 1955 this appeared:

"Viewers will no longer have to accept what has been deemed best for them. They will be able to pick and choose.

"And the new Independent TV programme planners aim at giving viewers *what viewers want – when they want it.*"

The editorial went on to assure the potential audience that ITV far from lowering broadcasting standards would actually raise them, and that it was genuinely independent of its advertisers – advertisements were a boon, they would enhance the medium by "combining information with entertainment".

No small boast, and one that would not look out of place today in a message from a press baron on the eve of a satellite launch – and it's just as meaningless. What did ITV offer to the viewers as and when they wanted it? On the first night an evening of opening ceremonies and programme samplers must have gone largely unwatched as the BBC Light Programme sent Grace Archer to her death in a burning barn. On the second night ITV offered *Take Your Pick* and *Dragnet* – two examples of what the channel would do best, game shows and American imports. But over the first week too much of the scheduling was quite clearly rooted in the older tradition of the theatre and must have looked odd against the American programmes – this applies to the variety shows, with music hall artists like Wilson, Keppel and Betty as well as to versions of Shaw's *Man of Destiny* and Lermontov's *A Month in the Country*. The first Christmas on ITV must have been edifying. At 2 p.m. their 'Christmas Afternoon' began – Nilakshi Ghose, a visitor from Bengal, would be in conversation with Anthony Wedgwood-Benn, followed by Peter Brook in Moscow with the Phoenix touring production of *Hamlet*. Even Channel 4 would gag on such a mixture. I am putting it gently if I say that it took ITV a while to get its formula right, and over the first eighteen months, despite the boast of Roy Thomson that his share in Scottish television was "a licence to print money", the companies lost money heavily. By 1958 ITV had re-thought and re-established itself and had reduced the BBC's share of the audience to a mere 30%. By 1963 the BBC had retaliated with fresh programmes and competitive scheduling, and held roughly equal shares of the audience with ITV. Out of this rivalry came the setting up of the 1960 Pilkington Committee of Enquiry into Television[35] and a stream of programmes and performers that, if not old favourites, are certainly old memories. Bill Maynard (a comedian then, rather than a straight actor) became the pullover kid and single-handedly caused the sales of sports coats to plummet. Billy Cotton (racing driver turned band leader) led Kathy Kay and Alan Breeze through tuneless renditions of the latest hits, but still managed to become one of the best loved of those 'on the telly'. George Mitchell's Black and White minstrels blacked up week after week until, in the late-sixties, the Race Relations Act was finally able to make clear that they were in fact the white and white minstrel show. Jack Warner forsook mindin' his bike for 'Evenin' all', and in *Dixon of Dock Green* offered an image of the British bobby that many people today would dearly wish were true. The nation trembled before *Quatermass and the Pit*, as Nigel Kneale played out his deeply anti-Establishment, anti-nukes drama in the guise of a good horror yarn. Hughie Greene offered contestants a chance to *Double Your Money* and follow the treasure trail. The stage at the Palladium revolved most Sunday nights. Johnny Speight gave us Arthur Haynes as the first of his Cockney philosophers, and Galton and Simpson gave us an actor of comic genius in *Hancock's Half Hour*.

Two programmes are worth a closer look – *Coronation Street* and *Tonight*. *Coronation Street* was not British television's first serial. The BBC had its weekly serial *The Groves* and ITV its daily *Sixpenny Corner* in the mid-fifties, but *Coronation Street* broke new ground and set new standards. It's misleading to compare it to any kind of TV soap that had preceded it – the origin of *Coronation Street* lies much more with the new cinema, and the similarity is more than just the evocative graininess of black and white photography. The first programme went out only as a regional broadcast on Friday, December 9th, 1960. In a series of blatant links the viewer was led from Florrie Lindley's corner shop (in which Florrie is the newcomer, and hence the vehicle of enquiry) to the Tanners, with delinquent Dennis fresh out of jail, and wayward Linda fresh out of marriage, and to the Barlows, where Ken (played then, as now, by William Roache) is just back from university for the Christmas break and feeling the angst of two worlds as fiercely as Hoggart's scholarship boy. Why does his father have to have tea with his evening meal, why do they have bread ready buttered? In its concern for representing the tension rather than just the bonhomie of working-class life early *Coronation Street* fulfilled some of the mission Sydney Newman had set himself when he took over ABC's *Armchair Theatre* in 1958, to capture Britain in transition. The scene in which Ken is embarrassed and angered to find his father and brother repairing the bike on the living room floor, while the posh girlfriend stands ready with the spanner, is a scene that would not be out of place, in terms of its style or subject, in the social realist cinema of the early sixties – in a film such as John Schlesinger's *A Kind of Loving*. Ken is reaping the rewards of the meritocrat, new opportunities and new oppositions, and hasn't a clue what to do with them. It's a perspective on how much Britain has changed since, when I say that the bike had a Sturmey Archer three speed, rather than ten gears, and that David Barlow rode it to work at the factory every day as his sole means of transport, rather than for the aerobic exercise it might offer.

Coronation Street, produced by Granada in Manchester, pointed the way north for television that *Z Cars*, the BBC's classic police drama of the sixties, would soon follow. In this it's in line with the sociology, the theatre and the cinema of its time. Television, curiously, became one of the few meeting points of high and popular culture, not only in such programmes as these but also in its one-off plays and in its new current affairs coverage, like *Tonight*. In music and in the performing arts generally, the avant-garde that had blossomed with the Angry movement, and the new popular culture that was emerging from rock'n'roll were at odds and stayed that way until 1967. It's not unfair to say that swinging London had to rise and fall before the avant garde surrendered its suspicion of the popular.

Tonight was the brainchild of Grace Wyndham Goldie and Donald Baverstock at the BBC Current Affairs Department, which had created *Panorama*. When ITV ended the toddlers' truce, which in their terms was a waste of good advertising time, the BBC had to follow suit, first with *Highlight* and then with *Tonight*. *Tonight* finally killed off the dinner-jacket style of news coverage, in which current affairs were allowed to stagnate for a fortnight before it was thought wise to air them, and a daily newsreel 'rounded up' events on film, and hence at a remove. *Tonight* took the cameras into the streets and the country and turned the polite deference of the traditional interview into a form of justified harassment. Baverstock dealt with the news and the people in it by, as he put it himself, 'being on the side of the audience'. The magazine format of the programme was a planned response to the mismatch of viewing conditions north and south. In the north it was teatime, in the south it was commuter time, hence *Tonight* was conceived as flow, that is separate but continuous items so that "any viewer who happened to be around could dip into it".[36] In this way a team of some of the best photo-journalists of the time (or any other) were turned loose – Fyfe Robertson, Alan Whicker, Trevor Philpott, Slim Hewitt, Macdonald Hastings, and, among the last to be recruited, Julian Pettifer: "There was an enormous amount of freedom left to individual producers and contributors. You literally went out and found your own material – you created your own style. It's been said that there was a *Tonight* style. There wasn't really – what there was was a lot of individual styles within it, and the individual directors and contributors all made very different contributions. You knew when you had a Robbie item it would have a particular Robbie style, and a Whicker item would have a Whicker style.

"One of the things that imposed discipline on us was the terrific peer pressure. At lunchtime everybody would go and view the newly cut films, and that was a complete free for all. People could rip it apart if they didn't like it – equally they were generous in their praise. If something was good it was 'wonderful'. What made this possible was the enormous esprit – what was said was said for the good of the programme."[37]

Tonight became the beneficiary of the demise of *Picture Post*,[38] from which Hastings, Hewitt and Bert Hardy had all come, and also the stable of some remarkable new talent. While Julian Pettifer was the youngest performer on-screen, off-screen were Ned Sherrin, Kevin Billington, Jack Gold and John Schlesinger as directors, and Bernard Levin as writer. The resulting mixture of hard interview, documentary film, and topical song looked like whimsy and anarchy wonderfully controlled. Over this Grace Wyndham Goldie pre-sided like a "dragon Great Aunt",[39] ensuring that *Tonight* was neither rebellious nor revolutionary, but "sceptical" and "anti-paternal".[40]

"In amongst the whimsicality there was serious investigative journalism – and at that time Tonight was the only programme doing this. They really did pioneer that sort of television. Robbie was marvellous at uncovering bits of bureaucratic nonsense. Nobody else did that. News doffed its cap at authority – even local authority."

Out of *Tonight* grew *That Was The Week That Was*, which re-spected authority even less. Although *TW3* was taken off the air before *Tonight*, Julian Pettifer's words on the esprit of the *Tonight* team might be taken to cover the fate of the BBC's most innovative phase in current affairs: "It was a great team if you were part of it, but it was thoroughly disliked by other people in the BBC – and with reason, because they were incredibly arrogant. I suspect that was how a body of resentment built up among other people in the BBC, which may have been responsible in the long run for the demise of the Current Affairs department."

The other programme that ran and ran is no programme at all – the adverts. The very first showed us a toothbrush and a lick of Gibbs SR encased in a block of ice, and over the years that followed we were instructed in Mrs Bradshaw's way with Surf, urged not to forget the fruit gums Mum, watched Katie crumble a thousand Oxo cubes into Philip's gravy, put Tigers in our tanks and utterly failed to distinguish Stork from butter. From the start there has always been the danger that the advertisements would be better made than the programmes. Joseph Losey, Lindsay Anderson and Karel Reisz all directed advertisements at some point. Such talent notwithstanding a *News Chronicle* poll in 1959 revealed that 81% of the population disliked advertisements in the middle of programmes, and I have to say I don't believe it. My memory is of children singing traditional songs in the fifties, but advertising jingles in the sixties, and I think the adult population were open to be flattered by association if the product advertised on television was used by them. Television conferred a degree of fame when there were only two channels that it did not do with three and certainly not with four. Fame by the merest association with the goggle box meant much more than it does today. Whatever the misgivings of the planners and the opponents of the coming of commercial television, advertisements were an accepted fact of the British way of life in 1963.

§

Sometime in the early sixties someone revived an old war cry from the days of *Picture Post* and asked What's Wrong With Britain? That I haven't been able to trace its first such use only adds to the mystical overtones the phrase carries, as though its question might not be a question at all but a statement of belief that the Great should still be in Britain – if only we could put it back. It spawned countless enquiries – Anthony Sampson devoted a sub-chapter of the *Anatomy of Britain* to 'malaise' – and Penguin Specials in their urgent red covers asked What's Wrong with the Unions, Church, Industry, Hospitals, Parliament? in volume after volume. It gave the early sixties an atmosphere of public breast-beating, and after Vassall, the defection of Kim Philby, and the resignation of Jack Profumo 1963 became the year of self-flagellation. Britain in 1963 was a land in need of heroes. Too often in the recent past we had 'lost the initiative', whether this be a failure to re-establish ourselves as a world power, to gain acceptance into the Common Market, to develop our own independent nuclear deterrent, to creep out from under the shadow of our rich Uncle Sam, to market the hovercraft, or to make television as sharp as *Dragnet* and *The Naked City* or rock'n'roll as compelling as Elvis. The heroes would be those who seized that initiative, whenever and whatever it might be. The first issue of the *Sunday Times* Colour Section on February 4th, 1962 disguised a long What's Wrong moan with nonsensical assertions that we had once again found a new national sense of purpose. It made no mention of the shabby unravelling of the tired, moth eaten era of Mr Macmillan, or of the threadbare economy and dogtooth contrasts that lay hidden beneath his leather elbow patch of afflu- ence. Further on the heroes of the near future were chosen, those young talents who were 'changing the mood of Britain' – amongst whom, quite rightly, were Peter Blake and Mary Quant. But who in February 1962 or even January 1963 would have guessed at John Lennon, Sean Connery or Marilyn Rice-Davies as those most likely to knock the stuffing out of the British shirt?

CHAPTER THREE

THE FOURTEENTH MR WILSON

"Though vain, [Harold] is certainly not conceited. Though enormously intelligent, he is *certainly not an intellectual*. He is a supremely professional politician – in this he resembles Kennedy."
Richard Crossman, 1963

"Harold can be tender-hearted, but he's also cool, careful, prim, non-conformist, *intellectual*: George is none of these things."
Richard Crossman, 1968[1]

"Two centuries ago when a great man appeared, people looked for God's purpose in him; today we look for his press agent."
Daniel Boorstin, 1962[2]

Britain, in January 1963, was a gerontocracy, but then so were France, the Soviet Union and Germany – Macmillan was sixty-nine, De Gaulle seventy-three, Khrushchev sixty-nine and Adenauer eighty-seven. The leader of the opposition, Hugh Gaitskell, was well into middle age at fifty-seven, and the youngest of Britain's leaders was Jo Grimond who had led the Liberals since 1956 and was only fifty. Behind Gaitskell lurked the two heirs apparent, George Brown and Harold Wilson, both in their mid-forties, both unlikely, in view of Gaitskell's age, to succeed in the foreseeable future.

The chance for the up and coming arose much sooner than expected. That month, in the depth of the worst winter in two hundred years, Hugh Gaitskell died. His illness had been sudden and mysterious – a virus infection with the complication of pneumonia. Gaitskell had been admitted to the Hampstead Hospital in December, allowed home for Christmas but admitted to the Middlesex Hospital on January 4th. His condition deteriorated, and on the 17th doctors tried connecting an artificial kidney. The following day Gaitskell's heart gave way, and he died on the evening of the 18th. Gaitskell had led the Labour Party for seven years, succeeding Attlee after the electoral defeat of 1955. He had led the party to a

41

surprise defeat in the 1959 election, and to several years of internal strife, but given the political climate of early 1963 he was widely expected to become Prime Minister in the course of the year. Roy Jenkins, writing in the *Daily Mail*, the day after Gaitskell's death, said: "In the last year of his life he was able to lead the Labour Party with an assured authority which no previous leader in the party's sixty years had ever attained . . . he was an immensely agreeable man . . . it was a pleasure to be with him."[3]

From start to finish 1963 was going to be an election year. Popular wisdom had it that the Tories couldn't possibly go the distance, could they? Where was the next "agreeable" man to be found?

§

Three candidates stood for leader of the Labour Party – Wilson, Brown and the outsider James Callaghan. They all held shadow cabinet posts, and they'd all first entered parliament in the Labour landslide of 1945. A straight fight might have favoured Brown in a contest in which he and Wilson represented right and left respectively, almost regardless of the similarity in their positions. The three-cornered fight split the right. Several influential MPs on the Gaitskellite right of the party, led by Anthony Crosland and Roy Jenkins, found Brown unacceptable and urged Callaghan to stand. Labour Party rules required a clear majority – so when the first ballot on February 7th yielded 115 votes for Wilson, 88 for Brown and 41 for Callaghan, Callaghan was eliminated and a second ballot called. At this point George Brown was, by his own account, urged to stand down and leave a clear field – Wilson after all needed only seven of Callaghan's votes – but he refused: "It's more than a matter of individuals or a question of personal policies or abilities."

So saying he barely disguised what was painfully obvious to him, that the contest had come down to personalities – the ebullient, larger than life Trade Unionist from Lambeth, famous for being indiscreet, emotional and, on occasion, plain drunk versus the "desiccated calculating machine",[4] former Oxford economics don, and professional Yorkshireman, about whom *Private Eye* could joke that his idea of a celebration was to open a bottle of Sanatogen.

Brown's autobiography *In My Way* (so called because most people were?) is a pitifully emaciated work for such a gargantuan personality and of Wilson's vast memoirs only two hundred pages deal with the years before he became Prime Minister – the contest for the leadership is covered in a couple of sentences. Of more interest, in the rush-to-print as Wilson headed towards No. 10, BBC producer Leslie Smith turned out a slim volume of hagiography, billed by its publishers as "authentic – Harold Wilson as a son, a husband, and a father". The main source appears to be Wilson himself, indeed there are few cited sources outside Wilson's immediate family and circle. During the campaign for the leadership the *Daily Mail* treated the public to 'The Inner Mind of Mr Wilson, by Marcia': "He is my ideal MP . . . even tempered, conscientious, understanding and like Mac he never flaps. He also always remembers my birthday . . . with chocolates . . . plain ones."[5] This does no justice to the mind of Lady Falkender, but it sets the tone for the ordinary bloke image that Wilson propagated at this time. Smith's Wilson is shot through with such nonsense, and it is best read as Wilson's closet autobiography.

Shortly after the death of Hugh Gaitskell, Herbert Morrison told Brown that the party would never elect a leader from the working class. Yet, however fine the differences between Brown the multilateralist, revisionist in favour of incomes policy, and Wilson the multilateralist, revisionist in favour of incomes policy, the parliamentary Labour Party could choose from two working-class candidates for the first time since the war. Each candidate was, of course, conscious of his working class credentials. Brown the child of London poverty was scarcely ever given a potted introduction[6] without some mention of Peabody Buildings, Lambeth.

Ted Eldred, for many years Brown's agent, recalled one of Brown's TV interviews from 1962: "George said 'When I was a boy we lived in Peabody Buildings – no bathroom, we didn't even have running water in the flat, just one tap at the end of the passage. I can remember my father coming home one day triumphantly holding a key – we'd got a council house! And we thought we were in heaven.'"

Wilson, from a more well-to-do Yorkshire family, the son of a works chemist, had seen hardship too. His father had not escaped unemployment during the depression. A version of the hardship he'd seen had been reported in the press in 1948: "The school I went to in the North was one where more than half the children in my class never had boots or shoes to their feet."

The Mayor of Huddersfield and some of Wilson's former teachers protested the untruth of this, and Wilson answered that he was quoted accurately, but had, of course, meant that they had worn clogs instead. The denial was nowhere near as effective as the legend – 'shoeless in Huddersfield' was trotted out by the newspapers at regular intervals – at times inflated into 'Shoeless Harold'

– the *Daily Telegraph* and the *Daily Express* carried the story early in 1963, and in October 1963, failing to secure publication in his own *News of the World*, Randolph Churchill took a full page advertisement in *Tribune* to tell the tale yet again. The irritation this caused Wilson in the hour of his image-moulding can be measured by the long reply he made to the *Telegraph*, and by the careful detailing of the anecdote in Smith's version – which carried the deciding, and previously unquoted, line: "They wore clogs because they lasted longer than shoes of a comparable price."[7]

In the struggle for the public creation of an image, Peabody George got off more lightly than Shoeless Harold. Privately he remarked to Eldred, "Funny thing, there's only my brother Ron agrees with me that we did live in Peabody Buildings. My sisters and my Mother deny we ever lived there."

The celebration of ordinariness is a bit like the sound of one hand clapping. The reader of the Closet Wilson is told the details of his mortgage, lest Harold be thought unlike the common voter, is emphatically told that he has never read a word of Marx, lest he be thought to be left-wing (this despite a career as an Oxford economics don), and is bombarded with trivia about his scout troop and his love of the Meccano magazine. The ordinary becomes the trivial, the trivial begets a bore: "He also read *Whitaker's Almanack* from cover to cover."[8]

The bore becomes an austere prig, the chancellor's apprentice: "He carried frugality to such extremes that he arranged for his mother to send him a joint every weekend; he thought the charge of tenpence for a plate of beef from the college kitchen was too high. He also grudged the college laundry charges, so sent his weekly washing home. The joint and the clean washing were regularly despatched to him in the same parcel."[9]

The prig becomes the puritan: "When I read press accounts of young people gambling away thousands, or living it up in cars they haven't bought for themselves, I remember how I bought my first car for £11, and I really had to earn those £11. I'd hate to see Robin or Giles [his sons] with a car they hadn't bought with money they hadn't earned themselves. I'd feel they'd missed something important in life."[10]

Smith traces the moves in Wilson's parliamentary career in such a way that almost everything Wilson does is seen as serving the interests of party unity or requiring a searing degree of soul-searching, the registration of which is, after Macbeth, loss of sleep, as the Ordinary Bloke wrestles with his conscience. Wilson is presented as a man of compromises – the past is rehashed for the ends of the moment – Wilson holding the party together in 1963-4.

At every turn self-serving tactics, sudden changes of allegiance and direction, are presented as linear, loyal and above all unifying. The Ordinary Bloke solidly plodding down the Middle-of-the-Road, dogged by extremists to left and right. His resignation from the government in 1951 over 'Teeth'n'Specs' – the imposition of National Health Service charges to fund the war in Korea – becomes not the triumph of Nye Bevan, the founder of the National Health, the Colossus of the Left, but of Harold Wilson, who has urged, nay proposed, compromises which have been rejected. The conclusion . . . "Bevan had in fact become a Wilsonite".[11] Wilson joins the Keep Left group but "never entirely identified himself with them", which skips over the fact that he chaired the group and also managed to remain a member of the Fabian Society at the same time, but leads easily to his rejoining the Shadow Cabinet when Bevan resigns again. Bevan is seen as inspirational but erratic, which justifies Wilson supporting Gaitskell in the 1955 leadership election, against his old mentor – Bevan cannot unite the party. Alas, nor can Gaitskell and it is in the interests of unity once again that Wilson opposes him for the leadership in 1960. No mention is made that it was without precedent for a sitting leader to be opposed – Wilson, after all, is only standing after much persuasion, loss of sleep, and to defend the sovereignty of Conference, albeit over the unilateralist issue which he does not support. Little is made of the candidature of left-wing, unilateralist Anthony Greenwood – who might have seized the heir apparent's crown. Nor does this challenge harm his relationship with Gaitskell, who batted him sideways out of his Chancellor's brief and into foreign affairs. As Wilson – or Smith – steadily disowns his left-wing past, the choice between him and Brown becomes implicitly, and accurately, one between two right-wingers. A neat sleight of hand elevates the choice. The discussion of the qualities of the candidates for the next leader of the Labour Party is suddenly changed into . . . "The choice, however, was for the likely next Prime Minister"[12] . . . and in the 'however' Brown disappeared. Which is exactly what Brown did in reality.

On February 14th the second ballot was announced by Brown himself as acting leader – he had lost to Wilson 103 to 144. Wilson called upon him to stay on as deputy leader. Brown declined to be rushed: "I shall have to consider very seriously the political and personal issues."

Brown cancelled his weekend engagements, saying that "nothing should be done to detract from the build-up of Mr Wilson as leader" and then he vanished, and to the delight of the press, no one, at least no politician, saw hide nor hair of him for a week.

Brown had flown from Heathrow to Renfrew, and had been staying near Loch Monteith. It's still a matter of speculation whether he was playing hard to get in taking a holiday at this time. Meanwhile, Wilson simmered, and with good reason. The last time the leadership contest had been so fought, Herbert Morrison, the incumbent deputy, had refused to continue once he'd lost to Gaitskell. If Brown was similarly petulant, the unity of the party, so hard won in Gaitskell's last year, could be instantly shattered. Morrison, fellow Lambether, had played mentor to Brown, and was rumoured to have told Brown that he should call it quits if he got fewer than a hundred votes. Brown's showing was better than this, but his intentions were not clear from his actions nor from his wishes. Before leaving, even before the result was announced, Brown had written to Herbert Bowden, the Chief Whip, saying that he would stay as deputy, but that he wanted a clear brief in the shadow cabinet – the post of shadow Foreign Secretary which Wilson now vacated – and to surrender his chairmanship of the Party Organisation Sub-Committee. Wilson chose to take this as an ultimatum, and as the week following his victory rolled on, a be-tween-the-lines reading of Richard Crossman's diary reveals the leader the *Express* had welcomed as "Machiavellian, shrewd, cunning, calculating and self-centred"[13] to say nothing of frustrated, angry and ruthless. In public he was plugging away at unity, saying that although the Labour Party has been without a leader for three weeks, he had "never seen a party more united or successful"[14] – which might be taken as a backhanded compliment to Brown – in private he was shelling out posts in his shadow cabinet and gloating over the defeat of his rival. Crossman records Wilson as saying on the evening of the 14th: "We've got him just where we want him. If he resigns now it is a private decision of no political signifi-cance."[15]

Andrew Roth, one of Wilson's more recent biographers, records that at his victory party Wilson was heard to remark: "He'll have to go . . . and when we drop him, you won't even hear a splash."[16]

In a matter of days such complacency has a tinge of frustration. On Monday the 18th, Wilson offered the job of shadow Foreign Secretary to Patrick Gordon Walker, thereby spiking Brown's re-quest: "I'm not going to be blackmailed by his going away like this."[17]

On Tuesday Brown, urged by his supporter Desmond Donnelly that he was putting his political future at risk, telephoned Wilson. This call was described by *The Times* as easing "the unmistakable discomfiture of Mr Harold Wilson" – easing it, I suspect, by turning it to boiling anger. Undoubtedly, Brown's behaviour was alienating even his own loyalists, but in frustrating Wilson's drive for the image of leader of a unified party it was clearly feeding a vindictive, if not megalomaniac, streak in the new leader. When, according to Crossman, Donnelly came to see Wilson, announcing he was George Brown's 'broker' (something Donnelly quickly denied having done)[18] he would not deal with him, and Donnelly, assuming he had Brown's implicit consent, gave the letter Brown had sent Bowden to the London *Evening Standard*. This "infuriated" Wilson, and Crossman's account of the conversation ends with Wilson threatening to give out the shadow cabinet list at a press conference the next day (Thursday, February 21st) to put an end to Brown's manoeuvring: "Everything George Brown has done has played into my hands."[19]

If Crossman is to be believed, this is a line worthy of Abanazar in a Christmas pantomime. Wilson has merely to be imagined rubbing sweaty palms together or twirling the ends of a Chinese moustache.

The appointment of the shadow cabinet was officially the joint task of the leader, his deputy and the Chief Whip. Yet there can be little doubt that by the time Brown chose to return on February 20th most appointments had been made. Whatever game Brown was playing with Wilson, it was not one he could win – it seems only to have had nuisance value. Yet when stopped by a sharp-eyed reporter at Renfrew airport on the morning of the 20th, he said: "Why is there all the fuss brothers? . . . I'm not saying where it was. I may need it again . . . I never sulk, I simply went away with my wife for a week's holiday"[20] – a line he stuck to ever after.

The next day Brown and Wilson met for two hours and the shadow cabinet list was finally worked out – although this can scarcely have amounted to more than Brown rubber-stamping all the decisions made in his absence – and announced. Gordon Walker was Foreign Secretary, Callaghan Chancellor, Healey Defence, Crossman Science and Brown Home Office. A huge headline in the *Standard* read 'BROWN AND WILSON SIGN PEACE TREATY'. All Brown had succeeded in doing was in giving Wilson a taste of his own medicine – the waiting game. This had been Richard Crossman's devising – the result of a wartime career as a specialist in psychological warfare. His technique throughout the election had been to do as little as possible, to restrain Wilson, to canvass quietly through the almost clandestine activity of George Wigg, and to give Brown's notoriously unstoppable personality enough rope to hang him. Brown had all but blown the campaign in the first move. His supporter Charles Pannell had suggested to Crossman that Wilson and Brown might enter into a pact – each agreeing to serve the other as deputy if he lost. This looked workable until Wilson leaked it to the press – the *Mail* ran the headline 'LABOUR LEADERS IN UNITY PACT' – and Brown promptly disowned it, seeing its publication as diminishing his position as the incumbent. Instead the disavowal tended more to show him up as putting personal pride before party unity. And Brown had finally blown it by the pressure that, in his insecurity, he brought to bear on the voting MPs. Whilst Brown, in his memoir, terms Wilson's campaign "bitter", there seems to be an agreed body of thought that Brown's tactics were "strongarm" (Crossman) or "armtwisting" (Tony Benn). As Anthony Howard and Richard West wrote in their 1965 book, *The Making of a Prime Minister*: "Tales spread of people being bludgeoned with threats or bribed with rewards."[21]

It's hard to imagine, for anyone who never met Brown, the combination of charm and monstrosity. He was loved, he was hated.

Ted Eldred: "He was a bully. And a lot of it was due to his own lack of confidence in himself – and this surprises a lot of people. I found George, in many cases, to be very unsure of himself. His public image wasn't that at all. When you were with him face to face, he'd express doubts – not about where we were going, but in his own ability.

"I remember when the party went unilateralist in 1960 . . . the following year George was due to make a major foreign policy statement at the Blackpool conference – the first item of business after the opening formalities. It was in the Winter Gardens and they were absolutely packed. I looked at the platform – everyone was there except George. I began to get anxious. I left my seat and went down to the foyer. There wasn't a soul in sight, and then the door opened and in came George. I walked to meet him, and he didn't say a word, he just got hold of my hand and gripped it right up to the entrance to the platform. I was saying 'You'll be alright, George, you'll be alright', and just as he opened the door to the platform he turned round and said 'Thanks'. Later, Sophie [Brown] told me that that morning he'd actually been physically sick at the prospect of making the speech. And he made a blinder. And conference reversed the previous year's decision. That was George."

§

During the leadership campaign Labour's 5% lead in the polls had almost doubled. The outward show of unity had had its effect, and unity would be Wilson's theme ad nauseam throughout the year. That which had been so hard won under Gaitskell could so easily fall apart. At the best of times Labour is a fragile coalition, or, as its members used to prefer to call it, 'a broad church'. Writing in the *Daily Mail* the day after Gaitskell's death, Walter Terry commented: " . . . of course if he had failed at the next election the rows would have started again."

At the 1959 Party Conference, Hugh Gaitskell, reeling from the loss of the general election, had suggested radical reform of Clause 4 of the party's constitution:[22] "It seems that this needs to be brought up to date . . . it implies that the only precise object we have is nationalisation . . . it implies that we propose to nationalise everything . . . but do we . . . ?"

He took another defeat, at the hands of his own party, as the left and the unions, the largest of which, the TGWU, was led by Frank Cousins, allied against him. This could have been the end of the matter, but such is the structure of power in the Labour Party that Gaitskell was able to work with the National Executive Committee and modify, if not drop, Clause 4 anyway. This brought forth the indifference of George Brown, who wrote in his memoirs "I didn't think it mattered a damn one way or the other"[23] and of Harold Wilson who, as Paul Foot wrote, had "never made a policy statement in his life which remotely resembles Clause 4",[24] both of whom thought the issue was ill-timed and divisive, if right. Left alone it might just die quietly. In a press conference held the following February Wilson managed to state his position without stating any position, when he reminded parliamentary journalists that the troublesome clause had been part of the platform at every election this century, but that he had no objection to "adding to our present statement of objectives". The phrase that told most was one that echoed throughout Wilson's subsequent rise to power: "Let us unite on policy not divide on theology."[25]

The reworded Clause 4 was eventually put to conference in 1961 as part of the putative election manifesto *Signposts for the Sixties*, and as such accepted. But in the two years that followed the party had undergone its greatest crisis since the war. The alliance of the left and the unions, once forged, found common cause in the Campaign for Nuclear Disarmament, and at the 1960 Conference a resolution committing Labour to unilateralism was passed by a slender margin. It looked very much like Cousins' revenge on Gaitskell. Gaitskell announced that there were "some of us . . . who will fight and fight and fight again to save the party we love. We will fight and fight and fight again to bring back sanity and honesty and dignity . . . "

Directly and indirectly, what Gaitskell fought was one of the most curious coalitions in British politics. A cultural force as much as a political one, CND in the years between 1958 and 1964 coalesced and dissolved, as it did so dominating the cultural life of the country – a broad spectrum, an almost indefinable hybrid of the avant-garde and Christian morality, born out of the uncertainties of an age which seemed at any moment capable of dissolving itself in the white heat of the hydrogen bomb. It was not confined to any particular age group or class, but the mix of ages, classes and cultures didn't prevent the movement being easily summed up or casually dismissed – the obvious respectability of such eminent figures as Jacquetta Hawkes and James Cameron could not stop the build-up of an image of youth, duffel coats and skiffle (all of which were true in part), even though the very presence of men like Cameron testified to CND's power to command a press hearing. Conservative MP Dudley Smith put a common, establishment view with: " . . . long haired advocates with their civil disobedience 'sittings' in public places negatived [sic] much latent goodwill for the nuclear disarmament campaign and saddled it with an unenviable reputation for attracting oddities and exhibitionists."[26]

Britain's acquisition of the H-bomb in 1957 had produced immediate repercussions in the Labour Party at that year's conference. Frank Cousins proposed disarmament with "There is no compromise with evil", and was answered by Labour's leading left-wing rebel Aneurin Bevan, with his most famous phrase, that to endorse such a resolution would be to " . . . send a British Foreign Secretary . . . naked into the conference chamber".

The following Easter saw the rise of the Campaign for Nuclear Disarmament, and the first Aldermaston March. By 1960 this had become an annual event capable of attracting 100,000 supporters, and the previously apolitical CND became a powerful pressure group within the Labour Party. Among its members were MPs Michael Foot, Ian Mikardo, Anthony Greenwood and Judith Hart. It was protest on a national scale, now seeking a national endorsement from the alternative government. At roughly the same time a CND splinter group, the Committee of 100, led by Bertrand Russell, became active. It was more confrontational than CND, and was treated more harshly. In April 1961, in Trafalgar Square eight hundred and twenty-six arrests were made, peaceably – only the numbers were shocking. It looked as though the government might be falling for a Gandhian tactic of filling the jails, but shortly before the major demonstration of September 17th 1961, justice itself became the shock. Refusing to obey an order to be bound over, thirty-six members of the Committee of 100 were given two-month jail sentences – among them eighty-eight-year-old Bertrand Russell. The twelve-thousand-strong demonstration went ahead. 1314 people were arrested, among them Fenner Brockway, John Osborne, Vanessa Redgrave, Shelagh Delaney and George Melly. The illusion of peace vanished in an explosion of police violence, as the truncheon came down and the boot went in, followed early the next year by the violence of the courts. Five members of the committee received prison sentences of eighteen months, and a sixth got twelve months, after a prosecution brought under the 1911 Official Secrets Act. What had begun as a crisis of survival had become a crisis of justice.

Within the Labour Party a Campaign for Democratic Socialism (originally and complacently entitled Victory for Sanity) was formed as a direct counter to the unilateralist decision, and initially was as much against Gaitskell as for him – there is a consensus among Labour memoirists that Gaitskell created divisions only for the sake of being seen to heal them, a process which had badly misfired with both Clause 4 and the H-bomb. Part of the power of CDS's campaign was to point out the logical consequence of unilateralism – could Britain possibly stay in Nato? At the 1961 Conference the decision was reversed with a majority of 2,418,000. Thus was Gaitskell's unity formed.

By the time of Wilson's election to the leadership, the forces contained by Gaitskell were not dead, nor were they even dormant, but CND and the Committee of 100 were in some disarray – they seemed to decline almost as their faith in justice itself declined. In January 1963 Russell resigned from the central committee, saying he would confine himself to working for his local branch in North Wales. Vanessa Redgrave resigned at almost the same time, suggesting that the Committee of 100 should now dissolve itself: "Protest marches and demonstrations have been extremely effective in the past, but I feel their usefulness has expired."[27]

In the *Daily Mail* on February 1st, Peter Lewis offered what seems to be a wake for CND, and an analysis of its failure. There had been 140 jail sentences served in the last four years, totalling some five thousand days . . . the government had outflanked the Committee of 100's tactic largely by avoiding arresting the many well-known figures in the movement and arresting en masse the unknowns who could safely rot in jail under long sentences. "Can ordinary people do anything effective to avert nuclear war? Or must we all sit in front of our television sets and hope for the best?" he mourned. The last CND demonstration had been cancelled, a crisis conference had been called. Lewis noted the splintering of the movement's aims, much as CND activist Jeff Nuttall had done " . . . the committee dissipating its force over the same wide area as CND to encompass world health, wild life preservation, care of ancient monuments and so on."[28]

In a very different way, Nuttall too mourns the end – but what grew from the CND/100 motley (a motley never better captured than by the late Jacky Gillott in her novel *War Baby*) was the loosing upon Britain of a diversity of social movements. The avant-garde element triumphing over the traditionalist element in the movement, and in so doing fragmenting itself, at odds with so much of the growing new culture until the late-sixties saw the hip, the pop and the political meet again.

There was much in both issues – Clause 4 and nuclear disarmament – that required careful handling, careful avoidance by Wilson. Disarray did not stop protest and as people continued to protest, so the abuse of justice continued. For example, for perhaps the worst example, on February 14th, 1963 – the day of Wilson's accession – two junior technicians, Edward Parker, aged nineteen, and Michael McKenna, aged twenty, from RAF Locking, Somerset, were sent for trial by court martial. A week later they were sentenced to eight months in prison with dishonourable discharge. Their crime? They had written a letter to the journal *Peace News* suggesting that a branch of CND might be started within the services.

The response of the party of 'ordinary people' to the prolonged abuse of 'ordinary people' in the courts of the land was left to individual conscience. There was no policy on such matters. Yet there was a perceived optimism in the new situation, a new confidence in the leadership. The day after Wilson's accession, five dissident Labour MPs (Michael Foot and Sidney Silverman among them), who had defied and thereby lost the whip by voting against the nuclear policy of the government, and in accord with their Conference decision, in the Service Estimates debate of March 1961, reapplied for the parliamentary whip.

In April thousands of copies of a secret document detailing the location of the Regional Seats of Government (bolt-holes for our masters when the bomb finally fell) were handed out on the last full-scale Aldermaston March. No prosecutions arose from the incident, but as Lord Russell recorded "the leaders of CND were shocked that secret methods should be employed by pacifists."[29] Russell had given the self-styled 'Spies for Peace' £50 to print copies, only to find that "a leading pacifist journal" would not handle material obtained in this way. This element of farce was rare. In July incidents that resounded through the next twelve months and the rotting, last days of Macmillan's government took place, once again in Trafalgar Square. Eleven members of the Committee of 100 were arrested after protests about the forthcoming visit of the King and Queen of Greece – so far had the movement spread from its initial aim – and of these George Clarke was charged with incitement to riot, Terry Chandler with conspiracy and Donald Rooum with possession of a weapon, to wit a brick. In November Chandler failed to appear at his trial, in September Clarke received an eighteen-month prison sentence (only to be acquitted on appeal), but on August 8th Rooum was acquitted at trial after forensic evidence showed no traces of dust from the crumbling brick the police claimed had been found in his pocket. The arresting officer was Det Sgt Harold Challenor. Now the complaints from above flew – the eminent followed time-honoured tradition and signed their petition to *The Times* and as Home Secretary Henry Brooke announced an internal investigation into the matter of Sgt Challenor,[30] a campaign mounted in parliament for a public enquiry. It looked as though the final fling of lunacy had at last brought forth coherent action from the guardians of democracy. Too late for the Committee of 100; too late for CND; its hour had passed.

"But it frightened its own leadership, scared the politicians stiff, and ranged against itself all the careful, unimaginative, conservative forces of all the establishments including its own. They fought it, and fought it, and fought it again, and beat it."[31]

§

The Ordinary Bloke spent much of 1963 barnstorming the country in his tartan-lined Gannex mackintosh, pipes at high port – delivering thirty-two major speeches[32] and roving his native Huddersfield with a team from ITV's *World in Action*. To be ordinary was not enough, the common touch had to be combined with a touch of brilliance, but the brilliance must not undercut the ordinariness and this demanded a "new frontier", the term Kennedy had coined at the 1960 Los Angeles Democratic convention: "a New Frontier . . . uncharted areas of science and space, unsolved problems of peace and war, unconquered pockets of ignorance and prejudice . . . " What was only the election of a leader he inflated into the future of mankind, but it sharply marked off his era from the one before. Wilson needed his frontier and, like Kennedy, who had thrown open press conferences to television, he needed to come to terms with the camera. In the forties as President of the Board of Trade, he had been filmed sporting a small moustache and speaking with painful refinement of a character called 'Stefford Crapps' – a young man trying to seem older than his years, and less northern than he was. For the Ordinary Bloke of 1963, this would not do. He revived the shadow cabinet Broadcasting Committee under Tony Benn, and on February 27th did his first party political piece to camera, with autocue – a device he could never work without on television. It is hardly the accomplished performer Wilson was with a live audience – live, he had 'naturalness' and an actor's sense of timing – but it was, as Tony Benn noted, 'competent', and drew an audience of nearly ten million. Wilson quickly learnt to play the man he wished to seem. He saw the importance of television as no other politician had done before.

In the USA in April he had the good fortune to arrive as the American photo-engravers' 114-day strike ended. He received substantial cover from a starved press in terms that must have been music to his ears: "Harold Wilson, the Labour pretender to the Prime Ministership of Great Britain, is of an age with JFK, on whom he is calling today. They live – though so differently – in the same world. Their psychological approach is similar. They will understand each other and feel alike on basic issues, even when disagreeing on details or minor problems. Both men are superb politicians in the professional sense of that word."[33]

The Kennedy factor can scarcely be overstated. In 1960 America had elected a forty-four-year-old President who looked like a film star and whipped up a storm when he spoke. Khrushchev once expressed his surprise at dealing with Kennedy by remarking that he had children older than the American President, but the real nub of the magic is that Kennedy himself had children, that he was young, that he was cultured, that he was married to a beautiful woman, that, for the first time in years, the White House echoed to the noise of kids, something it had not done in living memory, and would not do again until the time of Carter, fifteen years later. The Kennedys were the advertisers' ideal couple, the pollsters' basic unit, the sociologists' norm – in short, immense wealth, fame and limitless power easily set aside, they were pretty much *us*. The Hollywood image touched base in the notion of the family unit – a family which looked as though it would grow, Jackie Kennedy being pregnant at the time she moved into the White House. If this alone were not enough to promote the image of youthful dynamism, the President had appointed his brother Robert as Attorney-General, who at thirty-five still sported a mop of untamable hair, looked as slim as a teenager and scarcely seemed to fill out his clothes. American politics had skipped a generation. The Kennedys shook up the image of the politician, and in so doing served to make the British politicians of the early sixties image-conscious in a way they had not been before. Labour could feel it had a natural affinity with the Democrats, the party of Franklin Roosevelt, and, the torch having been passed to 'a new generation', as JFK himself put it, the generation waiting in the wings of the party could identify, however unrealistically, with the youth, vigour and dynamism of the new President. If nothing else Kennedy sent journalists and speech-writers scurrying to the thesaurus for the litany of youth. Dynamism is a much abused word outside the laws of physics. In the course of 1963 it was all but drubbed to death.

By the time of Wilson's audience with the man-god, Kennedy madness had reached absurd heights. The President had become, in the terminology of Daniel Boorstin, 'the human pseudo-event'. The bookish fan could now buy *The Wartime Adventures of President Kennedy, A Boy's Life of John F. Kennedy*, and *I was Jackie Kennedy's Dressmaker*. Wilson could hardly hope to compete – although Herbert Wilson's much printed snapshot of young Harold in cloth cap and shorts outside No. 10 in 1924 was being hailed as a form of prophecy – but at least he and Kennedy were photographed together. The identification with the man-god could not be borne out by appearances. Only a year older than Kennedy, Britain's bright young thing looks a generation apart. He is portly, prematurely grey, gap-toothed and pipe-stained. He has gone in a few short years from playing older than his age to looking older than his age – but then the myth of youth was no more real on the Kennedy side. Kennedy was kept alive by daily doses of cortisone, and by the subcutaneous pellets in his hip which counteracted the symptoms of Addison's disease. His father had funded the development of the drug, and even at the time of the 1960 election there had been talk in the family that this was 'Jack's last chance'. If elected in 1964 he was unlikely to live the term.

Tony Benn: "There's no doubt whatever in my mind that Kennedy and the One Hundred Days and all that did influence Wilson. [At that time] the feeling that we had to make a fresh start was quite strong – a feeling Kennedy had exploited – in his own context – in America, and Wilson did the same. At the end of his [political] life he thought of himself as Stanley Baldwin . . . in the middle he was a Lyndon Johnson . . . Wilson darted about, living in various guises . . . and at that time I think it's true that there was a strong [Kennedy] influence in his mind."

The *New York Times* spoke of Wilson's "mission to Washington . . . to proclaim his party's sympathy and support for the main lines of President Kennedy's policy."[34] In so proclaiming Wilson took risks that he might not have done so close to home – he spoke of "mucking about with this deterrent thing", and offered to build four new Polaris submarines when Labour came to power. In a televised address to the Washington Press Club on April 1st, Wilson had a chance to play President, and spoke of his own new frontier in his closing lines: "Our scientists are among the finest in the world. The tragedy is we don't produce enough of them, and those we do produce we do not use intelligently."

It was by no means a new theme in Wilson's thinking, but it formed the basis of his political attack and offered the prospect of much needed common ground between him and Frank Cousins.

§

On the morning of October 2nd Wilson, already the most observed, the most talked-about politician in Britain, became the most praised. The previous day he had opened the science debate at the Labour Party's annual Conference in Scarborough with the most memorable speech of his career.

Wilson gave a phrase to the language – "the white heat of the technological revolution" – and in broad, easy strokes created the new platform, the new sense of urgency with which to challenge the moribund Macmillan government.

He lectured, almost as though talking to children, on the new age in which we lived: " . . . 97% of all the scientists who have ever lived in the history of the world . . . are alive and at work today."

He invited our awe at the magic of technology: "[New computers] are in production [which] do their calculations at and take their decisions in a period of three millionths of a second."

He spoke as an enthusiastic layman, he did not pretend to understand more than the rest of us: "It was not easy for me at any rate to be able to appreciate what three billionths of a second . . . really means . . . until it was explained to me that if you were to set out to walk right round the earth at the Equator . . . taking a step every three hundred millionths of a second – that is one step every time these machines do their thinking process – then you would circle the entire earth in one second."

And proceeded to lay out the lines of a manifesto based on science: "The danger as things are, is that an unregulated private enterprise economy in this country will promote just enough automation to create serious unemployment but not enough to create a breakthrough in the production barrier . . . It is the choice between the blind imposition of technological advance, with all that means in terms of unemployment, and the conscious, planned, purposive use of scientific progress to provide undreamed of living standards and the possibility of leisure, ultimately on an unbelievable scale.

"First we must produce more scientists. Secondly, having produced them we must be a great deal more successful in keeping them in this country. Thirdly, having trained them and kept them here we must make more intelligent use of them when they are trained than we do with those we have got. Fourthly, we must organise British industry so that it applies the results of scientific research more purposively to our national effort.

" . . . we are redefining and we are restating our Socialism in terms of the scientific revolution . . . the Britain that is going to be forged in the white heat of this revolution will be no place for restrictive practices or for outdated methods on either side of industry."

The press response was rapturous. John Cole, in the *Guardian*, called it "the best platform speech of his career". The *Mail* saw the speech as Wilson "establishing his authority over the party with great impact". In the *Daily Herald* James Cameron wrote, "Wilson will not be just a good Prime Minister. He may well be a great one".

Wilson's interest in science went back a long way, perhaps even as far as to his father's occupation, certainly as far as his days at the Board of Trade, and figures considerably in Labour's *Signposts for the Sixties* – partly drafted by Wilson. Automation had been of increasing concern to the Labour Party since the mid-fifties, and by the early sixties the vogue for science had reached even the Conservatives. Macmillan had commissioned both the Trend report on Science and the Robbins report on Higher Education, which were due at the end of 1963. Dr John Poole, Commons Librarian for Science and Defence throughout Wilson's government, defines the moment: "It was in the air. It was an idea whose time had come. Something like it would have happened irrespective of who had been elected then."[35]

One, perhaps the only, reason it was in the air was because of the flying chunks of iron that had been orbiting the earth since the Russians launched the first Sputnik in 1957, so upping the ante in the cold war poker game and forcing the USA to embark on an accelerated space programme, and, along the way, seize the imagination of the watching world. The nearest we came to such expensive glory was our own sub-space, supersonic piece of flying junk – Concorde. Dr Poole describes the project as: " . . . A paradigm of much that has gone wrong in post-war Britain . . . in ten years the estimated cost rose from about £150 million to over £1000 million . . . a fruitless fantasy of technological achievement."[36]

It is worth noting that, in line with Dr Poole's view of the vogue for science, Concorde was conceived under the Conservatives and pursued so ardently under Labour. Today it flies in circles for the delight of gullible tourists. The *Queen Elizabeth* rots in Hong Kong harbour and the *Queen Mary* idles at Long Beach to much the same effect, but at least they have forty years of useful life behind them. Concorde remains a monument to the technofolly of successive governments.

To say that the speech was not new to Wilson's repertoire, or even new in terms of the general debate within British politics is not to belittle the achievement. The achievement was that Wilson took a recurrent theme in his own speeches, at the right moment to command popular concern and uttered it with enough skill, guts and energy to inspire if not a nation, then certainly an electorate. This the government, naturally, did not respect, but their response was feeble, effete and out of time. From a trip to Wiltshire Lord Hailsham, the Minister for Science and Lord High Everything Else, opined: "You could not do what Labour's policy demands without undermining the whole of the assumptions on which we live [by which he meant property] . . . they could, in effect, require control over the whole of industry."[37]

This was the gist of a dreary, unworldly tome Hailsham published that year, called *Science and Politics*,[38] in which he argued that science was its own master, and that direction from above was impossible. It lacks the clout and the directness of Wilson's approach, and reveals not the anxious, concerned layman that Wilson appeared to be, but the voice of the Senior Common Room of the inter-war years – "first class people", "promising minds", the odd Greek word thrown in for good confusion. If Hailsham knew as much about science as Wilson, which may be the case, he had not the style or the panache to convey it – and in that is a greater difference than any matter of policy or fact.

In the Labour mind all power is keyed to education – hence Wilson called for more universities, for a university of the air, for comprehensive education, as the first moves towards restoring the scientific and industrial achievement of Britain. He lamented the brain drain, and the foreign exploitation of 'British know-how and research' – although he spared the delegates the usual example of the hovercraft – and, in a moment of vision, called for what would now be known as intermediate technology. He said he would create new ministries – for Science (at last to be given cabinet status), for Disarmament, for Overseas Development, for Higher Education and for Planning. He pointed out how much scientific research was geared, wastefully, to defence. He anticipated the problems that getting out of defence would cause – he implicitly acknowledged that full employment was only possible because of military Keynesianism – and he speculated enthusiastically on the possibilities that redirection of this effort might create: " . . . if we could mobilise these scientists . . . we could within a very short period produce a major breakthrough in a whole number of fields: perhaps some new breakthrough in marine propulsion, in aircraft guidance, in electronics . . . " and in this his argument became peculiarly vague – the 'somes' and the 'perhaps' are telling – the dream had no substance. Wilson's moment has been demolished many times since, even by those who, at first hearing, were among the rapturous, but *The Times* ripped off the Emperor's new clothes immediately.

"Mr Wilson did far more to describe the problems of the future than to show exactly how his broad proposals could be worked . . . the speech scarcely did more than sketch the outline of what a Labour government will do for science and technology and then it amounted to no more than the creation of a new Ministry . . . the political significance . . . lies in the subtle skill with which he steered his rank and file away from sterile, traditional disputations . . . "[39]

Nor did Wilson define with any clarity the channelling of money into industry and science, nor would he have wished to. To do so would mean engaging with those 'sterile' arguments, nationalisation and Clause 4. The agenda for the conference did not set time for nationalisation, defence or foreign policy. The Gaitskell confrontation became the Wilson neat avoidance. Francis Boyd, writing in the *Guardian*, observed something of the behind-the-scenes compromise in the agenda: "In effect Labour has decided to abandon its rigidity which Hugh Gaitskell tried to remove by his attack on Clause 4 and which Mr Wilson, abetted by Mr George Brown, Mr Frank Cousins and Mr Harry Crane, chairman of the Conference Arrangements Committee, seemed to be removing while leaving Clause 4 intact."[40]

Intact? Mr Frank Cousins aiding and abetting? Two weeks previously Wilson had written a piece for the *New York Times*, stating more clearly the new position on these matters than he would allow at Conference. He had warned, as he repeatedly did, that British Socialism was not a revolutionary doctrine – after all its leader had merely read *about* Marx – and quoted in full the original Clause 4 and the Gaitskell revision: "Recognising that both public and private enterprise have a place in the economy, it [the party] believes that further extension of common ownership should be decided from time to time . . . according to circumstances, with due regard for the views of the workers and consumers concerned."

The presentation implies that this version has now wholly superseded the 1918 Clause 4 – which was not the case. No mention is made of Wilson's opposition to this wording, and of his attempts to shove it into Clause 5, thereby leaving Clause 4 intact.[41] The extent of the compromise was further revealed in Labour's five-hundred-page sledgehammer election document *12 Wasted Years*. By common consent of Brown and Wilson it concentrated on the Tory record, but here and there it made statements about the Labour party.

"The policy of the Labour party . . . is democratically determined by . . . annual conference . . ." *but* " . . . Before each election the NEC and the PLP decide which items from the party programme shall be included in the manifesto . . ." *but* " . . . The NEC . . . has no authority over the actions in Parliament of Labour Ministers or members."[42]

Fair warning for all who ploughed through that book that Wilson was taking the party right of Gaitskell, and right, right, right again, and the will of the party as a whole mattered not a damn. On the Friday before, the nature of conference and the impotence of the NEC was demonstrated in a heated set-to between Harry Crane and members of the NEC, in which Crane resisted attempts by the NEC to set the agenda for the coming week. Much in the style of the Conservatives, no one should mar the show of unity. Of course, there were those who could. Cousins had attended the September TUC conference, still seeking left-wing commitment from Labour. Yet he had given a press briefing only a few days before Scarborough, playing down any differences between himself and Wilson, and at the conference itself had approved even the contentious Labour incomes policy, and declared, poetically, that "science is a vision with its working clothes on". Between the two assemblies, somehow Wilson had been able to reassure Cousins. Perhaps the very nature of Wilson's approach was an appeal to the scientific interests Cousins was known to have? Cousins had, after all, contributed to the final draft of Wilson's speech. In the end, when Wilson created, as promised, all the new ministries,[43] the Ministry of Technology went to Frank Cousins. It seems beyond doubt that

Wilson did not offer the post to Cousins as early as this, and beyond doubt that a simple promise of power could never have swayed Cousins. His biographer, Geoffrey Goodman, is emphatic that this is not the point "when Cousins was being enticed to join a Wilson Cabinet . . . the truth is that the idea was not mentioned until the Summer of 1964".[44] Cousins, like so many, fell under the spell and pulled the wool over his own eyes. Crossman was an expert at such self-delusion. He sings the praises of Wilson's Kennedy image, celebrates the finding of Wilson's new frontier in the harnessing of science, but can only sum it up in the language of advertising . . . "Harold is onto something completely real" . . . as though he hadn't been at all sure before. Like Hailsham, Labour's own science spokesman read Greats at Oxford, and worried about being caught out as ignorant. And, above all, he reveals what lay beneath the illusion of unity – the contempt Wilson had for most of his colleagues. "I am running a Bolshevik revolution with a Tsarist shadow cabinet," said Wilson. What he thought of Brown is well known – Crossman added his own opinion that Brown was "a thug" – Patrick Gordon Walker, who was appointed to the post Brown wanted, gets the job simply because he "is stupid" and "would do as he's told" – Callaghan has "softening of the brain," although it's unclear who has formulated this opinion.[45] The unity bandwagon rolled on. As an anonymous supporter of Wilson's had been heard to remark in the summer: "Isn't it wonderful, now, for a change, to have a leader who can lie?"

When Brown opened his speech with the words "This is not a one man show," he twisted the liar's tail and put a minor convulsion through the assembly. He went on: "Though I had my doubts of the ways in which we reach our leadership decisions six months ago, I am very happy today sincerely to pay tribute . . . " and the remainder of his sentence was swamped in an uproar of cheering. In concluding he delivered Wilson's unity for him: "There are no enmities and no suspicions among the Labour ranks. We are men and women who have the same ideals, people who understand each other." With that, depending on which newspaper you read, Wilson seized Brown's hand and raised it aloft, or Brown seized Wilson's, in a gesture of victory tailor-made for the photographers and the television cameras – Wilson had, after all, delivered his own speech fully made up for the camera.

Ted Eldred, a regular at party conferences in the sixties, saw the gesture as Brown's: "Whatever differences George may have had with individuals . . . his loyalty to the Labour Party was never in doubt. The party was everything to George. The gesture was quite spontaneous and I don't think Wilson was expecting it at all. I think it was quite genuine."

As much as Britain was going to have it, this was it – the image of the new generation triumphant. In its way real enough. In its way the breath of political fresh air so long needed, so long delayed – the Kennedy touch.

§

Reality returned only six weeks later. On the evening of President Kennedy's assassination, the Rediffusion television programme *This Week* sought out a prominent Labour MP to pay tribute to the slaughtered man-god. They settled on George Brown.

Ted Eldred: "George had a long standing engagement to have a drink with an old friend who'd become Mayor of one of the London boroughs. George could not take his drink. On that night . . . I've no idea how drunk or sober he was . . . When the TV came along George, without stopping to think, said 'Certainly.' Sophie was saying 'George, you mustn't.' George was saying 'I must!' Being wise after the event he shouldn't have done it. But there was no faking about his emotions at all. The emotion was very, very real."[46]

Brown had wept openly on live television. He had spoken in personal terms of his relationship with 'Jack' – "Jack Kennedy was one of my best friends". He had said it would be necessary for him to go and see "Lyndon". The complaints poured in to Wilson from the constituencies. The *Mail* summed up the reaction as "Mr Brown's manner was out of keeping with the nation's sense of mourning and shock." Few seemed willing to believe in Brown's own sense of shock.

What the public had not witnessed was the scene in the hospitality room that preceded the broadcast. Also appearing were Carl Foreman, director of *The Guns of Navarone*, Eli Wallach, star of Foreman's latest picture *The Victors*, and American newspaper columnist John Crosby: "Straightaway he picked on Eli. Eli didn't know who Mr Brown was, but Mr Brown knew Eli from his films . . . Mr Brown asked Eli if he knew some scriptwriter and when Eli said he didn't, Mr Brown said something like 'Well, you don't amount to much' . . . Mr Brown kept needling Eli and started making wild statements about American domestic policy which I don't think he knew much about . . . finally Eli said 'Listen, I didn't come here to be insulted. I think we should step outside . . . I'll knock you on your can.'"[47] Clearly Mr Wallach didn't know *any* scriptwriters.

Brown denied that version of events. To him it was just "a strong discussion". It is possible that Brown's admiration for Kennedy – he kept a framed colour photograph of himself and the President on top of the family television set – was reciprocated, that there was a friendship. No one was inclined to believe him, or that he'd done anything but indulge in histrionics. Crossman wrote that he was certain Brown had met Kennedy only twice (Brown had spent forty minutes with Kennedy in Washington only a month before the assassination) and that his performance was "pretty dreadful." Wilson felt he had to discipline Brown. The press reported their meeting with headlines such as 'Brown Rapped' and he was said to be contrite, but in making amends Brown cleverly outmanoeuvred Wilson and ensured that Wilson's playing the headmaster was leaked to the press and that his formal apology was not to the leader but to the Parliamentary Labour Party as a whole. Wilson, Crossman concluded, came off the worse: " . . . Wilson has I think suffered. The view is now held that for the first time he really has misbehaved . . . the whole affair has clouded Harold's position."[48]

With Brown casting himself as the victim of an overbearing and insensitive leader Wilson found himself forced to act cautiously where Brown was concerned. Any shadow cabinet reshuffle was postponed and Wilson was unable even to stop Brown from appearing on television in the future.

§

Throughout October the Conservatives ran an advertisement in the press depicting a lone CND demonstrator sitting-doggedly-in, over the caption 'Meanwhile the Conservatives have signed the Test Ban treaty.'[49] At the end of the year several Labour MPs resigned from the CND Executive Committee, among them Judith Hart, Anthony Greenwood and Michael Foot. The last stragglers in the return to the fold?

Michael Foot: "We all wanted to see a Labour government elected and some of them didn't think that was so important. Well, we certainly thought it was and we wanted to assist in it. I was saying that I think that . . . it's not sufficient just to say that you are going to concentrate on this one issue, you have to get a Labour government elected, and we wanted it for a variety of other reasons as well . . . In CND there'd always been this argument about major matter discussion as to what were the tactics to be employed at any particular time, and some of us, right from the beginning had said we didn't think the Committee of 100 tactics were the sensible ones and were opposed to it. We didn't resign from CND or the rest, but we didn't think CND should be taken over by them . . . Then there was also the question of whether you were going to put up candidates against Labour party candidates, and of course, we were opposed to doing that too."[50]

The election did not happen. 1964 opened as 1963 had done with the same imminent prospect. Wilson took to the stump again in anticipation of a Spring campaign. In rapid succession he spoke in Birmingham, Swansea, Leeds, Liverpool, Edinburgh and London. The Scientific Revolution still formed the basic message of the speeches, in a less inspired, if still vigorous series, but the title had evolved. Taking his lead from a piece by Caroline Benn in *Look* magazine in October 1963 Wilson now addressed the nation on the topic of 'The New Britain'. Give or take the odd outburst from his deputy Wilson could boast that he had the party behind him, Gaitskellites, unions and the left. He had forged his fighting machine, he had created his new frontier, he had ditched the word 'revolution', he was ready for the next election, whenever it came.

Tony Benn: "He was a fixer really. Fixers have a part to play. I suppose one third of all leaders are fixers. Some are visionaries, who are brilliant but divisive, then after a visionary you need a fixer, who gets so shabby you need a straight man, and after a straight man who gets so boring you need a visionary . . . [Wilson] had a visionary element to begin with but on the whole he was a fixer – who 'fixed' labour in office for a long period."[51]

CHAPTER FOUR

SELF-EVIDENT TRUTHS

"I hereby enjoin upon the people so declared to be free to abstain from all violence, unless necessary in self-defense."

Abraham Lincoln, 1863

"In 1963 the Negro, who had realised for many years that he was not truly free, awoke from a stupor of inaction with that cold dash of realisation that 1963 meant one hundred years after Lincoln gave his autograph to the cause of freedom."   Martin Luther King, 1963

In 1963 the United States of America, particularly in its southern states, was a racially segregated country.

In 1963 the United States of America saw more than fourteen hundred Civil Rights demonstrations. In the 'conservative' estimate of Dr Martin Luther King demonstrations of solidarity with the Civil Rights movement that summer involved over a million people. Twenty thousand of those demonstrators were arrested. Ten people were killed over Civil Rights issues, and there were an estimated thirty-five bombings. In the second week of June alone twenty-three towns and cities experienced protest, from peaceful sit-ins to street battles, from Los Angeles to Washington DC, from Providence to Tallahassee, from sea to shining sea.

Whatever the disclaimers, a Negro revolution was under way. Awarenesss of this prompted *Newsweek* magazine to commission a Harris poll under that title. Statistics will always seem a bald way to describe the lives of men and women, but in the middle of 1963 there were 19,300,000 Negroes in the USA (this was the term in use at the time rather than the late-sixties' *Blacks*) just over half of whom lived in the Old South, in those states that had fought as the Confederate secessionist side in the Civil War of 1861-5 and which still[1] enforced racial segregation, and a third of whom lived in the seven major industrial states of the north and west – overall they made up some 10% of the country's population.

At more than 13%, unemployment amongst the black population ran at twice the national average, while the black wage was only

55% of the average white wage – although the southern white wage was only two-thirds that of the northern. This figure isn't offered as mitigation. It points up part of the spurious logic of apartheid, the common non-sense that there's always someone worse off than yourself, which scarcely conceals the wish fulfilment in making damn sure that there is. Segregation, as a caste system, could hammer down white wages with the phoney reassurance that 'at least you're better off than the niggers.' It's possible to view the course of southern history this century in the light of this notion – that they were desperate to ensure the reality of that wish in denial of their own hardship. To a large extent the American dream had passed the Old South by.

Of the black workforce 4% held skilled jobs, 60% 'menial' jobs and 9% were schoolteachers – since segregated schools demanded black teachers. The Harris poll revealed a wide dissatisfaction – 80% felt they were qualified for something better, but only 20% had joined a trades union and a mere 2% the National Association for the Advancement of Colored People.

In practical terms what these figures represents is the widespread poverty, exploitation and oppression of the Blacks, be it in the ghettoes of the northern cities or the sharecroppers' shacks of the South. In the South – and this chapter will be concerned almost entirely with the South – the Blacks had been disenfranchised, and from their lack of political power all other abuses followed – separate and unequal facilities in all aspects of life, housing (extortionate rents as well as ghettoes, slums and shacks), transport (sitting at the back of the bus and forcibly surrendering seats to whites), shopping (thousands of stores that would sell merchandise to a Black but would not sell him a cup of coffee or let him use the lavatories and drinking fountains) – and the ever present threat of violence. There were five thousand recorded lynchings between 1865 and 1959, to say nothing of the 'disappeared'.

Large numbers of rural black families lived under the sharecropper system – often described as slavery without shackles. The sharecropper lived in a wood and tar-paper shack, owned almost nothing and worked under a burden of immovable debt which 'sold' him in perpetuity to his white landlords, who advanced him his seed corn and fertilisers against the next summer's harvest and so perpetuated the debt. More often than not the sharecropper had never voted and had never even tried to vote. The Harris poll showed that only 30% of a potential southern black electorate of over five million registered to vote. 64% of Blacks did not attempt to register – hence Mississippi which was 42% black returned only 7% of the potential black vote, and Georgia, 28% black, only 6% – making a total of 850,000 unregistered black adults in just those two states. When asked, most Blacks who had attempted registration and failed gave 'intimidation' as the chief cause of failure. What this meant could vary enormously. At the registration office it could mean a voucher system – whereby the applicant had to be endorsed by a white, or show proof of 'good moral character', or it could mean having to take literacy tests, or possess knowledge of the state constitution that would tax a lawyer's brain (Mississippi's constitution had 285 sections – the questionnaire, in twenty-one parts, could ask about any of these), or pay a poll tax, or (until 1939) it could be the 'grandfather clause' which allowed automatic registration of voters whose grandparents had voted but put all others through tests – of course no recent descendant of a slave could take advantage of this. Away from the polls it could mean an end to credit, an end to local supplies of food, petrol and other necessities, police harassment – or night riders, the arrival of the Ku Klux Klan, the burning of homes and the beating or murder of 'uppity niggers'.

§

It's a measure of the seriousness of the North-South gulf that one of the ways the conditions in Dixie were brought home to middle America was by a white novelist skilfully passing as a Black and journeying across the South. John Howard Griffin's *Black Like Me* recorded his travels at the end of 1959 and ran to fifty editions over the next ten years. It abounds in the small details of segregation, the pettiness with which the fragile white superiority can be measured in having a black man walk a dozen blocks for a drink of water or a public lavatory that doesn't have a 'whites only' sign. Yet what most sticks in the mind is the total terror which seized Griffin on his arrival in Mississippi, the dread, the fear for his life that almost ruined the project, but which was the daily lot of every black man, woman and child in this the worst of the segregated states. After the book's publication in 1960, Griffin was hanged in effigy in his Texas hometown by outraged whites. He had touched upon a self-perpetuating Southern myth, one aired so often in the newsreels of the time – the Southern white hated outside interference, the arrival of agitators and troublemakers – he knew his 'nigras', they were all right, peaceable, so long as do-gooders didn't fill their heads with nonsense. This daydream of contented darkies, doubtless gently strumming banjos, extended all the way to Washington. Many a Southern politician could use his maid or his valet as a yardstick –

67

little doubting that they had long since learnt to tell him what he wanted to hear. 'We know our nigras' was a myth that would die hard.

The Harris poll asked whites how they saw discrimination. Even in the South 88% of whites appeared to approve of equal rights, so long as they weren't imposed on them from outside – but then they could have said the same in 1933 and under the veil of gradualism might have gone on being similarly positive in 1993 – but more closely, 91% would not want a member of their family to marry a Black and 97% did not want their daughter dating a black man. And therein lies the rub. As James Baldwin wrote: "It has to do with political power and it has to do with sex. And this is a nation which, most unluckily, knows very little about either."[2]

Throughout his travels Griffin was pumped by garrulous white men for details of his sex life – the black man appeared to the white bigot as a man who led a sex life unhampered by morals or diminished libido. From this fantasy springs the fiercely masculine sense of the southern honour that must 'protect our womenfolk'. Fantasy – because if this were not the line scored in the sand something else would be. In defence of womenfolk Blacks who looked directly at the white woman, spoke out of turn to the white woman or otherwise crossed the line, could be beaten, murdered and castrated. In the doctrine of the Klan this could be defended as the prevention of 'the mongrelisation' of both races, and biblical authority could be cited to defend the separation of the races sexually as it was cited to defend every other aspect of segregation. This too was a fantasy – the Harris poll put the number of Blacks who were part white as high as 71%. Mongrelisation was already a fact of life in America – as many white men would freely admit to Griffin when boasting of their own exploits, rape included: "We figure we're doing you people a favor to get some white blood in your kids."[3]

From this structured, if meaningless, doctrine it followed that one of the things most offensive to the white, male bigot was the integration of the races which allowed for the proximity of white women and black men. Inevitably the tactics of protest would put them side by side, and some of the most vicious acts of violence perpetrated against the Civil Rights demonstrators would be in response to the violation of this taboo.

Along with this fundamental sexual fear went the commonplace prejudices of smell, dirt and disease – all of which were widely thought, in the evidence of the Harris poll, to be typical of the negroes as a race, as were lack of ambition, inferior intelligence, tendency to laugh a lot and willingness to live on welfare.

It's an understatement to term the Blacks of early-sixties America second class citizens. Michael Harrington in his 1962 Penguin Special, *The Other America*, refers to the Blacks as outsiders within their own country, outsiders in a nation of immigrants, deprived of the sense of a common homeland which bound the immigrants together, and economically oppressed by their confinement to un-skilled work. These factors could undermine the sense of loyalty to the state in this the most patriotic of nations – the sense of depri-vation, of not belonging, was registered in very American terms in the Harris poll by the 20% of Blacks who declined to say that they'd fight for their country. This might not seem high now, some twenty years after a generation burnt their draft cards, but when bluntly informed of this fact by James Baldwin in the May of 1963, Bobby Kennedy was shocked. If the sense of belonging to America was weak, the sense of belonging to themselves was growing. More than half of Blacks questioned were willing to demonstrate for Civil Rights, and nearly three-quarters thought that 1963 was the time to make the big push for equality.

Whitney Young, head of the black National Urban League, told *Newsweek*: "What we need is a massive domestic Marshall plan that, for a period, will give special, preferential and expanded opportunities for Negro citizens in housing, employment, health, welfare and education – the same conscious effort to *include* which the society historically has exhibited in *exclusion*."[4]

§

America's Blacks had been organising slowly and sporadically throughout the century. The oldest of the black organisations was, and is, the National Association for the Advancement of Colored People, founded by W. E. du Bois in 1909 on the one hundredth anniversary of Lincoln's birth. Aimed initially at stopping lynchings, it became primarily concerned with litigation, with tackling segre-gation through the courts. In 1935 the NAACP successfully contested segregation in the University of Maryland, and in 1954 displaced the cornerstone of segregation by challenging the Plessy v. Ferguson decision of 1896 in the Supreme Court. Chief Justice Earl Warren overturned fifty-eight years of legal history with what became known as the Brown decision: "Separate educational facilities," he declared "are inherently unequal." The Brown de-cision was not easily or readily put into practice, but it's implication that all segregation was unequal and unconstitutional became ger-minal – the seed from which post-war black activism would grow.

The Congress for Racial Equality was founded in 1942 – like the NAACP it remained largely a northern organisation; unlike the NAACP it was committed to direct action rather than litigation. In its response to happenings outside America it also sounded a new note – its head, James Farmer, was influenced by the politics and actions of Gandhi. Without the teachings of Gandhi the course of the Civil Rights Movement in the following twenty-five years would have been drastically different – CORE introduced the two basic weapons of the movement, civil disobedience and non-violence.

In 1955 the bus boycott in Montgomery, Alabama had received national attention. The story of Rosa Parks' courageous refusal to give up her seat at the front of the bus, and of the fifty thousand Blacks who forced integration on the city's buses, quickly made the twenty-six-year-old Baptist preacher Martin Luther King Jr the movement's best known leader. Out of the boycott arose the Southern Christian Leadership Conference, founded in Atlanta in January 1957 around a core of ministers – Dr King and Rev. Ralph Abernathy of Montgomery, Rev. Fred Shuttlesworth of Birmingham – all Baptists – and Rev. Joseph Lowery of Mobile, a Methodist. In all some fifteen to twenty black churchmen attended the first SCLC conference. At last, the Southern Blacks had their own organisation. It was inevitable that the leadership would come from the church. Historically the church had been the only part of southern society in which the Blacks had autonomy. Blacks at prayer had not been thought threatening. Hence, as with school-teachers, the Blacks produced a high proportion of preachers. The education and the initiative was vested in such people. Yet, it was an initiative that was allowed to slip. Between 1957 and 1960 the SCLC did not build on the Montgomery success to develop a programme of direct action – this despite the obvious influence of CORE and Gandhi. Gandhi had been asked to speak in the USA as long ago as 1935. In 1957 his disciple Rammanohar Lohia had spoken at meetings in Alabama, and in 1959 Martin Luther King had visited the Gandhi Memorial Foundation in India. But by 1960, however strong his influence, Gandhi's tactics were not in practice.

On February 1st, 1960 a new generation took the initiative. Four black, male students attending college in Greensboro, North Carolina, and all still in their teens, revived a technique first pioneered by CORE in Chicago in 1942. They went to the whites only lunch counter in Woolworth's and when refused service simply stayed seated. The sit-in began again at Greensboro. Spontaneous though it was, it also fed back directly to the 'spiritual' home of non-violence and civil disobedience – Nashville, Tennessee.

70

Students at the black Nashville colleges had tried test sit-ins at the end of 1959. Under the tutelage of thirty-one-year-old James Lawson, a theology student at Nashville's Vanderbilt College, they had been introduced, over a period of two years, to the teachings of Gandhi and schooled in the techniques of non-violence. A conscientious objector in the Korean war, Lawson had spent the mid-fifties in India studying under Gandhi's followers. He became through these classes the primary strategist of the new youth movement. He believed in 'radical non-violence', in direct confrontation with segregation – most importantly he believed that if arrested and jailed the protestor should refuse bail – 'Jail – No bail' became a motto and a technique of the new movement. His classes taught resistance to abuse and violence. Students would sit, learning passivity, as their colleagues hurled insults, provoked and attacked them. Techniques of survival were developed – how best to avoid getting hurt without ever fighting back – fold hands over head to protect skull, cover face with forearms, assume foetal position to protect vital organs – such advice would be needed and heeded on countless occasions. Twenty-year-old John Lewis, son of an Alabama sharecropper, then a divinity student at Fisk College and now a US Congressman, drew up rules for the conduct of sit-ins – 'Don't laugh out loud, Don't swear, Be friendly at all times, Sit up straight and face the counter, Don't talk among yourselves, Don't hit back.'

"It was not just a tactic . . . for some of the people it became a philosophy . . . it became a way of life."[5]

Two weeks after the Greensboro sit-in the Nashville group mustered two hundred students and sat-in en masse in the main stores of Nashville. From there the sit-ins spread across the South and beyond, as a national boycott of stores, which, like Woolworth's, practised discrimination in the South, began to affect northern cities as far apart as San Francisco and New York– in the course of the year some one hundred cities and seventy thousand protesters were involved. There were more than three thousand arrests. The Nashville sit-in became the exemplar of the sixties protest movement, not only in the speed with which it spread, but in the pattern of retribution and negotiation that followed. After two relatively peaceful weeks the students were attacked by white mobs, while the police stood by, and afterwards arrested. Those arrested accepted jail rather than pay a fine, and, like a British square at Waterloo, a new line of students took their place at the sit-ins. Meanwhile the black professors expressed their disapproval of what the new generation was up to – Lawson was expelled from Vanderbilt.

" . . . the student movement galvanised the older organisations into a new dynamism, won the support of some of the established Negro leaders . . . and left far behind those leaders who could not break old habits of thinking and old ties with the white elite."[6]

White Nashville resisted with violence, even to the bombing of the home of the attorney defending the students, but integration came that summer to Nashville's public places, when the spending power of the increasing black middle class (which Nashville had in common with other southern cities, such as Atlanta) made itself felt in a boycott of downtown Nashville stores.

Out of this came a new organisation – the Student Nonviolent Coordinating Committee, convened for the first time at a special conference in Raleigh, North Carolina, during Easter weekend 1960. The SCLC had put up eight hundred dollars to fund the conference, and some three hundred student delegates attended. From its inception SNCC was not wholly southern, and not wholly black – the proportions being roughly 80–20 in each case. It was the first multi-racial Civil Rights group and by far the youngest, the mean age being between sixteen and twenty-two. Despite the willingness of SCLC to adopt the new organisation as its youth wing, the conference voted against any affiliation, believing firmly in its own independence and in its own tactics and ideals. Many former members have set down oral accounts (Julian Bond, John Lewis, Lonnie King, Diane Nash, Bob Zellner) or written histories (James Foreman, Howard Zinn, Mary King) of SNCC – they all have in common a belief in spontaneity, direct action, democratic structure and the rejection of personality leadership. This brought conflict with the older movement, now cohering around the figure of Martin Luther King, and they showed frequent distaste for the centrality King was achieving – nicknaming him 'de lawd'. King professed not to understand why they so dubbed him, and of all the older leaders King was probably the most responsive to SNCC ideas – his own actions and writings, in 1963 and 1964, show clear signs of his acceptance of their influence on the Movement as a whole.

From the beginning SNCC incurred the suspicion of the American Establishment – Marion Barry, lately the much-troubled Mayor of Washington DC, the SNCC delegate to the Democratic Convention of 1960, found himself defending his organisation against the charge of Communism made by former president Harry Truman – and very soon it evolved a position that was critical of, and in confrontation with, its potentially greatest ally, the administration of President Kennedy.

In his 1961 Inaugural Address John F. Kennedy said: "Let the word go forth from this time and place, to friend and foe alike, that the torch has been passed to a new generation . . . " by which he meant his own, the young men who had fought the last war in the front line. Yet in one context his words seem almost a year too late – in the battle that was raging within American society, the torch had already passed to a younger generation – the generation that was SNCC.

§

It's often been said that Civil Rights were a minor issue in the Presidential election of 1960 – but Jack Kennedy issued enough statements, pronounced on enough issues to make that view seem less than accurate. The Los Angeles Convention had produced a fairly wide Civil Rights platform – promising to end the poll tax and literacy tests, and offering executive action on discrimination in federal-aided housing and jobs. Kennedy had promised moral leadership and, with the most recent Civil Rights activities in mind, had said: "The next President . . . must support the right of every citizen to stand up for his rights even if on occasion he must sit down for them." More riskily, he had told the New York Liberal Party that Civil Rights were a moral issue and that he'd run without the South if that's the way it had to be. That's almost the way it was.

In the October of 1960 a Democratic Civil Rights weekend was held in New York, culminating in a Harlem rally in which the candidate shared the platform with the leaders of the Movement, and New York's black congressman Adam Clayton Powell. This was probably the electoral face of Civil Rights in the party, organised and manageable. Within a week of that rally the rough reality had broken through.

As the example of Greensboro took hold, sit-ins spread across the South. Almost at once students at Morehouse College in Atlanta, Georgia (the symbolic and emotional if not actual capital of the South, razed to the ground by Union troops in the Civil War) began to target public facilities in Atlanta. By the end of the summer the students had rocked the legal system with well over a thousand participants, but had failed to desegregate their targets. In that same October they decided to tackle the largest private facility in Atlanta – the whites only Magnolia Room of Rich's department store. They were aiming high in all possible ways – they could economically disadvantage Rich's by a campaign aimed at the better off black middle class, many of whom held Rich's credit cards, with the simple logic of 'you can shop there but you can't get a cup of coffee';

they could foster a national issue by the timing of the sit-in – only three weeks before the election – and they could ask the best known figure in the Movement to join in – Martin Luther King.

That King was free on October 19th was a remarkable coincidence and had consequences no one could have foreseen, though many have commented on. Among Jack Kennedy's campaign staff was a long term Civil Rights activist named Harris Wofford. Wofford was to keep the candidate informed of developments in his field. For the second of the famous television debates with Nixon, on October 7th, Wofford had briefed Kennedy – very much the Boston Irishman (in the words of Arthur Schlesinger "entirely devoid of racial prejudice but only intermittently sensitive to racial injustice")[7] – on the poverty of the southern Blacks. He was also an advocate of an official meeting between Kennedy and his friend Dr King. (King and Kennedy had already met privately twice during the primaries.) It was seen as advantageous if such a meeting could take place south of the Mason-Dixon line, and the date of October 19th was fixed for Miami, Florida. King wavered on the exclusivity of the meeting and suggested that it would be wise if he met Nixon too – at this point the Civil Rights Movement was not endorsing either candidate officially, and King Snr was openly for Nixon. Kennedy would not agree and at this point the proposed meeting fell through.

So, on the 19th Martin Luther King Jr sat down in the Magnolia Room at Rich's and, as expected, was arrested. King was on a year's probation for not possessing a valid Georgia driving licence. That he would be jailed immediately was beyond doubt. Fearing for her husband's life Coretta King wired both candidates. From the Kennedy camp, Wofford telephoned Atlanta lawyer Morris Abram, and Abram in turn called Mayor Hartsfield. Hartsfield, known as a shrewd fixer, interpreted the call as a request from Kennedy and agreed to the release of all those arrested at the sit-in. It was assumed that this included King. When, at last, Kennedy was told of his 'involvement' he was surprised, and a problem he was to face throughout his presidency came to the fore for the first time – he could not be seen deliberately to override the sovereignty of a state (wars were fought over that kind of thing) – more cynically he could not, as a northern liberal, involve himself too directly in the problems of the Deep South. A mild statement was issued, to the effect that Kennedy had asked for a report.

King was not among those released. He was returned to neighbouring de Kalb County, to the judge who had ordered his probation, and was sentenced to six months' hard labour – shocking in its brutality and out of all proportion to the original offence, this sentence gave weight to Coretta King's fear that the police meant to kill her husband. If King was to be set free more direct action would be required, tougher strings would have to be pulled. However mild the original statement JFK had made, Governor Vandiver of Georgia warned him that another such would cost him the South.

King's lawyers applied for bail. Days dragged by and still a minister of the church, held on a motoring offence, remained in Reidsville maximum security prison, in the wilds of Georgia, to which he had been taken in chains at the dead of night. Martin Luther King wore his prison stripes and shared a cell with the cockroaches.

Mrs King called Wofford. Wofford had the idea that a personal call from Kennedy might reassure her, but Kennedy was now campaigning in Chicago and was hard to reach. He got through to JFK's brother-in-law, Sargent Shriver. Shriver chose his moment and told Kennedy privately how serious the matter had become. Alone, free of more politic advisers, JFK called Mrs King at once. The call seems to have been much of nothing, the reassurance of knowing that someone cares – for there was little that Kennedy could do, despite his suggestion that she should call him if she thought he could help in any way, unless he surrendered his candidate's crippling sense of diplomacy. Nevertheless Mrs King was clearly touched by Kennedy's attention, as was her father-in-law who announced his intention to switch from Nixon to Kennedy. It was now the turn of Robert Kennedy to be surprised at the turn of events – he too invoked the threat to the Southern vote. Too easily 'natural' Democrats could switch to the Republicans; there had been Democrats for Ike and Democrats for Dewey, and there would be Democrats for Nixon again in 1972. Nixon was not indifferent to such events – he had made his own enquiries. If Civil Rights was not a major issue in the election then it certainly touched a matter dear to both candidates – they both wanted the black vote. Nixon raised King's imprisonment with the outgoing Attorney-General, Bill Rogers, only to find Eisenhower reluctant to make any statement on King's imprisonment in his less than wholehearted endorsement of his vice-president. The advantage now lay with the Kennedys. JFK's call after all had been a private one and had not offered any direct action. The Kennedy camp now urged King Snr to make his conversion public. King spoke to the press, told them of his initial opposition as a Baptist to the idea of a Catholic president and said: "I've got all my votes and I've got a suitcase and I'm going to take them up there and dump them in his lap."

Privately JFK remarked on the bigotry of holding a man's religion against him in the first place.

The issue still seemed ordered and contained, but the next move put the possibility of controlling it completely out of bounds – Bobby Kennedy received a call from Vandiver suggesting that a word from him to the judge, Oscar Mitchell of de Kalb County, Georgia, might do the trick.[8] Kennedy told Mitchell that a "decent American" would see to it that King was "out of prison by sundown". Later the same day King was released on a bail surety of $2000. More circumspect than his father, Martin Luther King Jr thanked Senator Kennedy, praised his courage, but declined to endorse him, and commented on the pleasing coincidence that the politically wise action had also been the moral one. Such measured comment was wasted. Much of the press reported that he had endorsed Kennedy, and it became widely believed among Blacks that he had. The direct involvement of the Kennedy campaign in a southern matter was now impossible to conceal. The risk had been taken and the news was beginning to spread. Robert Kennedy's call could be construed, since he was a qualified attorney, as unprofessional conduct, if not as interference in the due process of the law. Wofford's view was that the word was reaching the wrong people – the whites and the bigots were more in touch than the poorer, largely rural Blacks who needed to be told if the votes lost among the whites were to be recouped among the Blacks. Depending on your point of view the next step was either shrewd politicking or cynical self-serving – the Kennedy camp printed two million copies of a pamphlet entitled 'No Comment Nixon versus a Candidate with a Heart, Senator Kennedy: The Case of Martin Luther King' and distributed them nationally with the help of the black churches.

There is more to this than just background. It epitomises a tactic and quite possibly a principle of the Kennedy administration. The immediacy with which the Kennedy brothers could deal with people can be seen in this, the first example of their telephone diplomacy – a complaint that was probably common to all 'enemies' (I use that word lightly) of the administration was that they could be got out of bed at two or three o'clock in the morning by one brother or the other. The principle is better phrased as a question. Were the Kennedys overtaken by events? Dragged further into a Civil Rights issue than they might have wished? A yes to this is not necessarily cynical – it is not necessarily a question of the failure of leadership. Often in Jack Kennedy's presidency his administration was pushed by events in the Movement – the measure of his administration was not in the fact of being overtaken by events but in how they met the challenge – a phrase Kennedy himself might have used, and most probably did.

Kennedy defeated Nixon by 0.5% of the popular vote – and a significantly larger margin of the electoral college – and it's often said that the 68-78% (estimates vary widely) of the black vote he received won him the presidency – as might the thousands of ballot papers Mayor Daley fiddled in the city of Chicago – but what's undeniable is that the black population of America now looked to the new President for the promised executive action. Nowhere in the rhetoric of success did Kennedy's 'New Frontier' mean more than in the area of Civil Rights. Equally, whilst talking of the brightest and best as Kennedy myth, if the myth had reality it was in the young lawyers appointed by Bobby Kennedy to staff the Justice Department. Among these were Assistant Attorney-General Burke Marshall, described at the time as 'the brightest young lawyer in Washington', and Deputy Attorney-General Nick Katzenbach, a Professor of Law at Chicago, who like Kennedy was a veteran of the Second World War, and had studied for his degree whilst a prisoner in Germany.

§

Jack Kennedy's victory was not reflected in the elections for Senate and Congress where the Democrats lost two and twenty-one seats respectively, and the majority became marginal and fragile – particularly if the southern Democrats (the Dixiecrats) could not be relied upon to vote with their party and for the President. The seniority system on Capitol Hill inevitably left control of some important committees in the hands of southerners – Senators and Congressmen who could be returned time after time virtually unopposed from segregated constituencies where the Blacks were disenfranchised. Senator James Eastland of Mississippi chaired the all important House Judiciary Committee (and would do so for another eighteen years); the Housing Committee was chaired by two Alabamians, Senator Sparkman and Representative Rains; the Ways and Means Committee by Rep. Wilbur D. Mills of Arkansas; the Appropriations Subcommittee by Rep. Passman of Louisiana. In a parliament as finely balanced as this, men in positions like these could effectively 'kill' legislation by never letting it get past the committee stage. The appointment of Robert Weaver (a Black and a former NAACP official) to the Housing and Home Finance Agency was held up for two months, and his elevation to the cabinet in a newly proposed Department of Urban Affairs was allowed to die at committee level – a committee made up of five Republicans, five Democrats and two Dixiecrats, which mixture precisely illustrates the notion of balance of power. More than this, a filibuster on the issue of Civil Rights could create a log jam that would upset the administration's entire legislative programme, as the new President repeatedly explained to his visitors from the Civil Rights Movement.

Of course, some southerners could be counted among Kennedy's friends, campaigners and allies – Governor Patterson of Alabama, Rep. Boggs of Louisiana, Senator Smathers of Florida for example – but the inaction of the administration on new Civil Rights legislation in its first two years had nothing to do with political horse-trading. Patterson himself is on record as saying his support of Kennedy was without strings and no promises were given in return, and Burke Marshall, so often in the Justice Department's front line, adds: "I never once – and I was in charge of suing these people all the time – discussed that kind of thing [political deals] with a Southern Senator or Congressman."

§

All new appointments had to be passed by the House Judiciary Committee. Eastland indulgently gave a nod and a wink to Bobby Kennedy as he was confirmed in his post of Attorney-General, and reminded him of how little his predecessor had done; not one civil rights case had been brought in Mississippi under Mr Rogers. The next day, as Harry Golden, editor of the *Carolina Israelite* put it, "the Department of Justice received their standing orders from the President: *'Get the road maps and go'*" . . . soon . . . "Burke Marshall and his men were tramping the back roads and the back counties knocking on the doors of Negro sharecroppers and asking 'Did you ever vote? Did you ever try to vote? Did you ever try to register? What happened?'"[9]

Almost at once Kennedy doubled the number of lawyers in the Justice Department – by 1963 there were twenty-four, five times as many as the day he took office. His brother told every member of the new cabinet to look to the recruitment of Blacks, and Bobby began an active programme of black recruitment to the department, while Marshall recruited college students in the vacations to check the hundreds of voter registration records. In the seven and a half years Nixon had headed the Vice-President's Commission on Government Contracts he had brought six law suits against factories practising discrimination. By early 1963 Lyndon Johnson had brought some seventeen hundred. In the last three years of office Ike's Justice Department had instituted ten prosecutions over infringement of voting rights. In his first year alone Bobby Kennedy brought fourteen cases and set up investigations in sixty-one counties. Whatever the gap between promise and fulfilment, the new adminstration looked active by any comparison with the Eisenhower years – but, realistically, the piecemeal, painstaking approach was only just denting segregation. Fourteen cases, sixty-one counties? The Old South had eleven states – Mississippi, by no means the largest of the states, had eighty-six counties – some of which registered not one black voter. At the end of 1963 Sunflower County – the home of Senator Eastland, in which he owned five thousand acres of cotton plantations – registered hardly more black voters than it had done at the outset of the new voter registration drive.

What "tramping the back roads" really meant was explained in detail by Burke Marshall in a 1964 lecture at Columbia University in New York. He described the Justice Department's moves to secure voting rights. The example was Forrest Co. Mississippi, where no Black had registered to vote since 1954.

1. A suit is filed against the local registrar on July 6th, 1961.
2. The District Court refuses to rule on the Government's request for a preliminary injunction.
3. The Court of Appeal reverses the above decision. The injunction is issued, but with leave to appeal. It is now March 1962.
4. The registrar refuses to comply with the injunction.
5. The registrar is cited for contempt. It is now May 1962.
6. The Court of Appeal sits to consider the charge above. It is now January 1963.
7. The Court of Appeal finds the registrar guilty. The registration of 43 black applicants and the cessation of inhibitory practices is ordered, but is withheld for two months pending review by the Supreme Court. It is now July 1963. More than two years have passed and not one single black voter has been registered in Forrest County.

Burke Marshall: "I was responsible for sixty law suits like that, at least, over those two years. Even if we had a judge who was fairly active in enforcing Civil Rights, the registrars, the officials who were actually responsible for implementing federal orders, they still worked for the state, they worked for a system that was totally white dominated, totally committed to the notion of white supremacy and black oppression. You could remove registrar after registrar – but you'd end up with the same thing, people who had come up through the same system, whom the federal system couldn't supplant until the Voting Rights Act of 1965. It was the same with the schools. The school boards are state officials – they don't work for President Kennedy they work for Governor Wallace, and politically speaking for a white electorate dedicated to white supremacy. In 1963, cutting through that system was like trying to bring a law suit in Panama or London."[10]

Constitutionally there was no other way. Just as there was no federal police, there was no catch-all way to enforce anti-discrimination laws – it was a matter of taking each case as it arose. Without new legislation discrimination would have to be fought, as the phrase of the day had it, 'Negro by Negro'. And for two years this was the way the Civil Rights battle was fought by the Kennedy administration.

Burke Marshall: " It was impossible in President Kennedy's view – and I fully agreed with it – to get major Civil Rights legislation considered in Congress in 1961 and 1962. It wasn't the southern Democrats – they'd oppose it in a hundred years' time if it were still an issue – but the Republicans. We had to have a bill that could get bi-partisan support. We had a serious bill in 1962 – a minor voting rights bill we'd worked hard for – we needed two thirds of the Senate for the 'cloture' vote – we got less than fifty. You could not get the Republicans to go along with it. The Southerners were lost anyway."[11]

No one could doubt the commitment, the moral concern, the sheer sweat of the brow and, on occasions, the physical courage on the part of those in the Justice Department – it reads like a heartbreaking struggle – but an inescapable result of this slow process must surely have been a rise in the frustration of the black activists, a frustration that was born out of the very nature of the United States constitution?[12]

'Freedom Now!' – sometimes just 'Now!' – became a common slogan in 1963.

§

If the priority of the government and the Justice Department was to concentrate on voter registration, rather than legislation or the promised executive action,[13] viewing political power as the touchstone of equality, sections of the Civil Rights Movement did not agree. Where executive action was not forthcoming, direct action was. SNCC set out to create pressure, to force a strategy, to test the willingness of the government to enforce the law – if needs be to create a crisis. They worked for voter registration, but only as part of a larger structure of direct action. In this they were closer to CORE than to the NAACP.

In December 1960 the Supreme Court had, not for the first time, outlawed segregation on interstate travel and its facilities. On May 4th, 1961 CORE assembled thirteen young men – seven black and six white, some of them SNCC members – aboard two buses, one Trailways and one Greyhound, in Washington bound for New Orleans. Their plan was to sit at the front of the bus when travelling, and to enter as a mixed group the whites-only waiting rooms at all the stops en route. James Farmer's policy in this action is clear – he wrote to both the Kennedys, to the head of the Interstate Commerce Commission (whose job it was to enforce the Supreme Court ruling), to the presidents of both bus companies and to the head of the FBI, J. Edgar Hoover. The warning carried an implicit expectation of the protection of the law and of the Federal Government – the presumption looks to have been that no-one who mattered could say they didn't know. Yet, in an interview given in 1964, Robert Kennedy said he first learnt of the Freedom Rides only when they ran into trouble, just like any other citizen, from the newspapers.

Ten days later, outside Anniston, Alabama, the lead bus was stopped by a mob and firebombed. The second bus made it into Birmingham, where the police force of the Director of Public Safety, Theophilus Eugene 'Bull' Connor, let another mob beat up the Freedom Riders. The FBI's advance knowledge of this was not shared with the Justice Department.

Both Kennedys now intervened. Bobby Kennedy spoke to Dr King, urged him to use his influence to stop the Freedom Riders, and the President tried to talk to Governor Patterson At first Patterson made himself unavailable – Bull Connor had excused his police at Birmingham by saying he'd given them the day off, as it was Mother's Day; from the Governor's staff came the more traditional southern legend 'gone fishin''. Justice Department aide John Siegenthaler was sent down to Alabama. It was understood that he was the direct representative of the President. Patterson saw him, and when challenged by Siegenthaler on his power within his own state, declared that he had "the will, the force, the men and the equipment to fully protect everyone in Alabama". On a newsreel he ventured the opinion that the Freedom Riders were fools, and "you can't guarantee the safety of a fool".

The politics of the matter now dropped to grass roots level. No one would agree to drive the Freedom Riders on to Montgomery. All the drivers were white, but prejudice need not have entered into it – they had good cause to fear for their lives. CORE, with the exception of Farmer, now heeded the Attorney-General's request for a cooling off period, and the Riders took a plane to New Orleans. Almost at once SNCC replaced them with its own members, virtually doubling the number, and Farmer found himself with a new set of Riders, half his own age, drawn entirely from SNCC, and including both sexes and both races – among them John Lewis, Diane Nash, Kelly Miller Smith, Frederick Leonard, William Harbour and Jim Zwerg. Bobby Kennedy and Burke Marshall talked to the new Riders, to Smith and Nash, and accepted that they would continue. Patterson agreed that he would protect the highway, rather than the bus – a fine distinction, but then so much of the administration's dealings with the southern Governors rested on knowing when to let them save face.

Again Bobby Kennedy got on the phone – he called Greyhound's superintendent in Birmingham: "I think you should . . . be getting hold of Mr Greyhound or whoever Mr Greyhound is and somebody better give an answer to this question. I am – the Government – is going to be very much upset if this group does not get to continue their trip."[14]

The political price of this call was high. Greyhound taped it, and the tape was leaked. The association was formed in the minds of many people that Bobby Kennedy had been behind the Freedom Rides from the start. At the same time he was coming under fire from the Civil Rights Movement for suggesting the ride should be called off. Later Kennedy said of the incident: "I never recovered from it. That was damaging – just like waking the newspapermen up."[15]

More than newspapermen were awake. The violence surrounding the Freedom Ride was attracting nationwide coverage on television. The embarrassing potential of the situation could be measured in the President's calendar. Jack Kennedy was a week away from a meeting with De Gaulle and only ten days away from a summit with Khrushchev.

A driver was found and on May 20th the bus set off for Montgomery. Forty miles outside Montgomery, the escorting plane disappeared and the sixteen highway patrol cars vanished. The bus pulled into the terminal without protection. Another mob waited. Again the Riders were attacked with not a policeman in sight. Zwerg took a heavy beating – as the first off the bus, his white face proved very provocative to a mob already yelling 'Kill the Niggers!'

82

Siegenthaler was clubbed unconscious with a piece of pipe while trying to protect two of the young women Riders, and lay in the street for twenty-five minutes. Lewis was felled by a soda crate and as he lay on the ground the Attorney-General of Alabama stood over him and read out an injunction against him for breaking the laws on mixed interstate travel. Hospital treatment for the injured epitomised the problem. Montgomery ran segregated ambulances.

What SNCC and CORE sought by the Freedom Ride, and now needed, was the protection of the law, at federal level, if need be by a federal presence – what the administration wanted was to force the state of Alabama, or any other state, to enforce the law without a federal presence – there was no national police force[16] to which they had recourse, only the possibility of ad hoc posses of federal marshals, revenue men and border patrols, or the army. The effectiveness of the former was uncertain, and the use of the latter was a diplomatic sledgehammer no one in Washington wanted to use – but who in Washington could now take the word of a southern Governor? Dr King probably spoke for many in the Movement when he compared the federal marshals, at the disposal of the Justice Department, to the marshals of the old West[17] – professional lawmen in times of lawlessness. The *True Grit* image didn't square with the Justice Department's vision. Federal marshals were, as Burke Marshall put it, "only process servers working for the courts".[18] Bobby Kennedy mustered six hundred 'process servers', had them flown into Maxwell air force base and told the press: "As soon as the federal government is shown by action that the state of Alabama can deal with law enforcement on their own, those marshals will be out of there."

Martin Luther King flew to Montgomery the following day to address a rally in support of the Freedom Riders at the church of the Rev. Ralph Abernathy. That evening a mob besieged the First Baptist church. The marshals had split forces to guard the hospital and the church – even if they hadn't they would still have been outnumbered. The mob ran into thousands. It looked as though they might storm the church or set it alight. Through the night the phone lines buzzed – Kennedy to King, with King attacking Kennedy for lack of action – Kennedy to Patterson – a conversation lasting forty-five minutes – Kennedy to his brother, keeping him up to date on this, the first crisis of his presidency.

The mob lobbed rocks and a gas bomb into the church. Outside marshals were injured. King spoke calmly to the congregation. They sang hymns. Some time after 3 a.m. Patterson finally called out the state troopers and the national guard. The combined three forces dispersed the mob. Kennedy's tactics had worked, he had forced Patterson to accept responsibility for law and order and to protect the Civil Rights of black citizens. Patterson felt that "under the circumstances the sovereignty of the state of Alabama required that".[19] From the point of view of SNCC and the SCLC it could scarcely have been soon enough. Intervention too late, intervention that had to be squeezed out of the federal government and thrust upon the states, so guarded of their own sovereignty they could not guard the lives of citizens, had been measured in the suffering of their supporters – sooner or later someone would die waiting on a Kennedy call.

Hiding at the back of all this was the invisible fist. Kennedy had mobilised troops shortly after sending in the marshals. They had sat in planes, on alert, at nearby Fort Benning until the situation at the church changed for the better and they were stood down. Around six in the morning Kennedy too stood down and went home to bed.

The next stage took the Riders, under heavy escort and outnumbered by the press, on to Jackson, Mississippi. No overt violence awaited as they disembarked into the whites-only waiting room, only the guiding, commanding presence of Governor Ross Barnett's police force, ushering the Riders straight out of the back door into police vans. Avoiding further violence, and not trusting to Governors, Kennedy had done a deal with Senator Eastland – police protection was guaranteed and in exchange the Justice Department would not press for enforcement of federal law in accordance with the 1960 Supreme Court ruling. One set of Civil Rights were traded for another. The Riders went to jail and faced bail bonds and legal fees of more than a quarter of a million dollars. It's hard to view this as any kind of triumph, except that of media management. American television, and the American electorate, had seen too much violence.

Nick Katzenbach: "The Civil Rights Movement in this country was the first time that television was effectively used as an instrument of politics. The Civil Rights groups could not have succeeded had it not been for the television coverage of Civil Rights in the South. When you saw on your screen in the evening time after time, Blacks peacefully demonstrating, peacefully sitting-in, being arrested by white policemen, being attacked by whites, klansmen or otherwise . . . if you saw the time at Selma [1965] when they were attacked by Sheriff Clark and his troopers . . . beating them, using clubs, using cattle prods . . . this was what led to Civil Rights legislation in the United States. It was the first time that the power of television had been used for political purposes. That lesson was

84

not lost on other political groups. It wasn't lost on political candidates. We've almost got it down to a science at the South African Embassy – where congressmen tell them [television stations] what time they're going to be there, so they can get arrested and be back in time to make a vote."[20]

The Rev. Andrew Young of SCLC, Mayor of Atlanta in the 1980s, spoke to Morehouse College in 1986 and on the issue of Selma said: "We weren't callous about suffering – we really thought that the state of Alabama had better sense than to beat up people on television" – which acknowledges the power of television much as Katzenbach does, but seems to me to skate over the fact that the state of Alabama had been stupid enough to do so in front of the newsreels in 1961 and 1963.

In the 1964 interview Bobby Kennedy described his brother as being "fed up with the Freedom Riders who went down there afterwards",[21] by which he meant the three hundred odd who poured into Jackson's bus station and jails over the course of the summer until he convinced the ICC to enact the ruling in September. Too many chroniclers of the period have summed up this action as ending segregation on interstate travel, or leaving only 'mopping up' operations. No SNCC historian fails to point out what happened to a group of mixed interstate travellers on June 9th, 1963 in Mississippi. The following account is the most recent and is by Mary King, a white SNCC worker and later head of the Peace Corps under President Carter, but it could be James Foreman or Howard Zinn:

"The police arrested the entire group . . . in the Winona jail Annelle Ponder . . . a voter education worker for SCLC was separated from the rest of the group and she was beaten to the point that she could barely speak. Mrs [Fannie-Lou] Hamer was taken to another cell where there were three white men and two black prisoners. One prisoner was handed a blackjack and told to 'make that bitch wish she was dead'. He beat her all over her body with the blackjack while one of the other men held her feet down to prevent her from moving . . . Mrs Hamer was left unable to walk."[22]

This took place nearly two years after the desegregation of interstate travel.

The Freedom Rides bloodied both SNCC and the government. SNCC tactics and commitment had galvanised the Movement, putting them squarely in its vanguard – and had brought a significant, if complex, response from the Justice Department. Bobby Kennedy later said that it was important to "discover some new way of being of some help". The new way was to get Governors out of bed at three in the morning and to play strategically upon their sense of their own power in order to dredge up their sense of responsibility – to call demonstrators, to call bus superintendents, to call anyone who might help with a solution. In its way Government of the people, by the people was thrust back *at* the people in Bobby Kennedy's midnight calls, as the art of telephone diplomacy showed itself in a 'hands on' government of a style not seen in the Eisenhower years. Individually it may well have been the channelling of his notorious aggression – a Boston Professor described RFK to me as "little more than a thug when he was younger" – overall it was part of a perspective of being informed and being active where Civil Rights were concerned.

Burke Marshall: "I think it would be accurate to call it a Kennedy technique – though I wouldn't want to personalise it in that way – I think it was something activist – particularly in the Civil Rights Movement – that hadn't existed before and hasn't existed since."

Victor Navasky, now editor of the *Nation*, quotes an anonymous source as saying that Mr Marshall too had the art of the "interminable long distance phone call with Southern officials . . . down to a science."[23] And the science was indeed of its time – who at 1600 Pennsylvania Avenue in the eighties would have woken the Great Communicator up at three in the afternoon let alone three in the morning to tell him an activist Justice Department wished to inform him of what was happening in his country?

CHAPTER FIVE

GRINNING AT NOTHING

"One day it will all be over . . . John, Paul, George and Ringo will remember that bit about chains of pandiatonic clusters, laugh like drains, and nip off for a bevy in the nearest Lime Street boozer . . . none of them, it is said by those close to them, has much desire to leave Liverpool. Liverpool maintains a queer, rather sinister, hold over its people."[1]

Geoffrey Moorhouse

"We're not going to fizzle out in half a day. But afterwards I'm not going to change into a tap-dancing musical. I'll just develop what I'm doing at the moment, although whatever I say now I'll change my mind next week. I mean, we all know that bit about it won't be the same when you're twenty-five. I couldn't care less. This isn't show business. It's something else. This is different from anything that anybody imagines."[2]

John Lennon

I first heard the Beatles in the Autumn of 1962. My brother, disappointed at Mr Macmillan's abandonment of National Service, volunteered to serve Her Majesty in far flung Camberley and Aldershot and left me, as his legacy, a wireless the size of a small chest of drawers. It would be dignified too much by the label 'steam'. It ran on wet-cell batteries as big as bricks, which the brother kept alive by arcane processes known only to inhabitants of the wooden shed next to the school library that housed the cadet corps. Through the burble and faze (the signal came and went as though blown in the wind, and the stations crossed each other endlessly) I used to listen to Radio Luxembourg's evening programme of pop and rock. The BBC offered nothing like it – *Saturday Club* and *Pick of the Pops* on a Sunday afternoon were meagre concessions yielded to the British teenager by the Light Programme. It rarely seemed possible to hear a record clearly from start to finish, but in contrast to the era of the £7 tranny and Jimmy Savile's Listen-Under-The-Bedclothes-Club I heard through a thumping bass speaker, in part or whole, such as Frank Ifield's *I'll Remember You*, Joe Brown's *Picture of You*, Frankie Vaughan's *Tower of Strength*, adverts for Sta-Blonde and

Brunatex, Horace Batchelor of Keynsham ("That's Keynsham, spelt K-E-Y-N-S-H-A-M") offering his patent remedy for winning the pools week after week and a striking oddity called *Love Me Do*, by a group I'd never heard of.

Love Me Do, recorded by the Beatles on Parlophone, written by their own songwriters, billed at that time as McCartney-Lennon, topped the charts in their hometown of Liverpool – their manager Brian Epstein bought ten thousand copies for his NEMS record shops – and peaked in the national chart at No. 17 in mid October. It was short and simple, most singles were in those days, it was sung by Paul McCartney and featured John Lennon dubbed over with a catchy harmonica riff. It was different, but it wasn't dynamite.

At their first recording session at EMI's Abbey Road studios in London on September 4th, 1962, the Beatles had laid down *Love Me Do* and also tried out on their producer George Martin a song they thought might make a B side.

"We played *Please Please Me* over to our recording manager . . . It was a bit fussy, he advised us to smooth it out a bit."[3]

P.S. I Love You – another McCartney-Lennon original – became the B side of their first single. For the time being the incomplete, fussy *Please Please Me* was shelved. For their second single Martin sent the Beatles a song by a new writer, twenty-year-old Mitch Murray – until very recently Murray had been Lionel Stitcher, handbag salesman of Golders Green. He had taught himself the ukulele and composed songs on it which he had hawked in London's Tin Pan Alley, the traditional show biz bastion of popular music publishing centred on Denmark Street. *How Do You Do It* was only his second accepted song, and had been offered to Martin by the publisher Dick James. Martin felt that this was the song to make the Beatles a household name "like Harpic".[4] When the Beatles and Martin gathered again at Abbey Road in late November he expected them to record Murray's song. The Beatles resisted this. They had written a substantial part of their live act by this time, and Lennon estimated that he and McCartney has written about a hundred songs, although "some of them are rubbish, of course".[5] They insisted on recording their own material. At this time the unique, creative partnership of Martin and the Beatles that cut across age and taste was still in the future. Martin was in charge and, as he put it himself, read the riot act – "When you can write material as good as this, then I'll record it."[6] A version of *How Do You Do It* was dutifully taped.[7] After the session The Beatles asked him to listen to *Please Please Me* once more.

"In the following weeks [after *Love Me Do*] we went over

[*Please Please Me*] again and again. We changed the tempo a little. We altered the words slightly. And we went over the idea of featuring the harmonica, just as we'd done on *Love Me Do*. By the time the session came around we were so happy with the result we couldn't get it recorded fast enough."[8]

Martin listened as Lennon and McCartney played the song through on acoustic guitars. The early version had been a slow, blues-flavoured song which McCartney described as being like a Roy Orbison number. The new one was fast and short. Martin imposed a structure on it, doubling its length and adding an introduction. The Beatles recorded the first furious, fever-pitched take of *Please Please Me*. It was different, it was dynamite, from the opening double thump of McCartney's Hofner bass to Lennon's last 'Whoa Yeah' barely two minutes later. The touch of cuteness that had characterised the first single was gone. *Please Please Me* was raw with frustrated desire – Lennon screams and whines "C'mon" over and over again. The sexuality is unmistakable. The power of the record was startling. Martin spoke to them over the studio intercom: "Gentlemen you've just made your first number-one record."[9]

Indeed they had, but they had also made a revolution in popular music. They had seized the creative initiative and put the power of rock'n'roll back with the performers. Of course Tin Pan Alley didn't die – Mitch Murray's song went to No. 1 with Gerry and the Pacemakers – but its hold over music shrank that day in November 1962 and the pattern of writer-performers that dominated the rest of the sixties was set by the Beatles. Martin never again asked them to record a Tin Pan Alley song. Over the next seven years they recorded very little material that they had not composed themselves, and of their twenty-three singles one was by George Harrison and all the rest were Lennon-McCartney songs.

When the Beatles had first auditioned for George Martin, he saw them in the terms and style of the current success: "I went home wondering which one of them was going to be the star. My thinking was so coloured by the success of people like Tommy Steele and Cliff Richard that I couldn't imagine them being successful as a group. I felt that one of them was bound to come out as having a better voice than the others. Whoever that was would be the one, and the rest would become like Cliff Richard's backing group, the Shadows."[10]

To describe what had happened to music since the fizzling out of rock'n'roll and the drafting of Elvis into the army, is to describe the heyday of Cliff and the Shadows. They dominated the charts at the start of 1963. In turn they were overShadowed by their record company, Columbia, and their producer Norrie Paramor.[11] Music had become machine. The producers and the managers ruled. Cliff and the Shadows wrote little of their own material, and whatever life they had had in the heady early days of rock'n'roll had been tamed. Their greatest success was the 1962 film *The Young Ones* – a pop package of the worst kind, with almost as many songwriters as performers, and not a decent song to be heard. Their second film *Summer Holiday* gave 1963 its first No. 1, *Bachelor Boy*. This was toppled by the Shadows' instrumental *Dance On*, which was followed by a Shadows spin-off, ex-members Jet Harris and Tony Meehan, with *Diamonds* – another instrumental. The Shadows were the touchstone for both fans and producers. Any four-piece band would automatically invite comparison. The Beatles had been rejected by other record companies (Decca, Pye, Philips and Oriole as well as Parlophone's sister labels at EMI, HMV and Columbia) for being too like the Shadows (pretty ridiculous as the Shadows sang only to back Cliff and made instrumentals on their own) or because groups were felt to be on the way out, which in itself is a reference to the five-year success of the Shadows. Many acts copied the smooth presentation of the Shadows, the shining suits and the sang-froid, even imitating the precise footwork routine that three of the four members strolled through with every number – Freddie and the Dreamers began their high stepping madness as a send-up of the Shadows – and I'm sure that many guitarists of my own generation were influenced by Hank Marvin. For a long time Hank was the only model, and in the early years they had been pioneers on the music scene.[12] They were far from being *simply* pawns of the Tin Pan Alley music factory, but after five years at the top they had come a long way from *Move It* and *Apache*, and had come to seem very safe and very clean, standing – or strolling – behind the even safer and cleaner Cliff Richard. As far as the Beatles were concerned they had never liked or imitated the music of Cliff and the Shadows – it was 'antiseptic' – and huddling in the charts were lesser acts of unspeakable blandness – the Bobby-balladeers. Against this background, of a pop music gone stale through routine, polish and the unimaginative control of managers and producers, the Beatles burst as original and lively. Trying to answer the question 'Why the Beatles?' as early as September 1961, Liverpool DJ Bob Wooler wrote: "[They] resurrected original style rock'n'roll music . . . they hit the scene when it had been emasculated by figures like Cliff and the Shadows . . . gone was the drive that inflamed the emotions. This was studio jungle music purveyed skilfully by arrangement with the A&R men."[13]

If George Martin had difficulty in recognising the Beatles for what they were it's hardly surprising. Few recording acts were without a featured lead singer, fewer still insisted on and succeeded in recording their own songs. I'd go so far as to say there is a rock music cycle. Originality begins with writer-performers, lasts a few years, and then is recycled by the industry as pop-junk until the next wave of talent forces Tin Pan Alley, whether it goes by the name of Norrie Paramor, Mickie Most or Stock, Aitken and Waterman, to think again. Hence the appalling troughs that rock can sink into – the early sixties, early seventies and late eighties, the Craig Douglasses, the Donny Osmonds and the Kylie Minogues. The Beatles' brief, final brush with Tin Pan Alley remained in the stacks at EMI – their version of *How Do You Do It* has never been released.

Less than eighteen months after recording *Please Please Me* the Beatles were the biggest rock act the world has ever seen, bigger, as Brian Epstein had always predicted, than their first idol Elvis – their hair, dress, music and even their accent copied by and influencing millions. When Martin had first tried to interest Dick James in publishing the songs of Lennon and McCartney, James had replied with London scepticism about anything north of Watford: "Liverpool? So what's from Liverpool?"[14] – an answer that says a lot about the state of music in 1962, but one that prompts more questions . . . why them? . . . why then? . . . why Liverpool?

§

The beat boom which swept Britain in 1963 had been popular in Liverpool for several years. There were as many as a thousand amateur and semi-pro musicians in an estimated four hundred odd Merseyside bands in the early sixties.[15] Surprisingly few of them made the big time, but for a complexity of reasons they flourished locally.

"About the time of rock'n'roll in Britain – I think I was about fifteen, so I suppose it'd be 1955 – there was a big thing called skiffle, which was a kind of folk music, American folk music . . . with washboards . . . and all the kids from fifteen upwards had these groups, and I formed one at school . . . then I met Paul . . . then I met George and we changed to rock . . . that was all there was to it[16] . . . We started in the Buddy Holly days, when everyone thought they could turn out simple songs like his and we've been writing ever since."[17]

The Beatles (then known as the Quarrymen, after Quarry Bank School which Lennon infrequently attended) changed to rock when rock presented an imitable idol. Skiffle succeeded because it was easy, a proto-punk, garage and shed music (in Lennon's case the front porch). No one had really copied Bill Haley, it was too hard (try playing the lead on *Rock Around the Clock* – you need twelve fingers), no one had seriously copied Elvis, the power of his voice and the unenviable isolation of a solo singer were deterrent, but Buddy Holly and the Crickets offered a combination of rock's power, the sociability of a close-knit group and three-chord simplicity that seemed as easy to copy as skiffle had been. Buddy Holly in that one year of his success, 1958-9, probably inspired as many kids to take up the guitar as Pete Townshend did in the mid-sixties. Holly was also one of the most prolific songwriters to emerge out of rock'n'roll,[18] and one of the most imitated.

Arguably, the opportunities for working-class lads were the greater because of the unplanned freedom gained through state secondary education. Whilst Ringo had worked since the age of fifteen and had little proper schooling since he was twelve, Lennon, McCartney and Harrison all stayed in the system until their late teens, a system which theoretically offered a lot (an education in music if you wanted it) but in reality demanded little of them. After that the three of them managed to remain more or less full-time Beatles long before their income seemed regular enough to support them – others like Billy J. Kramer played and sang part-time while finishing apprenticeships. This prompts me to think that there had been a vital shift in the structure of the working-class family by this time. It's probable that, unlike the pre-war years, the family rested on a main breadwinner or on the parents, and that teenagers were not expected to contribute to the general upkeep of the household. Whatever the resistances the parents of such families had begun to recognise their children as distinctly teenagers rather than as young adults with devolved responsibilities.

Gillian Reynolds, five years older than Lennon, eight years older than Harrison, grew up in Liverpool in the forties and fifties. She sees a marked difference between her generation, with its memories of rationing and the parental pressure towards the newly available free, state secondary education – capable for the first time of putting a significant number of working-class kids into universities – and the one that followed so closely, experiencing new freedoms, including the freedom to ignore or take for granted what had seemed so precious only five or ten years before: "It was the generation whose parents had fought in the war . . . who had brought them up saying

'Go on enjoy it', knowing they'd lost their own youth in the war . . . the indulgence of children . . . I don't mean indulgent as a pejorative . . . became accepted. It wasn't 'go and get yourself a paper round', it was 'Oh, they're only kids.'"[19]

It has been often argued that Merseybeat arose in true Northern fashion as home-made entertainment born of poverty, but this seems less than the whole truth, and it's more accurate to say that Merseybeat flourished not so much in direct descent from Gracie Fields, cloth caps and clogs, but as a consequence of that fragile Macmillan affluence and the easy rise of hire purchase. Being in a band cost money. Never having it so good meant running up hundreds of pounds in HP debts for guitars and amplifiers. At the time Brian Epstein took over management of the Beatles they owed around £200 to Frank Hessy's music shop in Liverpool – the equivalent of a year's income for a teenage apprentice. In certain ways the traditional teenage 'job' of being apprenticed to a trade for a pittance directly served being in a band, as budding carpenters cobbled together guitars and speaker cabinets in woodwork shops, and the electrical apprentices soldered up valve amplifiers – George Harrison at one time trained as an electrician.

In *New Society* in February 1964, Colin Fletcher, a sociology undergraduate at Liverpool University and a former beat group member, wrote one of the few informed, intelligent analyses of the shaping of Merseybeat. He described how his band set about making their own bass speakers after they'd seen a local group (not named, but it seems likely they were the Big Three) create a massive sound with cabinets six foot tall:

"Even on the backing of soft chords there was a terrific pounding from the box. Immediately the group started to adapt its regular numbers to accommodate an accentuated beat. Many groups had done this before . . . and within a year it had become standard practice on Merseyside. As the bass note was bashed the drummer did the same and the whole line up of guitars stamped and shouted . . . what came to be known as the Merseybeat."[20]

To which he might have added that the only way a singer was going to be heard above the bash, the beat and the stomp was to shout. Merseybeat favoured powerful lungs and the combined efforts of two or three voices in harmony – the characteristic sound of the Beatles, the Searchers and the Merseybeats and dozens of less well-known bands.

Fletcher made the point that Liverpool was a city of gangs, and that the camaraderie of the gang lent itself to the forming of beat groups. Stanley Reynolds lived in Liverpool, while working for the

Manchester Guardian: "Things got much more peaceful. It became pleasant to go out. They'd stopped fighting and picked up the guitars . . . what I thought was a shame was that they [teenagers] were taking up following the bands as a vocation. They weren't learning any trade for themselves . . . they were learning to be fans . . . also there was a certain pride in their own ignorance that the Beatles brought in and that continued through rock and roll and pervaded the whole goddam place . . . we don't need no edukashun . . . leave us kids alone . . . that kind of thing . . . I think the Beatles were the start of that in a way . . . "[21]

Quite why rock should have survived in Liverpool isn't clear. The Cunard Yank idea is strong. Plenty of beat musicians testify to getting obscure American records from relatives on the ships – on the other hand Cunard was running down its Liverpool operation in favour of Southampton and few of the big liners now crossed from Liverpool. Lancashire had its fair share of American bases, with their own radio service, but so did East Anglia – neither Southampton nor Ipswich became famous as the cradle of British rock. There's more to be said for the isolation, the independence of Liverpool, even from Lancashire, let alone the tyranny of London – the cultural strength of an old industrial area, with a vast working class, that also characterises Newcastle.

Gillian Reynolds: "I do see it [Liverpool rock'n'roll] as a celebration – the ultimate celebration – of working-class life and working-class values, that embraced, that looked towards America as Liverpool always had. [There's] that statue in Sefton Park to Columbus – it says that the discoverer of America was the maker of Liverpool."[22]

The powerful sound and the American music were further refined in Germany. If Merseybeat was out of time in the rest of England, it was mainstream in Hamburg – dirtier and tougher than Liverpool itself. The Beatles were only the second Liverpool act to play the Hamburg clubs. Their manager in 1960, Allan Williams, sent over Derry and the Seniors to Bruno Koschmider's Kaiserkeller in Hamburg's notorious red light district. Koschmider asked for more groups, and Williams offered the Beatles, much to the distaste of the Seniors who considered the Beatles to be a "bum group" who could "fuck it up".[23] Playing to German audiences shaped the Beatles as surely as any American influence. Paul McCartney described the experience a few years later:

"We sometimes used to play an eight hour day . . . at the time it wasted us totally . . . I remember getting home to England – my Dad thought I was half dead . . . in Hamburg when we first arrived we were very green and there was a manager, a feller called Willi, and he used to say to us 'Mak Shau – Make Show – do something!' We used to just stand there and go through the riffs. That had been enough in Liverpool, but in Hamburg . . . people would poke their heads in and look at the beer prices, see a band there and we'd have to go 'Whoo . . . hee . . . hey. Look at us! And Come on in!' . . . it was good training for us . . . immediately anyone put their head in we'd Mak Shau."[24]

Lennon gave his account to Hunter Davies for the authorised biography: "The first Mak Show I did was to jump around in one number like Gene Vincent. Every number lasted twenty minutes, just to spin it out. We all did mak showing all the time from then on . . . We had to try anything that came into our heads . . . there was nobody to copy from. We played what we liked best. The Germans liked it as long as it was loud. But it was only back in Liverpool that we recognised the difference and saw what had happened to us while everyone else was playing that Cliff Richard shit."[25]

The prolonged 'rehearsal' of such live sessions, and the energy of making show changed the Beatles from a run-of-the-mill act to an accomplished band. Their image also changed. In Liverpool they'd been teds-manqué (largely jeans and winkle pickers – with black sweaters and two-tone sneakers as a makeshift stage uniform) never wholly adopting the look, never quite giving it up for anything else. In Hamburg they mixed with a more beatnik/existential set of people than they'd known back home. Photographer Astrid Kirchherr had created their stylish black and white image in her pictures of them, she had encouraged them to wear black, to wear leather suits and collarless Cardin jackets and to surrender the greasy quiff of the fifties' ted for the fringes that became the Beatle look. Deported from Germany, they returned home in ones and twos dispirited and saw little of each other until they played at Litherland Town Hall on December 27th, 1960. They wore their black leather suits, they shook their hair and they stomped their way into numbers just as they'd done in Hamburg. The Litherland gig was the turning point. Bob Wooler organised the concert: "When they came out they sang *Long Tall Sally* and the place went mad. I've never experienced anything like it."[26]

The adoration of the Beatles began that night in Litherland. For the first time they found themselves mobbed by their girl fans.

§

Six months later the Beatles had a large personal following and were residents at the Cavern in Mathew Street. At this time Liverpool's centre had upwards of twenty such clubs, survivors of skiffle and trad, uneasily making the transition to beat music. Billy Morton, a teenager in the era of the coffee bar, was a Cavern regular: "When I was a graduate apprentice . . . we'd spend lunchtimes in the Cavern picking up girls. If the Beatles were on there'd be more girls . . . You'd come in down the steps, there'd be a stink of sweat, a bit of drains, condensation. It was in three arches in a cellar . . . there was a bar selling soft drinks and crisps – no licence . . . People would stand on both sides, there'd be a row of seats under the centre arch, maybe fifteen to twenty seats across . . . they'd get in four to five hundred people . . . The condensation got so bad once it fused all the lights and somebody's amplification . . . About two thirds of the people were girls, and about two thirds of the men were predatory, picking up girls . . . there was no screaming then. You came to listen . . . *Some Other Guy*, *Mr Moonlight*, *Please Mr Postman*, a lot of Chuck Berry . . . and a lot of Jerry Lee Lewis . . . I'd always go out of my way to see the Big Three and the Beatles . . . and Rory Storm and the Hurricanes, because Rory was such a great character."[27]

As one of the Merseybeats Billy Kinsley played the Cavern dozens of times. When they formed the group in 1962 Billy was fifteen, and his partner Tony Crane only a year older. They were the youngest group to come out of Liverpool – and when they charted in September 1963 with their first single *It's Love That Really Counts*, Billy became one the youngest rock stars ever. At the time of their biggest success, *Sorrow* in 1966, he was still only twenty. After the Beatles they were the most long-lived of those Merseyside groups who made the big time. Six years younger than John Lennon, Billy Kinsley grew up in Liverpool – teenager, performer and fan:[28]

"When I first saw the Beatles I changed overnight . . . it was a Friday night at the Cavern. I was fourteen . . . I was very shy. I'd never been into Liverpool city centre, although I lived not far from it. Before the Beatles there was a jazz band. I didn't like jazz at all . . . I was totally dumbstruck [by the Beatles] – I thought this was the best thing I'd ever seen in my life. [They played] *Slow Down*, *Memphis Tennessee*, *Lucille* . . . George used to sing a lot of Elvis stuff – they'd do early Elvis – a lot of Buddy Holly, Bobby Vee – Paul used to do the Little Richard stuff, the out and out rockers as well as *Till There Was You*, *Somewhere Over The Rainbow* . . . John used to do more obscure songs that I didn't know . . . Dorsey Burnette . . . things I'd never heard of . . . they did a lot of songs I wanted to do, like Little Richard songs – but I was too embarrassed to do Little Richard songs. It was totally out of my league. I was doing Buddy Holly . . . he was the only one that was acceptable to both bands.

"There were about four or five bands that were really popular with the girl fans. No. 1 was the Beatles, No. 2 probably the Merseybeats and the Dennisons, then the Escorts and maybe Earl Preston and the TTs. But bands like the Big Three – although Johnny Gus was a great looking guy – I don't think they appealed to women. King Size Taylor and the Dominoes weren't a pin-up type of band – they were a band's band.

"There were usually four groups on. The one who was top of the bill would be third . . . The Cavern would start very early, about seven-thirty. There'd be records on first. If the Beatles or a big band were on there'd always be a queue outside, stretching a hundred or two hundred yards. Being in a band you could skip the queue – we were lucky in that respect – and I used to go to every lunchtime session straight from school. The sessions used to be split. It was always the Beatles Monday, Wednesday and Friday and Gerry and the Pacemakers Tuesday and Thursday [and vice versa the next week] . . . that was the norm until the Beatles and Gerry went to Hamburg, then you'd get other bands filling in – like the Big Three – then we took over, started doing lunchtimes. I had to leave school because of that situation – I didn't want to give up [music] . . . I left school in February 1962 because we were working five nights a week. I was getting home at midnight – trying to get up for school or do homework was just impossible . . . I didn't want to get a job, because I'd realised that the Beatles were professional musicians . . . working seven nights a week around Liverpool, making a lot of money . . . We came to that decision – Tony was working . . . he was eighteen months older than me – I was badgered and badgered by me Mam and Dad to get a proper job and when I did . . . Tony left his! – I lasted about three months. I only ever had one job – shipping clerk. [My parents] encouraged me by not discouraging me. They knew how into the music I was, but they didn't see it as a profession . . . We were totally taken over by the whole life, by the buzz – there was an incredible buzz in the city – we realised that we were part of it – I was just fifteen years old, Tony was sixteen, and we were playing at the Cavern alongside our heroes.

"If the Beatles were on second or third they'd use our gear, if we were on third we'd use theirs. After they'd been on they'd just go home, and Neil Aspinall would pick up the gear from our house the next day. We were the only band they'd let do that. They realised we were kids and would look after it. They knew we were big fans of theirs as well."[29]

Josie Neap, a couple of years older than Billy Kinsley, was a schoolgirl in Liverpool in the early sixties. Against the trend she was not a Beatles' fan: "I went to Merchant Taylors' as a sixth former, in Crosby, Liverpool 23. In 1960 or '61 we booked the Silver Beatles for the Sixth Form dance. Pete Best and Stu Sutcliffe were still with them. They wore leather jackets and jeans, they were pretty scruffy, not at all attractive, played rough American r'n'b – sort of Chuck Berry style – and they weren't very good. I think the best that could be said of them is that they were just raw, kind of unfinished. I didn't pay a lot of attention, they were just another band. Nobody raved over them. I suppose the truth is that I wasn't really into beat music.

"I saw them again in '63, at the Cavern. I was a student at Bristol University by then, and I used to come home regularly. You couldn't ignore the beat scene. Things had changed, and the Beatles had changed too. Mop tops, the Cardin jackets, and they played their own stuff, their own songs, and I don't think they played anything original when I first saw them. I think they'd already cut *Love Me Do*. Of course the girls went wild, but they still didn't do much for me. Maybe I was, or thought I was, too grown up for that sort of thing. I remember being very pissed off that you couldn't get a drink at the Cavern. I thought the Beatles were tame. I couldn't stand bands that wore uniforms. That was one of the silliest things about the beat boom – all those guys dressed up in suits playing very rough and ready rock music. I think I was too sophisticated for that even at seventeen."

It was in the Cavern that Brian Epstein saw the Beatles playing a lunchtime gig in November 1961. It was a meeting of needs. Epstein had studied at RADA and still had show-biz ambitions but all he was running was the record department of the family business, NEMS, and after another Hamburg trip and ten months rising to the top in Liverpool, the Beatles had gone as far as they could go without breaking into records and a national audience. Yet, if the Beatles were kicking their heels they also seemed to be doing little to break the deadlock. When Epstein began to use the power of NEMS (which stood for North End Music Stores, one of the biggest record retailers in the North) to get the attention of the London based record companies, he had only two examples of the Beatles work to offer – the German record they had made with London vocalist Tony Sheridan, *My Bonnie* – a standard chosen for them by producer Bert Kampfaert – and a home made tape of their Cavern act. Neither of these did much justice to the Beatles. Epstein resorted to telling producers to concentrate on the backing and forget the vocals on *My Bonnie*, which is like saying never mind the quality feel the width, even though the backing is good. What's surprising is that they were vying with Gerry and the Pacemakers, the Big Three and Rory Storm and the Hurricanes to be the top group on Merseyside, were only weeks away from having that status confirmed in the first Merseybeat Annual Poll, but did not attempt a demo tape or disc until nearly nine months later, when, at last, Epstein had the tape of their Decca audition of January 1962 made into an acetate. The Beatles performed at Epstein's insistence only three of their own songs (*Hello Little Girl*, *Love of the Loved*[30] and *Like Dreamers Do*), the rest were standards – not even rock standards – *September in the Rain*, *Red Sails in the Sunset*, *Your Feet's Too Big*, *The Sheik of Araby* and a cover of Bobby Vee's *Take Good Care of My Baby*. Their performance is less assured than on *My Bonnie* – George murders *The Sheik of Araby* to a pounding beat from the others – this is typical of Merseybeat at its worst: most groups mangled standards in this way – and the only sparks on the tape are Paul's vocal and the catchy guitar work of George on *Love of the Loved*. Lennon is hardly prominent and sings none of the leads – none of the chosen songs would have lent themselves to his voice. Decca turned them down in favour of Brian Poole and the Tremeloes, but Epstein kept a tape of the session, which he used as the demo tape for the next six months. It was this tape, or the acetate of it, which George Martin first heard the following summer. The Beatles, by this sample, weren't being presented as the originals they were. This was a failure of imagination on Epstein's part, a failure to see just what he had musically in the Beatles. He fared better with their image. The band he saw in the Cavern at that lunchtime session were magical to Epstein: "They were rather scruffily dressed in the nicest possible way, or I should say in the most attractive way – black leather jackets, jeans, long hair, of course, and rather untidy stage presence, not very aware and not caring very much what they looked like."[31]

They ate, drank and smoked on stage, talked among themselves, and to the front rows of the audience, and swore at each other. Epstein cleaned up their act, literally. At risk of their small-club intimate touch, he persuaded even the most rebellious and nonconformist of Beatles to 'behave', and bought them all lounge suits from Burton's the chain store tailor. As an anonymous Jeremiad in *Merseybeat* testifies the Beatles' influence on other bands was big and it extended to the image as well as the music: "Lack of originality is one failing . . . virtually all the groups learn to play from records . . . many turn out to be second rate carbon copies. Last year the Beatles made an impression. Closely following came groups on the 'Beatle kick'. Groups whose only aim was to be second hand Beatles . . . "[32] . . . by which the author meant other scruffy, foul-mouthed bands, who were advised that . . . "The Beatles have visited a tailor and will soon be having a new smart appearance when they visit London." The final advice offered to other groups was: "Get your hair cut".

Ironically what Epstein would not or could not change was the hairstyle – and the repartee, the mixture of cynicism and goonery, the Liverpool lip. Somehow, wrapped in the farcical garb of old show biz, the Beatles retained their personality and broadened their appeal in precisely the way Epstein had hoped they would. They played the same music, shook their heads and stamped their feet, but as long as they wore the shiny suits they seemed to be able to cross the age barrier.

§

The first major press the Beatles received was in the London *Evening Standard* two weeks after the release of *Please Please Me* and their first appearance on *Thank Your Lucky Stars*, in a piece by Maureen Cleave entitled 'Why The Beatles Create All That Frenzy':

"They wear bell-bottomed suits[33] of a rich burgundy colour with black velvet collars . . . their shirts are pink and their hairstyles are French. Liverpool lads of twelve and upwards now have small bouffant Beatle heads with the fringe brushed forward."[34]

Miss Cleave compared their patter and repartee to Max Miller rather than Spike Milligan, and quoted an anonymous Liverpool housewife: "Their physical appearance inspires frenzy. *They look beat-up and depraved in the nicest possible way*." If accurate, there could be no better tribute to Epstein's judgment in shaping the Beatles. The housewife who uttered these words was *Daily Telegraph* columnist Gillian Reynolds.

What Maureen Cleave and Gillian Reynolds saw, with a perception that would be almost impossible six months later, was the Beatle beneath the Epstein suit. Lennon had "a brutal upper lip", Ringo was "ugly but cute", and some of Lennon's remarks to Maureen Cleave can hardly have been pleasing to Epstein. They were either too honest: "We all want to get rich so we can retire. We don't want to go straight or get to be all-round entertainers." (The standard reply was that all the budding star wanted was to buy his

Mum a bungalow and become just such an all-round entertainer, preferably uttered in a sub-intelligent, deferential mumble.) Or they were already sceptical of the fame he'd always wanted: "We practice what we call 'grinnings at nothings'. 1-2-3 and we all grin at nothing."

The Beatles spent the next three years grinning at nothing.

Maureen Cleave caught the Beatles in Liverpool, not in their usual venue the Cavern but on a typical sixties package tour. They played third on the bill behind Helen Shapiro and Kenny Lynch. When *Please Please Me* hit No. 2, George Martin called them back off the Shapiro tour to record a 'Long Playing' record. The Beatles were already a phenomenon. It was not just a matter of a single hit record. The fanatical Liverpool following was spreading with startling speed. Martin, the music press (Fleet Street, Maureen Cleave apart, were slow to catch on) and the Beatles themselves may well have been wondering at this point whether they were one-hit wonders, but the reaction among the teenagers was much more positive. *Please Please Me* was not received as just another hit by someone new, someone else to join the long queue behind Cliff Richard. For all the reasons Bob Wooler gave it broke the mould. The Beatles, even in February 1963, stood like redwoods in the wilderness.

The pop convention at this time was to release an LP of the same name as the single padded out with standards – a cash-in. George Martin wanted to capture their Cavern act, and for a while considered making the record in the Cavern itself, or in front of an invited audience, but on February 11th they all met at Abbey Road again. Martin wrote in his memoir: "We started at ten that morning . . . and recorded straight on to twin-track mono. By eleven o'clock at night we had recorded the lot, thirteen new tracks. All we really did was to reproduce the Cavern performance in the comparative calm of the studio. I say 'comparative', because there was one number which always caused a furore in the Cavern – *Twist and Shout*. John absolutely screamed it. God alone knows what he did to his larynx each time he performed it, because he made a sound rather like tearing flesh."[35]

The LP *Please Please Me* shows the Beatles' early originality – eight of the fourteen songs are Lennon-McCartney compositions, and of them only one (*Ask Me Why*) seems to be a remnant of the hundred or so songs they'd written before *Love Me Do/P.S. I Love You*. They were now writing prolifically. The record also shows their absorption of American influences, the songs the Liverpool bands had taken up, and what they made of them. None of the six cover versions is a copy of an obvious hit – *Boys*, originally the B

101

side of a Shirelles single, *Baby It's You*, was a 1962 hit for the same group but not in England, *Twist and Shout* was a US hit for the Isley Brothers but only broke in England after the Beatles' version – and none of them are efforts to sound American. What Liverpool's isolated loyalty to rock through the desert of trad and Tin Pan Alley had achieved was the growing up of English rock'n'roll. The Beatles were not slavishly imitating America and certainly were no longer trying to be like Elvis. To the Mersey beat, to the American idiom of rock itself, and to the added harmonies inspired by Tamla's girl groups they brought something uniquely themselves. They weren't purists, they were innovators, working afresh in the rock idiom. From time to time this would cause critical difficulties for those who were purists. It didn't bother the fans, already they were screaming themselves hoarse, and it certainly didn't bother the Beatles: "We don't play real rhythm and blues . . . we try to change about as much as we can . . . one we do is *Twist and Shout* . . . I don't know whether you'd call that rhythm and blues?"[36]

§

The LP topped the charts, as did their third single *From Me To You*. *Twist and Shout* (an EP) also made the top ten. Promotion, touring, became a way of life for the next nine months – trundling across the country in coaches, from cinema to theatre to ballroom, backing acts they were clearly outclassing and outselling – until they got equal billing with Roy Orbison, who recognised the reality and let them close the show – writing songs like *From Me To You* and *She Loves You* across the aisle of the bus, throwing riffs and lyrics back and forth – Kenny Lynch was lucky enough to pick up *Misery* this way, the first ever cover of a Lennon-McCartney song, and unlucky not to make the top fifty with it.

At the end of March the Beatles appeared on the cover of *Melody Maker* under the headline "Is Liverpool Britain's Nashville?" By now Brian Epstein had signed other Liverpool groups – Gerry and the Pacemakers, the Big Three and Billy J. Kramer with (not *and*) the Dakotas. Gerry and the Pacemakers had gone to No. 1 only a few days before. On the centre pages an unknown Liverpool singer praised Epstein for opening up Liverpool to success. His name was Tony Jackson, lead singer of The Searchers. By Midsummer they too were No. 1 with *Sweets For My Sweet* – described by Lennon, at the time, as the best record to come out of Liverpool. The *Daily Mirror* gave the Epstein 'stable' a centre spread on June 21st. Epstein's groups stood shoulder to shoulder as a visual testament to his judgment – they held three of the first four places in the top ten and had sold two million records. The Searchers were not among them. London management had begun to pick up on Merseybeat – more than a dozen Liverpool bands were now making records,[37] and two Manchester acts, the Hollies and Freddie and the Dreamers had also emerged. The Searchers and Epstein had turned each other down. After the Beatles they were the most accomplished sound to emerge from Liverpool, and in Epstein's terms the band that got away. In the first issue of *Fabulous* the following year Epstein wrote: "If I could retrace my footsteps and add just one more Liverpool group to my list of recording artists I would choose to have the Searchers on my books."

Epstein became as famous as any act he managed – in 1964 he received the double accolade of a *Panorama* special and an appearance on *Desert Island Discs*. He founded a business empire on the Beatles, represented seven Liverpool acts by the Autumn of 1963, most of whom recorded Lennon-McCartney songs at some point[38] – and was mythologised as a man with a golden touch. He was not without his failures. Neither Lennon-McCartney songs nor regular television appearances could make a star of Tommy Quickly, and if any group 'got away' it was not the Searchers but the Big Three, Epstein's third signing.[39] On Merseyside the Big Three (Johnny Hutchinson, Brian Griffiths and Johnny Gustafson) were second only to the Beatles in popularity, and were the musicians' musicians. Their first single, *Some Other Guy*, was a song from the repertoire of almost every Liverpool group and crept into the charts at No. 37 in April. Lennon liked it enough to keep a copy on his jukebox. The Big Three hated it.

Johnny Gustafson: "I think my mother and father had gone out for a drink or something and my sister let me stay up till ten o'clock and I listened to a Radio Luxembourg programme called *Rock into Dreamland* – it was Jack Jackson – and he played Little Richard's *Rip It Up*, and I could not believe it – it was so exciting, so different. I was awake all night. I couldn't sleep a wink. I had to have this music . . . I had to do it. My brother was a pianist – not professionally, he played by ear, but he was very good – he was a painter and decorator professionally, and he knew about my leanings and I think he took pity on me and swapped a couple of cans of Walpamur for some old guitar . . . to me it was gold dust . . . had only two strings when it arrived, soon remedied that. That was the key to the door really.

"My life was segmented into changeable parts. I saw Buddy Holly live in Liverpool and he changed one of those parts for ever . . .

[My first gig] was on New Year's Eve 1959, Tower Ballroom, Blackpool . . . it was terrifying – this huge ballroom, two thousand people . . . after about three or four numbers you begin to realise that they're not looking at you all the time . . . so you start to enjoy yourself. I was paid – £2.

"Cass and the Casanovas – my first band – was a strange hybrid – kind of Latin-American tinged rock, standards, Johnny and the Hurricanes material thrown in for good measure, the odd Jerry Lee Lewis number . . . that developed more into a rock'n'roll quartet . . . we reformed as the Big Three and switched entirely to r'n'b and things that we really wanted to do. [Our speakers] were five feet high by about one and a half to two feet wide. Adrian Barber was a bit of an electronics wiz – he concocted these things. He got two Goodmans 15 inch speakers and made up this great big amp – it was only fifty watts, but he acoustically designed the cabinets to give it the most oomph, and they did sound very, very loud. We developed a one hundred per cent r'n'b format. This thing was happening in Liverpool at the time as a kind of fightback to the Shadows' material – and we developed through this and the big amps into a group with volume."

Johnny Gus left school at fifteen and didn't work for two years. He admits that only beatings from his father got him to take the string of odd jobs that followed. He says he was involved in street fights, but adds that that was just part of growing up in Liverpool.

"As soon as the rock thing started [Dad] thought I would get one hundred per cent worse – but it was exactly the opposite. I was so engrossed in it I forgot everything else."

By 1961-2 the Big Three were earning around £15-18 per week from their music. More, as Johnny says, than his father was earning. He remembers his father's repeated warnings that it wouldn't last, and that he wept when Johnny brought home a copy of the Three's first record.

"The image of the Big Three was really no image – just street clothes, smoking and drinking on stage, rough and ready, swearing, shouting at the top of your voice, insulting people in the front row. [Brian Epstein] reacted very badly. He forced us into suits. He gave us £80 or £90 to buy some band suits. We went to C&A across the road. There was a sale on and we bought these horrific suits – grey tweed things with odd trousers and spent the rest in the boozer over the next week or so. When he found out, Epstein went bananas. We were dragged down by the scruff of our necks and made to go to a real tailor – get measured up and all that – black mohair jobs, waistcoats, ties, pink collars and everything – made to have haircuts, get your fingernails trimmed, nicotine off your fingers with pumice stone . . . he thought it was professional, but we soon came unstuck.

"[Decca] gave us a song by Mitch Murray, and after playing it on the road we realised we hated these songs . . . we didn't want that kind of an audience . . . and we stopped playing them. Some representative of 'the office' would force a song on us at the beginning of a set, then we would revert to playing what we liked, to r'n'b – which was the reason we were there. We weren't there for suits or Mitch Murray."

If the Beatles were lucky in George Martin as their producer, the Big Three were unlucky in theirs. Martin's contribution to the Beatles' music can be exemplified by his piano playing on *Money* – it lends power to Lennon's performance, it furthers what the American critic Tim Riley calls the 'ethical hooliganism', it fits. On *Bring It On Home* the Big Three (after Johnny Gus had left the group) suffered a string quartet, applied fatuously to an r'n'b number. The Big Three's experience of record companies and producers was bad from the start, right from the recording of *Some Other Guy*.

"The last time we were in Hamburg . . . we'd been playing about six one-hour sets a night. Voices don't hold up that well over four or five weeks. When we came back . . . what was left of my voice was in tatters . . . we were taken down to Decca studios the next morning. Brian insisted that we all sang. I really couldn't do it. We sang part of our set as a sort of recording test. I stood back from the mike and let Johnny Hutch do most of it. You can hear a few croaks in the background if you listen carefully. We were accepted on the strength of this poor performance, partly because Decca were terrified of turning down another Beatles. Brian called us round and gave us the fantastic news – the single would be out shortly. 'What single?' '*Some Other Guy*, of course.' 'Listen, we've got to go back and record it *properly*.' 'No,' he said, 'they like it and it's going out.' . . . I think it's worth listening to now for the guitar solo – Griff was outstanding."

Epstein's understanding of their style and their music seems to have been slight. Only a few months later the inevitable split came.

"Our suits were wet from playing the night before. When I say wet I mean wringing wet – soaked. And we got to a TV show – *Thank Your Lucky Stars* I think it was – the suits were ruined, so we dumped them in favour of black polo-neck jumpers. That's what did the damage. Brian thought that was unforgivable – absolutely unforgivable.

"In the early days I was very suspicious. I'd never met anyone like that before. Very clean. Very dapper. I changed my mind after about six months. I decided he was a straight guy, honest and a gentleman. It was surprising, really, to transform three scallywags into some kind of an orderly unit that looked semi-reasonable, and to hoist us into the charts . . . it's quite a feat."[40]

Early in their career the Merseybeats had been managed by Epstein too. There's a much told tale that they left him because he refused to buy them stage suits, but, true though that is, there was more to it.

"We realised we were getting more of our own gigs than Eppy was getting for us."[41]

Epstein had, as so many of his acts have testified, less and less time for anyone but the Beatles. The Merseybeats had landed a record deal with Decca early in 1963 – but there was no follow-up. Two months later Fontana heard them playing a lunchtime session at the Cavern and signed them on the spot. Later in the sixties the Merseybeats considered returning to Epstein, and but for his death would probably have done so. Billy Kinsley adds that for all the 'goofs' he still thinks Brian Epstein was a great manager.

What had proved impossible with the Big Three was about to take the Beatles another step forward. The *Daily Mirror* of June 21st marks a turning point in the presentation of the Beatles. On the back page was a small story that must have caused Epstein no little worry. At McCartney's twenty-first birthday party in Liverpool, Lennon had beaten up Bob Wooler "because he intimated that I was homosexual".[42] Lennon was quoted as saying: "Why did I have to go and beat up my best-friend? I was so high I didn't realise what I was doing." It was the last time a realistic story of the off-stage life of a Beatle would make the press for some time. It would be years before the stories of drugs and whores began to circulate. With the success of their fourth single, *She Loves You*, at the end of the summer, there began a wider press interest in the Beatles, but also a curious conspiracy to present them as four lovable, working-class moptops – as George Harrison called them, the Fabs. In the *Mirror* on October 22nd Epstein openly admitted that he had cleaned up the Beatles, even that he had dropped one of his acts (though he did not name them as the Big Three, nor give the reason), but by now the myth had taken hold. Whatever Epstein had wished to promote them as, whatever they were or wished to be, the power of the press eclipsed totally. The Beatles were no longer a group of passable musicianship, outstanding composing ability and wide teenage appeal, they were a national treasure, a combination of asset, secret weapon and living monument. The age of Beatlemania was about to break, and with it nonsense of unparalleled, and unrepeated, proportions. In Harrison's nickname for the group is a measure of ironic distance, an assertion that it may have happened to him but wasn't really him.

§

Beatlemania, as a phenomenon distinctly different from the adulation of the fans, can be dated from the Beatles' appearance on *Sunday Night at the London Palladium* on October 13th. It was hard to ignore the Beatles by now – they had topped the singles and LP charts simultaneously with *She Loves You* and *Please Please Me* and would have topped the EP charts, if there'd been any, with *Twist and Shout* – but it seems that only their final entry into the bastion of 'Light Ent' with its sequins, its high kicking rows of dancing girls, its daft games and its revolving stage drew the full gaze of the national newspapers. It can be (and I'm sure it has been) argued that Beatlemania had to be invented to keep a press bandwagon rolling after the suicide of that summer's star turn Dr Stephen Ward in August and the publication of Lord Denning's enquiry into the Profumo scandal in September. But invented with such consonance, with such coordinated timing? As Lennon said, they seemed to click in the minds of fourteen different editors at once. Most papers carried similar stories of the siege of Argyll Street. The *Mirror* told of fifty fans who broke into the Palladium by the emergency doors and who were driven out by staff who threatened to turn the fire hoses on them. The Beatles spent the afternoon almost imprisoned in their dressing room. After the show a cordon of sixty policemen held back a crowd of a thousand 'wild' fans to enable the Beatles to escape with a motorcycle escort. The *Mail* had the same story of the girls and the fire hoses, put the number of fans at only five hundred but got a good quote from the doorman who had seen nothing like it since Johnny Ray's appearance in 1955. Yet, when interviewed by Philip Norman for the book *Shout*, photographer Dezo Hoffman said he saw no more than eight fans. It's a credible story. Worth checking. Neither the *Mail* nor the *Mirror* showed these screaming crowds. The *Mail*'s shots are cropped down into thin strips to show two or three fans at a time, with no indication, but an implicit suggestion, of what lay to either side. The reality was probably that the Palladium appearance had been selected as the moment to 'break' the Beatles. The fans had been pursuing and screaming over the Beatles for months now and it was tough luck on the press that on this occasion they failed to show up – but as with the death of

Liberty Vallance, 'when the legend becomes truth print the legend'.[43]

And the legend grew.

Beatlemania was only Beatlemania when it also drew in the grown-ups, the mums and dads, people who hadn't bought a record since they were ten inches across, spun at 78 rpm and broke if you so much as breathed on them. The old hands manned the pumps to introduce the Fabs to the frumps. First off the mark was the *Mirror*'s Donald Zec who got in a month before the official launch with "Four frenzied little Lord Fauntleroys who are making £5000 every week – THE BEATLES." Zec affected intimacy – "they breezed into my flat for tea the other day"[44] – but had no ear for the music – "four incomprehensible voices drowned by their own self inflicted 240 volt amplification" – nor any succinct grasp of the image – "with their long hair, drain pipe trousers and winkle picker boots the scene sort of resembled a teddy-boys' picnic." But then this is all part of the pose, the avuncular square somehow won over in spite of himself, who can reassure all the mums and dads that the Fabs are all right really, that their hair is clean and their manners impeccable.

For the *Daily Mail* Vincent Mulchrone wisely estimated that the Beatles earned a mere £2000 per week (such figures would continue to be rolled out with no sense of accuracy for months – Epstein, refuting £15,000 per week, said he had known one journalist to confuse the box office take with the Beatles' wage) and offered a dramatic vignette from Lennon that eventually found its way into Alun Owen's script for *A Hard Day's Night*. The scene, a first-class railway carriage – a crusty character (typecasting for Richard Vernon) closes the window and switches off the Beatles' trannie with the non-sequitur "I fought in the war" . . . "In reply," wrote Mulchrone "the Beatles chanted their most diabolical insult – 'Ah,' they said, 'you're one of those people who stay home at night and watch television'"[45] – which illustrated the generation gap Mulchrone was both emphasising and trying to bridge. Television was an object of contempt among the young. Within a couple of years the Who would be regularly smashing up TV sets as part of their stage act. In conclusion Mulchrone seemed to have had a close brush with divinity . . . "They are refreshing; they are fun; they are kind. I feel better about life for having been in their company." Pieces like this set the tone for most subsequent writing about the Beatles. They are held up as rich but lovable, clean, emphatically clean, fun loving, honest, harmless and inexplicably appealing – and as soon as that last fact is acknowledged the analysis of their appeal is attempted. Was this what Epstein had anticipated in his shaping of their image? Was this what he wanted, the broadest possible appeal? If so he could not have been more pleased than with the two major events of November. On the 1st the Beatles returned from Sweden to find two thousand fans waiting for them at Heathrow, and the Queen's Building draped with banners – and on the 5th the Beatles appeared once more at the Palladium, this time in the Royal Variety Performance before the Queen Mother, Princess Margaret and, when televised the following week, a huge home audience of twenty-six million. They shared the bill with, and stole the show from, such as Marlene Dietrich and Max Bygraves. They sang *From Me To You, She Loves You, Till There Was You* and ended on *Twist and Shout*. Barry Norman, then show-biz correspondent of the *Daily Mail*, was there, and wrote that if the Beatles had not made it before they had now. He recalls:

"Up to that point the older generation . . . had regarded the Beatles with a certain amount of suspicion. They were the first group who attracted the adoration of very young kids . . . and the older generation were not at all sure that this was such a good thing. Now, on this occasion, the streets all around were packed with screaming kids . . . you always got fans, but not like this . . . they were very young kids and they were screaming in hysterics both before and after the Beatles arrived. The doubt was whether they'd get across to the kind of audience that buys tickets to a Royal Variety Show, people who tend to be forty or fifty plus . . . and they did. That was the surprise of the whole evening . . . The audience just warmed to them. I met them in the afternoon at the rehearsal. They were very well behaved. Paul McCartney was the spokesman, always the most diplomatic of them, in fact always the most presentable in his language and in his manners. I can't recall much about Marlene Dietrich that evening. If you'd asked me who was the star of that evening I'd have said the Beatles. It was really rather triumphant."

Lennon introduced one song with his most memorable and misquoted line: "I'd like to ask your help. Would the people in the cheaper seats clap their hands. And the rest of you – if you'd just rattle your jewellery."

Barry Norman: "By that time the audience was ready to love them, because if it hadn't been it could have been death. People have died at the Royal Variety Performance. That got a huge round of applause."[46]

Epstein had spent part of the afternoon begging Lennon not to say "fucking jewellery".

The *Mirror*'s write-up of this event first used the word

Beatlemania. The Beatles had now become the regular press sensation that sold papers. The tales of sieges of music halls and cinemas all over Britain, of Beatles disguised as policemen to avoid mauling by thousands of girl fans, of the pounding they took from hundreds of jelly babies[47] each time they performed, and of the fabled millions of pounds ran and ran for the rest of the year. If this was the replacement for the Profumo scandal where then – good news being no news – was the merest hint of scandal? It was present in a ready juxtaposition of the celebration of, the grown-up pride in, the Beatles and the plethora of articles which pushed the analysis of the appeal of the fab four into questions of teenage morality and behaviour as a whole. The conspiracy of noise to present the Beatles as squeaky clean (who could even think that John knew a word like 'fucking'?)[48] was matched by repeated assertions of the seaminess of teenage life, explorations of a demi-monde and the trotting out of tame psychologists. At the same time as mum and dad were being reassured that the Beatles themselves were harmless, they were being unsubtly informed that Beatlemania, the press creation of which was neatly elided, was all part of a larger phenomenon that might not be.

The *Mirror*, in a very silly leader of November 6th, pitched an appreciation of the Beatles at the lowest common denominator, in a vocabulary that was years out of date: "YEAH, YEAH, YEAH . . . You have to be a real, sour square not to love the nutty, noisy, happy, handsome Beatles" – whose mops of hair were, of course – "WASHED [sic] . . . super-clean."

Nor did their in-house psychiatrist do much to raise the level of analysis: "We admire their freshness and innocence so much that it's almost like giving birth." Does that mean anything?

A month earlier the counterpart to this sense of adult pride in the young was aired in 'A *Mirror* Enquiry' into teenagers, under the headline "CALL THEM SPENDAGERS!", which allowed no room for pride but ample for resentment. The disposable income of Britain's five and a half million teenagers was estimated at £1000 million per annum – enough, in an absurd comparison, to pay for "twenty Polaris submarines" – but the teenagers had better ways of spending the money – they bought fifty million records a year, at a cost of 6/8d each.[49] A nineteen-year-old shorthand typist from Swinton, Lancs, was interviewed. Of her take-home pay of £7 10s a week, £2 went on clothes and "the rest is swallowed up in day-to-day make-up, nylons, bus fares that spell teenage living." There was no mention of food or rent – the girl still lived at home with Mum and Dad. Her lifestyle is average and unremarkable, but the *Mirror*'s enquiry is heading for a specific goal: " . . . they reckon that kicks for quids is a fair exchange."[50]

It's hard to believe that nylons, make-up and bus fares constituted kicks. Life in Swinton must have been exceedingly dull if the biggest buzz on offer was to blow half a crown on a pair of Pretty Pollys. In the follow-up article sociologist Mark Abrams[51] aired fears that the older generation could never have articulated for themselves: "Only a generation ago teenagers wanted to be identified as adults as quickly as possible. Now teenagers spend heavily so that they will stay the way they are. This is the awful thing about it – the Peter Pan mentality. They won't accept the responsibility of growing up."[52]

This is an extreme view, but Abrams' repeated theme was the shaping of a world of self-determining teenage values, an issue taken up by many less acute thinkers, as it dawned on them that baby boom was now on the verge of adulthood, and that they outnumbered every previous generation. The *Telegraph* developed the idea: "The cultural tone of society is normally set by the leisured and monied classes. Our teenagers have leisure and money. What sort of cultural tone are they setting?"[53] An answer to that question would not be fully apparent for another four or five years when the values of the new generation turned the world upside down. In 1963, for the *Mirror*'s purpose it led to one conclusion – trouble. The final interview of their enquiry was with a probation officer.

In November both the *Daily Mirror* and *Sunday Mirror* pursued the new youth. In the *Sunday Mirror* the Beatles gave what was billed as their frankest interview yet, but all it amounted to was them saying 'what's all the fuss about?' to the glut of teenage sex and morality surveys that now threatened to become a small industry. On the page opposite the paper printed the latest such survey. The *Daily Mirror* offered a potted guide to Mods and Rockers, some eight months before the seaside battles, and told you how to tell them apart. The mods were identified by their anoraks (not called parkas in this article), scooters, tab collars without ties, and their Italian fashions. The rockers were the polar opposite – scruffy, greasy bikers. The insight was in identifying most teenagers as Mids – kids of no particular style who used public transport and belonged to no grouping. It's hard to have a double-decker bus as an icon of power and sex. The trigger for the speculation on the sex life of the young – no real information was forthcoming – was that the screaming girl fans were perceived to be in a state of sexual hysteria, were rumoured to orgasm as the Fabs played, or to wet their pants. Attempts to explain all this reached the pits as the *News of the World* finally lumbered aboard the rollercoaster. Short of anything new to say, they pinched quotations from Maureen Cleave, drummed up phoney facts (the four now earned £7000 per week – John worked as a labourer to buy his first guitar) and headed resolutely for the conclusions of their own tame shrink, who offered this nonsense: "Subconsciously [the girls] are preparing for motherhood. Their frenzied screams are a rehearsal for that moment. Even the jelly babies are symbolic."[54]

Would that Lennon had expressed his preference for Bath Olivers.

§

In all this the fans were consulted less than the experts. In all the analyses of Beatle appeal, there are few direct questions as to 'why them?' Perhaps the fans were held to be inarticulate? Today they are thirty-something or forty-something.

Lizzie Bawden, double first Oxford, Ph.D, born 1952:

"I know the feeling of that record [*Please Please Me*]. The feeling's the same now as it always was. It's a yearning feeling, happy and yearning at the same time – which I suppose is very much like the feeling of being in love.

"I was in the Billy Fury fan club, and the Beatles fan club – I even wrote to John's Aunt Mimi. I bought *Fabulous* every week, for the marvellous pinups. I had one wall which was solid centre-spreads of Billy Fury, and one wall solid centre-spreads of the Beatles. I went for John Lennon. His image, just his physical image, was attractive. When their personalities became public property, I also found his personality attractive. He was weird, he was funny. I liked his books; they were funny in a way that no one else I'd come across had ever been. It seemed to make a lot of things possible. A lot of thoughts possible. The Beatles didn't seem 'clean' to me – they were very earthy. There was a granular quality to their voices. Something very personal – they weren't smooth or glossy – you could hear the breathing in their voices. They were individuals. Everybody had their favourite Beatle, and everybody could say in which order they loved them.

"It's very mysterious to look back on participating in that kind of mass hysteria. I screamed my head off, I cried and cried. I got tickets for the Hammersmith Odeon. It seemed very special to be able to get two tickets. I took a friend. It was very important to go with someone who was as crazy about them as I was. She was a little older than me – she was fifteen and wore make-up – which mattered. It was very much about being a teenager, which I suppose I

just was. It was impossible to hear them. They were just a phenomenon on the stage. We had a banner that said 'JOHN' and had an
enormous heart on it – we waved it as soon as the curtain went up.
The whole theatre was full of banners. Everyone was on their feet
and the screaming began. It was like a competition.

"Orgasm? I didn't know what they were at that time. No. I didn't
wet my knickers. I'd remember that. I'd have been embarrassed. I
never met anyone who did, and there wasn't a pissy smell about the
place.

"My brother was in show business. He was friendly with John and
Paul. He arranged for us to go backstage and meet the Beatles. 'Pull
the other one,' the doorman said – so we never got backstage. We
went to a coffee bar. There were two of the Dreamers – one apiece –
we got their autographs. A sort of second prize. We weren't terribly
impressed by them. We were equal to the occasion, we weren't
rendered breathless or weak at the knees.

"I was staying with my brother in London on one occasion. He
went out for a meal with John and Cynthia, to which, as a twelve-
year-old, I was understandably not invited. He casually remarked,
possibly after I'd egged him on, that he might bring the Lennons
back for coffee afterwards. I waited up, put on my best pyjamas.
Looking back that seems quite funny, being that cross between a
child and a woman that I was then. I've never been into négligés,
but I don't think I would later have thought my Norwegian pat-
terned, fleecy lined pyjamas were the most seductive dress for
meeting my hero in. I sat up until two in the morning. I was
disappointed. I never did meet John, although I did get his autograph.

"A friend of my brother's worked on a film with the Beatles.
Perhaps, being a woman, she was sensitive to what it was like being
a lovestruck adolescent and got me a signed photograph of them –
which I have to this day. I was delighted, so delighted that it was
John who had written my name on the photograph and added a kiss
at the bottom. I retired to my room when I got it and wept with joy
and stroked it and held it up to the light and looked at the thumb-
prints on it and hoped that at least one of them belonged to John.

"Any pop music was the route to adulthood. It was one way to
feel grown up and go through grown-up feelings – feelings like being
passionately in love with people one's never met. It hastened growing up in a particular way. It possibly inhibited maturing. It
hastened a sense of sexuality, I suppose. I was sexually active before
I stopped being a Beatles fan – I don't think I can attribute that to
the Beatles though. I didn't feel the lovers I had then were John

Lennon substitutes. I don't think kids today are so obsessed with boy-meets-girl stuff and I think it's a good thing. They're a lot more sensible about relations between the sexes."[55]

In the quality papers serious misgivings about youth were expressed – less obviously neurotic than the tabloids, more sweeping in their assumptions, but not notably different in meaning.

"The hysteria fills heads and hearts otherwise empty . . . is there not something frightening in whole masses of young people, all apparently so suggestible, so volatile and so rudderless?" asked a *Telegraph* leader.[56] A few months later, William Deedes, Minister without Portfolio, addressed the City of London Young Conservatives and seemed to have been a while on the road to Damascus: "[The Beatles] herald a cultural movement among the young which may become part of the history of our time . . . the young are rejecting some of the sloppy standards of their elders . . . ", which brought forth the wrath of Paul Johnson in the *New Statesman*. Johnson berated responsible adults – the church, the press, the politicians – for surrendering to the illusion of being 'with it'. It's one of the most scathing critiques of youth culture ever written. Teenagers are commercially exploited and culturally deprived – Johnson does not allow that the Beatles might be the teenagers' own choice, their own voice and culture – by cynical adults, and the price is the destruction of the precious sense of discovery: "It is a marvellous age, an age of intense mental energy and discovery. Almost every week one found a new idol – Milton, Wagner, Debussy, Matisse, El Greco, Proust . . . all springing from the mainstream of European culture."

Indeed it is. It wasn't the Beatles that screwed up my O levels, but lying awake nights listening to Debussy and Elgar on army surplus headphones – Lizzie Bawden seemed to find a love of the Beatles quite compatible with reading Henry James. None of which would make sense to Mr Johnson. The cultures are mutually exclusive. The worst is yet to come. Johnson has subjected himself to the torment of watching *Juke Box Jury* and *Thank Your Lucky Stars*, and as the cameras pan across the audience what circles of hell are revealed to his cultured gaze: " . . . a bottomless chasm of vacuity . . . The huge faces bloated with cheap confectionery and smeared with chain store make-up, the open sagging mouths and glazed eyes . . . the shoddy, stereotyped 'with it' clothes: here, apparently, is a collective portrait of a generation enslaved by a commercial machine."[57]

But there's something in this rant. Interviewed by Stanley Reynolds for the *Guardian*, Cavern compère Bob Wooler came closer to it: "They are afraid of sentiment. They are cruel to each other because they are trying to prove they have no hearts. They are trying to show that they are not affected by anything."[58]

Beneath such comment lurks a sense of the teenage dilemma articulated by Lizzie Bawden – how to be? It isn't as crude as simply rejecting the sloppy values of the elders, sloppy though they were. In a generation of such size and power, frontiers collapse to the touch. The centre cannot hold. What Johnson – as well as Tory MPs, other leader writers and Edgar Lustgarten – perceived as moronic might more generously be termed uncertain, unanchored, a generation with no knowledge of how to be, as culture distorted around their own image like Einstein's model of a universe curving under a single mass. Conceivably something like this happens in every generation – in which case it's a matter of scale. There has been no phenomenon like the Beatles since – whatever the hype of the record industry – there's been no such audience, big enough to buy records in millions,[59] big enough to draw in the generations around them and make the minority culture the main culture – if this includes the adults then it's not surprising that the problem becomes one of being. Possibly Paul Johnson was right to attack the adults for deserting their posts – for they did so even in the oddest corners of the national life.

Field Marshal Viscount Montgomery of Alamein announced that he would invite the Beatles to his Hampshire home to see 'what sort of fellows they were'. After the Beatles' first visit to the USA, the new Prime Minister, Sir Alec Douglas-Home, accustomed to playing second fiddle to the Beatles (held up at London airport while the fans welcomed them back from Sweden, delayed on his trip to Washington as the embassy held a reception for the Fabs), declared that they were his new secret weapon: "If any country is in deficit with us I have only to say the Beatles are coming . . . Let me tell you why they have had such a success in the United States – it is because they are a band of very natural, very funny young men."[60]

Wilson replied, aggrieved. Not only were they a Liverpool group, as he was a Liverpool MP, they were working class and hence the natural possession of the Labour Party. It was nonsense.

And the nonsense grew.

Soon you could buy Beatle badges, bags, guitars, posters, tea towels, mugs, T shirts, hats, ash trays, pencils, socks – and wigs . . . advertisements like this were common: "She'll love you in the MOD MOOD in the de luxe MERSEY BEAT WIG the latest, greatest Party rave! Only 19/11d plus 2/1d p&p. Dad, dig this new mod fad. It's a gas!"[61] . . . and, of course, suits.

Gillian Reynolds: "I bought miniature Beatle suits for little boys of four and five and put them on my stall in St John's Market, Liverpool, and I put tickets on them – Freddie and the Dreamers, the Big Three, John, Paul . . . people looked at the little corduroy suits with no collars . . . some London manufacturer's idea of what mothers would buy, and the mothers did . . . they wanted to share with their children the excitement of what was going on."

As the sales of Beatle jackets grew Edward Heath remarked, "Who could have forecast only a year ago that the Beatles would prove to be the salvation of the corduroy industry."[62]

Analysis in anxiety co-existed with pushing out the bandwagon, celebrating the resurgence of popular culture through the Beatles – themselves untouchable by the anxiety once their cleanness and niceness had been established by common consent. The trivia of Beatlemania was endlessly recorded For example . . . in an Accrington cotton mill there was a one hour strike by two hundred girls when the foreman turned off *Housewives' Choice*. The girls had screamed at the sound of *From Me to You* and it was feared they would be distracted from their work . . . or . . . on board HMS *Bulwark* an official memo was sent out ordering crew to cut off their Beatle hairstyles[63] . . . or . . . Clark's Grammar school in Guildford banned Beatle haircuts. According to the headmaster: "This ridiculous style brings out the worst in the boys physically. It makes them look like morons"[64] . . . happy, fun-loving, honest, natural . . . moronic? As one generation reminded the next that it had fought in the war for the likes of . . . et cetera . . . fashion became part of an inexplicable moral equation, the parts of which were known only to those who had fought in the war for the likes of . . . et cetera . . . the sum of which resulted in such profound moral dictates as 'no lad o'mine's goin' out wi' fourteen inch bottoms on his trousers.' It was reasssuring to know that with all wars safely over for ever, less than a year after Cuba, the serious problems of social order could now be tackled by the elder generation, and that Jerusalem would be built on the moral foundations of short hair and baggy pants.

At Christmas the pinnacle of respectability was reached. A hymn of praise from Dora Bryan singing *All I Want for Christmas is a Beatle*, a turn on the *Morecambe and Wise Show* singing *Moonlight Bay* in blazers and boaters, while Morecambe cavorted in a leather jacket (it's worth remembering that Elvis suffered far worse: he wore top hat and tails and sang *Hound Dog* to a basset hound on the *Ed Sullivan Show*), a ballet on Mods and Rockers performed to John and Paul's music, and a review of the Beatles' work to date by

William Mann, music critic of *The Times*. Too often in the analysis of the Beatles' appeal little or no attention had been paid to the music and the fact that the Beatles took the charts before anyone was aware of any image, long before they charmed the politicians or the royals with their wit.

"I am not concerned here with the social phenomenon of Beatlemania . . . the hysterical screaming of young girls . . . but with the musical phenomenon."[65]

Mann took the Beatles seriously, calling Lennon and McCartney the outstanding English composers of 1963, and paid the price of being sent up by many, even by Harold Wilson, for lines like "That Boy . . . harmonically one of their most interesting, with its chains of pandiatonic clusters" . . . or . . . "so natural is the Aeolian cadence at the end of *Not A Second Time* (the chord progression which ends Mahler's *Song of the Earth*)." He slipped too easily into the clichés of bewilderment – the screaming was a mystery, although girls had screamed at Tommy Steele, at Frank Sinatra and at Donald Peers, and so was the sound as distinct from the music – "I suppose it is the sheer loudness of the music that appeals to Beatle admirers" – as though amplification itself were new, and Crosby had never crooned into an electric microphone – but his conclusion was precise: "They have brought a distinctive and exhilarating flavour into a genre that was in danger of ceasing to be music at all."

*   *   *

The sudden shift north left London standing. It had been thought impossible to make it from anywhere else. Decca had signed Brian Poole and the Tremeloes instead of the Beatles partly because they were local (Dagenham) and hence handy for the recording studio. It was with Poole and the Trems that London first fought back and tried to create a southern Beatles – more in desperation than certainty. Their first hit, in July, was *Twist and Shout*, but owed more to the Beatles than it did to the Isley Brothers. Their second hit was even more derivative of Liverpool. *Do You Love Me?* (written by Berry Gordy for the Contours and recorded on Tamla) was first recorded in England by the Merseyside band Faron's Flamingos, who helpfully jotted down the lyrics for Poole after he heard them live in St Helens. Poole's version went to No. 1. Faron's version didn't even appear as an A side. In turn this was covered by the Tottenham group the Dave Clark Five – a group who'd missed already with four or five singles, and whose first taste of success was with a cover of a cover of a Liverpool cover of a Tamla song. So much for the originality of the 'Tottenham Sound'. When their next single – *Glad All Over*, written by Clark and singer Mike Smith – made No. 1 in January 1964, displacing the Beatles' *I Want to Hold Your Hand*, the fact was announced on television as news, and the popular press launched a brief spurt of London victory celebrations. The Beatles had been crushed, "Dave's the boy who beat the Beatles."[66] What mattered was not the quality of the Dave Clark Five (no personality and a sound like a Black and Decker hammer drill) or the non-existent Tottenham Sound, but the self-esteem of the south. The south's greatest asset, The Rolling Stones, were hard to promote in the press as an answer to the Beatles – they looked plain evil and played r'n'b rather than pop – and London had to wait until the Summer of 1964 for a band as immediately original as the Beatles, when the Kinks, from Muswell Hill, had their first No. 1, by which time the Beatles and NEMS had themselves moved south.

Although their success was hardly diminished by Merseybeat, 1963 was a tough year for Cliff and the Shadows. Towards the end of the year Cliff's interviews seem very much on the defensive, as though resisting premature attempts to write him off: "We are not going to contest the beat groups. We'll carry on doing what we are doing until the public stops buying our records."[67] Doubtless Cliff is still awaiting that moment. By the new year he was on the attack, saying to Donald Zec "in the manner of an A. J. P. Taylor tutorial": "All they've done is revert to rock'n'roll . . . five year old music . . . we've played the whole thing down, the screaming and the raving. The Beatles have stoked the whole thing up again . . . Their stuff is real homemade music. Anybody who can shout can be a Beatle."[68]

The pressures of being a pop star in 1963 are more visible in the story of the Shadows than of the Beatles at this point. Two of the Shadows had already left the group – drummer Tony Meehan to go into production, and bass player Jet Harris for a solo career. Harris had been the pin-up of the four, the one everyone said could make it alone. He left in the Spring of 1962, changed from dyed blond back to his natural, more attractive, brown and swapped his bass for a six string, which he tuned down for a bass sound. At the beginning of 1963, Jet and Tony, as a duo, had a smash instrumental hit, *Diamonds*, and were interviewed by Maureen Cleave for her regular column in the *Standard*: they were seen as two young men with a bright future, obviously cool, described as "taking it easy". Three weeks later Harris was in hospital suffering from exhaustion. He bounced back. Two more hits followed. In September, as *Applejack* slipped into the charts, Harris's chauffeur-driven car crashed in

Evesham. His girlfriend, singer Billie Davis, dragged him from the wreck. He was unconscious and needed twenty-two stitches – Davis herself suffered a fractured jaw and glumly predicted that Jet would never play again. In October he walked off the set of *Ready Steady Go* saying he had quit showbiz for good. Billie Davis told the papers that he was "on the verge of a nervous breakdown . . . he's been pushed too hard".[69] Jet retreated to Brighton. A few days later, on October 10th, he was arrested for being drunk and disorderly – the police had found him sitting on the seafront. Jet was fined £4. Trivial stuff – for anyone but the person to whom it happens. He reappeared sporadically throughout the sixties, but his career was over as surely as Terry Dene's. Whatever happened to Jet Harris? remains a perennial question for the nostalgic. Occasionally it is answered. In the late-eighties, Cliff played to a packed house at Wembley. At one point he summoned his bass-player to step forward and introduced Jet Harris to the audience. Time had scarcely been kind to Jet – he looked thin – so did his hair – but he was standing next to the Peter Pan of rock, and no-one in the business of rock has played Peter Pan quite as long or as well as Cliff Richard.

What happened to Harris wasn't unique. At the same time Bruce Welch announced that he too would leave the Shadows: "Doctors say I'll have a nervous breakdown if I don't . . . "[70] . . . and as Cliff defended his position against the northern onslaught Harris' replacement, Brian Locking, quit to join the Jehovah's Witnesses. Had Welch not returned, Hank would have been the only original Shadow left.

§

With a new market so readily apparent, magazines and television programmes aimed exclusively at teenagers sprang up. *Fabulous* and *Rave* were both launched in early 1964, and *Mirabelle*, a survivor from the first rock boom in 1957, relaunched itself in colour. *Juke Box Jury* lumbered on, on one occasion surrendering all four seats to the Beatles, and in January 1964 the BBC introduced *Top of the Pops* – but the real success went to ITV's *Ready Steady Go*, which took to the air in the Summer of 1963, hosted, as all such programmes were, by an 'uncle' – Keith Fordyce. By Christmas *RSG* had recognised the trend and appointed the first teenage presenter, Cathy McGowan, to be the typical teenager, not as the background figure Janice Nicholls had been on *Thank Your Lucky Stars*, but in the main role. It was on *Thank Your Lucky Stars* on July 6th that Britain caught its first glimpse of the Rolling Stones, miming to their first record, Chuck Berry's *Come On*. Britain had never seen anything like it. If Mum and Dad were slowly beginning to acknowledge that the Fabs were nice boys, even if their trousers were too tight, no such acknowledgment could ever be made of the Stones. They looked like a pack of dogs. The figure that struck the eye was not the singer – rumoured to be known as 'Jagger', a name that was surely made up, nobody had a name like Jagger? – but the harmonica player, Brian Jones, hunched over his instrument, be-fringed and blond like an old English sheepdog, breaking off occasionally to reveal a mouth wide enough to take a table spoon sideways. Too sophisticated for the Beatles, Josie Neap at last found the object of adoration: "Physically the Stones were just more interesting. The hair, they had such long hair. Brian Jones was so blond – I found that very attractive – men's hair was very sexy. The Beatles looked to me like the sort of guys you'd tell to bog off if they tried to pick you up, but the Stones you'd want to get to know. They had a much more dangerous quality. It was sex. I always fancied Brian Jones. I wrote to them at a theatre where they were perform-ing, and sent him a snapshot of myself. A manager rang up and said "Brian wants to meet you." I drove out to a country club near Bristol to meet him. We had a meal, something to drink, smoked a few joints. He said he wanted me to spend the night with him. Then he insisted that I went back to Bristol first, so I'd have something clean to wear the next day. He didn't think it was right for me to have the same clothes two days running. I thought it was odd even then. So he came back with me all the way to Bristol, and then all the way back out to the country. No – I didn't feel exploited. If anything I was doing the exploiting. I got what I was after. And then I couldn't sleep for all the speed I'd taken. It always was about sex. The stage act was very exciting but I never liked the music. Brian for me was the one with that slightly mysterious quality, almost James Dean type. He was much more intriguing than Mick who was flaunting it all over the place.

"When I met Brian he'd just got to the stage where everything was losing its charm for him. He said he could have anything he wanted. He could go into a shop and buy the whole shop. It had all lost its excitement with him. And it was the same with women. No, I don't mind the word groupie, and I've never done anything I regret. I never got asked into anything like group sex, I never got passed around – I suppose the sense of danger that I mean was simply another way of saying 'sex' – it was a straight het relationship, it wasn't 'dangerous'. He was a very possessive person. I had a terrible row with him once when I was seeing someone else. He got very angry about that. Towards the end, he couldn't put a sentence together, and he couldn't get it up – he'd ask me to do things like pee on him. I would oblige. Brian was the sort of person who would be destroyed by money – I think it would destroy anybody in that quantity. I suppose Mick was saved by the sheer power of his ambition. He wanted it all. Kept him sort of level? I don't know."[71]

There's a lingering belief that it wasn't done to like both the Stones and the Beatles. This wasn't the case. All that can be said is that in certain circles it was considered unsophisticated to like the Beatles. There's always the purist argument. The Beatles were rock imitators, while the Stones, at this stage, were true to r'n'b as practised in the London clubs, and practised well enough for Sonny Boy Williamson to cut an LP with the Yardbirds. I'm never sure where the purist argument leads. It presumes a pristine point of origin – any deviation from which is heresy, adherence to which is mere imitation, hence the new musician cannot win. It's a persistent theme, but it serves to set the point of departure like a bug in amber, when what matters is the journey. Under the Beatles' example the Stones began to write their own material too.[72] Arguments about the unoriginality of the 'so-called' Liverpool sound continued to be made in the reviews, but meant little.

§

Often in the analyses of the Beatles' appeal words like 'natural' and 'honest' crop up. It may be these words disguise the phrase 'working class'. Most pop and rock acts had been working class – Tommy Steele was, and with three of the four Beatles brought up in council houses,[73] they were too. What they were not was deferential. If class did not induce deference, usually showbiz did. The Beatles hammered this from the beginning. The forelock, of which they had plenty, was tugged for no one. This was new. No one should have been surprised at the Beatles' one liners,[74] at the irreverence, the stark humour, the vocabulary (gear, fab, judy, tatty 'ead emerged from Liverpool into the national argot)[75] – almost everyone was. It was as though working-class culture had once more reared up out of a void, as though no one knew it was there, as though the accepted pattern of behaviour in good fortune had been shattered. In their shiny Burton's suits, those who wished could believe in the image Epstein fostered. The teenagers didn't. To them the bad guys Stones good guys Beatles contrast meant nothing. (Once the Stones had established themselves the record releases were staggered by mutual consent of Epstein and the Stones' manager Andrew Oldham to ensure that the fans never did have to choose between the two.) You had only to look at the aggressive Lennon stance, the way he fronted the band, guitar high on his chest, head up, legs apart, bawling his lungs out with a voice that ripped and tore at the words, to know that Epstein had put only the thinnest of veneers over what was really natural about the Beatles. They could scarcely resist sending up the role of the pop star. McCartney teased the press with lines like: "[Our] sole ambition is to see [our] dear old mums living in nice houses"[76] – but of course neither he nor Lennon had dear old mums.

If the most crusty of complaints about pop was that it was 'mind-less', Lennon and McCartney showed at every turn that they had minds, and as they asserted their independence of both Epstein and Martin they sharpened their wits on anyone they chose to.

Stanley Reynolds: "They acted as if they'd been giving interviews all their lives. Ringo was a natural clown – George was very quiet, but Lennon and McCartney were like a double act. They could practically finish one another's sentences. They were really very pleasant. I never heard them say anything aggressive. I was quite surprised when I heard that John Lennon had an aggressive streak to him.

"I went down to London on the train with Maureen Cleave and the Beatles for the Palladium Show. We went into the dining car . . . there were lots of journalists there . . . it was very funny . . . people would come up and ask 'which one are you?' I was surprised by that. The faces had become so famous."[77]

'Which one are you?' plagued the Beatles. It became the symbolic exchange on the fleeting nature of fame, on the pervasive illusion that they were public property and loved by everyone.

The first book on the Beatles is still one of the best and the most ripped off. American journalist Michael Braun was one of the many reporters who followed the Beatles as they toured England, and eventually conquered America. He had few axes to grind and set himself faithfully to record their words. In Washington, at the British Embassy in February 1964 he heard the ultimate 'Which one are you?' exchange:

"Before the reception the Beatles met the Ambassador[78] and Lady Ormsby-Gore at the Embassy residence. When John is intro-duced to him Sir David says, 'Hello, John.'

'I'm not John,' says John, 'I'm Charlie. That's John.' And he points to George."

[Beatles lead one – nil.]

"'Hello, John,' says the Ambassador, turning to George.

'I'm not John,' says George, 'I'm Frank. That's John.' And he points to Paul."

[Beatles two – Ormsby-Gore nil.]

"'Oh, dear!' says the Ambassador. 'I'll never get these names right. My wife is much better at remembering names.'" [79]

[Coming from behind – game set and match to Ormsby-Gore?]

As they left the disastrous reception,[80] in which they'd been pawed like stuffed animals by a gathering of British hoorays, Ringo could not resist the last word and asked Ormsby-Gore what he did for a living. But there was a far harder edge to the jokes, more to it than strong personality, quick wits and a nose for pomposity – all of which had been sadly lacking in other pop stars and in most of their contemporaries. Lennon had always had a thing about deformity of any sort. It shows in his two collections of stories and in the cryptic 'cripples' reference the Beatles used with their roadies when they'd had enough of being public property and wanted the dressing room cleared. People in wheelchairs were brought backstage to the Beatles as though to Lourdes – much to Lennon's irritation – and the word became a derogative for anyone that bored them or pestered them. There is, in reading Braun's book, a mounting sense of the Beatles' distaste for being public property and contempt for the system that was making stars of them. As late as August 1963, they had been able to play the Cavern before audiences of the size and nature they'd grown up with. Within weeks that would be impossible ever again. In America they played venues the size of New York's Shea Stadium, and within a few years, after the final gig at San Francisco's Candlestick Park in 1966, they would play nowhere except to themselves and their tape recorders. The isolation, the creation of a wall around themselves is apparent even in 1963. Ray Coleman covered Beatles' concerts for *Melody Maker*: "Fans rush up the gangways, arms outstretched, pleading . . . the Beatles are visually unmoved and bash away. McCartney's announcements cannot be heard above the roar. 'You might know this next one,' he says to the crowd. 'Hush a minute.' Then, to Lennon, 'Oh never mind. Let's do it!'"

Afterwards in the dressing room their feelings are clear. Ringo says he does wish they'd be quiet . . . "but what can you do about it? The time to start worrying is when they don't make any noise." Paul tells John that there's no time to talk to the crowd, "We'll just have to get on with the stuff."[81]

The intimacy of the small club was gone, and with it something that mattered to the Beatles. Lennon was right, they were grinning at nothing. George told Derek Taylor in the *Express* in January 1964: "We hate it [*She Loves You*] as only we can hate our own hits. The excitement when we knew John and Paul had done it again just can't be described. Then, just as quickly, it goes to the top. We hear it and play it too often. The magic goes and we grow to hate it."[82]

The fifth Beatles' single went straight into the charts at No. 1 Their second LP *With the Beatles* became the sound of Christmas 1963, and sold over a million copies. In January they played to a poor reception in Paris, but while they were there news came through that *I Want to Hold Your Hand* had reached No. 1 in the USA. On February 7th the Beatles flew to the United States.

Nonsense reached a new peak.

The pilot wore a Beatle wig.

Everyone who got off the plane was given a free Beatle 'kit'.

An 'I Like the Beatles' badge, a signed photograph – a wig.

As they came down the steps at Kennedy Airport five thousand screaming fans drowned out the noise of the jets – many of them had been paid a dollar and a Beatles' T shirt by the company handling Beatles merchandising.

Almost the first words the Beatles heard were 'Which one is . . . ?'

Almost the first words Lennon spoke were 'Shurrup'.

The Americans took the Beatles to their own in a way few could have anticipated. It's not simply that so few British acts had made it in America, it's more in the excess, the Beatle madness that characterised the next two years, from the rapturous reception and idiots in wigs,[83] to their odd choice of Ringo as the favourite Beatle, to the Bible-belt backlash of burning hundreds of thousands of records as Lennon spoke his mind once too often for their comfort.

With the Beatles' arrival in America the year long boom in British pop culture, and the energy that drove it, was finally exported to the country of its origin. The era of the Bobby-balladeers was over. Rock'n'roll was back. The Beatles made the effortless transition from national asset to invisible earning on the balance of payments ledger.[84]

The end of the beginning. The beginning of the end. It had, as Lennon remarked, all got too far from the Cavern:

"You see we believed the Beatles myth too . . . we were four guys . . . I met Paul and said 'You want to join me band?' you know. Then George joined and then Ringo joined. We were just a band that made it very, very big, that's all. Our best work was never recorded . . . because we were performers . . . in Liverpool,

Hamburg and other dance halls and what we generated was fantastic, where we played straight rock, and there was nobody to touch us in Britain. As soon as we made it, we made it, but the edges were knocked off. Brian put us in suits and all that and we made it very, very big. But we sold out, you know. The music was dead before we even went on the theatre tour of Britain. We were feeling shit already . . . "[85]

CHAPTER SIX

UNHOLY JOY

"With a roar of unholy joy, the deprived flung themselves on the sated."   Bernard Levin[1]

"Even Suez was 'clean' – about war and politics. This was all 'dirt'."
                                                        Harold Macmillan[2]

There is an affair in the tides of men. At 11 o'clock on the evening of March 21st, towards the end of the fruitless debate on Foster and Mulholland, Colonel George Wigg, MP for Dudley, took it at the flood:

"There is not an Hon. Member in the House, nor a journalist in the press gallery who in the last few days has not heard rumour upon rumour involving a member of the government front bench. The press has got as near as it can – it has shown itself willing to wound but afraid to strike. This all comes about because of the Vassall tribunal. In actual fact, these great press lords, these men who control great instruments of public opinion and power, do not have the guts to discharge the duty that they are now claiming for themselves."

Hansard is not given to including stage directions, merely the nods and shakes of assent and dissent, but you can almost hear the deep intake of breath and the performer girding loins.

"That being the case, I rightly use the privilege of the House of Commons – that is what it is given to me for – to ask the Home Secretary, who is the senior member of the Government on the Treasury Bench now, to go to the Dispatch Box – he knows the rumour to which I refer relates to Miss Christine Keeler and Miss Davies and a shooting by a West Indian – and, on behalf of the Government, categorically deny the truth of these rumours. On the other hand if there is anything in them, I urge him to ask the Prime Minister to do what was not done in the Vassall case – set up a Select Committee so that these things can be dissipated, and the honour of the Minister concerned freed from the imputations and innuendoes that are being spread at the present time."[3]

126

'Rumour upon rumour' was more than a familiar turn of cliché. It was an accurate description of the state of political gossip in the Spring of 1963. Rumour had it, and had had it so for some nine months, that War Minister Jack Profumo had had an affair with the spectacularly beautiful, nineteen-year-old Christine Keeler, model and former nightclub showgirl. The rumour upon this rumour was that Christine had failed to appear, on March 14th, at the trial of John Edgecombe (who had discharged a revolver at her and Mandy Rice-Davies on December 12th) because someone, quite possibly – the rumour went – someone in high or very high places, had spirited Christine away in order to prevent her giving evidence that might prove embarrassing. In publicly citing the newer rumour, Wigg was also invoking the older, and with it what was known by every journalist in London, that Christine was also claiming to have had an affair with the Soviet naval attaché, Yevgeny Ivanov, at the same time. Wigg had called the press cowards for not printing what they knew to be the truth, and had set off a line of enquiry that would lead to two parliamentary debates, countless off-cabinet (as in off-Broadway) meetings, eventually necessitate an investigation by Lord Dilhorne, a report by Lord Denning and, arguably, bring down both the Prime Minister and the government. It was a tragedy for many players, but to find all three protagonists in this first act together you have to go back to July 1961.

§

Since the mid-fifties society osteopath Stephen Ward had rented a weekend cottage on the Cliveden estate of his patient Viscount Astor. As befits an estate like Cliveden, 'cottage' is an understatement to describe the large Tyrolean-style villa, nestling in the beech trees on the banks of the Thames. Spring Cottage was roomy enough for Ward to have house guests and weekend parties, and on the weekend of July 8th-9th, 1961 he had three or four guests, among whom was Christine Keeler – who also shared his London flat. At the same time, in the big house a mile away, Astor was entertaining more than thirty people including Lord Mountbatten, Nubar Gulbenkian, President Ayub Khan of Pakistan and Jack Profumo and his wife, the forties film star Valerie Hobson. At about ten thirty on the Saturday evening, after a hot summer's day, Ward and Christine drove up to the big house for a floodlit swim in Astor's pool. Christine, either because Ward had dared her or because her borrowed costume was too big, was swimming naked as Astor's guests began to drift out of the big house into the garden, at the end of dinner. As Profumo and Astor appeared, Christine grabbed a towel and reached for her costume, but Ward tossed it into the bushes, leaving her wet and dripping and scarcely covered. There was now one of those wonderfully ludicrous moments as upper-class manners coped flawlessly with the unexpected and the absurd, and Astor introduced his disparate guests to one another – the almost naked Christine shook hands with the dinner-jacketed Minister for War and his wife. (Ward and Profumo had met before – Ward had sketched the War Minister for the *Illustrated London News*.) Depending on which published account you read, there was also a scene from *Carry on Minister*, between appearance and introduction, as Astor and Profumo chased Christine round the pool. At the end of the evening Astor invited Ward and his guests to a Sunday picnic lunch by the pool, and Christine set off back to London to guide more of Ward's friends down for the Sunday – one them was Yevgeny Ivanov, whom both Ward and Christine thought was a spy, and on the logic of 'who in any embassy isn't?' it seems only common sense to assume that he was. So, at lunchtime on the Sunday a Soviet spy and the British War Minister were to be found racing each other the length of the pool, and competing for the attention of a teenage girl, watched by a member of the House of Lords and the President of Pakistan. Spy in clover? Minister in daydream? Reputation in peril? Security at risk?

Ivanov drove Christine home to Ward's London flat in Wimpole Mews, where, according to Christine, Ivanov got drunk on vodka and they made love. Profumo asked Ward for his telephone number, and two days later, on the Tuesday, he phoned and invited Christine out 'for a drive' around London in the chauffered ministerial Humber. Later the same week, Profumo called at the mews again in a less grand but very fashionable Mini. He took her to his house in Regent's Park, where they made love. In the weeks that followed Profumo and Christine continued to be lovers, usually using Ward's flat while he was out. The appeal of Christine Keeler to a man of forty-six is obvious, and for her part the affair seems to have had the buzz of risk and power – as she put it herself later, she felt as woman might feel "fucking Marlon Brando". Whether or not she was also fucking Marlon Ivanov during the same period isn't wholly relevant as detail – what is, is that as a close friend of Ward's, sharing his flat, she could scarcely avoid meeting Ivanov from time to time. A year later, long after the affair had ended, the proximity of Ivanov and Profumo via Keeler and Wimpole Mews was beginning to be the subject of gossip, and in the August 1962 issue of *Queen* Robin Douglas-Home (a nephew of the Foreign Secretary) put it into print for the first time in a spoof article entitled 'Sentences I'd Like to Hear the End of':

" . . . called in MI5 because every time the chauffeur-driven Zis drew up at her front door, out of the back door into a chauffeur-driven Humber slipped . . . " The brand names alone would indicate the status of the protagonists – even if the action of the drama seemed improbably well timed and a little too like a Brian Rix farce. Yet it was the unspecified possibility of contact between minister and diplomat that first drew the attention of the government to Profumo's private life. On August 9th, the cabinet secretary, Sir Norman Brook, asked to see Profumo. He warned him that Ward was an inveterate gossip – things said to Ward could find their way to Ivanov – and asked for his co-operation in an ongoing MI5 attempt to entrap Ivanov into working as a double agent. At this point there arises the first of many confusions between the moral and the security aspects of this affair – a dilemma which permeated most sixties' accounts of the matter, as well as the entire parliamentary response. Profumo seems to have taken this chat between chaps as fair warning that those in high places knew of his affair with Christine. He left Brook, not surprisingly declining to assist MI5, and dashed off a letter to Christine before joining his wife on the Isle of Wight, where he spent most of the summer recess. The letter began "Darling" and ended "Love J." It broke an engagement for the following day and said that he would not be able to see her again until the September. That Profumo took fright is obvious – but he seems to have fled not from the issue of his contact with a Soviet spy, but from the immediate threat of discovery in marital infidelity. Yet Brook and MI5 did not know of Profumo's affair at this stage, simply because their source had not known at the time he tipped them off. On the Monday after the swimming party, the day before Profumo first called on Christine (and the only time he did so in a ministerial Humber) Stephen Ward, recruited by MI5 only a month before as part of the Ivanov trap, reported to his case officer, a Mr Wagstaffe alias Woods, that Profumo and Ivanov had met. At this point Ward must certainly have had his suspicions about Profumo's interest in Keeler, but the affair had not yet begun. Ward was only reporting the arrival of Profumo as a spanner in the works.

Morality apart, what did it matter that a government defence minister had social contact with a spy? He was hardly likely to say – Beatles-style, 'listen, do you want to know a secret?' – nor, whatever the subsequent press speculation, was he likely to utter involuntary details of national security at point of orgasm, which his mistress might then pass to her other lover the spy. What then was at issue both in Norman Brook's warning and in Douglas-Home's exaggerated report?

I asked political journalist Andrew Roth: "It was still very largely a closed society in which there were received opinions about everything – the world was kept 'safe' by the Americans and Nato. Until the end of the fifties and the early sixties the Establishment had things very much its own way – it was a conformist society, very much like pre-war society. In the period we're talking about it was broken up, and the Profumo case had a very big impact because it showed that these people who were laying down the law for the rest of us were much worse than people had thought – they had no morality, no decency. Everybody had been told it was the worst thing in the world to have any contact with a Russian, and here he [Profumo] was sleeping with the same girl as a Russian and laying himself open to blackmail – all the things you're supposed to avoid if you're a sergeant in the armed forces. Here was the War Secretary doing the 'worst possible thing'. Of course there was a security risk as defined by the security people and the armed forces, of which he [Profumo] was a head. A lance-corporal, a private would not have been allowed to do this. It was about as bad as you could get. Anyone who'd been in the armed forces would recognise that."[4]

It's worth emphasising that in 1962-3 most adult males had been in the armed forces and would understand the context Roth is defining. Macmillan had abolished National Service only in 1960, and the last conscripts would not be demobbed until 1963. The security risk Profumo's private life engendered isn't objectively quantifiable, but even if it could be proved to be, as I suspect, virtually minute, Roth's point stands – Profumo was flouting the written and unwritten rules which every Tom, Dick or Harry lower down the chain of command would have been expected to follow. At the bottom of this slippery snake Sillitoe's Arthur Seaton was expected to get his hair cut like a private, at the top Jack Profumo had all the obligations that went with his 'rank'. It could all look unfortunately like double standards.

The August note was not the end of the affair, merely a cooling off. Keeler herself has said that Profumo sought a solution to the problem by offering to set her up in a place of her own later in the year. (With or without Profumo's help, she moved to Dolphin Square in the December of 1961, where she would, unwittingly, have been a neighbour of John Vassall.) However the evidence that Profumo did see Keeler right up to the December is his own, as it figures in the statement he made to the Commons the day after Wigg's speech.

Between the *Queen* 'story' and the shooting at Wimpole Mews, to which Wigg referred, the rumours about Keeler and Profumo circulated in Fleet Street. In November 1962 an anonymous informant called Wigg to tell him that he was wasting his time looking into the Vassall case and that he should look at Profumo instead. Wigg had no reason to heed such advice. He was on good terms with Profumo. Profumo and he had the common interest of the army, and although Profumo had had the difficult task of presiding over the change from a conscript army to a volunteer force, with all the problems of maintaining standards, until this point at least Wigg, as the Opposition's self-appointed barrack-room lawyer, had been more ally than opponent. No matter was closer to the heart of George Wigg than the lot of the fighting man. He'd joined the army as a teenager and risen through the ranks between the wars to end the Second World War as a colonel. Ten days later their friendship ended for ever when Profumo departed in the House from a line agreed between himself and Wigg over the supply of British troops landed in Kuwait. Wigg felt he'd been made to look a fool, worse he felt a fellow army man had betrayed him. The anonymous 'phone call, which Wigg had been inclined to regard as the work of a crank, suddenly became of great interest. He was out to get Profumo.

Whatever the source of the gossip about Profumo, Christine and Ivanov (and the most likely source was Ward himself) it was hardly a story the press was about to use while Macmillan's Radcliffe tribunal on the Vassall case was still looking at the role of the press. So, when a former boyfriend of Keeler's, West Indian Johnny Edgecombe, rolled up outside the Wimpole Mews flat on December 12th and fired bullets at the door and the window, it must have seemed to any journalist in the know to be a godsend. The story itself might have been worth some small coverage – a posh address, the violence and the involvement of young white women with a black immigrant must have appealed both to the fantasies and prejudices of the day – but as code for the Minister and the Model it was priceless. It allowed the press to hint at the very thing they dare not state.

Mandy Rice-Davies: "I cannot remember my terror and fear on that day. I can only remember certain aspects of it which I find funny still, which I found funny then and which we laughed about. It was obviously laughing from fear . . . The first thing I thought about, and the first thing that crossed Christine's mind I'm almost sure was 'There is a chap standing in the street with a gun, standing in the middle Wimpole Mews and Stephen is going to kill us!' . . .

131

Somehow it didn't seem real that that chap was going to fire the gun.
Now when he did fire the gun, it has, in retrospect, all the characteristics of a French farce, because, although we were terrified, now –
over the years – it's got mixed up exactly who did what . . . one of us
tried to hide under the bed, one of us stood behind the door with a
boot – he tried to shoot the door down downstairs – I remember
crawling, Indian fashion, into Stephen's bedroom to get the telephone and I did not first call the police, I called Stephen's office.
And I said, 'Stephen, there's a man outside and he's shooting!' He
said 'For God's sake call the police!'

"I'd washed my hair and my first reaction the minute Edgecombe
had disappeared was to get the bloody rollers out of my hair. So
while the police sirens were coming up, I'm battling with this head
full of rollers trying to get them all out, because I don't want
anybody to see me in curlers. The point I went cold was when the
Inspector said 'What's your name?' And I was going under the
name, I think it was Mandy Murray or something and he turned
round to me and he said, 'Otherwise known as Marilyn Rice-
Davies.' That was the giveaway. It was clearly written. I thought
how does he know my name is Marilyn Rice-Davies ?"[5]

Edgecombe was quickly arrested and charged not only with
'shooting with intent to kill' (does this differ in some vital respect
from plain attempted murder?) but also with wounding another of
Christine's West Indian lovers, Aloysius 'Lucky' Gordon, earlier on
– Gordon would himself be in the dock before long and play a vital
role in the undoing of both Ward and Christine. As Christine and
Mandy left the police station after making statements about the
shooting, a reporter from the *Sunday Pictorial* approached and
offered Christine £2000 for Profumo's letters to her, telling her he
"knew the lot". Mandy recorded their amazement in her autobiography: "We were both horrified, this seemed like very deep
water. Christine was even more concerned to know that the existence of the letters was common knowledge."[6]

§

To go further with this tale merely by incident is to miss the characters involved; in their juxtaposition is the 'meaning' of the Affair of
John Profumo. In the meeting of the principal characters is a meeting of worlds, and an exposition, however fudged and smothered, of
a world ill at ease with its own transitions. Stephen Ward was one of
those people who seem destined to act as a social fulcrum – through
Ward very different people from very different strands and classes

of society met. If that hackneyed and hammered word classless has any meaningful application, it is surely to Ward – a man to whom class did not matter, and whose undoubted charm made it easy for him to be socially flexible. That Ward was on friendly terms with nightclub showgirls, peers of the realm, cabinet ministers and Soviet agents was probably surprising twenty-five years ago and would be so again today, in a society that has once more dug in behind the sandbags. Ward himself attributed some of his openness to an American education – he had studied medicine and qualified as an osteopath at an American college in the mid-thirties. He was also, like Profumo, of the generation born near the outbreak of the First World War, that fought the Second. This changed British society more radically than had the First, and the class elisions and the combination of respectability and hedonism that seem to have been part of both their lifestyles again strikes me as a characteristic of men of that generation who never quite settled to the peace, men for whom the post-war years lacked the adventure and the openness of the war years. After the war (in which he rose to the rank of brigadier) Profumo resumed the political career that seemed to be his heritage – he was independently wealthy, a Baron of the Kingdom of the Two Sicilies, and on his election to parliament during the war had been the youngest MP in the House – while Ward began to build up his professional list. Within a few years of the war he was treating Churchill, Averell Harriman, Eden, Gaitskell, Bill Astor, Paul Getty, Joseph Kennedy and a good handful of maharajahs. Judging by this list, Ward must very quickly have risen to the top of his profession. He knew 'everybody' and treated most of them. The same hands that healed spines and necks also sketched faces – during the fifties and sixties many members of the Royal family, as well as political and show business figures, sat for him. His reputation as a portrait artist was high, and the mixture of his talents and tastes defined his world – he moved easily between the drawing rooms of Cliveden, his Devonshire Street practice, his cottage garden, the coffee bars of Marylebone and clubs of Soho – he was socially versatile and known for his charm. Parallel to this life was another, less open life in which charm was an inadequate catalyst – Ward's marriage had foundered after only a matter of weeks in 1949. His subsequent interest in women seems to have been less that of a lover or suitor than of a Pygmalion. He enjoyed the deception – the satire, perhaps – that Professor Higgins practised on London society with Eliza. Ward had 'made' the model Vickie Martin in the early fifties, transforming her from the working-class, homeless waif he met in a doorway in the pouring rain one night, to a top model pursued by the rich young men of the day. It was probably this potential in Christine Keeler that appealed to Ward when he met her in 1959. He did not seek to be and never was her lover. The stable relationships in Ward's life were with friends not lovers.

Christine came from the opposite end of society to Profumo. Her family home was a converted railway carriage in Wraysbury, lacking most facilities, like hot water or a flush lavatory. To her London was the opportunity to escape from a life that offered her nothing. She had little to trade on but her looks and at the time she met Ward was working as a showgirl at Murray's club in Soho's Beak Street. Ward moved her in with him, and over the next three years she came and went between bouts of independence, friends, lovers and Ward. During another spell at Murray's in 1961 she met and became friendly with Mandy, then earning her living as a dancer. Occasionally she too stayed at Ward's, and like Christine spent weekends at the cottage on the Astor estate. It was here that Ward the leveller was most apparent – the Astors and the Profumos met the Rice-Davieses and the Keelers. The combination has produced enduring myths – of orgies at Cliveden, and that Ward's constant association with women, some of whom were now thirty years younger than him, was for the purpose of satisfying the sexual needs of his friends. Ward's individual taste and curiosity certainly led him to break social barriers by having no qualms about who met who, and they also led him to pursue his own sex life with prostitutes – again I do not think this was unusual among his age group – but the myths are false all the same. He did not service the orgies of the aristocracy with a steady supply of 'gels'. Most weekends at Cliveden were spent pottering about the garden.

The Prime Minister himself cannot be discounted as a player in the melodrama – his opinions and decisions were part of the matter, part of the nexus of generations in the case of Stephen Ward. He was an old Etonian, a man of almost seventy whose picture of the world and its social divisions had been made before the First World War – he had been wounded at the Somme and had lain all day in a foxhole with a bullet in his pelvis reading Aeschylus in the original Greek, which says something about the man – and remade by the depression of the thirties. He was a man unlikely to come readily to terms with the upheavals of the sixties, nor, as a man who had endured a less than happy marriage, was he likely to wrestle willingly with the problems Profumo's affair presented to him. I doubt that the revelation of Profumo's adultery could ever have been less than shocking to Macmillan.

Lastly – Edgecombe and Gordon, the Rosencrantz and Guildenstern of the drama. The first major wave of Caribbean immigration was at its peak in the early sixties.[7] The social structure of London was changing, and London had adjusted badly. On the one hand West Indians were objects of suspicion – Ward is perhaps typical in his dislike of their use of marijuana and he discouraged Christine's friendships with West Indians – on the other they were seen as symbols of a post-war liberation, livening up coffee-bar culture with a new surge of music and energy, and it's in these ways that they figure in the fiction of the time, in the work of Colin MacInnes and Lynne Reid Banks. Profumo never met Gordon or Edgecombe, and Ward disliked both, yet it was part of the myth of dissolution that they had moved in the same world, that Profumo was somehow touched by the taint of the new underworld, represented by the West Indians, because he had shared a mistress with two of them. This, for the times, is as important as the presence of Ivanov in the same equation. The walls seemed in danger of tumbling down – later, the cartoonist Franklin would depict Christine at the walls of the Establishment like Joshua at Jericho.

§

What was good for the tabloids was not good for the practice of a Devonshire Street osteopath, and Ward suggested to Mandy that she move out of the flat until things had cooled. Mandy and Christine took a flat in Great Cumberland Place, and not long afterwards Ward himself left Wimpole Mews for good and took over a flat in Bryanston Mews, which had previously been Mandy's at the time when she and Peter Rachman (London's notorious slum landlord – although the notoriety was very much posthumous) had been lovers. This spell of musical flats may have been only a way of escaping the unwelcome attention of the press, but ironically it probably drove Christine into the hands that were waiting to sign the chequebook. For three years Ward had been a major figure in her life – for all his tightfistedness with cash, he had proved extremely reliable, putting a roof over her head in the bouts between lovers. It's as easy to lose track of the number of flats Christine had as it was for her (when asked in court) to lose track of the number of her lovers, but the pattern of her life since leaving home had shown one steady factor – the return to Ward and his 'open house' at frequent intervals. Now, without Ward, it must have been easy for her to feel both broke and lonely.

A month after the *Pictorial* made its offer, on January 22nd, 1963, Christine went to the paper and showed them the 'Darling' letter.

They offered £1000, half the previous offer. The immediacy of the matter had not entirely disappeared, but coverage of the case was trickier, now that Edgecombe had been charged and his case was sub judice. Christine tried the *News of the World*'s crime reporter, Peter Earle, who declined to get involved in an 'auction', so Christine went back to the *Pictorial* and accepted the thousand – £200 up front, the balance on publication, in return for the right to publish her story. Meanwhile Earle told the *News of the World*'s General Manager, Mark Chapman Walker – ex Tory Party Central Office – who, on February 1st, told the Prime Minister's Principal Private Secretary, Timothy Bligh. This, curiously, was only a day or two after the story had reached Macmillan's office by way of the FBI. Macmillan himself was told on his return from a visit to Italy on the 4th. However aloof from rumour Macmillan and his staff might have been over the past few months, they knew now. Afterwards he would say that this was the first he had heard of Stephen Ward, which skips lightly over the fact that Ward had sketched him some three years before, and makes me wonder about the looseness of what I had presumed to be a tight little world. It also says nothing for his memory. He had two connections with Cliveden himself – the second of Astor's wives was his god-daughter, and another of his secretaries also rented a cottage on the estate – he met Ward there too. In his Edwardian disdain for the 'new social world' in which "I recognised that the distinctions which had ruled in the past no longer obtained. Respectable and disreputable people now seemed to be all mixed up together."[8] Macmillan seemed loath to recognise that it touched him too, and that a bounder always was indistinguishable from a gentleman in dress and manner.

Ward, Astor and Profumo now tried various techniques to prevent Christine from publishing the letter. The most heavy-handed was Profumo's attempt to call in MI5 – who, now that Ivanov had returned to Moscow,[9] saw no role for themselves in the matter – the most obvious was the attempt to compensate Christine for the loss of her fee from the *Pictorial* – the most successful was the most simple, Ward's telephoning the paper, pointing out the risk of libel and offering them his own story in place of hers.

In the course of this Ward and Profumo met at the Dorchester. Profumo, according to George Wigg,[10] had already embarked on a course of denial even to those who knew – "Who is she?" he asked when Ward brought up Christine's name. "Ask MI5," Ward replied.

As well as to MI5 Profumo also told his version of the story to Sir John Hobson, the Attorney-General, and denied that there was any truth in the spreading rumour. Over the next week he saw Hobson three more times, met with Timothy Bligh – Macmillan's Principal Secretary – and with Martin Redmayne, the Government Chief Whip. These men with striped ties and three initials accepted what Profumo had to say, but I don't think it's simply a matter of believing Profumo, more a willing suspension of disbelief – a curious moral system whereby if someone you know insists on something you know to be unlikely, improbable or even untrue you ignore the prompting of intelligence. It helps no end if, like you, the party in question also has three initials and a striped tie.

§

Having bought Ward's story in lieu of Keeler's, and returned the original of 'Darling' to Profumo via Ward's solicitor, the *Pictorial* still kept a copy of the letter, and soon copies of the copy began to pass around Fleet Street. Tom Mangold, now frequently seen as a film-maker and reporter for *Panorama*, was an investigative reporter on the *Daily Express* at the time: "I got the letter from the *Sunday Pictorial*. Prima facie evidence of a relationship between Keeler and Profumo. I went to my News Editor. The next day he came back to me and said 'Beaverbrook says it's not for us.' Then the Deputy News Editor called me in and gave me a set of fake assignments, saying, 'But you'll cover Keeler and report directly to me.' I worked on the case surreptitiously for several months before it took off.

"The catalysts were *Private Eye* and *Westminster Confidential*. We needed them. The street would never have had the guts to go with it, but for them – God knows what pressure was put on their proprietors. Only when we could report other people's rumours could it take off."[11]

March 8th marked a turning point in the slow breaking of the story. Christine Keeler left for a 'holiday' in Spain on the very day the trial of Edgecombe opened (only to be postponed) and *Westminster Confidential*, a stencilled broadsheet of political gossip, available only on subscription, printed the rumour. Only two hundred or so people subscribed to the journal, but they were the *right* two hundred, and a copy ended up on Macmillan's desk.

"One of the choicest bits in the story was a letter, apparently signed 'Jack', on the stationery of the Secretary for W+r. The allegation by this girl was that not only was this minister, who has a famous actress for a wife, her client, but also the Soviet military attaché, apparently a Colonel Ivanov. The famous actress-wife, of course, would sue for divorce, the scandal ran. Who was using the call-girl to 'milk' whom of information – the W+r Secretary or the Soviet military attaché? – ran the minds of those primarily interested in security."[12]

I put it to the editor of *Westminster Confidential*, Andrew Roth, that, when all of Fleet Street chafed at the bits and thought of the writs, he was taking one hell of a risk.

"I knew there was some risk, but I didn't realise how large that risk was. I had no idea that anybody else had it [the letter] – as a newspaper man it wouldn't occur to me that the popular press could have something like this and suppress it!

"I'd been working on a piece about the floating of the pound – when that didn't happen my story collapsed. I needed something I could type directly onto a paper litho. The story of the Profumo case, which I'd heard, but hadn't had a chance to check out decently, was the only thing I had on hand that I could use. I went ahead rather incautiously – and in fact it was badly written by my standards.

"Essentially I pushed my finger through the dam wall. With this limited circulation newsletter I encouraged the big boys who'd been hesitant. The Government were angry with me – not because my influence amounted to a row of beans, but because I'd broken the dam. They began intercepting all my correspondence. Suddenly I didn't get any mail for three or four days."

A conventional prosecution was considered. Profumo consulted his solicitor and met, yet again, with Hobson, who advised that they should wait until a major paper dared run the story. The same considerations were weighed again only a week later when both the *Daily Express* and the *Liverpool Daily Post* pushed the 'code' to the point of transparency by juxtaposing the story of the 'missing' witness with an unsubstantiated rumour that Profumo had recently offered his resignation.[13] Rumour swelled to bursting point in Parliament and Fleet Street. As well as pirated copies of the 'Darling' letter, pirate copies of *Westminster Confidential* might even have outnumbered the authentic ones, as the enemy within – Macmillan's own right-wingers – pushed the story in the hope of forcing a legal action and ousting the leadership. Indeed Roth's source for the story had been right-wing Tory Henry Kerby, MP for Shoreham and Arundel.

"Henry was contemptuous of the old Establishment. He was never part of what he always called 'the kissing ring'. He despised people like Profumo – people who'd grown up together – same kindergarten, same prep school, same university – who looked down on everyone who hadn't. When he got this story, he passed it on to me. One day I happened to be sitting in the press gallery next to Harry Cousins, an English communist who worked for Tass – I asked him about Ivanov. He said he'd heard the same story. Getting it from two such disparate sources gave me a certain confidence in the story."

When, rather than if, the story broke it seemed very likely that Macmillan and Profumo would be caught in crossfire. As the popular press signed up Mandy's story and ran Ward's, *The Times*, not widely known for an anti-Establishment posture, ran an editorial under the heading 'It Is Happening Here' – this only a week or two after the Street had buzzed with rumours that a D notice had been requested to stop all mention of Ivanov.

The letters column of *The Times* had been filled with correspondence which defended 'liberty, but . . .' which would not extend the notion to Messrs Foster and Mulholland. The editor, Sir William Haley, a former Director-General of the BBC, had no time for muckrakers but felt that the threat posed to our civil liberties by the Vassall tribunal was very real and marked a worrying trend – "The executive has taken over power from Parliament," he warned, and went on to make a very timely statement: "Satire alone is not enough. Authority will, for a time, accept a few snooks as a cheap price to pay for the prohibitions it has been able to enforce in all countries without exception, upon sound broadcasting and television." Could this be Britain, land of the free? The letter writers, in the current high tide of homophobia, were concerned only with the Vassall case, but it seems impossible not to conclude that to Sir William, as to most journalists, the Vassall case had begun to merge into the Profumo affair.

In the *Sunday Pictorial*, Ward uttered the preface to the parliamentary rumpus: "Now it looks as though somebody – no doubt a loyal friend – has spirited her [Christine] away."[14]

§

March 21st: 11.05 p.m. George Wigg resumed his seat and the pursuit was taken up by Richard Crossman. As Crossman, old Wykehamist and Labour MP for Coventry East, crossed swords with Reginald Paget, old Etonian and Labour MP for Northampton, the elements of silliness and prurience that had been implicit came to the fore.

"What do these rumours amount to?" asked Paget. "They amount to the fact that a Minister is said to be acquainted with a

very pretty girl. I should have thought that was a matter for con-
gratulation rather than inquiry."

All that is missing from Paget's hearty, man's-world view of the
matter is the word 'popsie'.

Later Barbara Castle spoke, on the matter of the vanishing witness: "What if it is a question of the perversion of justice that is at
stake? . . . If accusations are made that there are people in high
places who do know and who are not informing the police, is it not a
matter of public interest?"[15]

Again Mr Paget intervened and denied having come across any
rumour relating to people in high places and the missing witness.
Mrs Castle replied that in that case he must be the only person in the
House or the press gallery who hadn't, and lobbed for game, set and
match with "I have no intention of revealing *my* sources."

At twenty to one Henry Brooke rose and offered no comment
other than to dare Wigg, Castle and Crossman to repeat their
questions outside the privilege of the House: "The Hon. Members
should seek other means of making these insinuations if they are
prepared to substantiate them." With that the matter closed and
Brooke went home to bed. Members of the government front bench
more finely attuned to the mood of the hour went into a panic.

§

What followed has often been referred to as a cabal. Five senior
Tories, Brigadier Martin Redmayne (Chief Whip), Ian Macleod
(Leader of the House), Sir Peter Rawlinson (Solicitor General), Sir
John Hobson (Attorney-General), and William Deedes (Minister
without Portfolio) met in Hobson's office. Between Wigg's opening
salvo and the necessity of Brooke answering, Hobson, Redmayne
and Rawlinson had gone into a huddle and drafted the one-liner
with which Brooke excused himself. Now they had to draft something of greater length, if not greater substance. Some time after 1
o'clock Redmayne had woken the Prime Minister and told him that
Profumo would have to make a personal statement. Macmillan
agreed and efforts were made to reach Profumo by telephone. He'd
taken a sleeping pill and didn't hear the phone ringing, so one of
Redmayne's assistants drove to the Regent's Park house and hammered on the door.

The personal statement is a parliamentary custom, which enables
members to offer apologies, corrections or, as in this case, denials
without interruption or cross-question. In the circumstances it was
an unusual measure to deal with the situation, and one that both

emphasised the 'truth' of what Profumo had to say, and, when he admitted it was untrue, the deceit. Once caught the sin was the greater for the device used.

Profumo brought along his solicitor Derek Clogg on the advice of Hobson. This was a move which Wilson would worry at like a dog with a bone in the June debate that followed Profumo's confession, and that would oblige Lord Denning to explain. If it was a personal statement why was Clogg's presence necessary? Denning wrote that Mr Clogg's presence was justified because Profumo had already embarked on litigation abroad (Dick Crossman had in his speech that night referred to the intention of *Paris Match* to tell the Profumo/Keeler story) and that the interests of a personal statement to the House had to be weighed against the demands of litigation. This doesn't go very far to explaining how a *personal* statement came to be drafted by a committee of Clogg, Hobson and Rawlinson, or why a *personal* statement should require the combined talents of three of the country's top legal brains. Rawlinson asked Profumo in a roundabout way if there was any truth in Mrs Castle's suggestion.[16] Profumo said there wasn't (and I think it's beyond doubt, by now, that the rumour to which Mrs Castle referred was groundless), and this would appear to be the extent of the investigation into the truth. It marks the turning point in the case. The sense of containment had up to now helped their acceptance of Profumo's denials, but it ought to have been obvious that containment was neither possible nor in the public interest. As Lord Lambton, backbench Tory critic, put it, "They were like five frightened mothers".[17] While the three wise lawyers worked in one room, Macleod, Deedes, Redmayne and Profumo cooled their heels in another. At about 4 o'clock Profumo was able to read through *his* statement. Within half an hour Profumo was on his way home to find the gentlemen of Fleet Street camped out on his doorstep.

The next morning the statement was offered to Macmillan who made a few minor changes of his own and deemed it "pretty clear and convincing". As far as he was concerned it was just a "silly scrape" – "Of course all these people move in a raffish, theatrical bohemian society, where no-one really knows anyone and everyone is 'darling'."[18] At 11 a.m. Profumo read his refutation to the House of Commons: "I understand that my name has been connected with the rumours about the disappearance of Miss Keeler. I would like to take this opportunity of making a personal statement about these matters. I last saw Miss Keeler in December 1961, and I have not seen her since. I have no idea where she is now. Any suggestion that I was in any way connected with or responsible for her absence from the trial at the Old Bailey is wholly and completely untrue. My wife and I first met Miss Keeler at a house party in July 1961 at Cliveden. Among a number of people there was Dr Stephen Ward, whom we already knew slightly, and a Mr Ivanov, who was an attaché at the Russian Embassy. The only other occasion that my wife or I met Mr Ivanov was at the official reception for Major Gagarin at the Soviet Embassy. My wife and I had a standing invitation to visit Dr Ward. Between July and December 1961 I met Miss Keeler on about half a dozen occasions when I called to see him and his friends. Miss Keeler and I were on friendly terms. There was no impropriety whatsoever in my acquaintanceship with Miss Keeler. Mr Speaker, I have made this personal statement because of what was said in the House last evening by the three hon. Members, and which, of course, was protected by privilege. I shall not hesitate to issue writs for libel and slander if scandalous allegations are made or repeated outside the House."[19]

It's hard to see why this required so many hands, but the fact that it did became contentious once Profumo had retracted it. By the time Lord Denning's report came to be debated in December, the wording and the authorship were being held up to scrutiny. Reginald Paget must have spoken for a wide body of Labour opinion when he said: "This statement was designed to deceive the House, it was drafted for this purpose by the Attorney-General." The statement seems to suggest that Profumo did not see Christine alone, and is so structured as to reinforce the sense of Mrs Profumo's presence at meetings she did not attend, while not actually saying that she did. The repeated emphasis on "my wife and I" carries forward from Cliveden to the home of Stephen Ward. It's a neat sleight of hand. It would be understandable if Profumo had written it himself, but he didn't and it laid the government open to accusations of collusion.

A friendly pat on the shoulder from the Prime Minister, who had sat next to Profumo throughout, completed the rout of the Opposition. For a while 'shut up or put up' would be effective. The questions members of the Opposition might have put would wait almost two months until the matter was the subject of a parliamentary debate, on June 17th – at which time a nagging point was raised that did not in any way depend on Profumo's confession – where in this meeting of the Famous Five was Henry Brooke, the man to whom the initial remarks had been addressed by Wigg? The government explained that Deedes had been asked to the meeting of the Five, as he had been present in the House throughout the debate. But, Wigg insisted, so had Brooke. Brooke is recorded as having left the House at 1.22 a.m. Denning offered the lame explanation that no one had thought to ask Brooke to attend the meeting – an understandable oversight, he was only the Home Secretary after all, and Mrs Castle's remarks concerned a mere matter of the perversion of justice. More likely is that the last thing anyone wanted was to have Henry Brooke around to interfere.

Andrew Roth: "Henry Brooke was a limited man from a different era. He was an honest, upright idiot – stiff, strict, blinkered, punctilious – the pre-war Conservative professional man. The Tories knew he was unbending and that he'd have no sympathy for a man like Profumo. If he'd been included in those evening discussions with Profumo to try and get to the bottom of it, he would have asked awkward questions – he would have gone to the police – he controlled the Metropolitan Police. They excluded Brooke, which makes it completely clear they wanted to build up a cockamamey story which would get Profumo and the government off the hook."

If this was the intention of the government, they failed. Five days later Brooke sent for Roger Hollis, head of MI5, and the Commissioner of the Metropolitan Police, without consulting Macmillan or Hobson. This action is typical of the whole case. As long ago as the end of January Christine had made a statement to the police, in what would seem to be a fit of resentment, alleging that Ward was a procurer and a pervert – this was not passed on to Brooke, or any member of the government. Norman Brook's meeting with Ward was not reported to Macmillan, nor was the information received by MI5 through Ward and Woods/Wagstaffe. In instigating this independent action, one half of the Tory Party was unwittingly working against the other half. Brooke had begun the meeting by asking about anonymous letters Mrs Profumo was said to have received – Hollis declined to be involved, saying it was a purely civil matter – but it ended with the decision to investigate the possibility of charging Stephen Ward with a crime – not that anyone knew what this should be at this stage. On April 1st Chief Inspector Sam Herbert began an investigation which eventually led to the framing of Stephen Ward. I do not think that the instruction to frame Ward came from Brooke (that would have been idiotic without being upright) but I do suspect that it all came down to 'who will rid me of this turbulent osteopath?'

Brooke blundered in. Ward already felt threatened. Once the pressure on him began to mount, his so far loyal, if dishonest, support for Profumo would be abandoned as he fought to clear his own name. The survival of Profumo's statement depended on Ward not changing his story. There was no more disruptive action Brooke could have taken than to begin the pursuit of Stephen Ward – an investigation which was conducted backwards in an effort not to detect a criminal but in the hope of discovering a crime.

There had been anonymous tip-offs about Ward, as well as Christine's statement – but none of these were what might be termed reliable sources, especially considering that half of Christine's statement (that which concerned Profumo) had just been refuted in parliament.

§

Profumo accepted a retraction from *Paris Match* and out of court damages from *Il Tempo*. The British press on March 23rd gave his denial front page coverage, but it wasn't all free from doubt. The *Daily Sketch* used the juxtaposition trick, recently tried by the *Express*, and ran the headline 'Lucky John Profumo' – which really referred to his 10-1 win at Sandown Park the previous afternoon, in the company of the Queen Mother, but made its point well enough. *The Times* supported the action of Wigg, Crossman and Castle as their airing of the matter had facilitated the denial of a rumour that might have gone on festering: "The best way to kill rumours is to confront them in the open." On which point they could not have been more wrong. The press were now free to report the rumour in reporting the denial. So long as they added a few crocodile tears they could relate most of the salacious detail they wanted. Ward had said in the *Sunday Pictorial* on the 17th that "It is incredible how such an innocent word as friendship can be misconstrued." In which statement he was prophetic. In the weeks that followed friendship would be a much abused word, as would innocent.

On the evening of the 23rd Ward appeared on ITV. "I know where Miss Keeler is, or roughly where she is," he said, and backed Profumo vigorously. That same night the first example of kudos by association, of which there'd be plenty later, was tried out on *That Was The Week That Was*. Randolph Churchill, sometime politician and flagging journalist, found himself bested in a debate on the freedom of the press by Bernard Levin. The next morning his column in the *News of the World* defended the privacy of the individual against the muckraking (in which his own paper indulged), attacked the editor of *The Times* for his defence of the freedom of the press and invited responses to his appearance on television. The public duly replied and Churchill quoted letters of support the following week, dismissing those who did not agree with him as 'loonies'. Meanwhile his paper continued its serialisation of Christine's story and one of its journalists took it upon himself to reinforce Ward's sense of privacy by burgling Spring Cottage.

On the 25th the *Daily Express*, aided by Mandy and a postcard from Madrid, found Christine in Spain.

Mandy: " . . . Here I am – I don't know this chap shooting at me on the street and next thing I'm the only witness in the court. Christine's disappeared and everybody's looking at me . . . I really was worried to death and I thought Christine had been bumped off. I really did . . . Now we had spoken about disappearing together of course before that, but then we had a small falling out in between and by the time the trial came up I was no longer friendly with Christine. So I wasn't ringing her up and speaking to her. But suddenly she disappeared. Now I know . . . she never liked going abroad, I'd had to twist her arm to come with me to France . . . so I thought it was unlikely that she had 'disappeared'. At the trial when she . . . couldn't be found anywhere I really had this terrible feeling that she might have been disposed of in some way. But then Christine's mother had a postcard, and it was only when I went down and spoke to her mother and she was absolutely adamant that Christine was all right.

"The *Express* came to me and said 'Would you like to go to Spain, we think she's in Spain, do you want to go and look for Christine?' Daft I'm not. I said 'I'll go to Spain.' So did I go to Madrid or did I go to Barcelona? No I went to Majorca and sat on the beach on expenses from the *Express*. The press found her . . . in Madrid."

Christine returned home saying that she had been frightened and that no one had given her a definite date to appear in court. No more plausible explanation of her disappearance has been offered. The *Express* reaped its reward. Christine's story of her jaunt around Spain ran in the paper the following day.

§

In the first week of June Profumo cut short a holiday in Venice, returned to England, owned up, and resigned. The story was released to the press at five o'clock on June 5th. There has been much speculation as to why Profumo did this when he did. In the six or seven weeks following his statement to the House, circumstances had changed rapidly. Christine had begun to tape record her memoirs and in so doing had at last set down the truth about herself and Profumo – news of this had reached the police. Ward had begun a frantic search for allies as old friends and MI5 deserted him – the

145

police had interviewed almost a hundred and forty people (Christine no less than thirty-eight times), his practice had been ruined by the presence of the police outside his consulting room, and Astor had asked for the keys to the cottage – he saw Wigg, wrote to his MP, to Wilson and Brooke, and saw Bligh, all in an effort to establish his innocence of any crime and to stop the police from hounding him. As a result of all Ward told Wigg and Wilson, Macmillan had reluctantly asked the Lord Chancellor, Lord Dilhorne, to look into the matter – at some point soon Dilhorne would want to interview Profumo. Speculation has varied from a confessional impulse to tell all to his wife – yet she was the one person who could not have been deceived by the wording of the statement in parliament – to a fear of facing Dilhorne – yet he had faced so many other top Tories – to simple exhaustion from the pretence. The most logical explanation is a combination of the latter and Profumo's increasing awareness that Ward cornered was Ward dangerous. The truth was no longer containable if it formed Ward's only defence. Brooke's response to Ward's letter had been to say that he could not interfere with a police investigation – but it had started with Brooke, and Profumo had plenty of cause to regret the streak of honest idiocy that has traditionally been part of the Conservative character.

The papers exploded with cries of national disgrace, collapse of public morality, failure of government, and about it all hung an air of the unspoken and unwarranted 'I Told You So'. Several ran potted histories of scandals in high places from Kitty O'Shea onwards, most recapped with mini-biographies of all the major characters in the current scandal. Stories began to change hands and papers at the speed of light – Christine, as Tom Mangold expressed it, being "bought and sold like cocoa futures", eventually accepted £23,000 from the *News of the World*. Less than three months after they had given front page coverage to her denials, and sizeable coverage to Randolph Churchill's attack on journalistic muckraking, they printed her admissions of her affairs – Ivanov was "this wonderful, huggy bear of a man" to whom she had "yielded" – beneath a photograph of her sitting naked astride a plywood chair. The *Sunday Pictorial* (recently renamed the *Sunday Mirror*) had little to go with other than its copy of Profumo's letter, which it printed alongside a few feeble excuses for not doing so sooner – to wit, they had not regarded the letter as "evidence of any substantive nature" and had been wary of ruining the career of a Minister – with not a word about the problem of libel.

Yet again rumour packed its bags and took to the streets. A score card of the stories in circulation might prove difficult, but . . . most of them concerned cabinet ministers and if even half had been true Macmillan had assembled the biggest team of, I believe the term is, 'goers' ever to gather in one room . . . a masked man serving dinner naked to his guests was rumoured to be a cabinet minister, as was the man seen receiving fellatio in Richmond Park, another was rumoured to be guilty of gross indecency with little boys, yet another had been involved with Christine, the *Mirror* ran a 'Prince Philip and the Profumo Scandal' headline simply for the sake of being able to refute it "utterly" in smaller typeface, the naked man in a photograph produced in the concurrent scandal of the Duchess of Argyll's divorce case was rumoured to be Duncan Sandys, and at the peak of inventive fantasy the High Court also got its share of the action as the nation turned into a latter day Sodom.

"He [Macmillan] was in a terrible state going on about a rumour of there having been eight High Court judges involved in some orgy. 'One,' he said, 'perhaps two conceivably. But eight – I just can't believe it.'"[20]

It was a time for retribution. "The pent-up lake of disappointment sought an outlet; deprived of scandal once by the fact that there was no scandal, it seethed and bubbled and waited. When the dam went the second time, with the announcement of Mr Profumo's resignation, the flood waters poured, unchecked, into the valleys of public life, sweeping everything before them in a great release of joy in the depravity of others. Mr Profumo had been to bed, not once but several times, with a girl who, whatever else she was, was undeniably attractive, at any rate to judge from the newspaper photographs; sexual envy, if nothing else, demanded that he and the whole world he moved in be accused of corruption."[21]

And for sermonising. "Clichés came out from under stones," as Wayland Young put it in his excellent book on the Profumo affair, "fathers, return to the values of our; stables, cleanse the national; Denmark, something rotten in the state of."[22]

The Times once more rose to the occasion with a memorable leader headed – 'It Is A Moral Issue'. It bore little resemblance to Haley's defence of press freedom, but it continued the attack on Macmillan's government. Eleven years of Tory rule had " . . . brought the nation psychologically and spiritually to a low ebb . . . nothing else, they seemed to think, mattered, compared with the assertion that the nation had never had it so good. Today they are faced with a flagging economy, an uncertain future and the end of the illusion that Britain's so-called greatness could be measured by the so-called independence of its so-called deterrent. All this may seem a far cry from Mr Profumo . . . " – the but cannot be far away

– "but his assertions could be the last straw." It hardly seemed necessary, still the message was spelt out – "affluence is about played out".[23]

In its fundamental belief that well-being must surely corrupt anyone not born to it, and even a few of those that are, *The Times* stood at the threshold of Swinging Britain like Canute before the North Sea. It spoke for the middle-class far-from-silent majority who would, any minute now, be outnumbered and shouted down.

The most pertinent statement of all was probably that made by satirist Willie Rushton in his Lookee 'Ere column in the *Sunday Mirror*, when he predicted that "Profumo will be drowned in printer's ink."

§

Ward appeared on the ITV programme *This Week*, on June 6th, and revealed a misplaced optimism. Asked by Desmond Wilcox if he had been running a call-girl racket he replied: "No, indeed, I wasn't. This my friends know and I think the police know now." It's doubtful whether Ward had all that many friends left after the police inquiries, and far from knowing the truth the police arrested him in the street less than forty-eight hours later. He appeared before Marylebone magistrates and was charged with three counts of living on immoral earnings – those of Christine, Mandy and the hitherto unknown Ronna Ricardo – two counts of procuring – a charge so arcane, the nature of it would baffle the legal journalists as well as the jury – two counts of helping to procure abortions, and one of conspiracy to keep a brothel. He was remanded for trial and spent the best part of a month in jail.

For a while Christine was the most famous woman in the country, at a time when instant fame could offer instant reward, and instant reward still carried instant condemnation – Nick Luard and Dominic Elwes put the film *The Christine Keeler Story* into production, in which Christine would play herself, though in the end never did as Equity objected – offers to appear in cabaret were reported to be in the region of £5000 per week, which prompted much criticism along the lines of 'it's a scandal when a disreputable woman can earn more than a Prime Minister', and the witness box at the Old Bailey provided good press copy and a foretaste of the trial of Ward. On April 17th Christine had been punched by the brother of one of her girl friends. At this time Chief Inspector Herbert was making his case against Ward, and when Christine reported the assault to him he saw an opportunity to coerce a reluctant witness – Christine's old boy friend Aloysius 'Lucky' Gordon. Christine was persuaded to accuse Gordon of the attack, and he was charged. When his trial opened at the Old Bailey, the timing could not have been better – June 6th. Nor could the performances have been better staged. Christine, dressed in a simple mauve outfit, arrived at the Old Bailey in a hired Rolls-Royce, and Gordon gave the press everything they might have dreamed of by dismissing his lawyer, asking to call Profumo as a witness and saying that Christine had worked as Ward's call girl for years. He was not the only one to be seized by histrionics in the heat of the moment.

A week later Lord Hailsham also made a television appearance, on the BBC programme *Gallery*. The BBC had initially approached Macleod, who had passed them to Hailsham – Macleod being the Leader of the House, there's some case to be made for saying that Hailsham was the party choice for the interview with Robert Mackenzie, and hence 'official'. The BBC had also asked Patrick Gordon Walker to speak for Labour, but he had declined, so the piece became a two-hander between Hailsham and Mackenzie. It's hard to know how close to the heart of things Lord Hailsham felt himself to be – he had denied being the man in the mask, just as he had denied being the naked man in the Argyll divorce case,[24] although it does not seem to have been suggested that he was either (again, kudos by association?) – and his anger, revealed so sharply in the course of the programme, requires some understanding. Mackenzie remarked that the Profumo affair was a strange reflection on the state of the Conservative Party and the leadership. In a matter of seconds Hailsham called Profumo a liar no less than nine times – "lied and lied and lied – lied to his colleagues, lied to his family, lied to his friends, lied to his solicitor, lied to the House of Commons." If the government tactic in handling the mess was to emphasise the moral issue at the expense of the security issue, then Lord Hailsham had his own, unique way of doing this.

"It is silly to talk of not being interested in Mr Profumo's morals. Mr Profumo's morals are a great public issue . . . Of course there's a security problem. Don't be so silly! A Secretary of State for War can't have a woman shared with a spy . . . The question is not whether there was a security risk, but whether there was an actual breach of security. Be sensible!"

His views thus far, the obvious rattiness and lack of charity apart, might be the truest reflection of what most impartial people really thought – however what most incensed him was not the impartial but the partial. The Conservative Party was not to be brought down by "a woman of easy virtue and a proven liar".

"It is silly to make a party issue of this," he told Mackenzie.

But wasn't it already a party issue? Hadn't the Conservative Party issued a three-line whip for the debate on the 17th? Here Lord Hailsham parted company with the courtship of popular opinion. The three-line whip was not a summons to vote, but merely to attend – while this might be constitutionally accurate, it was a remark few could credit as logical or truthful in defining the practice. In the institution of the office of the whip is the clearest symbol of the transition from parliamentary democracy to parliamentary oligarchy. It was a fudge of the first magnitude and one for which he would not be let off lightly.

In the debate that followed Wigg and Paget made easy meat of his necessarily absent Lordship.

On his lack of Christian charity, Paget: " . . . a virtuoso performance in the art of kicking a fallen friend in the guts . . . it is easy to compound the sins we are inclined to by damning those we have no mind to. When self-indulgence has reduced a man to the shape of Lord Hailsham, sexual continence involves no more than a sense of the ridiculous."

On the three-line whip, Wigg: "The three-line whip is the final appeal to party loyalty, and Lord Hailsham knows it. Whether I am in order or not, I call Lord Hailsham a lying humbug."[25]

Humbug? Without a doubt. Humbuggery – be it vice or virtue – is something for which Lord Hailsham has shown a predilection, and to which corpulence is no obstacle. Lying? Performing would be more generous. The programme's producer – Grace Wyndham Goldie – noted in her record of the programme that Hailsham was remarkably affable and friendly once he was off the air. Was this only the good manners on which his class prides itself, at least when dealing with those it recognises as equals, or was his 'uncontrolled fury' more like a simple ploy? What Hailsham almost succeeded in doing was in shifting the moral prerogative, the moral outrage from Mackenzie, as the spokesman for the public, onto himself, spokesman for the Tories – for whatever this might be worth in terms of evading the issue. But . . . he blew it.

Bernard Levin has described Hailsham as a "brilliant, passionate and in many ways likeable man" . . . but just beneath the brilliance and the passion is a streak of unrefined adolescence that can make him reduce serious interview to asinine bonhomie, permit him to indulge himself reading his poems on teenage television programmes or to say 'bollocks' to the bishops from his seat on the woolsack. This is important not simply because of a single television interview, but because, as Macmillan's esteem fell within his own party – even before the scandal in question – Hailsham was often mentioned as a Prime Minister in waiting.

After this outburst *Private Eye* ran a spoof headline asking "Is Hailsham Mad? . . . We are forced to conclude that he is not. He is simply a conceited, boring, anachronistic, deluded and arrogant old gentleman." Before the year was out all that passion, brilliance, conceit and arrogance would take to the boards again as Hailsham played heir apparent to his party. In a world made up of player kings and princes would the princess kiss this frog?

§

It hardly needs to be emphasised that the Tory leadership was now in crisis. Rumours of a palace coup were rife. One newspaper printed a photograph of the man most often named as chief conspirator – Enoch Powell, whose rivers were as yet unblooded – labelled the conscience of the Conservative Party. But Mr Powell's recollections are not of any conspiracy.

Enoch Powell: "I was at first incredulous that he [Macmillan] had been unaware of what he was doing when he decided to ignore the allegations against his Secretary of State for War. However, by the time I spoke on the subject in public for the first time, which I think was on Saturday [June 15th], I was convinced that, improbable or not, he in fact had not been aware of, or had not actually credited, the allegations. That being so, his fault was an intellectual fault and not a moral failure. He hadn't been failing in any duty apart from the general duty to apply one's mind correctly and efficiently to the data presented to it. I did not regard therefore, by the end of the week which ended on June 15th, Macmillan's government as a place where no respectable man would stay. I did stay. And as near as possible to the debate on the following Monday I took the opportunity publicly of stating my conclusion. It was at a sort of garden party in Norfolk."[26]

On June 10th a hastily summoned cabinet was dragged in from its travels – Macleod from the USA, Home from Scotland, Brooke from the Channel Islands. Whatever the rumours to the contrary, whatever the backbench rumblings, the cabinet appears to have supported Macmillan, and more meetings and soundings followed as the June 17th debate approached. On the 13th a delegation from the National Union of Conservative Associations came calling from sad shires and was received at No. 10. They too seemed disposed to side with the Prime Minister rather than with the editor of *The*

Times – and on the morning of the debate the chairman of the 1922 Committee met with his restless flock and was able to report back that only a few rebels would fail to answer the whip.

In the afternoon the House was packed. Members overflowed into aisles and galleries.

At half-past three Wilson opened for the prosecution by hamming up the decency angle and playing on Labour's refusal to cash in on rumour.

"We are not here as a court of morals." This despite the fact that "many of us have witnessed the ceaseless interweaving of innuendo and rumour."

It would not be Labour's tactic to go for the jugular – Wilson would concentrate on the issue of security.

"When we say that there was a security risk we mean that through a personal defect of character . . . " – this was the official language of the government's white paper on security – " . . . or a perverted political loyalty, or through the possibility of intolerable pressure, or through cupidity or financial need, or through a personal or family relationship, an individual is more liable than his fellows to disclose information. That is what we mean by a security risk."

Wilson asked at what point the security services 'knew' and didn't wait for an answer.

"I believe the first the security services knew or even guessed about this very big security risk was when a Sunday newspaper told them a few months later. If this is true – the Prime Minister must be frank about this – this would imply that the £60 million spent on these services under the Right Honourable gentleman's premiership have been less productive than the security services of the *News of the World*.

"So, though I personally acquit the Right Honourable gentleman of foreknowledge or complicity in this matter – of course I do; of course, we all do; I mean complicity in the misleading of the House – he cannot be acquitted of a grave dereliction of duty in failing to find out."

Having made his point – that Macmillan didn't know soon enough and now would probably never know the extent of the security risk or the nature of any leak, Wilson turned his attention to the country at large. His oratory slumped into pomposity, the rallying, spine-stiffening vocabulary of a *Times* leader writer manqué.

" . . . A canker at the heart of our society . . . a diseased excrescence . . . a corrupted and poisoned appendix of a small and unrepresentative section of society that makes no contribution to what Britain is, still less what Britain can be . . . There are, of course lessons" – read sermons – " . . . the replacement of material-ism and the worship of the golden calf by values which exalt the spirit of service and the spirit of national dedication."

It would not be the last Old Testament reference that day.

Macmillan's defence was plaintive, simple and inadequate. No-body told him. He presented himself as the unworldly victim of actions and standards no one could reasonably expect a man of his generation to understand.

"I know that I have acted honourably. I believe that I have acted justly." The important issue was surely whether he had acted wisely?

He repeated the litany of Profumo's denials and admitted that his error in prematurely accepting the resignation of Thomas Galbraith "was certainly in my mind". This had predisposed him to believe Profumo, but then so had his own professed, if uncharacteristic, unworldliness:

"The letter began with the word Darling. This was volunteered by Mr Profumo who explained that in circles in which he and his wife moved it was a term of no great significance [Laughter]. I believe that might be accepted – I do not live among young people much myself."

Macmillan was playing for sympathy, but in so doing was expos-ing himself to the charge that would be made many times over the following weeks – that he was out of touch or too old for the job, and certainly too old for the nation. Profumo was forty-eight. If this was a generation of mystery to him how on earth could he possibly relate to people in their twenties?

The striped tie had also predisposed the Prime Minister to believe Profumo: "I would ask the House to consider what alternative I had except to believe what I was told by Mr Profumo. Here was a man who had been for a long time a member of the House; who had a good war record; who had been appointed originally to a junior post in 1951 and had worked his way up the ladder. Why, then, should I disbelieve what he told me?

"My colleagues have been deceived, and I have been deceived, grossly deceived – and the House has been deceived – but we have not been parties to deception . . . I am entitled to the sympathetic understanding and confidence of the House and the country."

The Prime Minister, as Norman Shrapnel put it, "quavered like some restoration cuckold".[27] The sense of his personal shock and bewilderment at goings on in low places had been strongly com-municated. The security issue had been glossed over.

The first of his backbench critics to speak was former minister

Nigel Birch, who had resigned over the 1957 budget and had been a thorn in Macmillan's side ever since. He too saw little mileage in the security issue, but felt that Macmillan's competence was an issue, as was morality. In tackling this he finally stated what should have been obvious all along:

"Is it really credible that the association had no sexual content? There seems to me to be a certain basic improbability about the proposition that their relationship was purely platonic. What are whores about?" He called upon Macmillan to resign with a quick flourish of Browning: " . . . let him never come back to us!/There would be doubt, hesitation and pain./Forced praise on our part – the glimmer of twilight,/Never glad confident morning again!"

Neither Ward nor Christine came out well in the privileged representations of their characters and deeds. The generosity the Hon. Members extended to each other did not reach beyond the walls of Westminster. If Ward was wondering what the courts held in store for him, Hansard for June 17th might have given him a few pointers. To Wilson, George Wigg's account of the story Ward had told him was "a nauseating document". Wigg was only the most prominent among a group of speakers who seemed to attach blame more to Ward for his support of Profumo than they did to Profumo himself. To Birch Christine was a "professional prostitute", to Charles Loughlin "a dirty little prostitute", to Wilson, with his biblical sensibility, "a harlot". It was left to Ben Parkin, working-class MP for Paddington, to sound a more humane note, even if that too contained a few words of abuse: "Is no one in the House today going to say a word of compassion for the poor little slut who is at the centre of all this?" . . . and to the so-far-reticent George Brown to offer a timely reminder with "Vengeance Is Mine Saith The Lord", although I suspect he was prompted by Tolstoy's epigraph to that other tale of adultery and vengeance, *Anna Karenina*, as much as by the Old Testament itself.

In 1963 the television cameras were not allowed within the precincts of the Palace of Westminster. *Panorama* covered the debate and met the public demand as best it could. Robin Day and his camera crew stood in Parliament Square in the pouring rain, trying for a blow by blow account as MPs and journalists dashed back and forth. Wigg, Gerald Nabarro, Woodrow Wyatt, Jeremy Thorpe and William Rodgers all came to huddle under a BBC umbrella and drip into the microphones.

§

The majority for the government was sixty-nine – as Wayland Young would have it, more appropriately, soixante-neuf – less than was needed to constitute a vote of total confidence. Twenty-seven Tories abstained, Lambton and Birch among them. Macmillan congratulated himself on his modest success – his diary offers no insight as to why Labour had behaved with such restraint. Crossman's does. From the first surfacing of the story Labour had pussyfooted. At a dinner party given by Barbara Castle on March 10th, Wigg had aired the Profumo story, only to be told to shut up by most of his peers. The Galbraith fiasco was still an embarrassment to Labour – the front bench recalled too well how Brown's attack on the government had fizzled out. When the story was eventually raised in the Commons on March 21st it was not the result of any concerted action. Barbara Castle had decided, unilaterally, to mention the Profumo affair; Wigg and Crossman had nipped in smartly in an effort to ensure the story was broken "in a reasonable way".[28] Still, Wigg was annoyed to lose control of the matter and at the emphasis Mrs Castle had been able to put on it. Between that revelation and Profumo's confession, both Wigg and Crossman had shied away from public involvement – it seems hypocrisy for Crossman to have attacked the *Sunday Pictorial*'s decision not to print the 'Darling' letter as "dereliction of journalistic duty"[29] when his own account shows how unwilling he was to take up Henry Brooke's challenge.

Between Profumo's confession and the debate a policy decision was taken. Labour wanted to avoid Macmillan being replaced by a younger man, like Maudling, who, with a year or more to go, might lead the Tories refreshed into the next election. They much preferred to see Macmillan stay on and decline. Yet at the same time they could not unduly reinforce his position by delivering a sympathy vote. So, the policy became one of no attacks below the belt, by no references to anything below Profumo's belt. His morals were to be seen to be his own affair. Once again parliament applied its privilege standards. While Jack Profumo was not to be publicly castigated for his lifestyle by the Opposition, George Wigg was helpfully co-operating with the investigation by Chief Inspector Herbert into the lifestyle of Stephen Ward. Wilson effectively gagged comment from his own side. His own remark to reporters in Ottawa summed up the hoped-for effect of this policy: "No comment – in glorious Technicolor." That he got George Brown to abide by this seems little short of a miracle. On June 6th he dissuaded Patrick Gordon Walker, Manny Shinwell and Crossman from appearing on the same *This Week* as Ward – so it's hardly surprising that *Gallery* could not find a Labour speaker for the following week. In the Commons, *Hansard* records the occasional 'Laughter' and odd 'Oh', but Labour did not harass or barrack any of the Tory speakers on an occasion when you might expect the traditional 'Uproar'. I wonder if such tactics might be considered 'dereliction of an Opposition's duty', which, as Crossman himself put it several years earlier, is to oppose. By shifting the emphasis of the Profumo affair from the man himself to the shadowy world in which he moved, Labour surely contributed to the atmosphere of moral retribution that now wrapped itself around the figure of Stephen Ward? Instead of being responsible for his own actions, the lie to the House apart, Profumo had had the misfortune to fall in with a bad lot. It could be argued that that shadowy world was allowed to remain shadowy, critically unexplored, by the timing of the arrest of Stephen Ward. Sub judice rules permitted suggestive references to the demi-monde in which Ward lived, but prevented any serious discussion. It allowed nebulous allegation without the necessity of evidence or answer.

After confession and debate, Dilhorne's report seemed less than adequate – it had taken him a mere fortnight – and Macmillan was determined that the flood of rumour should be stopped by an official move. He asked for a new report from the Master of the Rolls, Lord Denning.

Enoch Powell: "The social phenomenon which I recall from the months of May to July 1963, is the manner in which it was a remarkable demonstration of a phenomenon illustrated by Titus Oates or the South Sea Bubble, the way in which actual events promote a collective state of mind which almost becomes a thing on its own, an autonomous thing. I was very struck by the autonomous nature of the public excitement. I suppose you can't dissociate self-perpetuation from autonomy in the sense in which I'm using that word – but it becomes something which is apprehensible, and observable apart from particular events. The resignation of John Profumo was a particular event and it was dissociable to an observer at the time from the general sense of credulity, alarm, excitement. But it was with this autonomous thing that the Prime Minister was hoping to cope by appointing Lord Denning. Denning's appointment was designed to puncture the balloon, the self-inflated balloon."

As well as his brief to consider the operation of the Security Service, Denning was also told to look into rumours affecting "honour and integrity in public life". Macmillan sent a memo to his ministers inviting suitable rumours. Labour opposed this, and a long letter was drafted by Wigg and the prominent London lawyer Arnold (later Lord) Goodman for Wilson to send to the Prime Minister. Again Labour professed to be concerned only with the security issue, worries were expressed about 'McCarthyism' – Macmillan's preferred bogeyman was usually Titus Oates – and the letter ended with: " . . . may I say how strongly I deplore the statement by ministers that the whole country is alive with gossip and slander."[30] Well, it was wasn't it? The letter is a masterpiece of buckpassing. Wigg's memoir notes the "essential facts", after his meeting with Ward, including "Profumo was not at any time a security risk". Yet Labour continued, largely under Wigg's advice, to press the security issue, while in the case of Vassall and Galbraith it had little compunction in playing on the gossip. Once again, the public and the private issues were being manipulated – the security issue, if both sides knew it was a non-starter, could only sooner or later give way to the moral issue, which Labour could not be seen to raise directly, but which, since they were too 'decent' to tackle a cabinet minister on his conduct, would require some other scapegoat. It would be interesting to know what Wigg put in his 'nauseating' report to Wilson, after his meeting with Ward, and what account of Ward Wigg gave Chief Inspector Herbert. The only time you can clearly see the full span of Establishment ranks is when they close.

Tony Benn's diary for July 3rd records his feelings about the investigation Wigg had set in motion: "This is quite mad. I am terrified that George Wigg will be made Minister for Security and given power over all our lives."[31] Wigg became Wilson's Paymaster General, known to his own party as Spymaster General, or as one reporter more succinctly put it 'the sneak of the remove'.

§

On June 28th the preliminary hearing of the case of Stephen Ward was held at Marylebone Magistrates Court. Ward chose to go for trial by jury. Logically – but the law is far from logical – this should be all there is to it, but the magistrate was obliged to hear the evidence against Ward in order to determine if there was a case against him that would warrant trial. He does not customarily hear the case for the defence, nor, at that time, would there have been restrictions on press reporting. Hence the first the public would hear of such a matter would be the unanswered case of the prosecution. From somewhere twelve impartial ratepayers would have to be found to form the jury. The proceedings in court and out had such strong elements of showbiz that twelve illiterate Esquimaux would have been needed to guarantee Ward a fair trial. The court and the pavements were packed with people. Public reaction to the affair was strong. Mandy recalls that people in the crowd shouted hellos to her, as they might to a star of *Compact* or *Coronation Street* – when Christine arrived someone lobbed eggs at her, and as they both left women booed and hissed and beat the top of the car with rolled umbrellas. Inside the court Mandy uttered a line that is now in the *Oxford Book of Quotations*; when told that Astor denied having slept with her she replied, "Well, he would wouldn't he?" The limelight that had favoured Christine for the last few months proved itself fickle and found another favourite. Ward was freed on bail – the excessive sum of £3000 – and the trial was set for the Old Bailey on July 22nd.

The Old Bailey was a disproportionately grand venue for such charges, but was justified on the grounds that public attention could overwhelm a lesser court. In fact the crowds were large enough to block the street, the queue for the public gallery topped the hundred mark, and any photograph of Christine, Mandy or Ward taken during the comings and goings from the court shows another twenty odd lenses reflecting back at the photographer. As with the debate of the previous month the only means that would have satisfied public interest would have been live television coverage of the proceedings.

New dramatis personae now took the stage. Ward had retained the services of James Burge as his defence; even though the shrewd move might have been to switch to a QC at this point, Ward felt that Burge had conducted a good case at Marylebone and remained loyal to his barrister. The prosecution brief had gone to Mr Mervyn Griffith-Jones QC, famous for the prosecution at the 'trial of Lady Chatterley' – the prosecution brought against Penguin Books under the new Obscene Publications Act two years before – in the course of which he had revealed himself to be a man singularly ill at ease with the mores and vocabulary of the twentieth century. Presiding was Judge Sir Archie Marshall, a man in his mid-sixties with a lifetime of criminal law experience behind him.

The abortion charges having been set aside for the time being, Ward faced only the first five counts – three of immoral earnings, relating to prostitution by Mandy, Christine and Ronna Ricardo, to which list was added a new name, Vickie Barrett – and two of procurement, that is of using and being a third party in the persuasion of a woman under the age of twenty-one to have sex. I said this was an arcane charge. Ludovic Kennedy, in the press gallery throughout the trial, sums up the contemporary response to it: "I must here confess that in my *naïveté* I did not know (and other journalists I met did not know) that if a man asks a friend to introduce him to a girl over the age of consent but under twenty-one, and he subsequently has a romp with her, that constitutes a criminal offence."[32]

As Mandy put it – if this was illegal you might as well arrest all the bachelors in London.

Rereading Kennedy's account, rather than proving that Ward was living off the immoral earnings of Mandy and Christine, the trial of Stephen Ward proved the opposite – that they had taken more money off him than he'd ever got back. Nor did the rest of the prosecution evidence stand up to scrutiny. Ronna Ricardo withdrew the testimony she had given at the Magistrates Court, backed this action with an affidavit, and now denied that Ward had ever introduced her to men and taken money from her for it – and Vickie Barrett's evidence that she had whipped total strangers at a pound a stroke in Ward's flat was exposed as a badly constructed invention.

What all four had in common, as I think Burge proved, was that the police had subjected them to intense pressure to testify against Ward. Christine's twenty-four interviews with Herbert – to say nothing of the dozen or more meetings over the cases of Edgecombe and Gordon – would, to someone of a different class or intellect, have called for a letter to an MP about police harassment – it's hard to imagine anyone with a grasp of the law putting up with it, but over Christine the police held the threat that they might also charge her with aiding Ward in the procurement of women. Chief Inspector Herbert also, I presume, held the unspoken threat that she could be exposed as a liar in the case of Lucky Gordon. Vickie Barrett, a professional prostitute, was told that the police would take away her livelihood – quite simply they would bust her every chance they got. The pressure brought upon Ronna Ricardo was, perhaps, the most sinister of all, they threatened to take away her daughter and to have her younger sister committed to a remand home. But the pressure put upon Mandy Rice-Davies was the most concerted and the toughest. Twice Mandy was arrested at Heathrow – on April 23rd and June 16th – on a variety of charges.

Mandy: "They needed my evidence . . . obviously they'd re-searched my character a little and decided simply visiting me and knocking on my door saying 'Please Miss Davies may we have a few words with you?' wasn't going to work. So . . . they arrested me on these charges, which were after all quite valid – I was driving with a forged driving licence, it's perfectly true, and I was driving without insurance. The [stolen] TV was totally trumped up and they knew it anyway, that's why it was dropped. [But] they'd been gathering information for months before that."

The previous year the police had interviewed her about her lover Peter Rachman.

"They asked me an awful lot of questions about Peter. He'd been dead about two months, less actually, and they asked me questions about Peter which amazed me. How did they know that I knew Peter Rachman? . . . There were all these . . . small mysteries all building up somewhere. Obviously I was not very cooperative . . . I think that when I was leaving for Spain they had two reasons for stopping me . . . because in Spain there was no extradition even though they told me there was – which was a lie – and . . . to slap me in the cooler for a few days so I would have time to think about it.

"And I was put in there for something like eight days because the court was in recess – normally I would have been taken the next morning to the court – so I stayed in there, I was left in there, I didn't hear a word from [Chief Inspector] Herbert . . . until about four days later when I had a visit from him – 'You don't like it in here very much do you? You help us and we'll help you.' All they did was have Christine's statement . . . and they . . . asked me to verify certain facts in it. Did I know this person, did I know this, did I know that, did you have an affair with Lord Astor, did he give you any money?' That kind of thing. And the Indian doctor who I never named – he wasn't Indian at all.

"It's pretty effective thumb screws on an eighteen-year-old girl isn't it? A very salutary experience going into a jail, I can tell you."

Out of some hundred and forty people interviewed, these four and the three women involved in the procurement charges, were the only ones the police could use to build their case.

Of the three women cited in the procurement charges, one denied having sex with Ward at all, and the other two admitted only to the most ordinary and voluntary of love affairs – with no third parties involved. It is hard to see now why the case was not thrown out on the third day. The evidence of the prosecution had totally collapsed, and by any standard the police had prepared their case very badly indeed. But this was not a trial of facts and actions, it was a trial of Ward's sexual mores and of the lifestyle he represented. It was a lifestyle shared by many – Lord Astor and Profumo for example, neither of whom were called – but which, in court, was devoid of context and hence alien to those on whom Ward's freedom depended. When Judge Marshall offered the wisdom that barristers and judges were men of the world, there must have been few outside the court who believed him.

The evidence of the two women who admitted to sex with Ward is indicative. Both, on cross-examination, said that Ward had not been their first lover. I suspect that however worldly the court professed itself to be, this very ordinary fact of life was a little shocking. Not only were these women not prostitutes, they did not even appear to have led lives similar, in the pursuit of hedonism, to Mandy or Christine, and it was not suggested that they had. They seemed, in short, to be 'respectable'. But they did represent the mores of a new generation, and with the substance of the prosecution's case dissolved, Griffith-Jones' cross-examination of the defence – Ward himself in the box – began to look more and more like an attack on the general morality of Ward, an issue over which Ward and Griffith-Jones, although roughly the same age, were not the same generation. Ludovic Kennedy recorded Griffith-Jones' performance:

"The outraged tone of voice in which he delivered his strictures did nothing to increase their appeal. He seemed to be assuming a part, not merely as the state prosecutor of public criminals, but as the state guardian of private morals; to be acting as a sort of Establishment front man for an ethos which few people besides himself any longer believed in."[33]

For some reason, perhaps it was inescapable, Burge chose, in opening his defence, to warn the jury: "You are not concerned I hope – because if you are, we might just as well plead guilty – you are not concerned with the standards of moral conduct of this man. That is far short, and the accused will be forced to admit it, of anything you will approve of."

This, I'm sure, was accurate. In answering the questions of his own counsel Ward admitted he had paid prostitutes for sex, and had been in a foursome with Ronna Ricardo. With his character 'established' it was natural for Griffith-Jones to see him and question him as a corrupter of youth, and with his repeated arithmetic on the ages of Ward, Astor, Mandy and Christine, he played upon one of the folk panics of the time – the degeneration of youth.

"In your view would it be right for the jury to have a picture of you aged forty-eight, corrupting an innocent girl of sixteen?"

"I did not corrupt her and she was not innocent at all."

As much as he could, in the face of articulate and intelligent answers from Ward, Griffith-Jones tried to hold Ward responsible for the lifestyles of the girls – not only had he not been charged with this, it wasn't illegal. The trial had moved smoothly into the court of morals. As Ward was about to step down the judge intervened and asked Ward for a definition which is crucial to the times and to the issues of the Ward case, even if it was ignored in the course of the verdict.

"When do you say a woman is a prostitute?"

" . . . When there is no element in the relationship between the man and the woman except a desire on the part of the woman to make money – when it is separated from any attachment and is indeed just the sale of her body." To which he might have added – no other desire on the man's part but self-gratification.

In his summing up Griffith-Jones seemed oblivious to the evidence and steamed along in high dudgeon as though points which had been demolished had been proved. Ward was portrayed as "this filthy fellow", a phrase he used repeatedly, and Mandy and Christine became, for the purpose of conviction, "two girls of sixteen, just over, recently in London from their homes in the country". He painted a picture of Ward as some latter-day Dorian Gray sucking the youth and innocence out of two wayward, but innocent, rustic girls.

In the course of Griffith-Jones' speech news arrived of the outcome of Lucky Gordon's appeal against his conviction for assault on Christine. The tape recording of her 'life story' had been reported to the Attorney-General by Wigg. In it Christine had set down the true version of the attack, and once this was known to the court Gordon's conviction had been quashed. Since this affected the credibility of a major witness, you might assume it was now a matter for Judge Marshall and that the proper course of action would be for the whole of Christine's testimony to be discounted. Instead Chief Justice Parker's curious wording of the outcome was relayed to the jury by Griffith-Jones:

"That does not of course mean to say that the Court of Appeal have found that Miss Keeler is lying." Yet, that was exactly what it meant, and a report had already gone to the Director of Public Prosecutions with a view to charging Christine with perjury. At this point the few scraps in her testimony that told against Ward were surely invalid?

At this point it looked as though the jury were bound to acquit Ward. Those watching and conversing with Ward think his confidence was still high, and there was only the judge's summing up to come before the jury retired. Judge Marshall relied more on tone and emphasis than on a blatant neglect of the facts. Throughout the trial he had played a curious game with the defence – pausing between the Mister and the Burge when addressing counsel, as though Burge was of no real significance (the jury could scarcely have failed to pick up on the unconscious suggestion) and venting his frustration with schoolmasterly impatience when Burge – a little hard of hearing – had occasion to ask the softer spoken witnesses (Christine in particular) to repeat their answers. Kennedy observed: "When he came to matters which told against Ward, his tone changed: his voice and bearing became brighter, livelier; he held the attention where elsewhere he had lost it. It was this that made the summing up sound so one-sided."[34]

The judge also chose to point out that Ward's friends had deserted him, as though this were a sign of guilt, of the sure judgment of society upon Ward, rather than evidence of the cowardice and faithlessness of Ward's friends. Perhaps Ward understood this better than anyone else, that it might mean nothing in terms of the law but everything in terms of his own life and the world in which he moved.

When Ward left the court on Wednesday, July 31st only the verdict was left to come. Around midnight he took a huge overdose of nembutal. On August 3rd he died, without regaining consciousness. In his absence the jury returned a guilty verdict on the first two counts – finding that he had lived upon the immoral earnings of Mandy and Christine.

He seems to have spent most of his last evening writing letters – to Judge Marshall, to Griffith-Jones, to Denning, to his solicitor, to his literary agent, to Henry Brooke and to many others. The desire to explain, to be understood, that had driven him obsessively for months, burst out one last time. In the middle of the evening he sent for Tom Mangold:

"He gave me a bundle of suicide notes. Including one addressed to me. It's nonsense to suggest that Stephen was murdered. He killed himself. He had no hope left – they took away his vision of himself. In his note to me he asked me to thank Ronna for trying and to see she got a couple of hundred from the estate."

In his letter to Noel Howard-Jones, in whose flat he was staying at the time, Ward said that he had given up hope in the face of Marshall's summing up. Suicide, surprisingly, "required no guts". The next day the *News of the World*, righteous to the last, wrote that he "did not have the guts to face his nemesis" – a word which must have sent most of their readership scuttling to a dictionary – he was "a central figure of evil, a diabolical mischief maker" who associated with "lying whores, frightened scrubbers, irresponsible little tarts". His crimes could not readily be dealt with "under earthly law" – and with that they condemned him to hell and history, and themselves to hypocrisy.

163

Two more equally unofficial obituaries are more interesting. At the cremation in Mortlake, the following week, a wreath was sent by twenty-one artists, including John Osborne, Kenneth Tynan and Joe Orton, who was at this time beginning his final burst of hard-won success. Three years later, collecting an award for his play *Loot*, Orton remarked that there were probably people who thought his play a fantasy, his bent copper, Truscott, to be a work of pure imagination, "but, of course, the police know it's true". And on the war memorial in Cheltenham a wreath appeared, labelled:

"We three girls from Cheltenham Ladies' College have laid this wreath as a tribute to dear Dr Stephen Ward, who dared to live his life as a human being and not just as a dummy. An outraged society revenged itself upon him."

§

In this latter view is the perspective I seek. It seems to me that the anonymous authors of that note spoke for a generation.

A few months after the death of Stephen Ward, Colin MacInnes wrote in a piece for *Encounter* called 'Sterilities and Virilities': "The equation, in England, of sexual morality with morality in general is philistine (and irreligious) in the extreme." This sums up what had happened in England at that time, and it had happened to such an extent that at the age of eleven or twelve I assumed all moral issues to be issues of sexuality. Sexuality and sexual morality had been easily displaced on to the young. If nothing else endless articles on the sin of pre-marital sex sold sleaze-rags like the *News of the World* and *Today* – but as an issue it went further than simple titillation – it was, as I said earlier, on the scale of a moral panic, and like Salem, paradigmatic of all moral panics, it required sacrifices and demons. It is a truism that each new generation invents fucking, but my feeling about the early sixties is that it was less invented than discovered on their behalf as a newly chronicled statistical concern with sex (evident in the 1957 Wolfenden report in Britain, and the Kinsey report in the USA) inflated the sexual practices of the young into scare stories that fed the fantasies of their parents' generation. In this respect the case of Stephen Ward provided meat aplenty. He was the perfect scapegoat not only for the chinks that had opened up in the Establishment armour, but also for the moral rot of the young.

The popular press of 1963 is littered with examples of a burgeoning adult sexual crisis – as though the unconscious message was that the teenagers should hammer the ethics of the miserable post-war years and set their elders free.

The voyeuristic – in March 1963 the *Sunday Pictorial* reported how porters at St John's, Cambridge had burst in on a student ten minutes after curfew to find he had a girl in his room – they "stripped back the sheets" (why? either the bed was obviously occupied or it wasn't, or perhaps this was a visit from the Understain Squad masquerading as porters?) and reported finding "female underclothing scattered", as though it were nuclear fallout. The student faced disciplinary action, but the Dean felt obliged to engage with the terms of the day and point out that it was "not a moral issue".

The bizarre – the *Express* in July told of the case of John Mallet, Tory agent in Wokingham, who had ordered eighteen-year-old David Gillman, treasurer of the Young Conservatives, to remove his trousers and receive six of the best with a fly swatter after a poor report from Central Office. The prosecution said that "the trousers were removed without question because Mr Gillman thought it was a test of character." Clearly the way into the Tory hierarchy for a young hopeful was much the same as the way out – perhaps trousers are a source of mystery and power like the masonic apron? An essential requirement for Tory leadership – 'Carleton-Browne here, sir. Eton and Balliol, outright ownership of own trousers, ready for off.'

The masturbatory – the film *Yellow Teddybears* was reported in *Today* in July. The title refers to a badge worn to boast of lost virginity, supposedly based on the Gollies of 1961. The film packaged teenage sex for the adult market, simultaneously playing on the desirability of teenage girls and the moral censure of the parent – look, leer, and lament. The only such badge I can remember bore the arcane inscription 'Young Liberals'. In the same issue coverage of Ward and Profumo focused on the inevitable chain of connection, in a series by Judge Gerald Sparrow on 'Vice', prostitution – blacks – drugs. Since the trial was still in progress the piece did not mention Ward by name, but the inference was obvious – the sexual laxity of Christine led her to associate with blacks and blacks use 'hemp' and so on and so on – and at the back of it an evil Svengali? Even when asking the reader for compassion for Christine, the magazine was able to tease out the moral: "No story more dramatically reveals the sickness of our times than the Christine Keeler story." The sickness, of course, being the moral decay of the young – some of whom were so far gone they would pose wearing only a striped towel and magazines like *Today* would print it on their covers, perhaps hoping the public would think they had had a photographer at Cliveden on the fateful day.

Amongst the humbug were a few small voices of sanity. In the *Mail* in the previous October Levin tackled the problem by asking "Do you honestly think a four letter word can corrupt you?" and we would wait three years to find out – until Ken Tynan finally said 'fuck' on television in 1965. And in the Reith lectures for 1962 Dr G. M. Carstairs, Professor of Psychological Medicine at Edinburgh, asked "but is chastity the supreme moral virtue?" only to find that the *Mail* reported his otherwise obscure Home Service lecture. He received over a hundred letters, which on any other issue but teenage morality might have been more than the actual audience.

"I believe that we may be quite mistaken in our alarm – at times mounting almost to panic – over young people's sexual experimentation. Contraception is still regarded as something wicked, threatening to chastity, opening the way to unbridled licence . . . it seems to me that our young people are rapidly turning our own society into one in which sexual experience, with precautions against conception, is becoming accepted as a sensible preliminary to marriage."[35] The last clause excepted, Dr Carstairs' statement seems to be one of the most level-headed uttered on the subject.

Adam Faith is probably as well remembered for his 1962 BBC interview with Dr Coggan, then Archbishop of York, as he is for a handful of breathy singles. Faith was questioned as a representative of the new sexual mores – part of the audience reaction was surprise that pop singers could be articulate, part was that Faith did not appear to be a monster of depravity, but the point is that it was thought interesting and necessary to make the programme in the first place. Speaking as someone who was a teenager in 1963, of the same generation as those three girls from Cheltenham College, Faith was not the hero we sought. To be articulate to the adults on their own turf was not enough. If we discerned a new sexual ethos in the life and death of Stephen Ward, it called for defiance, and defiance threw up a new hero – eighteen-year-old Mandy Rice-Davies.

With her "He would wouldn't he" she announced a fact that was supposed to break worlds. She had fucked, and seemed not to care who knew it. Her testimony at the Old Bailey added to this. Christine had been shy and confused, as she had every right to be, Mandy had – or so it seemed at the time – stood tall and spoken up for herself and the ethics of a new generation. The confidence with which she dressed helped this impression. A hat of pink petals and a sleeveless grey gaberdine dress, specially tailored for the occasion, that seemed to combine modesty with a hint of revelation – concession to the time and the place with her own personality. Her impact on Ludovic Kennedy was dramatic: " . . . a marriage of the brazen and the bashful. She was in turns pert, cool, innocent, tearful, giggly. Unlike Christine she was never pathetic; unlike her too she was not in the least abashed either by the company or her surroundings. She was one of the very few female witnesses one was able to hear. She smiled at Ward, at Mr Griffith-Jones, at the judge . . . at one moment she was calling the counsel 'sir' from behind lowered lids, the next she was trying to split a joke with the judge. She was in short wholly unpredictable."[36]

Mandy's account shows tensions that were not apparent to the press:

"I cannot say I really arrived [in London] and thought 'Boy oh boy this is the great big city, isn't it wonderful'. It just seemed like my natural environment, it was like walking from the beach into the sea. To a degree I believe I was escaping that small marooned life. It was a comfortable life, it was rather pleasant in fact. It was the life of, let's say, a semi-detached house. You never went hungry, there was always food on the table, always a bit of money in your pocket. I had a pony, had the country life, the pony club. I wanted more and also I suppose, in that particular area that I came from, I suppose one's only real hope was marrying a guy that owned an MG and polished it every Sunday.

"It was adventure I was interested in, adventure. Since I was a kid I've always liked adventure stories and I've always read things like South Seas tales – Albert Schweitzer, I've followed his stories with great interest and rather wished I could be one of these wealthy young things that could go over into the jungle and run around hugging leopards. When I was very young being a missionary appealed to me. Something I would never admit to in my auto-biography in case everybody laughed up their sleeve, or down their sleeve. But that appealed to me, not so much from the re-ligious aspect although I was religious, although I could not find my niche in religion, but because it was the adventure, the travel . . . I felt as though I was in training for something, I didn't know quite what, but I felt I was gaining an experience, gaining an education which I had missed.

"I think I always had something in my character, though, that if ever [I'm going] through a bad experience, I always feel as though I'm a character in a play. I somehow can divorce what's happening, something else takes over. Perhaps its the survival of the sub-conscious, that wonderful survival instinct which comes into play . . . and then acts out the part, that actually you are playing but it's not really you it's something else. Even now that whole time then has an aura of fiction about it.

"You can see it quite clearly, in some pictures. The hardback version of my autobiography [is] very interesting. On the front you've got me in *the* hat and inside it you've got pictures of me leaving the court smiling. But on the back page is where I've turned a corner – and it's obviously a . . . candid picture, just snapped – and I'm leaning against a wall and my face is . . . you can read everything on that face. I looked dreadful, I look absolutely awful. Nobody could understand why I allowed it on the back of the book . . . I've walked round the court, I've come out big smiles, the hat, I've turned round the corner, I think nobody's looking and then you see . . . ? And the mask and the front dropped.

"In the years since, so many people have come to me and said 'Oh God I was at school when this was going on, and I had pictures of you . . . and I thought you were wonderful' and the whole thing. But at that time the only thing that was in my head was that everybody's against me. I didn't think that anybody liked me at all, because after all, the only feedback I had was from the press, I had no feedback from the public whatsoever . . . I was divorced from the public, the public were these wild animals out there, as I saw them. If you'd walked out of that court and you'd seen the mob pictures . . . The way I handled that, and I nearly didn't, was purely instinctive. When I arrived there was this mob, thousands and thousands of people, and I'd heard on the radio that they'd thrown tomatoes, and cabbage and eggs and God knows what at Christine. You can imagine . . . we used to have this racehorse in the stables who was vicious . . . and everybody was terrified of this bloody horse and nobody wanted to go in and feed it, nobody wanted to go in and groom it, but I used to go in and do it, I used to march in and I would conquer my fear . . . I realised that he could smell or he could see that I was afraid, and that brought it out . . . Everybody who walked in [to the court] – their fear was so apparent, so when I got out of the car I put on this immensely brave front and I smiled and I waved.

"I really was alone, so I fought it alone and I didn't bother fighting the press. It was totally useless. I realised that I had enough intelligence. So if I ever saw the press hanging around – they'd followed me around for months on end – and if it was pouring with rain and they were standing outside I'd give them a cup of coffee. The thing that was really odd, that I found unjust, was that the very people [who] in private were talking to me and saying 'What's happening in this country, why don't they throw this case out of court?' were writing something totally different the next day. Of course, the next day in the newspapers would be the headline, 'All for the love of Mandy' or something, instead of writing what they should have done. Now 'Does the press report the truth, or does the press report something what the public wants to hear?' was a question I asked myself at the time. And of course the answer had to be they reported what the public wanted to hear."

Mandy is only a few years older than me, but with hindsight I am less inclined to see her as a spokesman for my generation – if only because I've looked more closely at the one that preceded us, and I'm more aware that the death throes of an old culture are too easily mistaken for the birth pangs of the one you anticipate coming into being – a fine distinction, but it matters. I said, nearer the beginning of this chapter, that in the meeting of worlds lies the 'meaning' of the case of Stephen Ward – and if the Affair of John Profumo has slipped effortlessly into being called the Case of Stephen Ward, then it simply reflects what happened at the time and quite probably defines the purpose in Ward's trial being held at all on such flimsy evidence. For once Mr Macmillan's reflections on the matter are near enough right: "It was, I must admit, as much a surprise to me as to ordinary folk to hear of this strange environment in which men of some importance, even holding high positions, were led to mingle with crooks, charlatans, pimps and courtesans. In my youth, good manners, although not necessarily good morality, made such a confusion impossible. The *monde* and the *demi-monde* were kept strictly apart."[37]

Ward, the social fulcrum, symbolised to the Establishment the breaking of barriers they would rather see kept in place. I doubt that many people would have expressed it with the Edwardian bewilderment of Macmillan or with the innocence that was strictly his own, but the meeting of ages, classes and races in the life of Stephen Ward brought *monde* and *demi-monde* together in a way that could, given the times, scarcely be less than criminal. It looked like the breaking of worlds. It's been said often, and it's become a large part of the myth, that Profumo inadvertently performed a service to the nation – the sacrificial victim in a ritual of national cleansing that set us on the way to a moral and intellectual health. The lancing of the boil, as so many have called it – they may be right. We differ on whom we emphasise.

All this had more to do with the old morality than with the new. In the Old Bailey the world of Ward was judged by the world of Profumo. Profumo behaved as men of his class have always behaved and had the tough luck to get caught – and a most apposite comment was made in a photo-cartoon in *Private Eye*: 1st woman "Is that Mr Profumo? But he looks perfectly normal." 2nd woman: "Yes that's the problem." And, critically it has remained the problem. The question of why a man's (and it usually is men in questions of this sort) private morals should affect his public role crops up every so often, and founders – no one wanting to think we any longer have or need an elite which must be above normal human feeling and behaviour and the certain intelligence that context is a differential in every case. The principle in the matter of Mr Profumo is not the principle in the matter of Mr Parkinson. There was from the Profumo Affair onwards, pervading the Sixties, an understanding that private versus public morality was no longer an issue – the marital infidelity of the late President Kennedy became a celebration of cock-artistry. We had, through Profumo, freed ourselves from all that and from the crisis of sexuality that had obsessed the early sixties. We had at that time, so the legend goes, lost an empire, found no role, and with pristine Freudian psychosis turned in on ourselves with the threat that we would eat ourselves alive or tear some new being loose from a rough caesarian. An optimistic view of the mid-sixties would be that Britain did indeed become a new creature – one that now scurries headless down the yard like the anecdotal chicken.

The matter of blackmail nestled in this context. It was raised time and again – in the Commons, in the press, and in Denning's report. There was a much repeated story of Christine being asked by Ward to ask Profumo about the date when Germany would receive nuclear warheads from Nato. Yet, none of it seems plausible. The journalists I talked to, who covered the affair at the time, agree on one point – the risk of blackmail, over a heterosexual affair, was negligible even in 1963. The risk for Profumo stemmed from the contact with Ivanov – and until he told the truth about his private life the nature of that risk could not be discerned – and since he did not tell the truth when asked to do so by his party, the Opposition and his leader, the real risk of blackmail lay not in the violation of accepted moral standards in an affair with Christine Keeler but in the violation of more rigorous, more traditional moral standards in a lie to the House of Commons.

The judgment of Profumo's world upon Profumo led to disgrace and a productive exile from public life. Stephen Ward ran the greater risk, and paid the higher price. He had evolved his own style, socially and sexually – risking accusations of corruption, depravity, possibly abnormality – but it too was very much part of the interregnum, the grey years between the war and swinging London, very much a man's world and one that differed drastically from the sixties in its surface respectability. Christine probably was what Macmillan meant by a courtesan – if so she fulfilled a centuries old role. Mandy didn't – despite her comparison to Lady Hamilton. She was by no means, as I might have thought twenty-five years ago, the prototype of Sixties' sexual liberation, but she was her own woman, independent, shrewd, ambitious, older than her years and would not play down responsibility for her own sexuality to suit the tenor of the times. Not surprisingly in the eighties she seemed very much a woman of the eighties. Christine has, by her own admission, floundered – she has described her life in the seventies as existing rather than living. All these different generations, moving in different worlds that met in Ward came under the judgment of three old men – Macmillan, Marshall and Denning, none of whom could have had much grasp of the sexual crisis that found its focus in the panic over teenage morality, none of whom is likely to have grasped in that juxtaposition of the generations the sense of a world in transition, that the last fling of fifties' scandal, and our willingness to be thus scandalised, would break the mould. A generation that had grown up accustomed to strict social divisions saw them threatened by the very existence of a man like Ward. He brought the demi-monde, however reluctantly he did so, to the fore. It must have seemed to these men as though he'd strolled up the gravelled drive and pissed through the letter box.

Tom Mangold speaks for his generation when he says: "In 1963 we were all coming out of our closets – not just the homosexuals and the swingers. There was a sense of liberation. Britain was pregnant with change. 1963 was a year of revolution – round one of '68, the social revolution. Things changed. It was exciting – it was great simply to be in your twenties in 1963. Of course there were people who resisted it – the church wouldn't like it – the backbenchers wouldn't like it. Stephen's lifestyle was at the cusp of that. Neurotic, happy-go-lucky. No roles. There was an aura of sex."

Ward, not Profumo, was the last sacrifice to the god of closet morality. The old Edwardian wrote that "men of some importance were led" – and it's more than carelessness. It says what he really meant.

"Profumo couldn't be evil. Ward had to be. All the people who regarded themselves as the guardians of our morals had to justify bad behaviour by finding a devil – there had to be a devil leading Profumo astray. Stephen fitted the bill. It was theology more than conspiracy. The Establishment in Britain was not at that time conspiratorial. There had been since Victorian times a class which felt it

171

had a duty to rule – their class, breeding and education all pointed them inescapably towards public service. It only worked if they were *seen to be different*, incorruptible. For Jack Profumo to be caught in the act was bad news for the Establishment – their duty to rule rests on the principle that they behave better. It would have been a non-conspiracy that trapped Stephen. The word was Stephen Ward was a nuisance, a ponce who led people astray. It would be two men talking in a club – it could happen that way. Ward wasn't *one of us.*"[38]

There were too many ways in which Ward could be discounted as not one of us. He earned high fees from his practice – enough to make the idea of him pimping absurd – but had no income without working. He went to a public school, but Canford was a very minor public school – not the sort of place where friendships made at thirteen last a lifetime and permeate the entire top drawer of society. He was a doctor, but only a doctor of sorts with a foreign qualification. He could pass for one of us, he could make acquaintances and friends in that top drawer, and while his friendship with Astor may have been genuine (as well as asking for the key to the cottage back, it should also be pointed out that Astor paid for Ward's defence) how many others were?

It was cogently argued in the first book on the matter – Wayland Young's,[39] written between the publication of the Denning report and the debate on it, and hence part of the matter in the immediacy of its response – that Ward's acceptance into such a society was possible only because he served them in a particular office – that of procurer. I find that hard to accept today, at least as precisely as it was put. Tom Mangold's view is this: "It's inconceivable to me that Stephen procured. He was a bohemian, a sexual voyeur."

From which two points follow – it's possible that Ward was so misperceived by a repressed society because he was that rare being who knew what he liked, and his friends were fortunate in being the beneficiaries of his harmless practice of surrounding himself with beautiful women. Yet, if *they* saw him as *their procurer* the reality matters little – he was as disposable as any other functionary in a system which had as its highest status of all no function and no work (the notion of 'public service' satisfies the desire for self-aggrandisement without actually reducing a member of the Establishment to working, hence their obituary notices habitually disguise avaricious self-seeking under this phrase). Ward was not so blessed, and the Establishment non-conspiracy, that malevolent theology – like a machine on automatic – rejected him, trapped him and destroyed him.

172

§

Since the unholy joy of this chapter's title was largely that of the press, and since I've quoted them many times, some view of their role is necessary. It would be fatuous to go on illustrating the ease with which tabloid journalism can propagate and celebrate on its front pages what it condemns on its inside pages. In that respect what was true a quarter of a century ago is true today. If there was any truth in the legend of a nation throwing off the shackles of outmoded moral conservatism, the press were behind the times in their appraisal of the Profumo affair. They had a role beyond commentary, however. So many stories were 'bought up' that it became an issue in the trial of Stephen Ward, and the value of evidence given by people who had already negotiated deals with the press was questioned. It follows, therefore, that there's a case to be made for precipitating action by the newspapers – that their intervention influenced the course of the unfolding of the case, and perhaps the course of justice. Was it possible for Stephen Ward to receive a fair trial after weeks of sensationalism? Was he not as likely to be sacrificed by the press, in their gung-ho Mac Must Go attitude, as he was by the politicians? In the papers following his death and conviction I didn't find anyone arguing about the miscarriage of justice. The most vital issue of all got lost in the ballyhoo.

Against this it must be said that Ward seems to have adored both gossip and conspiracy – months before he needed to seek political allies he had written to Wilson to point out that he and Ivanov had attempted mediation during the Cuban missile crisis, and I can see no other purpose in this but that joy in conspiracy. Why Ward should ever have expected to find an ally in Wigg is also a mystery. Ward appears, from Wigg's own record of the meeting, to have given a less than truthful account of the matter, but why he should want to give any account is a puzzle. And Ward told the true version to, of all people, Willie Rushton at *Private Eye*. His natural propensity to gossip seemed compounded by a desperate loneliness. Ward's friends would have deserted him anyway, and the loneliness he felt was lessened by the company of journalists. He would not have left notes at his death for Mangold and Barry O'Brien of the *Telegraph* had this not been the case.

§

173

The last word came not from the press but from the unlikeliest of tabloids – called simply *Lord Denning's Report*. Railway station bookstalls all over the land found themselves besieged by customers on its publication in September. Cmnd 2152 is probably the only bestseller Her Majesty's Stationery Office has ever had. In the USA it was reprinted as a mass market paperback. Lord Denning had the measure of his audience and wrote under chapter headings that augured well for him if he ever wanted to edit the *News of the World* . . . The Slashing and The Shooting, The Man in the Mask, He's a Liar . . . and for those who'd been slow on the uptake he gave a checklist of rumours – at one point packing a member of the government off to see his GP so that he could be certain he was not the faceless, naked man in the Argyll case. It must have left many people wondering whether it was a matter of circumcision or the size of the ministerial schlong. Denning interviewed many people, asking them about rumours in circulation.

Andrew Roth: "The story he'd asked me about concerned a well known man who took Christine Keeler for a ride in his open car and she'd performed fellatio. Denning said 'What's that?' I looked at the verbatim reporter, a middle aged, very spinsterly lady . . . and for the life of me I couldn't think of anything but 'cocksucking'. I said he'd have to look it up in a dictionary. I was so surprised he'd asked me that question I went and looked up his record – he'd been in the divorce courts for a long period! It was all just judge's technique."

The purpose of the report was to back Macmillan's belief that nobody told him. Ward emerged as the villain of the piece – a man Lord Denning could describe as one of the most evil men he'd ever met. The report hardly scrapes the surface of the subject, reprimands Profumo in passing, doesn't mention the trial of Ward at all and offers criticism of the government on only one count. The meeting of the Famous Five asked only whether Profumo had committed adultery, not whether his conduct "had been such as to lead ordinary people reasonably to believe he had committed adultery." When it came to the issue of ministerial responsibility Denning sidestepped almost everything that needed examination by saying "they are matters for parliament not for me", lamenting that parliament had no mechanism for coping with "moral misbehaviour" once MI5 had satisfied themselves on the security issue.

And in the end Denning too felt it was time to assess the breaking of nations: "It might be thought . . . that these rumours are a symptom of a decline in the integrity of public life in this country. I do not believe this to be true. There has been no lowering of standards."

If that was an earnest statement of Lord Denning's belief that life after this would go on much as before, he has lived to know how wrong he was.

CHAPTER SEVEN

BISHOPS IN OUTER SPACE

"This so-called new morality is too often the old immorality condoned."
                                                    Lord Shawcross, 1963

An abiding figure of this period is the much-criticised, much-satirised 'trendy' vicar – the priest who came to his flock with his message, on their terms. The Reverend William Shergold of London's East End,[1] who set up a bikers' youth club and dressed like a biker himself, was perhaps typical of that small band of missionaries to the home country, sent up by more than one cartoonist in sketches depicting motorbikes roaring up to the altar rail while the vicar intones lines like "Oh Gawd in Heaven, bless this Norton 650."

Less typical, better remembered, but wholly fictitious was the Reverend Smallwood – an invention of the Boulting Brothers and Malcolm Muggeridge, portrayed by Peter Sellers in the 1963 film *Heavens Above*. Smallwood is an unwelcome revolutionary as far as the Church of England of the early sixties is concerned – he is as his name suggests, a minor version of the second coming, a simple, literal, working class Christian who loves his neighbour and gives all he has to the poor. The result is chaos. Capitalism at its most basic begins to break down – the shops lack customers, the factories lack trade. The vicar is conned by the poor, abused by the well-off and hated by the clerical hierarchy. He cannot be crucified – if only – but he meets a modern day sanction, he is promoted into oblivion, and appointed to the even more fictitious British space programme as the first Bishop of Outer Space, and is last heard of orbiting the earth, singing hymns in his broad brummie accent. Smallwood was nothing like the Bishop of Woolwich, but without priests like the Bishop of Woolwich it is hard to imagine that Muggeridge would have thought up Smallwood.

The Rev. Dr John Robinson, one-time lecturer in Theology at Cambridge, and since 1959 Suffragan Bishop of Woolwich in the diocese of Southwark was the most controversial clergyman of his day. To my knowledge, the Bishop was not trendy in that he had

176

ever blessed a motorbike, but he most certainly saw himself as a missionary and a Christian revolutionary.

Dr Robinson was a member of the Labour Party, a founder of Christian CND, an Aldermaston marcher, and a campaigner against apartheid and capital punishment – he also favoured the ordination of women, and was one of the translators of the much-criticised, unpoetic if accessible *New English Bible*, which first appeared in 1961. Politically he was of the same stamp as his superior the Bishop of Southwark. Even *Tribune* could afford a tongue-in-cheek appraisal of spiritual life across the river: "London south of the Thames has become the Red Belt of the Church of England. Mervyn Stockwood, Bishop of Southwark, is mild enough himself but he enjoys the company of turbulent priests, and behind every other dog collar in the pulpits under his charge you will like as not find a secret Aldermaston marcher, a furtive abortion-law reformer, or a militant campaigner for the Socialist Kingdom of God. That is the environment in which Dr John Robinson, Suffragan Bishop of Woolwich . . . has written *Honest to God*."[2]

Honest to God is a fairly difficult work of modern theology. During the Spring and Summer of 1963 it was outsold only by the paperback edition of *The Kama Sutra*. Its first print run of six thousand sold out on the first day. It is still in print and has sold over a million copies in seventeen languages. When it was first published on March 19th, 1963, the pump had been well primed by an article written by Robinson for the *Observer* of March 17th, under the headline "Our Image of God Must Go": "If Christianity is to survive it must be relevant to modern secular man, not just to the dwindling number of the religious . . . Modern man has opted for the secular world: he has become increasingly non-religious; the churches have deplored this as the great defection from God, and the more they write it off, the more this movement has seen itself as anti-Christian.

"But . . . Man . . . is 'coming of age' . . . for good or ill he is putting the religious world-view behind him as childish and pre-scientific . . . I believe that Christians must go through the agonising process in this generation of detaching themselves from this idol. For to Twentieth Century man the 'old man in the sky' and the whole supernaturalist scheme seem as fanciful as the man in the moon."

"Our Image of God Must Go", however much it was invited by phrases like 'the old man in the sky', was not a line that pleased Robinson, and was seized upon by the press and public alike – for the bishop was no newcomer to controversy and to statements that made headlines. In 1960 he had appeared for the defence at 'the trial of Lady Chatterley' – more correctly Regina v. Penguin Books. Examined by barrister Gerald Gardiner, later Lord Chancellor under the Wilson government, the Bishop offered his views on the morality of the long-banned book:

"Clearly, Lawrence did not have a Christian valuation of sex, and the kind of sexual relationship depicted in the book is not one that I would necessarily regard as ideal, but what I think is clear is what Lawrence is trying to do is to portray the sex relationship as something essentially sacred . . . For him flesh was completely sacramental of spirit."[3]

In conclusion Mr Gardiner asked: "Is this a book which in your view Christians ought to read?"

"Yes," Dr Robinson replied, "I think it is. Because I think what Lawrence was trying to do . . . "

The Bishop never did complete the sentence. Interruption and objection from the prosecution, Mervyn Griffith-Jones, who would also be prosecutor at the trial of Stephen Ward, put paid to that. But the Bishop, by no means the star of the trial – that was Richard Hoggart – made newspaper headlines with the less than accurate "A book all Christians should read". What had been merely approval was turned into instruction.

Levin's tongue-in-cheek comment on the instant success of *Honest To God* may well be a true reflection of the fame of Dr Robinson:

" . . . The number sold suggest that many who would not otherwise have ventured to tread upon the thin ice of theology may have bought it to find out what he was up to now, and perhaps in a few cases because they were sufficiently confused to believe that he was the author of *Lady Chatterley's Lover* and that this might be a sequel."[4]

Sex was the aspect of *Honest to God* that proved most newsworthy, but there was more, much more, to this difficult book than that. Fully aware that it would bring the cry of 'heretic' down upon him, the Bishop said at the beginning that: " . . . I can at least understand what those mean who urge that we should do well to give up using the word 'God' for a generation, so impregnated has it become with a way of thinking we may have to discard if the Gospel is to signify anything . . . not infrequently, as I watch or listen to broadcast discussion between a Christian and a humanist, I catch myself realising that most of my sympathies are on the humanist's side."[5]

The most constructive of his critics, Alasdair MacIntyre – fellow of University College, Oxford, and appointed shortly afterwards to the first chair of Philosophy at the new University of Essex[6] – answered in September's *Encounter* by saying: "What is surprising about Dr Robinson is first and foremost that he is an atheist". This conclusion is hard to escape as Robinson peels away the layers between the Christian and humanist positions. Notions such as God is 'an old man in the sky' are easily challenged – it's too rich even for children: "For in place of a God who is literally or physically 'up there' we have accepted, as part of our mental furniture, a God who is spiritually or metaphysically 'out there' . . . a God who exists above and beyond the world he made, and to whom we 'go' when we die . . . But the signs are that we are reaching a point at which the whole conception of a God 'out there' . . . is itself becoming more of a hindrance than a help . . . perhaps after all the Freudians are right, that such a God – the God of traditional theology – *is* a projection, and perhaps we are being called upon to live without that projection in any form."[7]

The Bishop acknowledged that in conventional terms this might be construed as atheism – but his wish is not to advocate atheism so much as to challenge the constructions based upon the notion of *theos*. Hence he must redefine his God, and so strange are these definitions, so rooted in the new German theology of Bonhoeffer, Tillich and Bultman, that they were bound to outrage whether understood or not. God is 'ultimate reality', 'that which we take seriously without any reservation', 'the ground of our being'. But, as of old, God is Love. The attacks were swift in response.

The Archbishop of Canterbury, Michael Ramsey, said in a television interview: "It really is a caricature of the ordinary churchman's views on God. When the ordinary churchman speaks of God as being 'up there' or of God being 'beyond', he does not literally mean that God is in the place beyond the bright blue sky. He's putting in poetic language, which is the only language we have, that God is supreme . . . "[8] And Ramsey told the Convocation of the Church of England: "The considerable liberty of thought which we enjoy as a Church does however carry with it certain obligations of consideration and restraint . . . the initial method chosen was a newspaper article, crystal clear in its argument and provocative in its shape and statement, to tell the public that the concept of a personal God as held in popular Christianity and in orthodox doctrine is outmoded, and that atheists and agnostics are right to reject it . . . the message which the Bishop succeeded in disseminating in the country was the negative one which I have described. No other result could have been reasonably expected."[9]

In the *Sunday Telegraph* T. E. Utley regretted that there was no way of getting rid of the Bishop except by the extreme measure of prosecuting him for heresy, and here he spoke for many who would have loved to see the Bishop unfrocked: "Can the Church of England, in the name of intellectual liberty, be content to allow its bishops to use the authority of their office, and by implication that of the Gospel, to support any trend of the opinion they happen to favour? I cannot see how, on this occasion, the church can avoid the duty of facing the question squarely – yes, even at the risk of being thought 'square'."[10]

And in the *Observer*, C. S. Lewis pinpointed one of the major problems: "Any entity describable without gross abuse of language as God must be ultimate reality, and if ultimate reality is personal, then God is personal. Does the Bishop mean that something which is not 'a person' could yet be 'personal'?"[11]

Eric James, Robinson's biographer, describes himself as being at that time a "sort of lieutenant of John's": "It was a marvellous time, and it feels very different [now], because it never occurred to me that we weren't on the crest of the wave that would roll forward and forward . . . It was bliss to be alive in terms of the reform of the church and the reform of the world. You felt the stuffy old world was opening up. It never occurred to me that there would be anything like the Thatcher years . . . Everything was up for re-evaluation . . . It was a very exciting time . . . I was appointed to go round the country and . . . whip up the reformers, and what amazed me – and this is very important – it was the most painful time of my life. I only stood it for three years before becoming Canon of Southwark, because I was damned if I was going to go around being hated any longer. It was the most painful thing because at that time there were at least twenty-five thousand clergy – now there are ten – and as one went around in the rural parts all one got was the hatred there was for . . . John Robinson, and I found I was receiving it all. And I realised after a very short time that the radicals were in a very small minority – a voluble minority but quite small."[12]

The weakness in the bishop's argument is that he argues for but cannot himself countenance the surrender of the idea of a personal God – even to the point of endowing his non-person with the human characteristic of 'love', as the ultimate good and the ultimate reality. In compromising his own belief in this unsatisfactory abstraction, Robinson hoped not to convert the atheist but to catch the marginals, those amongst us who were the newly secular, who would love to be able to believe if only it weren't for the sheer corniness of that ole time religion. Hence the Bishop was at pains to separate

God from 'the religious' and the religious from the moral – and in doing so he could please neither the orthodox nor the indifferent and caught it from all sides.

As MacIntyre put it the Bishop was trying to create an atheism with the vocabulary of theology, "an atheist christology". It's called having your cake and eating it. And what remains is the question of any role or purpose for worship and prayer. Why not abandon them altogether? One, cynical, answer might be that the Bishop was out to herd in the marginals, and his purpose, as the word 'marginal' implies, was political at heart. If worship and prayer are abandoned what would be left for that political entity the Church of England? No worship, no flock, no power.[13] So, Dr Robinson must explain how to worship the non-entity and pray to the non-person.

"The purpose of worship is . . . to open oneself to . . . that which has the power to penetrate its superficiality and redeem it from its alienation . . . The function of worship is to make us more sensitive to these depths: to focus, sharpen and deepen our response to the world and to other people beyond the point of proximate concern (of liking, self-interest, limited commitment etc.) to that of ultimate concern; to purify and correct our loves in the light of Christ's love: and in him to find the grace and power to be the reconciled and reconciling community. Anything that achieves this or assists towards it is Christian worship. Anything that fails to do this is not Christian worship, be it ever so 'religious'."[14]

Prayer is "openness to the ground of our being."[15]

All of which leads inevitably to the line with which MacIntyre concluded: "The creed of the English is that there is no God and that it is wise to pray to him from time to time."

The most puzzling aspect of this debate, which ran many weeks in the popular and heavy press – the heavies all gave the book lengthy reviews, and in the populars trendy vicars were trundled out to answer Robinson under misleading headlines, which Robinson himself took on with an essay in the *Sunday Mirror* – is the ease with which the Bishop accepts secularisation, the scepticism of a scientific age, as though the exploration of space itself proved the absence of a heaven. It seems too statistical a view to insist on the godlessness of modern man – and it's significant that Robinson's German mentors wrote not so much in the space or atomic age, but in the age of Auschwitz – having witnessed the demonstration of a potentially faith-shattering abdication of God and justice. It strikes me, against all certainty, that the Bishop, despite his appearance at the Chatterley trial, could not have been a man who bothered much with literature – he's read Lawrence, but has he read Blake? –

'Everything that lives is holy'. His reassessment of the God 'out there' as the 'ground of our being' might have been usefully illustrated with some of the world's other, Eastern religions – but *Honest to God* carries its C. of E. politics to the point of mentioning no other religion. Only a few years later the sixties saw a religious resurgence (probably a spurious one in the eyes of the church), a willingness to believe, in the revived interest in Hinduism, Zen and Buddhism. It seemed short-sighted of the Church of England to write off the religious impulse in modern man. But, statistically – as reported by *New Society* – the church was in trouble: 67% of the British were still baptised, but only 24% of them made it to confirmation. MacIntyre provided a sense of context: "Imagine it [*Honest to God*] directed to . . . a church which chose the right moment to get out of gilt-edged and into equities as Dr Robinson's church did." To which he might have added a church that also sold off its housing in street-loads to the likes of Peter Rachman.

After 1944 and Rab Butler's Education Act, religious services, so long a part of school traditions, became compulsory. I have a less than fond memory of a Senior Mathematics Master standing, bellowing, during a rehearsal for a carol service, to the boys of the Lower Fifth, "SING!" with his admonishing finger upraised, tone and gesture identical to that with which he would threaten you with physical violence or offer to spike your chances of a university place by refusing you a reference. For all the compulsory church and scripture forced upon me at school I cannot recall a single visit from a churchman of any denomination to see what was being done in the church's name. The church's real problem was that it had allied itself so closely to the educational and political system that it could not be taken seriously on any matter of ethics or religion – such alliances, such examples, bred several generations of atheists.

Dr Robinson titled a chapter of *Honest to God* 'The New Morality'. This more than anything exercised the critics. Sex again. The Bishop pointed out that "the sanctions of Sinai have lost their terrors" and came perilously close on the general issue of morality to advocating 'do your own thing', but he pulls away from this into an injunction which begs the notion of a permissive society, in that it focuses not on freedom but on permission (the paradox in the misnomer 'permissive society' was that the society in question needed no permission). Again the half-measure could please no one: "To the young man asking in his relations with a girl, 'Why shouldn't I?', it is relatively easy to say 'Because it's wrong' or 'Because it's a sin' . . . it makes much greater demands to ask and to answer, the question 'Do you love her?' or

'*How much* do you love her?'"[16]

"I have to be in love first," is usually a line uttered only in jest, but the approval of extra-marital sex outraged the orthodox, confirming the worst suspicions that could have been harboured since the Chatterley trial – the Bishop could be portrayed as a man who condoned immorality – and its qualification merely irritated the intellectuals. To MacIntyre the Bishop was "intensely conservative" in his moral attitudes, and an anonymous reviewer in *The Times* wrote that "it is rather consoling to see how this most latitudinarian of bishops still retains the old Protestant suspicion of fornication."[17] And it is surprising just how much of the New Morality[18] was concerned with matters of sex.

As the new moral crisis grew matters of censure became matters of censorship – and the power of the courts and Her Majesty's Lord Chamberlain were exercised. The correspondence between John Antrobus, Spike Milligan and his Lordship, over *The Bed Sitting Room*, may well be, as Kenneth Tynan termed it, "the strangest single document in the history of theatre censorship."[19] Where twelve good men and true could reach a verdict that might reflect the times or the public interest, as in the case of *Lady Chatterley's Lover*, the Lord Chamberlain's wishes were absolute and arbitrary, never more so than this, which Antrobus recycled as part of his contribution to *That Was The Week That Was*: "Act III, pages 12-13: Omit the song 'Plastic Mac Man' and substitute 'Oh you dirty young devil, how dare you presume to wet the bed when the po's in the room. I'll wallop your bum with a dirty great broom when I get up in the morning.'"[20]

Who, one is forced to wonder, wrote such lines for the Lord Chamberlain? Milligan was also warned, some three years after Peter Cook's prime ministerial address in *Beyond the Fringe*, that representations of the Prime Minister or references to the royal family would not be permitted. There was dignity at the end of the world. Milligan vented his frustration with: "I'm sick. People like the Lord Chamberlain, the people who make the rules, are turning us into a race of zombies. I don't care any more whether the play goes on or not. In fact I'm seriously thinking of leaving this country."[21]

Ghosts that might have been presumed laid to rest at the trial of Lady Chatterley were revived by the seizure and prosecution of John Cleland's eighteenth century romp *Fanny Hill*, in November – or, to be precise, in the prosecution not of its publisher but of a bookseller, a Mr Gold. Reviewing, if that's the word, *Fanny Hill* for the *Observer*, Marghanita Laski engaged with the moral tone and moral target of the times: " . . . we do have to ask what we feel about it in the hands of the young . . . In any normal person it will arouse sexual desire. But it is already normal for sexual desire to be easily aroused in young people, whether corruptly, as I see it, by many advertisements, films, songs, comics, or directly by say, spring or the opposite sex, and because *Fanny Hill*'s appeal is direct, not furtive or covert, I would not call it harmful on this ground. Then because what it has to say about the practices of sex is realistic and true, it could, I think, be helpful rather than harmful."[22]

The court, sitting without a jury, did not agree. *Fanny Hill* went into circulation as a covert, coveted bestreader if not bestseller.

In March Associated-Rediffusion TV presented as a network transmission Harold Pinter's *The Lover*, an original work for television. The play depicts a married couple, played by Alan Badel and Vivien Merchant, whose pretence is that they are illicit lovers. In the *New Statesman* it was described as " . . . an hour of real brilliance . . . spoiled only by some tedious would-be erotic camera work, gloating up and down Vivien Merchant's body inch-by-silk-covered-inch." The *Mirror* referred to the play as "Pinter's plunge into sex on ITV . . . to the less mature it could be a continuous display of erotic emotion, quite meaningless in purpose", while the *Sunday Times* reviewer described it as "the sexiest play I remember seeing on television" adding " . . . it was certainly not pornography". All the same one company chose to opt out of the network. Border TV declined to show *The Lover* as "unsuitable for family viewing". Its broadcast time was nine forty-five in the evening. The most surprising defence of the play was to be found in the pages of the *Catholic Herald* – "I would appoint Harold Pinter Sex Programmes Controller because of his good taste in dealing with his subject."

The moral panic of a nation could be ascribed to sex, as I chronicled in the previous chapter, but, prostitutes and homosexuals excepted, the retribution could hardly be meted out to the sexually immoral. Yet, in the flurry, the speeding up of 1963, the unfolding of the Profumo case, the unravelling of the Macmillan government, the rise to wealth and fame of the immoral (Ian Fleming) or the undeserving (the Beatles, the Stones) there was a scarcely suppressed mood of national retribution lurking in the criticism levelled at such men as the Bishop of Woolwich. God was still Love, Justice was still Retribution. Sex itself was only the most provocative symbol of a moral collapse that began with the slashed cinema seat and ended in nebulous notions, a catechism of cliché: 'respect' – of which no one had any, 'discipline' – which could only be qualified as lax: 'national service' – which should never have been abolished: 'six of the best' – which made me the man I am today – liberally peppered with 'in my day no-one would have dared', while the bold and the bluff could resort to 'two world wars' – in which they fought for the likes of . . . In the *Observer* the Archbishop of Wales, replying to Dr Robinson, spoke for England (and Wales): " . . . Modern man worships gods many and lords many. The vast majority worship the god called Money, using Stock Exchange lists, football pools coupons, bingo cards or betting slips as prayer books. Many worship the transient gods and goddesses of the film world, or the current pop singers. Sex is another popular goddess with a whole range of pornography as the bible of her devotees."[23]

When exactly did the church get out of gilts?

The national decay was caught in compelling terms once again by Harold Pinter in Joseph Losey's film *The Servant* – a screenplay written in 1961, based on Robin Maugham's novel of the late forties, but which, in 1963, found its perfect time. Youth, promise, nobility, wealth are destroyed by a scheming manservant (Dirk Bogarde, cast inventively against type – when first shown the screenplay he had assumed he was being asked to play the victim) who uses sex and drugs to lure the young master (James Fox) into the circles of a modern hell. Since the film was not an expression of the national outrage, it's clear that the young master is responsible for his own downfall – he cannot deploy his wealth, he can only spend it – but then so was Mr Profumo, yet the scapegoats were women and blacks, easy virtue and drugs. At the end of the film the rejected symbol of the 'done thing' (Wendy Craig as the fiancée) has no choice but to turn on her heel and walk away from the waste and corruption, leaving the young master to do it in the street and frighten the horses. As a nation we had better resources. What was needed was a transgression so real, so unambiguous that retribution could be done and seen to be done.

On August 8th such a crime occurred. At around 3 a.m. the Glasgow to London Royal Mail train was stopped by a gang of a dozen men at Linslade in Buckinghamshire and robbed of £2,631,784. This was a record sum, and that alone entitled the crime to the name of The Great Train Robbery, and to the excitement of extensive press and public interest. It became less a matter for the papers, who after all had only to report the facts of the crime and the pursuit of the thieves over the next few weeks, than for a general atmosphere, the sort of conversations overheard in pubs and cafés. Almost at once the crime became seen as in some way romantic, the thieves in the popular imagination in some way admirable. The owner of the farmhouse they had used as their base was reported as saying only a few days later that he planned to open the farm as a tourist attraction. *Life* magazine asked Ian Fleming to write the story of the train robbers – he declined – and Granada restaged the crime for *World in Action* – the rigging of the signals, the stopping of the train, the ambushing of the fireman, the coshing of the driver who was knocked out cold until the robbers had to revive him to drive the train onto a bridge across a road, from which they all escaped with a fortune in used banknotes to the hideaway at Leatherslade Farm. The commentary summed up the robbery as: "All . . . precision and planning." Interviewed afterwards, with his head still bandaged, driver Jack Mills said it was like "an army manoeuvre". It was a short step to unofficial national heroism. Yet, these latter day Robin Hoods, these master criminals, were arrested within a few weeks largely because most of them had left their fingerprints all over Leatherslade Farm and the mail bags in the garden. And the man they knocked senseless did no work at all for the next nine months, never worked again as an engine driver and died only seven years later.

At the trial of the train robbers the following April exemplary sentences were handed out – most of the thieves received thirty years apiece, although the papers, the *Mail* for example, lumped them all together to produce the headline "307 YEARS." And the judge left no doubt that Establishment England took a dim view of the romanticisation of crime: "Let us clear away any romantic notions of daredevilry. This is nothing more than a sordid crime of violence inspired by vast greed. All who have seen that nerve-shattered engine driver can have no doubt of the terrifying effect on law-abiding citizens of a concerted assault of armed robbers. Leniency would be a positively evil thing. When a grave crime is committed it calls for a grave punishment, not for the purpose of mere retribution, but that others similarly tempted will be brought to the realisation that crime does not pay and the game is not worth even the most alluring candle."

The nerve-shattered engine driver was shattered once more: "I'm shattered. I never expected them to get such long sentences. I thought they would be severe, but this has shaken me."[24]

And as for retribution, up and down the land, in the pubs and cafés it was said that the sentences were out of all proportion, criminal in themselves. The *Mirror* raised the matter in a leader, pointing out that the sentence for murder was only fifteen years: "Does this mean that stealing banknotes is regarded as more wicked than murdering somebody? What is the real purpose of punishment

. . . to mete out retribution? To deter others? To reform the criminal?"[25]

Even the robbers, in interviews given since their release, have opined that they took the rap for the state of the nation as represented by the Profumo affair. Buster Edwards, the man who wielded the cosh that ruined the life of Jack Mills, said in one of those tedious, frequent interviews he gave publicising the film version of his life story, that he knew the money involved would attract attention that would be reflected in the sentences if they were caught, but expected nothing like thirty years. He didn't get thirty years himself. He was never caught, and gave himself up in 1966. Again Mills came out to give his evidence, and at the end of his trial Edwards received only fifteen years. Allowing for the effect of his surrender, the disparity in the sentences must reflect a change in the times and a change in the national mood. Even on appeal in 1964, most of the original sentences had been upheld.

With *Fanny Hill* and the train robbers the old morality had found an indirect way of striking back at the new. Heretic priests, sexual intercourse, raucous rockers, sexy plays and mucky books notwithstanding, God was still in his heaven – all might yet be right with the world.

CHAPTER EIGHT

IN THE MIDDLE OF THE BEAST

"The real reason that nonviolence is considered to be a virtue in Negroes – I am not speaking now of its racial value, another matter altogether – is that white men do not want their lives, their self-image, or their property threatened. One wishes they would say so more often."   James Baldwin, 1963[1]

"You North Americans are very lucky. You live in the middle of the beast."   Che Guevara to Jerry Rubin and others, 1964

In January 1963, in the United States, the measure of the Student Non-Violent Co-Ordinating Committee was set by the segregationist lobby which asked HUAC – the House Committee established in the fifties to tackle the bugbear of Communism – for an investigation. By this time SNCC had grown to have an annual budget of $250,000 on which it ran a force of a hundred and twenty field workers, each of whom was paid around $10 a week. The average age was still under twenty-five, and the organisation retained its racial mixture. Their policy had developed into one of putting field workers into communities, working for voter registration, sharing a lifestyle that was often poor and rough – constantly harassed, constantly underfunded. They were evolving into what *Village Voice* writer Jack Newfield called " . . . this battered brotherhood of organisers, poets, hipsters and visionaries . . . unburdened by obsolete blueprints for Utopia from other generations or countries . . . the best of the SNCC workers sound more like teachers or therapists than organisers and agitators."[2]

At the heart of the organisation was a small office over a tailor's shop in Atlanta geared to information and publicity, run by Mary King and Julian Bond. With two phones and a newsletter their task was to see that no Civil Rights action in which SNCC was involved went unreported – most of the time they seemed to be prodding at reluctant media.

"To the national press these were local stories; to the news corps in the region they were not stories at all because of whom they were about – members of the black community . . . few of the big-city southern daily papers . . . carried mention of the stories we were trying to break . . . most of the time neither the AP nor UPI would make any mention of the latest violence."[3]

The development of extensive television coverage helped. If television saw fit to cover an incident it became harder for the press to ignore it, and harder for the line of a single local stringer to become the common story of a national network. With the networks a useful practice was to call the northern office with a story that they could then refer 'from above' to an uninterested local office in the South. There were also countless telephone calls to the FBI and the Justice Department – and telegrams to the Attorney-General and the President.

Few incidents were as 'media friendly' as the Freedom Rides. Much of SNCC's activity was continuity rather than incident, but their work in early 1963 is peppered with confrontation and reprisal. They were active across the South in such places as Albany Georgia, Danville Virginia and Greenwood Mississippi. From 1961 onwards SNCC had kept a constant presence in Mississippi. The town of Greenwood in the cotton belt became a focus of activity in the winter of 1962-3. The Board of Superintendents of LeFlore County cut off the supply of federal aided food to the poor – although the food was free, they claimed they could no longer afford the $37,000 a year it was costing them to distribute it. It was a direct blow against the impoverished black population that was involved in the voter registration drive, and an indirect one at SNCC who were organising the campaign. SNCC found itself simultaneously trying to enfranchise the twenty-seven thousand unregistered Blacks, and cope with growing queues for food. They organised food gathering and distribution from across America. Chicago comedian Dick Gregory raised money and had 14,000 lbs of food airlifted into Memphis, Tennessee and then trucked into Greenwood. By February 20th SNCC were recorded as distributing food to queues six hundred strong. The backlash was almost immediate. On February 28th field worker Jimmy Travis was shot in the head from a moving car. On March 6th the SNCC office was blasted by a shotgun, and on the 24th set ablaze. On the 27th ten members of the SNCC staff in Greenwood were arrested and held for a week. Such situations as Greenwood furthered the politicisation of SNCC, the extension of the struggle from the politics of race to politics per se – which increasingly put them at loggerheads with both the other Movement groups and the Administration.

John Lewis: "Long before we started talking about the voter

registration campaign, back in '61 or '62, we said we were struggling for more than a hamburger and a Coca-Cola.

"There was always tension between SNCC and some of the other groups because we represented the people on the front line. We were in a sense the footsoldiers in a non-violent army. We were there in the Deep South, going where other organisations dare not go. We were always pushing, applying pressure for groups like the NAACP and the Urban League to move further. We had to get Dr King (and CORE from time to time) to come with us."[4]

Part of this tension stemmed from the long term nature of SNCC's commitment – a policy of not withdrawing from a town into which they'd sent their staff until they had succeeded. When Dr King pulled the SCLC out of Albany at the end of 1962, SNCC stayed put. In April the next year, in Birmingham, where the NAACP had been virtually driven out and SNCC had scarcely established themselves, Dr King initiated a campaign that was entirely run by the SCLC. It would attract coverage once again on the scale of the Freedom Rides, and take on the proportions of a national scandal. It was, in a sense, the retaking of active leadership from the younger, more provocative organisation. The targets for direct action were the downtown stores and businesses – to get at the political leadership of Birmingham through the till and the wallet. The strategy rested on the predictability of Bull Connor, the Commissioner of Public Safety, and recently unsuccessful candidate for mayor. Birmingham in 1963 was virtually Connor's personal fiefdom – the city had a record of seventeen unsolved bombings in the six years up to 1963, and its police force was one of the most brutal in the South. The purpose of the campaign – called Project C for Confrontation – was to provoke Connor into a show of force and violence that would shock America. The risks in this were obvious, and James Lawson came to Birmingham to instruct the volunteers in the techniques of non-violence as he had done in Nashville in the late fifties. All volunteers had, by King's own account, to sign a long declaration of their commitment to Christ and non-violence before being accepted. For the best part of a month recruitment was sluggish, marchers moved downtown in dozens rather than hundreds, and the police arrested them without violence. By the end of the month press interest was beginning to wane, and King adopted the most controversial tactic of his life at the suggestion of James Bevel – an SCLC member, but also one of the original Nashville sitters – and the Movement began to recruit not just students but high school kids. The logic of this was that the campaign could finally fill the city jails to the point where no more arrests could be made. The black schools of Birmingham were flooded with leaflets, and on Thursday, May 2nd hundreds of schoolchildren set off in waves from the Sixteenth Street Baptist Church. This day also passed without violence – five hundred were arrested under the gaze of press and television. The next day when the children marched Connor turned his police dogs loose and brought out high pressure water hoses. The photographs of this atrocity were flashed not just around America, but around the world. At close quarters high pressure water can tear flesh, pop eyes and break bones. Children rolled down the streets of Birmingham like broken dolls. Dr King wrote in his account that he had rejected the very young from the ranks of the marchers, but Dick Gregory found himself sharing a cell with a child he estimated to be no older than four. Writing later the same year King still considered that involving children was "one of the wisest moves we made", and although they volunteered in hundreds he still maintained that the Movement had found the time to teach them the philosophy of non-violence. By May 4th the danger that had been inherent from the start began to surface – the Blacks began to fight back. James Bevel took a police bullhorn and appealed for the crowd to disperse, but on the 7th serious fighting broke out.

Dr King's account was written for his book *Why We Can't Wait*, as the essay 'Bull Connor's Birmingham' and probably dates from the summer of 1963. It lacks the power of his contemporary 'Letter from a Birmingham Jail' and it lacks the capacity to convince – there is the blinkered innocence with which he writes of the oath of non-violence, insists on control and then reduces both to meaninglessness with the leaflet campaign of mass recruitment. It becomes impossible to believe in his 'command' in Birmingham. He avoids confronting the consequences of the events he has fostered rather than led. He is inclined to dismiss or disown the violence on the streets – saying that it was the work of people "not trained in the discipline of non-violence", which again begs the question of how he had expected to train and screen people on this scale. The black reaction attracted a lot of attention, in the press, in the Movement and in the White House. Kennedy had sent Burke Marshall to Birmingham on May 4th, after the first such conflict, to bring the two sides together. On the night Mr Marshall succeeded in producing an agreement on desegregation two bombs went off – one at the home of King's brother, A. D. King, and one at the motel where King had been staying. A full-scale riot followed as Blacks fought the police in the streets. Again rather than recognise that this possibility had been an inherent risk in his tactics King chose to

191

ascribe it to "Saturday night drinkers".

At a White House meeting two days later Bobby Kennedy described the scene in Birmingham to his brother, Robert McNamara, Nick Katzenbach and Burke Marshall in a sub-cabinet meeting. The President's analysis is startling: "The group that's gotten out of hand has not been the whites, it's been the Negroes by and large."

This emphasis figures repeatedly in the long discussion that followed. The knowledge that it was black violence, for the first time, was considered in arguments over what federal Civil Rights had been breached, what action could be taken, and how effectively troops could be used. President Kennedy continued: "This could trigger off a good deal of violence around the country now. If they feel that the federal government is their friend we could head some of that off. It's back to the strongest argument of doing something."[5]

More precisely Bobby Kennedy predicted that the black reaction would spread to the cities of the north, with cries of "What's the President doing?" What the President did was to dispatch federal troops to army bases near Birmingham. As Bull Connor's electoral defeat was confirmed by the Alabama Supreme Court, and a new city government took over, Birmingham began to cool, but the black demonstrations spread – to New York, New Jersey, Rhode Island, Ohio, Texas, California, Florida, Missouri, Maryland . . . and on June 14th Bobby Kennedy faced a crowd of three thousand hostile demonstrators at the Justice Department's own building in Washington. These demonstrations were not, by any means, all violent – although the water hoses were out again in Danville – but America had been rocked, the eyes of the world had turned upon her, and the black backlash had proved successful, the white businessmen had responded. Dr King had mastered the art of using television, but he had also strained the limits of non-violence and the example was there, in print and on screen, for every Black in America to see.

In the May 12th meeting Bobby Kennedy had suggested to the President that the situation called for "a strong statement from you". There were reasons why this would have to wait a while.

§

In January 1963 Alabama had sworn in a new Governor – George C. Wallace. Short and stocky, with a wide, wicked curving mouth, he looked like something central casting had dreamt up to occupy Edward G. Robinson for a few weeks, but he became in a matter of months the most potent demagogue the South had seen in several generations. A racial moderate, he had been a Kennedy man as far back as 1956, when he backed JFK in the race for the vice-presidency that Adlai Stevenson had thrown open, and during his time in office he would practise liberal economics, but he had lost to Patterson in 1958 and had vowed, in the parlance of his state, never to be 'outniggered' again. In his move to vociferous racism he quickly learnt never to call a man unprincipled when 'scallawaggin'' would do, and brought the intimate force of the cracker-barrel philosopher and spittoon marksman to the age of television. He made his first stand within seconds of taking office: "Today I have stood where Jefferson Davis stood, and took an oath to my people. It is very appropriate then that from this cradle of the Confederacy, this very heart of the great Anglo-Saxon Southland, that today we sound the drum for freedom . . . in the name of the greatest people that have ever trod this earth, I draw the line in the dust and toss the gauntlet before the feet of tyranny. And I say, Segregation now! Segregation tomorrow! Segregation forever!"

In the campaign he had promised to stand in the door of any school that was threatened with integration. Alabama was by now the only state not to have integrated its state university. In the early spring two black students were cleared for registration and accepted by the University of Alabama authorities at the Tuscaloosa campus. 'Cleared' is literal – the history and records of black applicants were vetted by an Alabama State Detective, answering to Wallace – no white students were so critically examined. The registration of Vivian Malone and James Hood was backed by a federal court order.

Publicly Wallace prepared for a confrontation, and made a show of not taking any calls from Bobby Kennedy; privately he sent messages to the government via Senator Sparkman asking that Alabama be given more time. On April 25th, as the Birmingham campaign escalated, Bobby Kennedy paid him a visit at the Governor's mansion in Montgomery. If the inaugural speech had not revealed the theatrical nature of the new Governor this visit made it inescapable. Wallace had renamed the State Patrol 'State Troopers', and had issued them with white steel helmets emblazoned with the Confederate flag. Bobby Kennedy and Burke Marshall had to walk a line of these storm troopers to Wallace's doorstep, on which Jefferson Davis had been declared President a hundred years before – one of them rapped Kennedy in the stomach with his nightstick with more than playful force.

Kennedy had one purpose in mind, to dissuade Wallace from any

193

opposition to the enrolment of Hood and Malone. Wallace had more complex matters to work around – moving from subject to subject, and feigning deafness when it so suited him – for most of the conversation he avoided any overtly racist remarks, but could not resist taunting Kennedy with the racial problem of the capital: "You don't have [integration] in Washington. Everybody's fled to Virginia. Why don't the government make all them officials come back from Virginia and Maryland and go to school in Washington. Wouldn't that be ah . . . they flee integrated schools?"

In so saying he jibed personally at Kennedy who had made his home at Hickory Hill, Virginia, and emphasised the fact that the federal government had never seen fit to entrust the population of Washington (70% black) with a city government, which lent a slight irony to Kennedy's statement of the, by now familiar, federalist position: "I'm in favour of the people, and the President is, and this administration is, trying to get people to make these decisions, to remedy the situations themselves . . . I just don't want it to get into the streets. I don't want another Oxford, Mississippi, that's all I ask."

At this Wallace homed in on his subject and seized on it like a dog with a bone.

GW: "I don't want another Mississippi myself, but . . . you're going to bring *troops* into Alabama."

RFK: "No, I didn't say that, Governor."

GW: "You didn't? Well you said 'all the *force* of the federal government.'"

RFK: "To make sure that the orders of the court are obeyed."

GW: "But 'all the *force*' includes *troops*, doesn't it?"

RFK: "Well I hope that would stay in the courts and be litigated."

GW: "But it does involve *troops* if the law is not obeyed?"

RFK: "I'm planning and hoping that the law will be obeyed."

GW: "But I mean, if it's not in your interpretation of obedience, you will use *troops*?"

'Another Mississippi' to which both Wallace and Kennedy refer was the shadow that hung over the registration of Hood and Malone from start to finish. What Wallace was doggedly seeking was what Ross Barnett had sought, in countless phone calls to the Justice Department and the White House, and had achieved the previous September. James Meredith had been enrolled at the University of Mississippi only by the use of some five hundred US marshals (again the ad hoc posse) and twenty-three thousand federal troops. Barnett's inevitable defeat at the hands of the courts had been turned into a 'moral' Southern victory by the degree of intervention

194

that had been necessary in enforcing judgment. A riot in which some twenty-nine marshals had been hurt and two people killed had been a Kennedy nightmare and had forced upon them the one move they had wanted to avoid.

Nick Katzenbach: "President Kennedy felt that when Eisenhower sent troops into Little Rock[6] it had been a great mistake, and had caused a lot of resentment. We never wanted federal troops sent in if we could possibly avoid it, because we didn't know how to get 'em out. Once you had federal troops enforcing federal law, how were you ever going to make the transition so that local police would, in the normal course of things, enforce that law?

"[When the State Police left Ole Miss] all hell broke loose – lots of outsiders were coming in. I guess it was squirrel hunting season in Mississippi, there were an awful lot of people with rifles. I kept a line to the President open all night, telling him what was going on – but it was clear – there was shooting and the marshals wanted to use their guns. I wouldn't let them. Then I told the President he'd have to send in the troops, which he did."[7]

In the course of this conversation Katzenbach had relayed the marshals' feelings to the President. Kennedy had authorised them to fire only in protection of Meredith.

Burke Marshall: "I was with the President and Robert Kennedy in the White House when that call came in. From that point of view one could look to the future and think what it would look like if federal marshals fired on a bunch of students and killed someone. That kind of trauma is irremediable. The psychological consequences to the country seemed to them to be intolerable."[8]

On June 5th, 1963 Federal Judge Seybourne H. Lynne issued a personal injunction against Wallace to prevent him obstructing the registration of the students. Avoiding any repeat of scenes at Ole Miss had become of paramount importance to the government. The mistakes had been studied and plans were drawn, redrawn, scrapped and improvised. Katzenbach, going in again as the Justice Department's front line, ordered the campus at Tuscaloosa to be photographed from the air. At Oxford a building under construction had provided bricks to be used as weapons, and not knowing the layout had hampered the marshals. Troops had taken hours to arrive. This time they would be on hand – across the line at Fort Benning in Georgia, according to most White House accounts, or at Vance schoolhouse only miles from Tuscaloosa, according to Wallace's detective Ben Allen – the last resort if used would be used effectively. How quickly the Alabama National Guard could be placed under federal control became the major issue. Wallace had

called the guard out, but they were not on campus. What would
happen if Wallace turned Katzenbach and his two marshals away at
the schoolhouse door and it took a whole day to bring in the guard?
The clash between Wallace and the Kennedy administration, more
than most incidents, reveals the tactical workings of the Justice
Department.

BM: "I think our being turned back by the Governor and letting
that situation exist throughout the country and the world for even
twenty-four hours . . . "

JFK: "All right. Well I don't mind going. Let's go with the
Guard."

RFK: "Well, it's a step – because what we've tried to do is to put
it on his back completely. We're trying to get this worked out."

JFK: "Well, of course he called up the Guard . . . which indicates
that he thinks the situation is very critical. He's produced a situation
which necessitates calling out six hundred guardsmen, I'm therefore, to meet my responsibility, prepared for any situation . . .
because of 'you' [Wallace] we're going to federalise this guard and
so on and so forth . . . he may announce that he's not going to be
responsible for law and order – but that could come any day – then
we would have the guard ready . . . We could just put up with
the twenty-four hours. We could nationalise the Guard in that
period, we could make the speech on television, we could take other
action which would indicate that we are not permitting him to get
away with this line and it's inevitable that we are going to be
successful."[9]

If possible the National Guard was to be brought on campus by
mid-afternoon, within five hours of Wallace's refusal – the risk of
nationalising the guard beforehand was too provocative to be taken.
The government could be seen to react, but not to act, in this
matter. Hence the television coverage of any possible incidents was
also assessed.

RFK: "It's unfortunate that these pictures go abroad. I don't
think there's any question that it affects our position throughout the
world. But that's only a secondary reason for doing what we have to
do. The first reason is that because it's the right thing to do."[10]

If Wallace really did mean to stand in the schoolhouse door (and
in all this planning Wallace remained the unknown quantity) he
would not be given the chance to reject the black students face to
face and certainly not in front of the television cameras.

Behind the scenes the administration drew up its 'Alabama Note-
book' – the names of executives in every Alabama company with
more than three hundred employees. A member of the cabinet

spoke to every one of them – some three hundred and seventy-five people in all. By June 10th – the day before registration – Wallace, so Robert Kennedy claimed, was receiving fifteen to twenty calls a day from local businessmen urging him to avoid trouble. Meanwhile the President hesitated about making 'the strong statement' – a national address on television. His brother urged him on – there was a lot to be gained by it, it would help to convince the Blacks that they were doing something – perhaps convince them that they should in turn recognise their own responsibilities, by which he surely meant, as Lincoln did, that they should 'abstain from all violence'.

At 9.53 on the morning of the 11th, Wallace roared up to the Foster Auditorium at Tuscaloosa with a huge motor cycle escort. One hundred and fifty of his Confederate-style State Troopers sealed off the building. Over the telephone, Katzenbach outlined his plan to both Marshall and Kennedy: "He won't step aside, he'll be carried off by soldiers . . . I've every indication that he'll drama-tise to that group of reporters and that crowd the fact that he's been forcibly removed. The alternative is simply that we reduce going through that door to nothing, and they start attending classes. Now the Governor simply cannot block all those classes . . . The only danger with that plan – and it's one that ought to be weighed – is that the Governor's resentment at being made a fool of will be such that he will move way over to the segregationist side and make life much more difficult and dangerous in the future. Of course that might happen anyhow."

Shortly afterwards Kennedy obtained the reassurances he needed from National Guard General Graham – the guardsmen could be on campus in a matter of a few hours – and at some point Graham conveyed to Katzenbach Wallace's message that if he could just make his speech there would be 'no problem'. Kennedy and Katzenbach finalised the plan. Katzenbach had obtained keys to the dormitories with a bluff about 'security reasons'. He would let Wallace turn him down, then he would take the students to their dormitories and return later with the National Guard. Kennedy advised that Wallace shouldn't be allowed "to make a stage pro-duction out of it". Yet this was precisely what Wallace had in mind. Outside the schoolhouse door his theatrical prop, a lectern, was set up. Inside Wallace repeatedly asked his staff "Do you really think they mean to arrest me?" – which feeds speculation that word of Judge Lynne's intention of jailing Wallace not for a token forty-eight hours but for a minimum of six months had reached the Governor.

Kennedy gave last minute advice to Katzenbach: "Almost dismiss him as being rather a second rate figure for you – he's wasting your time, he's wasting the students' time, he's caused a big scene up there . . ."

At 10.48 a.m. Katzenbach arrived with the students, Deputy Assistant Attorney-General John Doar and the US Marshal and US Attorney for Alabama. Leaving the students behind, Katzenbach emerged from his car with his suit creased, feeling hot and tired, already sweating in the ninety-eight degree heat – "He stood me in the sun, while he stood in the shade. I resented that . . . I'd been up all night" – and walked the row of State Troopers towards Wallace. Wallace stopped him with a raised hand, a theatrical gesture like a traffic cop. Katzenbach at six foot two and two hundred pounds towered over Wallace and seemed to be stooping just to catch Wallace's words – although Wallace had been wired for sound to make sure no one missed a syllable.

NK: "I'm asking from you an unequivocal statement that you will not bar entry to these students, Vivian Malone and James Hood, and that you will step aside peacefully and do your constitutional duty as Governor."

GW: "I have a statement to read. As Governor and Chief Magistrate of the state of Alabama I deem it my obligation and duty to stand before you representing the rights and sovereigntry [sic] of this state and its peoples."

Wallace spoke for eight minutes, largely on sovereignty, that last refuge of a despot. There is a photograph (by now surely a famous photograph?) of Katzenbach listening patiently, arms folded, as Wallace speaks his piece over the lectern. Patience? Boredom, musing, perhaps a combination of the two, but I cannot presume that the Deputy Attorney-General's stance indicated patience. Seeking clarity on the matter of law I asked Nick Katzenbach, "Was there a word of truth in Wallace's speech to you?" "I don't know," Katzenbach replied, "I wasn't listening."

Wallace ended on: " . . . I do hereby denounce and forbid this illegal and unwarranted action by the central Government."

NK: "Governor I'm not interested in a show. I don't know what the purpose of this show is. I'm interested in the orders of the court being enforced. That is my only responsibility here. I ask you once again – *the choice is yours* – there is no choice that the United States government has in this but to see that the lawful orders of the courts are enforced . . . it is a simple problem scarcely worth this kind of attention in my judgment . . . From the outset, Governor, all of us have known that the final chapter of this will be the admission of these students."

Wallace stayed put – silently. Katzenbach walked off with Vivian Malone, keeping the press guessing about their destination until they reached the door of the dormitory block.

By 3.30 p.m. the National Guard was under federal control and on campus with a force of some hundred men. The State Troopers began to shout "Yankee go home!" General Graham faced Wallace in the doorway, informing him of his "sad duty". Wallace continued to posture for a minute longer, saying "I am still your commander in chief" and deploring the "trend towards military dictatorship" – but at 3.35 he simply stepped aside as he must have known he would do all along, and was off the campus before Malone and Hood were registered only a few minutes later.

Even before Wallace had stepped aside spokesmen for the Justice Department were defining the incident to the *Washington Post* – Wallace did not obstruct them, there would be no citation for contempt, no use of the army. There was a distinction, however improvised, between letting Wallace save face and making any kind of martyr. Wallace's speech seemed empty, posturing – the rhetoric rather than the stuff of opposition. He didn't and couldn't resist or refuse – he could merely state his dissent. Hence it scarcely seemed necessary for Katzenbach to listen to him:

"It was a distasteful show – he was using it for political purposes we could not sympathise with. The night before I'd said to Bobby, 'Why are we going through with this charade? – the kids can be registered without that – they can start going to classes – the court can just order them *as* registered.' Bobby said, and I think he was absolutely right, 'If we don't give him this day, this show, then I think there'll be a real danger of violence.'"[11]

It's an argued point that what the administration had learnt from Ole Miss was not how to win in confrontation but how to avoid confrontation.[12] At Tuscaloosa not only was there no violence, there was no visible confrontation (despite the presence of television cameras) between black and white – and even the presentation of Hood and Malone in this limited way had been screened; John Doar telling them to dress like it was Sunday, and the NAACP coaching them in what to say to the press. In such avoidance the administration was helped by Wallace's own demagoguery, his theatrical swagger – a natural braggart eventually hoist with his own petard. He could not fail to offer defiance to Katzenbach, but nor could he accept the humiliation of being physically tossed aside (according to his detective, Ben Allen, troops at Vance had rehearsed this very action)[13], neither of which need have troubled him had he not asserted repeatedly that *he* would stand in the schoolhouse door. Although precisely what Wallace would do remained unknown until he did it, Katzenbach had no doubts about the outcome. Had not Wallace placed himself so firmly in the limelight victory might not have been so easy. On the other hand, defeat did no harm to Wallace's political prospects. His parting shot to a documentary film crew: "The South will decide who the next President is, because you cain't win without the South and you gonna see the South's gonna be agin some folks."

Agin some folks, but for Wallace. In 1968 Wallace ran for President.

§

Much depended on the outcome of the Tuscaloosa crisis. The President did not decide until the last minute whether he would make his television broadcast – whether it would be explaining violence or welcoming a peaceful resolution, or whether it would mention the new omnibus Civil Rights Bill he now proposed to send to Congress. Burke Marshall and the Attorney-General had been working on the bill since the middle of May – but in the first week of June as national disturbances followed the bombing in Birmingham the President had told his team that the bill should be held over until after Tuscaloosa. At about 6 p.m. on June 11th the Kennedys, Marshall and speech writer Ted Sorensen met in the cabinet room with only an hour to go before broadcast. Sorensen wrote as the Kennedys threw out ideas, with Kennedy himself making notes, since he intended to improvise parts of the speech. A few minutes before the President went on the air, Sorensen was able to hand him a draft speech – all the same Kennedy improvised his own conclusion.

"The Negro baby born in America today, regardless of the section of the Nation into which he is born, has about one half as much chance of completing high school as a white baby born in the same place on the same day, one third as much chance of completing college, one third as much chance of becoming a professional man, twice as much chance of becoming unemployed, about one seventh as much chance of earning $10,000 a year, a life expectancy which is seven years shorter, and the prospects of earning only half as much.

"We are confronted primarily with a moral issue. It is as old as the scriptures and is as clear as the American Constitution.

"The heart of the question is whether all Americans are to be afforded equal rights and equal opportunities, whether we are going to treat our fellow Americans as we want to be treated. If an American, because his skin is dark, cannot eat lunch in a restaurant open to the public, if he cannot send his children to the best public school available, if he cannot vote for the public officials who represent him, if, in short, he cannot enjoy the full and free life which all of us want, then who among us would then be content with the counsels of patience and delay?

"One hundred years of delay have passed since President Lincoln freed the slaves, yet their heirs, their grandsons, are not fully free. They are not yet freed from the bonds of injustice. They are not yet freed from social and economic oppression, and this nation, for all its hopes and all its boasts, will not be fully free until all its citizens are free.

"We preach freedom around the world, and we mean it, and we cherish our freedom at home, but are we to say to the world and much more importantly, to each other that this is a land of the free except for the Negroes; that we have no class or caste system, no ghettos, no master race except with respect to the Negroes?

"Now the time has come for this nation to fulfil its promise. The events in Birmingham and elsewhere have so increased the cries for equality that no city, no state or legislative body can prudently choose to ignore them.

"The fires of frustration and discord are burning in every city North and South, where legal remedies are not at hand. Redress is sought in the streets, in demonstrations, parades and protests which create tensions and threaten violence and threaten lives.

"We face, therefore, a moral crisis as a country and as a people. It cannot be met by repressive police action. It cannot be left to increased demonstrations in the streets. It cannot be quieted by token moves or talk. It is time to act in the Congress, in your state and local legislative body, and, above all, in all of our daily lives."

This speech, of which the above is only the central piece, has long been acclaimed Kennedy's finest. It offered, at last, the moral leadership his election had promised. There's probably less of Sorensen in it than was the practice – certainly less of his symmetrical aphorisms – but Sorensen's memoir well sums up the speech's quality and impact:

" . . . It drew on three years of evolution in his thinking, on at least three months of revolution in the equal rights movement . . . but the moving force of that address was the unequivocal commitment of John Fitzgerald Kennedy, his office and his country to the proposition that race has no place in American life or law."[14]

Whilst well received, this speech is undeniably less well known than the 'Ich Bin Ein Berliner' speech that followed a month later. After Kennedy's mistimed speech during the Ole Miss crisis – mistimed in that he had gone on the air thinking the situation had been brought under control, only to have it get worse as he spoke – maverick Washington columnist I. F. Stone had asked in his *I.F.'s Weekly*: "When's the President Going to Mention Racism?"[15] The President mentioned it soon enough, in the long, carefully detailed address to Congress that accompanied his February 1963 Bill on Voting Rights and Equal Employment.[16] Stone's other main criticism bears further examination: "this stale cold war rhetoric was offensive on so serious an occasion" – by which Stone meant " . . . healing these wounds that are within, we can turn to the greater crises that are without, and stand united as one people in our pledge to man's freedom."

In this is a strong pointer to the mixed philosophical basis of John F. Kennedy and his times. Too easily the most well meaning and most moral of stances is collapsed into cold war posturing. In the February 1963 speech the issues of Civil Rights and Cold Wars seemed inseparable in his mind: "Race discrimination . . . hampers our world leadership by contradicting at home the message we preach abroad" – as though the validity of the issue in its own pressing terms cannot be fully admitted. Nor is the June 11th speech free of this mental clutter: "Today we are committed to a worldwide struggle to promote and protect the rights of all who wish to be free, and when Americans are sent to Viet Nam or West Berlin, we do not ask for whites only" – which must seem savagely ironic in the light of subsequent policies which clearly favoured the wasting of black lives rather than white in futile defence of what Noam Chomsky calls America's Fifth Freedom. In its way the more polished, less spontaneous speech in Berlin that July was a more accurate, less confused reflection of the Administration's thinking – and its effect on the people of Berlin cannot be doubted. Yet how much more effective would the June 11th speech have been if its spontaneity had been matched in the choice of location, if Kennedy had spoken not only on the medium of which he was master, but to a live audience on racism's front line – somewhere south of the Mason-Dixon line? Macmillan, after all, had made his Wind of Change speech in South Africa. Significantly Lyndon Johnson, the highest placed Southerner in the administration, opposed the speech.

"If he made a commitment in Jackson, Mississippi 'it would be worth a hell of a lot more than it would in Harlem.'"[17] (Johnson expressed this only to Sorensen, but that's hardly surprising.)[18]

The Berlin speech is Kennedy drawing the line in the sand, just like Wallace, but on the world scale – saying he who oppresses the free German oppresses me. The Civil Rights problem demanded no less. A President of the United States could, as I think Johnson's remark implied, have made a better identification with the oppressed of his own country. Even his inaugural speech, so startling at the time in the power of its oratory, reads, twenty-five years later, like another piece of cold war bombast. Nowhere does it mention the problems of race and Civil Rights, unless it be that "those people in the huts and villages across the globe struggling to break the bonds of misery" to whom the new President pledged his best efforts be construed to refer also to the poor of his own country. The rhetoric, the remorseless illogic of the Cold War dogged Kennedy, even at his best. He seemed, as Stone put it less than a month after the inauguration, to have "a weakness for seeing an Armageddon everywhere".[19]

The speech went on to outline briefly the provisions of the new bill:

"I am, therefore, asking Congress to enact legislation giving all Americans the right to be served in facilities which are open to the public – hotels, restaurants, theatres, retail stores and similar establishments.

" . . . to authorise the federal government to participate more fully in lawsuits designed to end segregation in public education.

"Other features will also be requested, including greater protection of the right to vote."

Robert Kennedy is adamant in the 1964 Lewis interview that his brother's awareness of Civil Rights was active, and was not, as had often been said, merely awoken by events in Birmingham. I've no doubts that this is true, but the case made by RFK that only now, after Birmingham, were the American people ready to support legislation needs examination. They were ready, by the Attorney-General's account, because they had been exposed to unacceptable violence by the TV coverage of Birmingham – but there'd been two years of televised violence, almost all of it white on black.[20] Did John Kennedy decide that the people had decided only when TV showed them black violence? (Which his speech seems to indicate by repeated references.) In which case, it would seem as though white America was indifferent to white violence and responded to the threat of black reprisal rather than to injustice itself, and unfortunately for the Movement, that non-violence was less effective than violence, direct action less effective than reaction – in which case there was a dreadful lesson for the late sixties here.

A few hours after Kennedy finished his broadcast NAACP field worker Medgar Evers, a man described by co-workers as being as important to Blacks in Mississippi as King was to the Movement as a whole, was shot in the back by a sniper outside his home in Jackson, Mississippi. There had been many murders in the history of the Movement, but this was assassination, the first in the wave of political assassinations that eventually claimed the lives of both Kennedys, Martin Luther King, Malcolm X and Lincoln Rothwell and put George Wallace in a wheelchair for the rest of his life. (No one was successfully brought to trial for the killing of Medgar Evers, although the chief suspect was twice charged – by the time of writing [May 1991] the same suspect had been charged for a third time and was in jail in Tennessee awaiting extradition.) Any thoughts the President might have had that the black backlash was over vanished. The week following the death of Medgar Evers saw a continuation of demonstrations that merged seamlessly into the aftermath of Birmingham.

In July SNCC organised a folk concert in Greenwood – the Freedom Singers came from Georgia – Theodore Bikel, Pete Seeger and someone reported in the *New York Times* as Bobby Dillon came from the north.

"They sang in the yard of a Negro farm home on the edge of a cotton patch three miles south of [Greenwood] . . . The festival was attended by 250 to 300 persons. Most of them were Negroes. There were a score or more of young white people, plus several white newsmen and a television camera crew of four white men from New York."[21]

Folk was begetting a new genre. The protest song grew out of the Civil Rights Movement. Some of the footage shot by the camera crew ended up in D. A. Pennebaker's film *Don't Look Back*. Dylan sings his protest on the death of Medgar Evers, *Only a Pawn in Their Game*, behind him stand black farm workers in straw hats and dungarees, looking slightly perplexed by it all, looking as though time has not moved on in this Mississippi cotton patch since the turn of the century.

Privately Kennedy said many times that the new bill might cost him the North – the South being, as Burke Marshall said, already lost – and that it might be his political swan-song. The following day he met with Ike. Ike declined to talk to the press, but the *Washington Post* quoted him as saying that "passing a whole bunch of laws" would not solve the problem – but then he had said throughout his presidency that 'you can't legislate for the minds of men', something Kennedy could not afford to believe. Rumour had it that

Ike was advising his party not to vote for the bill – and Senator Russell (Democrat – Georgia) promised a filibuster, saying he was "shocked to hear the President justify if not encourage the present wave of mass demonstrations."[22] In a series of meetings over the next few weeks the President and the Attorney-General, rallying support for their bill, saw over fifteen hundred people – from the Republican Party, without whose co-operation the bill could not possibly succeed, from their own liberal wing, from the clergy, the Movement, the unions and from business. There's a distinct hint of judicious blackmail in Robert Kennedy's own account of meetings with the businessmen: "There was going to be more violence . . . because the students were getting out of school for the summer. They were the ones who were going to be actively involved . . . If we could get the businessmen and the community leaders to take action and desegregate . . . then the chance for these kind of disorders would be greatly lessened"[23] – which sounds very like 'If you don't deal with us you'll have to deal with them.' Which was accurate.

Arguably, the first of these sessions was held a little earlier, on May 24th at the Kennedy apartment in New York. Burke Marshall and Bobby Kennedy met, at Kennedy's own request, with 'prominent' Blacks – James Baldwin, Dr Kenneth Clark, Lorraine Hansberry, Harry Belafonte and Lena Horne among them. Also present was a young veteran of the first Freedom Ride, CORE worker Jerome Smith. His anger expressed itself in the terms that seemed current – Baldwin had, after all, only recently published his apocalyptic message for the sons of Ham and the sons of Cain:

"If we do not now dare everything, the fulfilment of that prophecy, recreated from the Bible in song by a slave, is upon us: God gave Noah the rainbow sign, No more water the fire next time!"[24]

By Baldwin's own account and by Burke Marshall's, Smith talked of the prospect of armed resistance by Blacks in the South, and his anger fired up everyone else, and Kennedy in turn grew angry at their anger.[25] In the 1964 interview he speculated on the rich Blacks "having complexes about the fact that they've been successful" whereas Smith had so clearly suffered for the cause. To a degree Lena Horne's account supports this view: "You could not encompass [Smith's] anger, his fury in a set of statistics, nor could Mr Belafonte and Dr Clark and Miss Horne, the fortunate Negroes who had never been in a southern jail, keep up the pretence of being the mature, responsible spokesmen for the race any more."[26]

If meeting Smith's fury was Kennedy's low point in his long relationship with the Movement then it seems most unlikely that he didn't know it and the reason why: "Careful explanations of the historic limitations on the federal government's police powers are not satisfactory to the parents of students who have vanished in Mississippi, or to the widow of a Negro educator shot down without any reason by night-riders in Georgia."[27]

As Navasky put it, "During his years as Attorney-General, Robert Kennedy's popularity with the Civil Rights Movement was inversely proportional to his deepening involvement and commitment."[28]

But there is also the view of Baldwin himself. He was quoted as saying of Robert Kennedy: "He didn't get the point. He was naïve. He doesn't know pain. He just doesn't know."[29]

On June 22nd most of the Civil Rights leaders gathered at the White House. Prominent among them was A. Philip Randolph, founding president of the Brotherhood of Sleeping Car Porters, then well into his seventies, tall, white-haired, distinguished, the elder statesman of the Movement, looking, as Burke Marshall said, like God. In 1941 he had challenged Roosevelt over discrimination in the defence industry, saying he would lead a 100,000 strong march on Washington. Roosevelt met him by setting up the short-lived Fair Employment Practices Commission, something now mooted again with the new bill – Randolph revived his idea too.

John Lewis: "The first mention of the march itself that I can recall came from A. Philip Randolph at [that] meeting in the East Room of the White House – a meeting with Martin Luther King Jr, Whitney Young, Roy Wilkins, James Farmer and me, representing SNCC. During a discussion with President Kennedy about what was going on in the South, Mr Randolph said, 'Mr President' – in his baritone voice – 'the masses are restless, and we're going to have to march on Washington.' That was the first time that somebody said something *serious* about the possibility of a march on Washington. At that point, I think, in that group, the march became an unofficial plan – there'd been no former discussion among the people who called the march, but Mr Randolph was so respected, the Dean of Black leadership, that when he spoke all the other members of the so-called leadership tended to listen.

"The purpose of the march was to dramatise to the President, to the Congress, to the American people the need for a strong Civil Rights Act – but it was not in support of any particular piece of legislation.

"One reason that pushed us was that President Kennedy had a real problem with the idea of a march. He said, in effect, he didn't think it was a good idea – he couldn't see how it would be orderly or peaceful. 'If you bring all those folks to Washington how are you going to control them – they'll get out of hand, there'll be disorder, there'll be violence.' There'd be a [congressional] backlash."[30]

Also present was that assiduous note taker, Arthur Schlesinger, who records Randolph's eloquent answer to Kennedy's complaint. "The Negroes are already in the streets. It is very likely impossible to get them off . . . is it not better that they be led by organisations dedicated to Civil Rights and disciplined by struggle rather than leave them to other leaders who care neither about Civil Rights nor about non-violence?"[31]

The march was planned for August 28th, just before Congress broke for the Labor Day holiday. Since the administration could not stop it, they chose to back it. The march committee appointed Harlem Civil Rights worker, and veteran of the first Aldermaston march, Bayard Rustin as deputy to Randolph and march organiser, but Bobby Kennedy appointed Assistant Attorney-General John Douglas to organise from their side, with a brief to play down the administration's worries about the potential for violence. The involvement of the government this closely, and their 'approval' of the march, has become as contentious as it might have been had they continued to oppose it.

America is fond of ballyhoo. A gathering can be turned into a parade with remarkable ease. It needs only three men in shirt-tails and waistcoats, a fife, a drum, a flag and a few bandages. It's one of the ways in which an essentially conservative nation can harmlessly remind itself of its once radical origins. A change of ownership mistaken for a revolution. It can also gut serious protest by over-organisation, by the excision of meaning and the levelling of spontaneity. More than fifteen hundred extra buses were laid on, twenty-one special trains, and the man 'counting the cars on the New Jersey turnpike' estimated some sixteen thousand people had headed out of New York for Washington by 3 a.m. on Wednesday August 28th. The expected one hundred thousand marchers rose rapidly to a quarter of a million. If Mr Rustin had rallied the people, Mr Douglas had laid on the loos . . .

"Talk about 'integrated'! It was like salt and pepper and . . . there wasn't a single logistics aspect uncontrolled.

"The marchers had been instructed to bring no signs – signs were provided. They had been told to sing one song, 'We Shall Overcome.' They had been told *how* to arrive, *when*, *where* to arrive, *where* to assemble, when to *start* marching, the *route* to march. First aid stations were strategically located – even where to *faint*!"[32]

New Yorkers worked through the night preparing eighty

thousand 50 cent lunches, to be shipped south in refrigerated trucks. As bus loads of Blacks poured in from the Deep South, and planes jetted in the famous from Hollywood, it looked as though all America would be represented – including those who had been officially excluded. A permit to parade had been refused to Lincoln Rothwell and his American Nazi Party – at 6 a.m. seventy-five neo-Nazis gathered at the Washington Monument, the starting point for the march, only to be moved on and penned for the day by a squad of two hundred police and national guards. These were but a drop in the ocean – nearly six thousand police, guards and marshals were on duty – and four thousand marines were put on standby at bases just outside the city. The operation, from the Justice Department's side, was as smooth as Tuscaloosa, but beset by the same fears. Tuscaloosa was not to be another Ole Miss or Birmingham – nor was Washington.

The threat of counter-demonstration popped up sporadically. In Austin, Texas, Governor Connolly asked the White Citizens Council not to march – they remained defiant in their words, and eleven people showed up. In Burbank, California, a hundred neo-Nazis attended a demonstration, and in Washington itself Malcolm X held a news conference in the Statler Hilton hotel, denouncing the march as "The Farce on Washington – seeking favours from the white man's government."

From nine till eleven, the leaders of the march visited the majority and minority leaders on Capitol Hill. Randolph stated the case for a stronger bill than the one presently stuck as HR 7512 in Representative Emmanuel Celler's House Judiciary Sub-Committee. Afterwards Celler was non-committal in his comments, as were Senators Mansfield and Dirksen.

The cool summer morning began to warm up as the marchers gathered at the Washington monument for 'freedom singing' – the temperature would soon rise to the mid-eighties and some 2000 people would need to know where to faint. Halfway through Bobby Darin's song, the march began to drift towards the Lincoln Memorial, at the opposite end of the long, Taj Mahal reflecting pool. The *Washington Post* noted that the march had started ten minutes early "with a sizeable portion of the crowd upsetting programme plans by getting in front of the ten March leaders. Some saw this as symbolic of the Negro movement for Civil Rights today."[33] However, the television cameras had no difficulty picking out Dr King or Mr Randolph. CBS, NBC and ABC all carried live coverage and a satellite link via Telstar II took the pictures into seventy-two countries, Moscow withdrawing from the link-up at the last minute. It was hailed as the biggest TV spectacular since the inauguration. Among those watching 'at home' was the President of the United States. Often in the previous months he had been asked to make a personal appearance for Civil Rights – Tuscaloosa being only the most obvious example – but of the Kennedy memoirists only Sorensen reports that he was asked on this occasion, and he does not say by whom. His afternoon was kept free, as though he intended to watch the Lincoln part of the march, but in the morning he had attended a White House meeting about a small country, on the other side of the planet, called Viet Nam, in which the secret police of Ngo Dinh Diem had taken to military attacks on Buddhist temples and the monks had demonstrated by turning themselves into human torches. It was becoming impossible for the USA to support the regime any longer.[34]

The march assumed a holiday air. On the podium erected in front of the vast memorial to the Great Emancipator, the Freedom Singers, Joan Baez and Peter, Paul and Mary sang *Blowin' In The Wind*, Bob Dylan's alternative anthem for the Movement. Dylan himself performed *Only a Pawn in Their Game* and marchers paddled in the reflecting pool, an action that I suspect would be considered irreverent on any other occasion. Some seventy-five or so Congressmen attended for the speeches – among them three future presidential hopefuls, Senators McGovern, Humphrey and Eugene McCarthy. Roy Wilkins of the NAACP said it was "like a Yankees game", Dick Gregory recalled that it was a picnic, "whitey expected violence and he had a picnic on his hands."[35] Hollywood's representatives appeared – Moreno, Heston, Brando, Newman – Burt Lancaster read a statement from fifteen hundred people in Europe and Harry Belafonte read a statement on behalf of actors. Josephine Baker appeared before the crowd, wearing her Free French uniform and the Légion d'honneur, and once Marion Anderson had sung the national anthem the speeches began. As the Catholic Archbishop of Washington, Patrick O'Boyle, read his invocation a small huddle of people met next to Lincoln's statue and argued over the problem the man now speaking had posed for them. O'Boyle had threatened to get up and leave if John Lewis, the chairman of SNCC, gave his speech as written. Lewis's speech was the only one of the eleven to offer direct criticism of the government – O'Boyle wanted it changed and wanted to see a fresh draft before Lewis went on.

John Lewis: "On the evening of the 27th, Julian Bond, the communications director for SNCC, made advance copies available to the march leaders. Several hours later I received a knock at the door of my hotel room – saying 'Come downstairs to a meeting – we have a problem with your speech.'

"Part of the speech people had concern about was the use of the words 'revolution' and masses,' It was too inflammatory, too social-istic. A. Philip Randolph came to my rescue – said 'there's nothing wrong with the use of 'revolution' and 'masses.' I use them myself sometimes.'

"In the original text I said 'With good conscience we cannot support the administration's proposed Civil Rights Bill. It is too little and too late.' There was nothing in the bill that would protect old women and young children involved in peaceful non-violent protest. That was changed to 'We support the bill, however with reservation.'

"[The next day] there were several people – James Foreman, Courtland Cox, A. Philip Randolph, Dr King, Roy Wilkins – all sort of sitting there. I had written 'Patience is a dirty word. We cannot be patient.' I think it was Bayard Rustin who suggested I should drop this – because it may offend the Catholic church. It was the Catholic Archbishop of Washington who'd said he'd refuse to give the invo-cation if I didn't change my speech. We later learnt that it was the Kennedy administration which, in a sense, was using the Arch-bishop, getting him to take this position, but there were other people within the march leadership who were siding with the admin-istration.

"We worked there – on a portable typewriter – to the side of Mr Lincoln. While the programme was held up, while the people were singing, there were people saying 'Can we drop this, can we change that?' I remember shaking my finger at Roy Wilkins and saying 'Mr Wilkins, this is my speech. It represents the feelings of the people we've been working with in the Student Nonviolent Co-ordinating Committee. I have a right to deliver my speech, you have a right to deliver yours.' That's the only time I got . . . not angry . . . a little incensed. A. Philip Randolph said 'John, we've come this far to-gether. For the sake of unity can we change this?'"

It is significant that John Lewis, twenty-three-year-old veteran of the Movement, with twenty-four spells in jail behind him, the gentlest and most pacifist of men, a former divinity student, should be cast in the role of 'hothead and a quasi revolutionary'. The reality is more closely revealed in his conceding not to the political postur-ing of O'Boyle or Wilkins or to the clandestine pressure of the government, but to the elder statesman of his Movement who'd waited all his life for the unity of a march on Washington. Randolph was the first speaker after Cardinal O'Boyle. He delivered a tough speech, asking for a social and economic programme:

"It falls to us also to demand new forms of social planning to create full employment . . . we have taken our struggle into the streets as the labor movement did. Until we went into the streets the Federal Government was indifferent to our demands . . . look to the enemies of Medicare, of higher minimum wages, of social security . . . there you will find the enemy of the Negro . . . "

Lewis's speech, even in its revised version, is a blast: "We march today for jobs and freedom, but we have nothing to be proud of. For hundreds and thousands of our brothers are not here. They have no money for their transportation, for they are receiving starvation wages . . . or no wages at all. While we stand here, there are sharecropppers in the Delta of Mississippi who are out in the fields working for less than three dollars a day for twelve hours of work. While we stand here, there are students in jail on trumped up charges. Our brother, James Farmer, along with many others is also in jail. We come here today with a great sense of misgiving . . . Do you know that in Albany, Georgia, nine of our leaders have been indicted, not by Dixiecrats but by the federal government for peaceful protest?[36] But what did the federal government do when Albany's Deputy Sheriff beat Attorney C. B. King and let him go half dead? What did the federal government do when local officials kicked and assaulted the pregnant wife of Slater King and she lost her baby?

" . . . All of us must get in this great social revolution sweeping our nation. Get in and stay in the streets of every city, every village and every hamlet of this nation, until true freedom comes, until the unfinished revolution of 1776 is complete. In the Delta of Mississippi, in southwest Georgia, in Alabama, Harlem, Chicago, Detroit, Philadelphia and all over this nation – the black masses are on the march. You must go home from this march and help us to get our freedom.

"We will not stop now. All the forces of Eastland, Barnett, Wallace and Thurmond will not stop this revolution. If we do not get meaningful legislation out of this Congress, the time will come when we will march through the South – through the streets of Jackson, Danville, Cambridge, Nashville and Birmingham – with the dignity and spirit we have shown here today. By the force of our demands, our determination, and our numbers, we shall splinter the segregated South into a thousand pieces and put them back together in the image of God and democracy. Wake up America!"

Next on was Walter Reuther of the Auto Workers' Union. At a time when organised labour was still sceptical of the Movement (the

AFL-CIO had declined to endorse the march) Reuther had been among the leading white supporters of Civil Rights[37] and had worked to ensure that the march was integrated. Estimates interpret the 'salt and pepper' tag, so often applied, as indicating that approximately a quarter of the crowd was white. His speech received very loud applause:

"If we fail the vacuum created by our failure will be filled by the apostles of hatred . . . and the spirit of brotherhood will yield to bitterness and bloodshed." In so saying Reuther seemed to utter what the administration was collectively thinking. Reuther had been instrumental as a mediator between O'Boyle and the Civil Rights leaders over the Lewis speech. Reuther was followed by Floyd McKissick, reading a letter from James Farmer of CORE, who was in a Louisiana jail with "231 other Freedom Fighters". Like Lewis and Randolph, Farmer also pursued the problem of equality in economic terms:

"We will not slow down, we will not stop our militant pacifist demonstrations. We will not come off the streets until we can work at any job befitting our skills . . . until our kids have enough to eat and their minds can study without being cramped in Jim Crow schools."

In the middle of the afternoon the crowd, according to the *New York Times*, grew restless and began to drift off. Gospel singer Mahalia Jackson seized their attention with *I've been 'buked and I've been scorned*. Sometime after 3 p.m. Randolph stepped out onto the podium and introduced "the moral leader of the nation", Dr Martin Luther King Jr. King was what the crowd had been waiting for, and most likely the viewer in the White House too. Where Lewis had the potential to alarm, King could do the opposite. He could skilfully align the Blacks not with revolution, but with the mainstream of American history. Kicking off with a reference to Lincoln was only the first move in this alignment: "Five score years ago . . . " is a deliberate echo of the opening sentence of the Gettysburg address, a deliberate pacifier for the words that follow, in which King says much the same things that Lewis and Farmer had said, pointing out, in his own way, the plight of the Black in "the midst of a vast ocean of material prosperity" he cannot share – and warning of the price that will have to be paid if justice is delayed – "the whirlwinds of revolt will continue to shake the foundations of our nation until the bright day of justice emerges." It is a less direct, more poetic language than Lewis used, and less provocative for such imagery. Halfway through King began to improvise around words and themes he had used in previous speeches, and the power of his ecstatic oratory and his soaring voice combined with his masterly use of the language and images of the American myth:

" . . . I still have a dream. It is a dream deeply rooted in the American meaning of its creed, 'We hold these truths to be self-evident, that all men are created equal.' . . . I have a dream that my four little children will one day live in a nation where they will not be judged by the color of their skin, but by the content of their character."

One of King's biographers, Stephen B. Oates, records that the crowd were crying out "Dream some More!" On the other hand John A. Williams reports hearing a dissenting "Fuck that dream, Martin. Now, goddammit. NOW!"[38] The most noted response was "Tell us! Tell us!"

The beauty of King's technique is that it was a Kennedy technique. King did what Kennedy had done in 1961, he accused America much less than he *challenged* it.

"This will be the day when all of God's children will be able to sing with new meaning, 'My country 'tis of thee sweet land of liberty, of thee I sing. Land where my fathers died, land of the pilgrim's pride, from every moutainside let freedom ring.' And if America is to be a great nation, this must become true."

And with this King launched into a geography of patriotism and his reputation soared into history.

"So let freedom ring from the prodigious hilltops of New Hampshire, let freedom ring from the mighty mountains of New York, let freedom ring from the heightening Alleghenies of Pennsylvania, let freedom ring from the snow-capped Rockies of Colorado, let freedom ring from the curvaceous slopes of California. But not only that. Let freedom ring from Stone Mountain of Georgia, let freedom ring from Lookout Mountain of Tennessee" – and when America ran out of mountains – "Let freedom ring from every hill and molehill of Mississippi. From every mountainside let freedom ring.

" . . . When all God's children join hands and sing in the words of the old Negro spiritual: 'Free at last. Free at last. Thank God Almighty, we are free at last.'"

Dr King had told the 250,000 strong crowd and the watchers across the nation, *the black man is not only black, he is American*. He had not simply wrapped himself in the flag, he had enfolded the movement in the red, white and blue. Up on Pennsylvania Avenue the President turned from the screen and remarked, "That guy is really good".[39]

In the cabinet room Kennedy and Vice-President Johnson received the march leaders. Hearing they'd missed lunch he had tea, sandwiches and cherry cobbler brought up from the kitchens. What followed had a formal surface, containing the tensions. It was less a conversation than a structured debate. They proposed, he answered. Randolph, courteously referring to a man half his age as sir, outlined an economic programme couched in the concepts of his own time – it was in effect a request for a black New Deal. Kennedy spoke of a coalition of all 'men of goodwill' and proceeded to hammer in the brass tacks of getting the bill through congress. He went through the Congressional list state by state, and then through the list of Senators, saying how each would vote and leading inevitably to the necessity of at least sixty Republicans voting yes – or as he put it 'right'. This must have been obvious and tedious for those present – still the requests came from his guests, asking the President to strengthen the bill by provision for a Fair Employment Practices Commission and extending the powers of the Attorney-General to allow him to prosecute across a wide area of Civil Rights. Randolph perceived the problem in heroic terms – it required a crusade that only Kennedy could lead. This too brought forth blunt pragmatism. Brass tacks having failed, Kennedy turned to the steel hammer and invited Johnson to speak. Johnson, the ultimate Capitol Hillbilly, told the Civil Rights leaders that the President could not run Congress, he could only cajole and persuade: "The President can't get those sixty votes if he turns the White House upside down and he pleads on television an hour every day."[40]

The photographs show smiling faces and the White House statement read: "The nation can properly be proud of the demonstration that has occurred here today."[41] But the Civil Rights leaders could hardly have been as pleased with the meeting as Kennedy was with the march. The *New York Times* described Martin Luther King as "both militant and sad".[42]

David Garrow, King's most recent biographer, writes of the general effect of the march: "Robert Kennedy's and Burke Marshall's efforts to influence the march toward moderation and away from angry condemnations, toward a legislative focus and away from an economic one, had been an overwhelming success."[43] The first part of this seems true, but several speeches and countless placards made the economic equation clear: 'Civil Rights + Jobs = Freedom'. There had been no direct clash between the march and the administration, not even between SNCC and the adminstration – rather they had shifted it to SNCC versus the other groups. Although they had seen to it that O'Boyle and Reuther had been

214

informed of Lewis's speech, it had hardly been necessary for them to intervene thereafter. Had O'Boyle been less predictable, I've no doubt there would have been confrontation between SNCC and Bobby Kennedy.

Nick Katzenbach: "We ran that march . . . there were so many people coming in from out of town – there was a real danger of violence. We were concerned about the speeches. We got the right to review all the speeches. We also had control of the loudspeaker system. If anything had happened, if any speech was made that was not the speech that was meant to be made, but somebody started calling for things that would lead to violence, the sound would have been cut off."[44]

At some point an alternative speech seems to have been prepared for John Lewis by the Justice Department. Burke Marshall was driven to the Lincoln Memorial in a police sidecar, but he has no recollection of where the speech came from, and Lewis has no recollection of ever receiving it.

John Lewis: "That's the first I've heard of it, but I wouldn't be surprised. The administration was concerned, over concerned, about what would happen. They wanted to get it over with, to control it. There was so much apprehension and fear – most of the citizens of Washington stayed home, because they'd been told that something could happen."

Most SNCC commentators share a common view of the march – it was ineffectual and a waste of precious resources that would be better spent at the front line of the struggle, on organisations fighting segregation in the Deep South, but their sense of conflict with the government goes beyond that. Howard Zinn, the first of SNCC's own historians, writing in 1964, said: "The sit-ins stimulated, among other things, a re-thinking about the sanctity of 'private property' . . . the slogan 'private property' has long disguised the fact that so called private enterprises drastically affect the public interest and the public therefore has a right to make certain demands upon them . . . Civil Rights groups, then, may begin to argue for a planned American economy."[45]

Such radical thinking was ahead of the administration's position – hence SNCC were tagged as 'very radical' – it's almost a dismissal – but there was simultaneously a fear of Black revolution in the wake of Birmingham, and an old apprehension of the post-war bogeyman – the commie. The cold war illogic reasserts itself – the fear of black demands becoming more militant folds into the cliché of the red peril. After the June 22nd meeting Kennedy took Martin Luther King into the Rose Garden to tell him he should drop a man suspected of being a communist from his team. Several minutes of Anthony Lewis's 1964 interview are given over to Bobby Kennedy's views on communist infiltration of the march on Washington, and the *New York Times* reported that "authorities" estimated there were one hundred and fifty New York communists in the march. It all seems like a misperception of the nature of black demands and the direction black frustration was taking – a confusion of propaganda with a burgeoning reality. This is not to say that there were no communists in the Movement. That's not the point. The point is that when an American politician or policeman invokes the word communist the symbolic power outweighs the perceptual or analytic. It's left to a Southerner, Harry Golden, to show this for the bunk that it is and to point up the common denominator, the common limitation on the thinking of Americans in power:

"Such accusations are part of the segregationist's technique in isolating the Negro and those who support him . . . soon the telephone lines are alive with a rumour that has been most effective throughout Alabama, Mississippi and Louisiana: 'There were two big black cadillacs in front of his house all night' . . . It is always two Cadillacs, and of course they are both *big* and *black* – and supposedly filled with outside agitators, 'Communists from New York'."[46]

Looking back, several writers have remarked on the unity of August 28th – the 'purity' of the day as Arthur Schlesinger put it. John Lewis speaks of it as "consensus building" the acknowledgment that it was "time to change". Others hold the view that it was the high point, the last time such peaceful unity was possible in the struggle for Civil Rights. Two weeks later the Sixteenth Street Baptist Church in Birmingham was bombed, killing four fourteen-year-old Black girls. In the demonstrations that followed two more children died as Bull Connor imposed his idea of law and order. Between September 15th and October 2nd three hundred people were arrested at Civil Rights protests in Selma, Alabama. One of them was John Lewis, in jail for the twenty-fifth time.

On November 22nd President Kennedy was assassinated. Five days later Lyndon Johnson addressed both houses of Congress: "No memorial oration or eulogy could more eloquently honour President Kennedy's memory than the earliest possible passage of the Civil Rights Bill for which he fought so long. We have talked long enough in the country about civil rights. We have talked for one hundred years or more. It is time now to write the next chapter – and to write it in the books of law. John Kennedy's death commands what his life conveyed – that America must move forward."

The bill became law on July 2nd 1964. Not one Dixiecrat Senator voted for the bill, and only seven Dixiecrat Representatives, four of them from Texas. Nick Katzenbach, acting Attorney-General in the absence of Bobby Kennedy, recalls being up on the hill every day that Spring "largely in Senator Dirksen's office". Dirksen delivered the sixty, and more, Republican votes that the bill needed. Even allowing for SNCC's dissenting view, it would be hard to believe that the march of 250,000 people on the nation's capital was not in some way influential.

§

Shortly before his death Medgar Evers spoke to the press on the future of the South: "One day whites and Negroes will live here in Mississippi side by side in love and brotherhood. And we know each other better in the South, that's why it should work better here than anyplace else."[47]

This is a startling remark – a curious inversion of the white 'we know our nigras', but it echoes throughout the considered thought of the South. Robert Penn Warren toured his native South in the mid-fifties, researching his book *Segregation*: "If the South is really able to face up to itself and its situation, it may achieve identity, moral identity. Then in a country where moral identity is hard to come by, the South, because it has had to deal concretely with a moral problem, may offer some leadership."[48]

Speaking in 1988 John Lewis, Congressman for the Fifth Congressional District of Georgia, feels that Evers' words have been put into practice. Georgia, he says, has "a greater optimism than anywhere else" in the USA – the South "put it into the light, [the North] never had that moral confrontation, the cleansing effect on the psyche. That's what we've been doing the last few years, laying it down, laying the burden of race down, putting it behind us."

On the burden of race, Robert Penn Warren quotes an anonymous Nashville cab driver: " . . . It ain't our hate, it's the hate hung on us by the old folks dead and gone . . . we don't know how to shuck it."[49]

On the laying down, Howell Raines quotes this: " . . . I promised to hate every white face I ever saw when I got to be a man. Well this ain't no more. I don't hate anybody . . . I read that book as best I could, the Bible. I read where you don't hate anybody, and I came up then changin' from that. But nobody helped me more than Martin Luther King Jr." Raines is quoting Martin Luther King Sr,[50] which pinpoints something of the relationship between the generations in the sixties' struggles.

In the Spring of 1988 I talked to a black policeman in a bar in Harlem about the changes of the last twenty-five years. New York born and bred, his summing up contains a perspective on the way the moral problems that faced North and South have worked out: "People think Lincoln freed the slaves. That ain't so. Lincoln said if he could unite the country without freeing a single slave he'd do it.

"When I got home from the Army in '56, I still couldn't go to the cinema, I still had to sit in the back of the bus, walk on the other side of the street – and I was in uniform – serving my country. White America don't know what it owes to black people who fought for America.

"In New York it's different now. I don't sit in the back of the bus – but not that different and not everywhere in America.

"In '63 I was in the Harlem riots[51] – don't remember the month – but it was summer – I saw people smash up and throw things. I was a rebel – I fought the system, but then I found out you can't fight the system. I got married. I got kids. And now I got grandchildren. I joined the NYPD when I was thirty-five. I done seventeen years. There's no equality. I know guys speak out against racism – they got themselves suspended. What NYPD has is a points system for hiring minorities. Black cop counts a point, black woman cop counts two points. Every time they hire a black or a hispanic they can hire three white guys. New York is 25% black. The Police Force is almost totally white. We don't volunteer? Ain't a matter of volunteering. They got ways of making you not count.

"I'm retiring soon. Bought me a plot of land down in Georgia, just outside Atlanta. That's a place Blacks count."

CHAPTER NINE

CLOTH CAPOCALYPSE

"The 'telly-glued masses' do not exist; they are the bad fiction of our second rate social analysts." Raymond Williams[1]

"It has been pointed out that, in the country of the blind, the one-eyed man is not king. He is taken to be an hallucinated lunatic." Marshall McLuhan[2]

With *The Uses of Literacy* in 1957 Richard Hoggart set off a new wave of empirical British sociology. From under the old flat cap in Hunslett, West Riding, an immediately fashionable rediscovery of working-class life and culture burst forth. Studies such as *Family and Kinship in East London* (Peter Willmott and Michael Young, 1957), *The Insecure Offenders* (T. R. Fyvel, 1961), *Education and the Working Class* (Dennis Marsden and Brian Jackson, 1962), *Adolescent Boys of East London* (Peter Willmott, 1966) and *Working Class Community* (Brian Jackson, 1968) followed. Judging by the book blurbs Young and Fyvel were not working class. Arguably, all the others were. A generation that had obtained its university education against tradition and odds turned its attention and its talents to the class and culture that had produced it. And they found it in dissolution and disarray. The processes that had set them free threatened to destroy that from which they were free, or at the very least change it beyond recognition. The buzz and whir of the washing machines, the fridges and all those lawnmowers was drowning out the still sad music of humanity. In the new sociology there was defensiveness, and nostalgia. They weren't second rate social analysts, nor was what they wrote necessarily bad fiction, but fiction it was nonetheless. The purpose of sociology has always been to tell the monied classes what the rest already knew – the form of telling most popular was established in this new wave as the novel-by-any-other-name.

Brian Jackson's book, the result of research which began as early as 1958, strays vividly into the territory of fiction – or is it cinema, as informative by then as any empirical observation, the opening

219

tracking shot of any one of half a dozen early-sixties films?

"Watch a working class boy walk along one of his home streets –
he taps on a window, rings a bicycle bell, picks up an orange at the
grocers, throws it up in the air and puts it back. In the pub he
doesn't just order a pint he asks the landlord if it's free beer tonight
– he makes a tiny incident, and his path is a trail of minute happenings. It's as if the horizons of life are firm and immutable, and
interest can only come from a series of lively kicks within the too-
settled structure: vitality within fatalism."[3]

The threats to the working class were twofold – what was
interpreted as a new affluence but might be better termed
employment stability (the basis of the credit boom) and the com-
mercialisation of entertainment. Hoggart looked at popular songs,
popular magazines and pulp fiction. Compared to the old order, this
'Candy-Floss World' was the cultural robbery of working class
people:

"The strongest objection to the more trivial popular entertain-
ments is not that they prevent their readers from becoming
highbrow, but that they make it harder for people without an
intellectual bent to become wise in their own way . . . These
productions do not contribute to a sounder popular art but discour-
age it. They make their audience less likely to arrive at a wisdom
derived from an inner, felt discrimination in their sense of people
and their attitude to experience. It is easier to kill the old roots than
to replace them with anything comparable."[4]

Statements like this, so immediately striking, so immediately
supportable, have far reaching effects. The sense of nostalgia is
inescapable, made worse by the fact that Hoggart admits that his
description of working-class community and culture is based on his
own youth before the Second World War. That the thirties tele-
scope into the fifties is acceptable, but what remained after a first
reading of this book, some fifteen years after its publication, was a
feeling of being trapped. Hoggart's nostalgia was my prison. There's
something damning about it. The working class at this moment in
the fifties, as they became the sixties, is in deadlock. It cannot go
back, and to go on seems like a betrayal of all that made it what it
was. The moment Hoggart captures is the shift from a compliant
workforce to overstimulated over-consumers, from a culture that
was of the working class, ritualised and self-defining, to mass culture
which was of no-one and nothing but commerce. It's a position that
can slip too easily into an uncritical anti-materialism. Mass culture,
and with it mass media and mass education, became, in the wake of
Hoggart's work, the subject of the dominant critical debate of the

early sixties, a debate dogged by both nostalgia and puritanism. The issue of mass versus minority culture wasn't new, it's implicit in the critical stance of the Leavisites, in their notion of an 'organic community'. It was not a clear-cut issue of opposing class cultures or even of gradations of class culture, but of the dissolution of these cultures into mass and minority – a reductive, simplistic opposition that, from the critical point of view could serve and satisfy no-one. On the one hand there would seem to be a minority 'natural' culture defending taste, morality and meaning in a state of siege, on the other a synthetic, commercial culture passively accepting whatever junk mass-media put in front of them. The obvious culprit, the obvious target for such criticism, was television.

Television was a subject barely touched on in *The Uses of Literacy*, but over the next five or six years it became the most acute focus of the argument Hoggart had triggered. In *Encounter* in January 1960 he wrote:

"Spend a week regularly watching television on either or both channels and you can almost feel the cakes of custom being cracked open . . . What we see in all these media . . . is a sort of processing of attitudes . . . It is a processing which tries to produce a cultural classlessness (and I do not mean, as I have already said, an economic classlessness)."[5]

The new mass culture, as Hoggart so often argued, grew from nothing and offered no consideration of the lives and mores of ordinary men and women – in its creation it usurped a culture that, whilst born out of economic impoverishment, rooted itself in the lived structures of the working classes. At its crudest we no longer 'made our own entertainment' but, in the American phrase, sat like 'couch potatoes'. A prevailing view held that ITV had fulfilled the worst fears of the anti-commercial lobby of the early fifties – standards had dropped, serious programmes had been pushed into the late hours by a plethora of game shows and easy money quiz games. At the heart of this canker was advertising[6] – a disruptor of continuity in programmes and an unacceptable pressure on quality and scheduling. Nor was the BBC free from taint – it had met the challenge of ITV by competitive scheduling (so much so that they had roughly equal shares of the market by 1963). It was argued that this was unnecessary, as the BBC was not commercially dependent, but the BBC contributed to a movement towards the lowest common denominator in broadcasting.

Later in 1960 academic debate received political form – a rare enough event in itself – as the Pilkington Commission of Enquiry into Broadcasting. The committee took two years to hear the evidence and report. Meanwhile the debate moved on. To meaning-lessness and triviality, as the ills of commercialised entertainment, could be added that it drew heavily on American influences and, in terms of its organisation, offered no choice or power to the con-sumer. Raymond Williams, another working-class boy, the son of a railway signalman from Pandy, argued in *Communications* (Penguin Special, 1962) for a democratisation of culture, posing the ironic question "Surely we get the culture we deserve?" and answering it by asserting that we didn't because there was no mechanism for finding out what anyone wanted. The justification so often offered by the programme makers and broadcasting authorities, that they knew people wanted game shows and imported cop series because they watched them in their millions, was readily dismissed by Williams, even as it was blandly being offered to the Pilkington Committee. There is in his argument, as in Hoggart's, something terminal. Not Hoggart's sense of deadlock, but the sense of immi-nent breakthrough, to an accountable media, the end of a 'long revolution'.

"Isn't the real threat of 'mass culture' – of things like television rather than things like football or the circus – that it reduces us to an endlessly mixed, undiscriminating, fundamentally bored reac-tion? The spirit of everything, art and entertainment can become so standardised that we have no interest in anything but simply an indifferent acceptance . . . We can conceive a cultural organisation in which there would be genuine freedom and variety, protected alike from the bureaucrat and the speculator . . . We would be using our means of communication for their most general human pur-poses."[7]

In his attack on synthetic, rootless culture, Williams' call for democracy in culture outstripped anything that could be offered in his lifetime. Much of what he proposed sounds as radical today as it did twenty-five years ago, while such ideas as national culture or a national voice seem neither old nor new but simply startling in their irrelevance – but it all rests on a difficult, if not discredited idea – the passivity of the audience. Hoggart had pointed out the working-class habit of 'staying in'. It was a short cultural hop from this to seeing the working classes, as the advertisers surely did, as passive consumers. So much of this early-sixties argument overstates the power of television per se, in stating the very real power of the broadcasters. This failure in perception, amounting almost to the paranoia of the educated, informed the Pilkington report, when it eventually appeared in the Autumn of 1962, from start to finish.

How the Pilkington Commission of Enquiry into Broadcasting

managed to come into being is a mystery. Asa Briggs argues, in *The BBC: The First Fifty Years*,[8] that the composition of the committee reflected the ideas of Macmillan, but where in the philosophy of 'you've never had it so good', the fast buck and the never-never was there room for a Leavisite critique of the decline of culture and the rise of commerce? Dons did not predominate in the dramatis personae of Pilkington, but distinctions did – *Sir* Harry Pilkington, the glass manufacturer, H. Collison *CBE* (General Secretary of the National Union of Agricultural Workers), Joyce Grenfell *OBE*, W. A. Wright *CBE* (the footballer), *Professor* F. H. Newark, R. L. Rose-Smith *CBE* (a radio research engineer) and five others, one of whom was its driving force, Richard Hoggart.[9] I point out this bias not simply to emphasise the lack of ordinary people on the committee (although I suppose Billy Wright was taken to be one) but because it is reflected in the evidence the committee took. The bulk of this came from organisations with vested interests – that small portion which came from named individuals tended to come from academics, politicians (there were no serving politicians on the panel) and from lots of people with titles or distinctions of some sort. It's tempting to ask whether there was any real intention to find out what the 'average viewer' thought or watched, and whether the committee members themselves owned sets or watched programmes other than for the purpose of compiling their report.

The full report ran to 296 pages, with appendices totalling a further 600. Some 636 submissions were received, including 57 from the BBC amounting to more than 150,000 words. It held no surprises. It reads like an extension of the work of Hoggart, and it seems to represent no significant advance in his thought. It could have been written in 1959 or 1960. It was as transparent as Pilkington's finest. Neither Hoggart nor Raymond Williams, who gave evidence, ever argued for the innate superiority of print over broadcast media, yet the Pilkington report seems to rest upon such an unspoken notion in so far as it is shot through with contempt for television and for the act of watching it. At the level of primary education – and it surely was an educational debate? – such ideas filtered down as an injunction to children not to watch TV and an assertion of the superiority of print: a view I deplored publicly at the time, but have practised ever since.

The report's conclusions were that the Independent Television Authority, rather than the companies, should prescribe on violence, that the companies should observe the 9 p.m. line for 'family viewing', that they should be reconstructed with the advertising controlled by the ITA and, most sweeping of all, that the ITA

223

should be responsible for programme planning. The prize, the third television channel, went to the BBC. The report whitewashed the BBC and pasted ITV: " . . . the general judgment is unmistakable: it is that the [ITV] service falls well short of what a good public service of broadcasting should be . . . We conclude that the dissatisfaction with television can largely be ascribed to the Independent Television Service. Its concept of balance does not satisfy the varied and many sided tastes and interests of the public. In the field of entertainment – and not least in light entertainment – there is much that lacks quality. It is these facts which largely account for the widespread opinion that much on television is trivial."[10]

Looking at the evidence given by individuals rather than by spokesmen for organisations, this conclusion cannot be borne out. Advertising is universally criticised, but the BBC is not spared – the most representative comment is this, from Miss Grace Greiner, lamenting:

" . . . The competitive programme planning of BBC and ITA, resulting in the showing of similar programmes at precisely the same time."[11]

How this came about is indicative of the times, as are the leading men involved. The BBC had a new Director-General in 1960, Hugh Carleton-Greene, the younger brother of the novelist Graham Greene, a career journalist and broadcaster, and an expert in the use of propaganda. A post as Berlin correspondent of the *Daily Telegraph* in the thirties had led him to the BBC in the war, where he specialised in propaganda to Germany. The chairman of the ITA was Sir Ivone Kirkpatrick, former head of the Foreign Office, who had been Chamberlain's translator at Munich, whose war years had been spent in a similar field alongside such as Burgess and Blunt. Their evidence to Pilkington might be seen as a battle of the spooks, but their approaches could hardly have been more different. Greene took the debate of the day on its own terms and engaged directly with it. From the advantages of not being culpable on the matter of advertising, and of speaking not for thirteen companies but for one, Greene built up a sense of the national position and responsibility of the BBC, through a shrewd mixture of self-praise and self-blame: " . . . even in a competitive situation it remains a national voice, 'an extra member of the family'."

Greene had wined and dined the 'influential' at informal lunches from the start of the enquiry – when the new television centre was opened in 1960 he gave a special screening of Richard Cawston's celebratory documentary for the members of the Pilkington Committee. Unlike Kirkpatrick he took the hearings, and the sociological context in which they were rooted, completely seriously. His attack on ITV maintained that only the BBC had prevented things from being worse than they were:

" . . . with standards of broadcasting established in Britain in the course of a generation . . . a steadfastness on the part of the BBC in maintaining its standards in the last five years against considerable odds."

Such statements scarcely begin to admit to the BBC's role in the ratings race – some programme "clashes" are, the BBC evidence says, "inevitable in a competitive situation", which conceals thinly that what is objected to are not clashes but similarities, lack of choice. Greene was adamant that the new channel should go to the BBC:

"A second service would enable the BBC to increase the number of serious, cultural and informational programmes . . . further opportunities handed to commercial television . . . could create a mental and spiritual poverty . . ."[12]

Confronted with that central argument – lack of choice, cultural impoverishment, the ITA, in the person of Ivone Kirkpatrick, seemed scarcely to know that the debate existed, let alone that it had been running for several years.[13] The ITA, the report concluded, were "disposed to regard as exaggerated the commonly held view that television exerted a high degree of influence." Kirkpatrick comes over as a man of patrician indifference to anything as red-brick as a sociological argument. He told the committee that "society would be largely what it was with or without television . . . he would hesitate to accept a dictum that society was going to be in any way moulded by it."[14] To such as Hoggart this must have sounded like heresy. At best it was stupidity. A wilful ignorance of the moral basis of the intellectual life of the last thirty years. What Kirkpatrick could not see was that the intellectual argument mattered more than the actual programmes. He argued for the role of television as merely a "mirror of society" – a statement quashed by the Pilkingtonians with the unadulterated Leavisism, "Broadcasters must accept as part of their responsibility a constant and living relationship with the moral condition of society."[15] He stood firm where he should have admitted culpability (TV violence, largely in the imported American cop series, defended with reference to the violence in Shakespeare), backtracked where he should have stood firm (on the issue of kitchen-sink plays, termed by the report "these sordid domestic dramas", he offered to cut back – the BBC had made the same defence initially offered by the ITA that writers must write about what moves them, and in retrospect ITV's track record in drama at this time was excellent and worth the fight) and on the vital issue of trash and triviality made no defence at all. The BBC won hands down and shuffled off their own contribution to the trivialisation of our national culture onto the opposition. Triviality itself was defined by the report. It was more than a matter of low-brow television it was: " . . . A failure to respect the potentialities of the subject matter . . . a reluctance to be imaginatively adventurous."[16]

The BBC's second channel (opened as BBC2 in 1964, and 'advertised' well before by a pair of kangaroos known as Hullaballoo and Custard) was awarded in recognition quality: "We found in the BBC an all-round professionalism . . . [which] shows itself not least in their dissatisfaction with performance, in their sense of the unrealised possibilities of the medium."[17] What Hugh Greene did with his unrealised possibilities and his imaginative adventure is the subject of another chapter. But he had got away with murder – he had fought a ratings war and emerged from it with a blessing as the voice of the nation.

"The ITV . . . were lazy in the public presentation of their case and fatally casual, even, I believe, contemptuous, in the preparation of their evidence . . . They got what was coming to them."[18]

Apart from creating BBC2, the Pilkington report achieved virtually nothing. No other recommendation became action, although they all became the subject of further debate. Whilst it might be expected that the Conservative government would not tamper with the licence to print money, the Labour response was equally ineffectual if more subtle.

In *Encounter* Richard Crossman, writing up his observations after three bedridden months as a captive viewer, described the report as "out-Reithing Reith in its governessy attitude to popular entertainment",[19] and spoke of a "right to triviality". For him the model of Light and Home services, as practised on radio, needed to be applied to the television service. In the November issue, Tony Crosland joined the debate, somewhat more acutely: "The picture of the atomised mass-viewer, with a tabula rasa of an empty mind, is a snobbish intellectual's nightmare" – but to the same conclusion, pointing out that the radio model of Light-Home-Third, in itself a reproduction of the basic class model, was set up in the hope that people would ascend through the channels via education and discrimination to the better service, and that BBC2, with this in mind, should become the minority channel. When George Brown referred the report to the shadow cabinet they shelved it, just as the government had done. No changes in the structure of ITV followed, and in

1963 the new head if the ITA Sir Charles Hill, lately of Macmillan's cabinet, renewed all the franchises of the old companies. Five years of debate came to nothing. Crossman and Crosland took the easy way out. What their conclusions amount to is that as long as they – in all the expansive inclusiveness of the word – got a channel they could watch BBC1 and ITV could remain as they were, slogging it out in a pointless contest. Rather than tackling the problem of mass v. minority culture they endorsed it as a two-nations division and the most far reaching part of Raymond Williams' argument, that mass and minority failed to recognise gradation and variety in taste and value by seeking a bland audience on the one hand and a siege culture on the other, received no support from the quarter where it might most have been expected. Williams himself seems to have anticipated this:

"At best, a minority culture, in keeping the works available, offers the best that has been done and said in the world. At worst it translates the best into its own accents, and confuses it with many inferior things. I see no real evidence that it is a permanent and reliable means of maintaining a living excellence."

Hoggart had pointed out in *The Uses of Literacy* the damage done to working-class communities by the hiving off of the brightest into an educational system that isolated them and then assimilated them. Television was about to get its grammar school.

§

The weakness in this prolonged debate is that, whilst seeming to judge the whole national culture, none of the participants were capable of looking at the new medium except in old terms. Nobody took on television as though it operated in any way that had not been previously defined in other media. Giving his evidence Sir Kenneth Clark, TV producer and former head of the ITA, said, "I have been struck more than ever by what a limited medium it is."[20] He feared it might run out of material for programmes. The Leavisite backlash was a volume that disowned Pilkington – *Discrimination and Popular Culture* – and it's odd to think that these words, so rooted in the snobbery of print culture, were being written at the same time that Marshall McLuhan was writing *Understanding Media*: "The whole experience of listening and viewing is turned into a glorified version of *Tonight*. And the point about a programme like *Tonight* is that item follows item too smoothly and rapidly for any one item to engage the attention or grip the imagination for more than the moment of its passage. Comical items and serious items, the calamitous and the diverting parade before us in unending processions."[21]

McLuhan took television on its own terms, and refuted the passive audience argument in terms that were outrageous. From the simple act of viewing he made a pyrotechnic leap to declare that television wasn't merely visual it was tactile and restored man to his lost synaesthesia, to unified sensory perception.

"Just as TV, the mosaic mesh, does not foster perspective in art, it does not foster lineality in living. Since TV, the assembly line has disappeared from industry. Staff and line structures have dissolved in management. Gone are the stag line, the party line, the receiving line, and the pencil line from the backs of nylons.

"Television has changed our sense lives and our mental processes. It has created a taste for all experience *in depth* that affects language teaching as much as car styles. Since TV nobody is happy with a mere book knowledge of French or English poetry. The unanimous cry now is 'Let's *talk* French' and 'Let the bard be *heard*.'"[22]

This is as big a load of gobbledegook as his global village, but it acknowledges a transforming power of the new medium more than any of the print-bound British critics did. Television for McLuhan is not just a poor substitute for a book. That 'mosaic mesh' was a perception that eluded the Leavisite critic. Without it it's impossible to come to grips with television as a form in its own right.

The events of 1963, most of which were recorded by television programmes, some of which were television programmes, did not so much resolve the debate as smother it. Issues that had seemed so important disappeared into McLuhan's mosaic – for example, Williams' argument on the cultural dominance of the King's English wasn't tackled by any educational process, it was knocked for six as Beatle scouse and Terence Stamp cockney became fashionable. But for all the sweeping power of fashion and the repeated clichés on classlessness and the new Britain it's worth remembering that all this resolved nothing, resolved none of the issues of culture and class that Hoggart had pointed up, and that the New Britain's climax – Swinging London – was, to paraphrase George Melly, merely old capitalism with a trendy new suit.

§

In the Spring of 1962 two policemen met at the grave of a recently murdered colleague. There ought, they agreed, to be a better response to armed robbery than simply a bobby on a bike. What they needed were new-fangled patrol cars – which would be known as *Z cars*, from the call signs Z Victor 1 and Z Victor 2. At the graveside they symbolically buried not just their bobby on a bike, but with it the prevailing image of the policeman on television, Constable George Dixon, of Dock Green, London. This wasn't London. It wasn't even the South, it was Newtown and Seaport, a mythical Merseyside.

The originators of *Z Cars*, the BBC's head of Drama, Elwyn Jones, and writer Troy Kennedy Martin, took the decision that the time had come to take a police series out of London (even if it continued to be made there, with Wood Lane masquerading for stretches of northern highway) and to follow the lead set by ITV with *Coronation Street*. With the move, the comfortable image of the British bobby changed. On and off Dixon had been around since he was shot to death by Dirk Bogarde in *The Blue Lamp* in 1951, only to be revived as a widower for television. The avuncular Dixon, with a friendly local nick, where every villain was on the 'manor', where 'the lad settled down nicely in the end', and the Chief Inspector was nicknamed 'father', co-existed with *Z Cars* and in the end outlived it, but its style was outmoded even with the changes that came in the sixties – no more domestic life, the dropping of the character Mary – Dixon's daughter and the Detective Sergeant's wife. The coppers of Newtown were a harder, more human, flawed bunch of heroes.

Given two patrol cars, Inspector Barlow and Sgt Watt (Stratford Johns and Frank Windsor) have to man them from the beat force.[23] One by one, the camera revealed them. Bob Steele (Jeremy Kemp) the wife-beater, Bert Lynch (James Ellis) slyly placing an illegal bet, the cocky, outrageous Fancy Smith (Brian Blessed) and the displaced Scot Jock Weir (Joseph Brady). They were too real for comfort. The police, from the wives to the Chief Constables, protested, but the public and the critics loved it, from the catchy theme tune (Fritz Spiegl's arrangement of a Liverpool folk song) to gritty realism and the hard edge of aggression. By 1963 it had fourteen million viewers, the actors were household names, and Jeremy Kemp was a heart-throb who could move on to better things.

Z Cars represented a new peak in television realism. It anticipated the Wednesday play and drew on the fragmented editing techniques of the cinema – as many as two hundred and fifty shot changes in a single fifty-minute episode, many of them less than twenty seconds long – and on the semi-articulate dialogue of recent British theatre.

Graham: "Ten minutes."

Lynch: "I still haven't found my gloves."
(There is a pause)
Lynch: "It's annoying, a thing like that."
Graham: "I know."
(Another pause)
Graham: "How about a last drag?"
Lynch (shrugs): "If you like . . ."[24]
Alan Plater – with a tip of the hat to Harold Pinter?

From the start *Z Cars* concerned itself with social issues and aimed at being much more than just a cops and robbers drama – at dealing with the representation of Britain in the sixties. It was, as Peter Black wrote, "the first television series not to reflect back to its working class audience a flattering, fundamentally insulting picture of itself as making the best of things."[25] On the other side the opposite trend was in motion, a drift to the fantastic that would seize a larger slice of the popular imagination.

The Avengers was first aired on ITV in October 1961. It starred Patrick Macnee and Ian Hendry. When Hendry left to make films, he was replaced by Honor Blackman, an actress who'd waited the best part of fifteen years to become 'an overnight sensation'. The second series that began in December 1962, and ran until March 1964, was *The Avengers* in its definitive form – the bowler-hatted, old Etonian John Steed and his formidable, black leather-clad, karate kicking assistant Mrs Gale.

ABC producer Sydney Newman thought up *The Avengers*, and also had the idea of replacing Ian Hendry with a woman. In a newsreel he'd seen a widow of the Mau Mau crisis, wearing both a papoose to hold her child and a revolver with which to protect it. The combination of femininity and firepower appealed to him.

"There had been this chemistry between the jaded, sophisticated killer, Macnee, and the innocent police surgeon full of morality and noble purpose, played by Hendry – it was the conflict of moralities that made *The Avengers* work . . . I thought why not make the moral purity one a woman, based on this character I'd seen in the newsreels. So, when we used Honor Blackman she was a widow, she worked at the British Museum as an archivist . . . and she had learned to protect herself when she was living in Kenya in the days of the Mau Mau, so she knew ju-jitsu, she knew how to shoot. Honor Blackman's character was prissy and proper. Pat Macnee's character was always trying to lay her and she'd brush aside his sexual advances, and yet there was a kind of devotion by which he drew her into his causes. Again the conflict of moralities made it work – but it had the conflict of sex, which gave it an extra patina.

And then, of course, there was the question of dressing her. In rehearsal, when we did a dummy run and she was doing the ju-jitsu we could see her pants, and once her blouse was torn off – well, I couldn't have that on the air . . . so we made this a problem for the costume department. They knew leather would be in vogue that autumn, so she was dressed in black leather, with those split skirts or long pants."[26]

If there'd been a realistic intent in the first series it slowly evaporated in the second and third. As cops – of a sort – the two secret agents lived in a different world from *Z Cars*, a world that resembled Kafka more than Newtown. Who they worked for was never made clear, and they fought the agents of shady foreign powers. That said, for the benefit of anyone who saw *The Avengers* only with Diana Rigg or Joanna Lumley, it's worth emphasising that it was played seriously and had none of the high camp that became its later trade mark. At its peak it drew a larger audience than *Z Cars*, and was put out in direct competition with *That Was The Week That Was* – before the invention of the video tape recorder such competitive scheduling could lead to family bloodshed.

The press adored Honor Blackman. Stories of her karate skill made the papers as role reversal, with her actor husband Maurice Kaufmann described as having to dissuade her from lashing out on occasions. Together she and Macnee featured in spin-off books and annuals, and in early 1964 made a pop record together – *Kinky Boots*. Television could not hold her. Blackman left to star in *Goldfinger*, the third film based on the novels of Ian Fleming.

§

There'd been efforts to film the James Bond books since the first appeared in 1953. *Casino Royale* was made into a one-hour play for American television, and the film rights eventually sold for a mere $6000. Fleming's idea of success meant bestsellers and films, yet throughout the fifties no film offer came to fruition. In 1959-60 the most constructive effort yet petered out unsatisfactorily. Fleming met the Irish film producer Kevin McClory, who had the idea of a creating a Bond story especially for film rather than filming one of the novels – Fleming had written seven by this time, the most recent being *Goldfinger* – and the idea for *Thunderball* was conceived and turned into a treatment by screenwriter Jack Whittingham. When the film project came to nothing, Fleming reworked the storyline as his eighth novel, published the following year. Only then, in 1961, did successful film interest arise. Harry Saltzman and Albert Broccoli decided to film *Dr No*, which had been Fleming's sixth novel in

1958. But, the films were not precise renditions of the books – by the time Bond reached the screen so long had elapsed since his creation, each medium, each version was of its own, distinctly different era.

Early editions of Fleming's books show the time to which Bond really belonged. It is easier, looking at old Pan paperbacks, to imagine Bond played by David Farrar or Eric Portman than by Sean Connery. Fleming's own descriptions are rare: "His grey-blue eyes looked calmly back with a hint of ironical inquiry and the short lock of black hair which would never stay in place subsided to form a thick comma above his right eyebrow. With the thin vertical scar down his right cheek the general effect was faintly piratical."[27]

"He looks a nasty customer . . . height 183 centimetres, weight 76 kilograms; slim build; eyes blue, hair black; scar down right cheek and on left shoulder; signs of plastic surgery on back of right hand . . . all-round athlete; expert pistol shot, boxer knife thrower; does not use disguises."[28]

He is, as so many critics have remarked, a 'clubland hero', an improvement on but a descendent from the heroes of Sax Rohmer and Sapper, and despite the Smersh dossier less than expert in most of the ascribed spy-arts. Bond may be less than gentlemanly in much of his behaviour, but there's also a touch of the gentleman amateur about him.

The era of Bond is the era of Dan Dare, the immediate post-war period, in which both present and future are defined by the backward glance. Dare explored new galaxies in the vocabulary of the Battle of Britain, Bond fought the Red Menace with an ethos that harked back to the war, but twisted and turned into a new ruthlessness and vulnerability, a style that was purely Fleming's.

The distinctive characteristic of Fleming's work is a sensual, almost tactile prose of remarkable intensity,[29] and a skill with branded objects that creates a world-picture that seems underexplained by the word so often applied, consumerism. Bond's cars are the most obvious such objects:

"Bond's car was his only personal hobby. One of the last 4½ litre Bentleys with the supercharger by Amherst Villiers, he had bought it almost new in 1933 and had kept it in careful storage through the war . . . Bond drove it hard and well with an almost sensual pleasure. It was a battleship-grey convertible coupé, which really did convert, and it was capable of touring at ninety with thirty miles an hour in reserve."[30]

By the time of *Thunderball* this had been replaced. It's only a couple of years before Eon films equipped Bond with his Aston

Martin battlewagon, but its an eon away: "Bond had the most selfish car in England. It was a Mark II Continental Bentley that some rich idiot had married to a telegraph pole on the Great West Road. Bond had bought the bits for £1500 and Rolls had straightened the bend in the chassis and fitted new clockwork – the Mark IV engine with 9.5 compression. Then Bond had gone to Mulliners with £3000, which was half his total capital, and they had sawn off the old cramped sports saloon body and had fitted a trim, rather square convertible two seater affair, power-operated, with only two large-armed bucket seats in black leather. The rest of the blunt end was all knife-edged, rather ugly, boot. The car was painted in rough, not gloss, battleship grey and the upholstery was black morocco. She went like a bird and a bomb and Bond loved her more than all the women at present in his life rolled, if that were feasible, together."[31]

The car is the object of a love-affair, not a complex weapon to be used and abandoned. The references, so obviously sensual, move slyly into the sexual, as Fleming qualifies 'rolled' with the wholly unnecessary phrase that follows. It is knowing rather than flash consumption – who or what are Mulliners? It is the language of the old Etonian that both Bond and Fleming were, a pre-inflationary vocabulary in which having money in the bank is 'capital', in which cars have chassis and 'tour' rather than simply 'go'.

The most disturbing aspect of Fleming's sensuality was the depiction of sadism. In the *New Statesman* in April 1958 Paul Johnson tackled the matter of Ian Fleming's 'Sex, Sadism and Snobbery'. *Dr No* was, he wrote, "the nastiest book I have ever read . . . Fleming deliberately and systematically excites and then satisfies the very worst instincts of his readers." Johnson dwelt at some length on the brutality of *Dr No* – Honeychile Rider strapped down naked to be the lunch of giant land crabs, Bond's tunnel of torture, with it's red hot metal and 50 foot squid, and the reported killing of a rapist with a black widow spider – but the perspective from which Fleming wrote was of greater interest, Fleming the establishment figure: " . . . Our curious post-war society, with its obsessive interest in debutantes, its cult of U and non U, its working-class graduates educated into snobbery by the welfare state, is a soft market for Mr Fleming's poison. Bond's warmest admirers are among our Top People."[32]

With the film of *Dr No* in production, *Today* magazine ran a campaign to persuade the public to reject James Bond, and resurrected the old argument, in terms close to plagiarism. *Today*'s 'leader' of April 21st, 1962 was headed "Why Britain Should Say

'No' to 'Dr No'" and attacked "the strange disease which afflicts many of the Top People in Britain today."

" . . . a bunch of would-be 'in the mode' intellectuals has huffed and puffed this nasty writing into respectability . . . Rome was rather like this in the last days of Nero."[33]

Today then proceeded to identify Fleming, yet again, as an establishment figure and added to Johnson's examples from *Dr No* snippets of other "sagas of filth" – the keelhauling scene from *Live and Let Die*, and the climax of *Casino Royale*, in which Bond is tied naked to a bottomless cane chair and struck repeatedly across the testicles with a cane carpet-beater. The scene peaks with the possibility of pleasure beyond any pain: "He had been told by colleagues who had survived torture by the Germans and the Japanese that towards the end there came a wonderful feeling of warmth and langour leading into a sort of sexual twilight where pain turned to pleasure and where hatred and fear of the torturers turned to a masochistic infatuation."[34]

I can't help wondering whether, without doubting Mr Johnson's conviction, the revival of his argument by a magazine as tacky as *Today* was just a publicity stunt. On the day the article was published Fleming was interviewed on *Tonight* by Kenneth Allsop, and said that *Today* were getting at him because he had not let them have his next book for serialisation. Ten days later Cliff Michelmore broadcast a correction. Fleming's novel had been turned down by *Today*, and an apology was offered by Fleming to the appalling rag which had vowed never to publish his work again.[35] Yet, by December *Dr No* had the cover of *Today* in the shape of Eunice Gayson, who played Bond's girlfriend, and in July 1963 they ran a two-week spread on Connery with stills from the new film *From Russia with Love*.

The moral minority need not have worried. Scenes of sadism were not filmed. In *Dr No*, Bond crawls along the undersea pipe not as a form of torture, gloated over by Dr No, but to his escape. The same applies to sex. Filming Honey Rider's rising from the waves naked but for an army belt would have got the film banned or at least an uneconomic X certificate – but in other ways Fleming's treatment of sex was changed. In *From Russia with Love* six pages elapse between the appearance of Tatiana in Bond's bed and the seduction – six pages largely of dialogue. Film scarcely had the time to spare for such slow consummation, Bond's epicurean consumption of women was replaced by speed and quantity. What Eon filmed were less the novels than the strip cartoon Bond that had run in the *Express* since the first flush of success, when the press began to notice Fleming, after Anthony Eden's use of his house Goldeneye, on Jamaica, as an escape from the strains of the Suez crisis.[36] With the first film imminent, the *Express* ran a competition to see who their readers wanted to play James Bond. Eleven hundred replies failed to produce anyone acceptable to Fleming and the producers. Fleming had given up the idea of a star name like Richard Burton, James Mason, Trevor Howard (who perhaps most closely resembled the Bond of the novels) or Peter Finch and now favoured an unknown. Legend has it that Mrs Albert Broccoli spotted Sean Connery in a 1959 Disney film – *Darby O'Gill and the Little People*.

Connery had begun as a body builder, and had got his first break as an actor in the British production of *South Pacific*. Television and films followed – a small part in *Hell Drivers*, in which he threatened to steal the show from Patrick McGoohan, the lead role in *The Frightened City*, in which he stood head and shoulders (metaphorically – as well as literally at six feet two inches) above the other dogged Brit actors of his generation, and the television plays *Requiem for a Heavyweight* and *Adventure Story* – playing Rattigan's Alexander the Great.

Barry Norman first encountered Sean Connery when the *Daily Mail* sent him to do a location report on the film *The Longest Day* which was being filmed in France in 1962. He travelled down with the cast of British stalwarts: "There was Norman Rossington, Michael Medwin, my photographer, me and this guy Sean Connery, whom I'd vaguely heard of but never met before . . . when the train came in for La Rochelle it was already fairly packed . . . it was a long journey and there was a mad rush to get on the train. Rossington, Medwin and the photographer were quick off the mark and they all got seats. I was talking to Connery on the platform. By the time we got on there was not a seat left, so the whole journey we sat on the floor of this third class compartment from Paris to La Rochelle. I was just making conversation, I didn't know Sean . . . I didn't know much about his work, and he only had a spit and a cough in *The Longest Day* . . . I said 'What are you going to do after this?' And he said, in a fairly sheepish way as I remember, 'Oh, I'm playing James Bond.' And I said, 'Bad as that is it?' And he said 'Oh well it's a job.' We didn't discuss it any further. It was meant to be a sympathetic remark from me, he genuinely didn't sound very keen on [the part]. Maybe he thought it was going to be made cheap and cheerful. It was the first starring role he'd ever been offered. I don't think he saw himself as a movie star in those days, in fact I'm quite certain he didn't. I think he looked upon it as just another job. I don't think he expected too much from it. The next time I saw him was after *Dr No* had opened and he was on his way to becoming a superstar."[37]

A cautious, curious beginning to the establishment of one of Britain's most enduring film stars, and the finest screen actor since Gary Cooper, or as Barry Norman prefers to put it, "Second only to De Niro". But, if Connery was James Bond he was James Bond for a different era. He was working class, noticeably Scottish (however much he toned down the accent) whereas Bond was an Anglo-Scot and presumably spoke with the U accent of Eton and Fettes. Had it mattered any more it would have been hard to believe in Connery as an old Etonian – but it didn't matter. Fleming is quoted as seeing his character as only two dimensional, a "cardboard booby": "I did not mean him to have any character, except to be a blunt instrument in the hands of the government . . . I quite deliberately made him anonymous . . ."[38]

In his later books Fleming pulls back from this intention, just as the films take the opposite tack and propel the character of James Bond into a world of exaggerated style, presumptive classlessness and increasing fantasy. Bond is pared back to his original two dimensions, he scarcely suffers, never loses – the book Bond is always perilously close to being a loser – and behaves like a super-hero . . . Superman, Spiderman, Bondman. One of the reasons that James Bond – so much a character of the fifties – succeeded in the sixties was that he lent himself to the great British self-parody. What, above all, the Bond films gave to the sixties was their first sense of 'Style'. The style was not just the de-classing of the hero, it was about the opening up, the sending up of British society that could be represented in the Baccarat-playing, vodka-martini drinking James Bond, with the labourer's physique and the trace of a tenement accent – there's a chic cheek in Connery weighing up a disappointing brandy to M in *Goldfinger* with: "I'd say it was a thirty-year fine indifferently blended, sir. With an overdose of bonbois" without the slightest pretence of accent. That style was Connery's own – he was, whether or not you noticed his extraordinary ability as an actor, a great shape, possessed natural grace of movement, and had a voice that you could listen to reading the Edinburgh telephone directory out loud. He filled a suit with that tapering, fat-free body in a way that itself made clothes look good. After many years in which male fashion had been a matter of shapeless conformity, the very shape of Connery helped to redefine fashion for Britain in the early-sixties. Beyond that the films had style of their own. Compare *Dr No* or *From Russia with Love* with *The Frightened City*, which, whilst good in its own way, is as drably domestic as the stock British B film churned out in dozens at Merton Park. *Dr No* is international in cast and setting – there is a near parodic contrast between the stalwarts of British film – Bernard Lee and Desmond Llewellyn – and Jack Lord and Ursula Andress. Jamaica is a far cry from the Soho of *The Frightened City*. *Dr No* opened outwards from the confines of British film, not simply in imaginative casting and finding a location that wasn't the River Platte or the Burma Railway, but in the attention to detail – the theme tune by Monty Norman, played not with lush orchestration but rather like a beat group by the John Barry Seven, the enigmatic opening shot down the barrel of a gun and the elaborate title sequences by Maurice Binder, the theme songs beginning with *From Russia with Love* sung by Matt Monro and *Goldfinger* written by Bricusse and Newley to create a standard for Shirley Bassey, and Ken Adam's colossal sets – Dr No's rocket toppling base on Crab Key, or the recreating of Fort Knox on the backlot at Pinewood for *Goldfinger*. Compared to anything else made in the early sixties these films had 'Style'.

As the films romped on, with *From Russia with Love* breaking all British box-office records, the sense of style rippled outwards – often in small absurd ways. In sharp contrast to discreet orange and white Penguins, for example, the 1963 Pan edition of *Thunderball* sported a cover with two black bullet-holes, and the slugs could be found nestling in what appeared to be a pool of dried blood on the pre-title page. Only then did it become clear that the beige cover was an image of human skin, as though the whole book had been bound especially for the delight of a sadistic villain in a Graham Greene novel. By 1964, if you so desired, you could plaster the rear window of your Ford Anglia with stick-on bulletholes at 4d a sheet and pretend it was an Aston Martin DB5 with machine guns in the bumpers and an ejector seat. By 1965 you could buy Slazenger 'Goldfinger' golf clubs, Rosa Klebb dolls, or drink vodka-martinis that were shaken-not-stirred in 007 bars in Paris and London, buy 007 toothpaste in the USA or 007 clothes in France. But in one respect merchandising failed – the Burton idea for a line of Bond clothes for the British came too late, in 1965. By this time Carnaby Street had taken over, and such mass-merchandising could hardly dent Swinging London. Burton's line, designed not by Fleming's tailor but by Connery's, never made the high street shops. The 'Style' that was Bond had rolled on into the hype that was British pop culture in the mid-sixties – somehow to wear a copy of a suit worn by Sean Connery was not to share the joke of plastic bullet-holes or the 'Style' that the Bond films had generated. It would have been like wearing a Beatle wig, and only middle-aged Americans ever did that.

Fleming was now almost as famous as his creation. In August 1963 the *Sunday Times* could make a lead article out of its coverage of a meeting between two of the greats of crime, as Fleming visited Simenon in the south of France. The film of *From Russia with Love* (far and away the best film of any Bond book) was released in October and in November *Thunderball* returned. Kevin McClory took Ian Fleming to court to establish his part in the authorship of the story. After ten days Fleming and his business partner settled out of court along the simplest lines – McClory received the film rights to *Thunderball*, Fleming retained the book rights with an acknowledgement to Whittingham and McClory.

While the superhero of the films leapt from exploit to exploit, Fleming's paper hero lurched into crises that reflected the author's own failing health. At the start of *Thunderball*, he is seedy and unfit and told by M to report to a health farm. At the start of *On Her Majesty's Secret Service* (published in 1963) Bond is mentally drafting his letter of resignation. In *You Only Live Twice* (completed in March 1963 and published the following year) he is the distraught widower, driven by vengeance and deathwish to confront his wife's assassin in a Garden of Suicide. The James Bond of the apocalyptic *You Only Live Twice* is spiralling down towards his end – Fleming himself died in the August of 1964, leaving a last novel unrevised.[39] The cult of Bond – so independent of the character he had created – had boosted sales of Fleming's books almost beyond belief. The early novels had sold ten to twelve thousand worldwide. At the time of his death forty million copies of the Bond books had been printed.

§

Among the films Ian Hendry appeared in after *The Avengers* was *Live Now Pay Later*, based on Jack Trevor Story's novel of 1962-3. It's hardly great literature, but taken in contrast with an equally minor novel – Dave Wallis's 1963-4 novel *Only Lovers Left Alive* – it shows the before of a crude before and after.

Story's hero, Albert Argyle, is a hire-purchase tallyman, selling and living on the slate, juggling consumer goods, debts and sex-starved housewives like some living embodiment of a theory of perpetual motion. Around a week in the life of this feckless smooth-talker Story creates a comic picture of Macmillan's Britain, the nation that had come into being with 'You've never had it so good'.

It is a nation tied to its own past, crying into its beer and contemplating its navel. It is a world enjoying the novelty of unaccustomed possessions – the bedside lamp, the chiming clock, the picture of the green woman, to say nothing of the harder hardware. At the heart of this tawdry empire is Albert's boss, Mr Callendar of Callendar's Warehouse.

"The young woman, pretty, nicely-shaped, was plainly ill at ease and had not yet been indoctrinated into credit buying. The state of strain which resulted from this was composed of many subtle elements. Many contributory factors of which they were all aware, but which could not be allowed to emerge baldly. She wanted some things and she hadn't the money to pay for them. She couldn't admit this outright. If she had had the money she would not have come to Callendar's at all but would have gone to one of the many shops in town which offered a wider choice and lower prices. Mr Callendar couldn't admit this. She had been recommended to Callendar's by a similarly hard-up friend who consistently defaulted on her payments. Neither of them could mention this."[40]

Story makes it quite clear that the Britain he sees is a house built on sand, yet the worst of it is that this flimsy world has an air of permanence even in crisis.

"And ever since the possibility that Britain might join the European Common Market Mr Callendar had kept a case ready packed in anticipation of the kind of national prosperity which would demand higher quality and competitive prices for exportable goods, wages in accordance with work done – regardless of tea breaks – and unemployment for those who disliked hard work – regardless of their hire purchase commitments . . . the dark possibility of a nation living according to its means and on an orderly cash basis was terrifying to Mr Callendar and he had made his plans to get out."[41]

Britain did not join the Common Market. On January 14th, 1963 General de Gaulle said a final "Non" to the persistent efforts of the Lord Privy Seal, Edward Heath,[42] and it's almost without point to speculate on how much people ever believed Britain would join at that time. What matters is the sense of national isolation, of our own self-appraisal as a second-rate nation. Dean Acheson remarked, famously, on December 6th, 1962 that "Britain has lost an empire and not yet found a role." Of course we had a role – breast-beating and lamenting the good old days before the war.

"'Call anybody a working man today and he's insulted. He surrounds himself with the left-offs of his betters – second hand Jaguars made for somebody else, big houses built for gentlemen,

239

refrigerators, washing machines – well you know better than I do. Half the riding schools are full of snotty-nosed gorblimey kids from the council houses – you don't know where you are these days . . . you see who comes up here golfing at the weekends – ruddy shop-keepers, factory foremen, cloth-cap oafs who don't know one end of a club from the other. Never have done before the war, you know. Nothing sacred now.'"[43]

The sense of permanence lies in the obsession with class, or at least with the dread that previously clear class lines were dissolving under the illusory affluence. At the end of the novel, Callendar's world is unchanged by a week of chaos, a long time in politics is a gnatspan in hire purchase. Albert Argyle, deeper in trouble, deeper in debt, ends the book in the same state of sloppy optimism that he began it. For all that he's only in his twenties, it's a middle aged world – *Live Now Pay Later* is an adult world of home owners and renters, of table lamps and nylon carpets. The voice of '63 simply isn't heard. Teenagers are in school or on the shop floor. In *Only Lovers Left Alive*, it's their world, and theirs alone.

Dave Wallis's third novel was published in early 1964 to remarkable critical attention. Wallis seized upon the voice of '63 and hypothesised a world in which all the grown-ups did 'it' – that is, committed suicide, leaving the young to fend for themselves and tear each other apart:

"All the oldies wouldn't talk about 'The Crisis' as it had come to be called. The more conspicuous the signs of the Crisis the more it became impolite to mention them. The gap in the generations became even wider because young people on the contrary were always talking about suicide and saying, 'Go and do it,' to bus-conductors, teachers, policemen or shopkeepers who had a brush with them. The phrase came to replace 'Drop dead!' . . . "[44]

It reads like a pasty, limp fulfilment of the worst teen fantasy – a world to themselves, with no one to yell 'getyererrcut!', a world in which the concerns of Macmillan's Britain, of Jack Trevor Story's novel, simply do not figure, in which hire purchase, CND, class and party politics are all equally insignificant. Consumer durables are treated as disposable. When everything's up for pillage nothing is of value . . . until the food runs out. As such, it's a poor novel, but an interesting response to the shift in the national focus that had taken place since Macmillan ushered in the age of the tallyman. Such was its fame, such was it thought to be of the moment, that stories began to circulate that the Rolling Stones would make it the basis of their first film.

There's a sense in all this that Wallis was taken as speaking for the teenagers themselves, or at the least had so well observed the year of the youthquake that his simple act of picking up on the obvious rebellion of the teens made a second rate sci-fi novel into a major insight, a form of prophecy. The scene that so exercised the critics was this: "Meg advanced with her eyes bright and a thin slither of saliva dribbling from her half open mouth. Ernie wanted to shout, 'No! Stop!' but then they might not think he was a real tough leader any more; so he stood and watched.

"To use the scissors properly, surgically, would have meant handling the boy and this she would not do, for some reason, and so she went at the job stabbing, pecking and tearing like a starving vulture. The boy screamed and screamed and couldn't faint. When she had done she slumped and lost her tenseness and handed the scissors over to a boy who stabbed the King behind the ear so that the blood spurted and jerked and then fell like a jet from a garden hose when the tap is wrenched shut."[45]

And all without the use of the word castration, let alone prick or balls. The sex and the violence are all unimaginatively tame – it's a milk shake kind of decadence: "The girls took off their shoes and the boys their jackets. The jugs of cider and bottles of beer were drunk and spilt. When they were hungry they ate cold baked beans from a stack of tins Ernie had carried up there from the stock of a storekeeper who'd done it last week. Then they paired off. A few boys, left out in the mating musical chairs, took a last drink and slouched off into the silent streets in search of another party."[46]

As the teenagers gang up, tool up and inherit what's left of the earth they are occasionally flummoxed by the question of why their parents did it, and once or twice sense that they've been deserted.

"'Then they had nothing much left but getting hold of things to show off with, better cars, projectors to show their holiday films to each other. It's a good thing really they started doing it. They were all getting so bored without another war they'd soon have started one, H-bomb or not. Look at the way they kept going on about the war, films about it, parades, bugles on November 11th, plays, TV films, the lot. Making out how brave they were once, living in the past. When we wouldn't sit around and clap any longer they made out there was something wrong with *us*.'"

The war comes anyway, and with it pestilence and famine – freedom tips over into apocalypse. Here the book becomes more readable, less like an unwitting parody of a Sunday newspaper enquiry into teenage life, as the survivors of glorified gang battles head north and rediscover agriculture and animal husbandry with painful slowness.

Even this minor work now seems almost central to the ideas of the time. If nothing else the teen apocalypse points out forcefully that the teenagers had arrived, that 1963 had been their year.

§

Apocalypse figures strongly in the arts of the year. It's rare that it's played out as solemnly as it is in *Only Lovers Left Alive*. More common is the joke wipe-out of *The Bed-Sitting Room* or *Dr Strangelove*, the latter subtitled *How I learned to Stop Worrying and Love the Bomb*.

The Bed-Sitting Room opened at the Mermaid Theatre on January 31st. In *Strangelove it* is about to happen – in *The Bed-Sitting Room it* has happened and the semblance of normality is to be found everywhere. It's a gag that wears thin too quickly, but the world created by John Antrobus and Spike Milligan is a world of remnants masquerading as the whole – our national institutions reduced to the loyal – if stupid – service of lone individuals, a one man BBC, a one man National Health Service. It is an extension of Milligan's passion for the ephemera of British life, his gas stoves, batter puddings and upright pianos of *The Goon Show*, here piled up in mountains – a furious satirising of bourgeois stability directly rooted in Milligan's experiences of the Second World War. The survivors of the Third World War, the nuclear apocalypse, satirise the society of the day as they go through the rituals of the pre-apocalyptic society, as though the wipe-out were some temporary event, as though the practices and institutions were not the same practices and institutions that had led to the unthinkable (so often thought) Third World War – a war which lasted a mere two minutes and twenty-eight seconds. The problem and the solution are, the play seems to say, in our hands.

The angst of bomb culture had, in 1963, its finest flowering not in bomb-tragedy but bomb-farce. *Dr Strangelove*, Kubrick's polished black comedy, completely eclipsed the film version of the 1962 novel *Failsafe* – the plots of the two films were basically the same, a missile is launched at the Soviet Union in error, and in compensation America has to destroy one of its own cities. *Strangelove* is Sellers' film all the way (he plays three roles) but the most memorable image comes as gung-ho airforce officer Slim Pickens plummets to earth over Russia, riding his nuclear bomb, whooping and roaring like some rodeo cowboy, a parody of all the parts he'd ever played in countless Hollywood westerns.

Yet, the most striking attempts to deal with the prolonged presence of the nuclear threat came in two works which didn't mention it at all. In Joan Littlewood's *Oh, What a Lovely War!* and Bruce Lacey's *An Evening Of British Rubbish.*

An Evening of British Rubbish opened at the Comedy Theatre on January 24th. Nothing quite like it had been seen before in a 'legitimate' theatre. Not even the Crazy Gang were this crazy. It was performed by (it seems impossible to say written by) Bruce Lacey, spuriously if aptly titled Professor, the Alberts, Joyce Grant and Ivor Cutler. They had put the show together at the suggestion of William Donaldson and Michael Codron, but Lacey and the Alberts had been 'doing their own thing' (a use of the phrase which I don't mean as a cliché) for many years by then. Few figures of the nineteen-fifties prefigure the imagery of the later sixties as strongly as Bruce Lacey – a self-taught master of mechanical chaos.

Lacey had been a performer since the age of nine, and an inventor since his teens. Much of his act revolved around his unique ability with robots, animations and self-destructive machines. Too young to serve in the RAF in the war, he had constructed what must have been one of the world's first flight simulators out of torch bulbs and the innards of wind-up gramophones, to enable him to fly night raids over Germany without leaving the comfort of his bedroom – the first of what he called "environmental fantasy experiences". This aptitude was sharpened by a post-war training in electronics in the Navy, where he first ventured into what he calls 'performance art', and focused by a long spell in a TB sanatorium, where he took to painting and drawing. After this he enrolled at the Royal College of Art, where, accomplished in electronics, painting, tightrope, trapeze and robotics, he and Jeff Nuttall began 'the happening' some ten years before the word achieved its vogue. In the early fifties Lacey could be seen on the London Underground dressed in the armour of a Japanese warrior. At the RCA he founded the Dodo Society (so-called because the RCA was, he says, dead as a), to the first meeting of which he invited the model who had spent the day posing for the life class, but whose naked presence at a social gathering caused alarm and walk-outs. (When John Calder pulled the same stunt at the 1963 Edinburgh Drama Festival, it was held to be the first recorded happening, and resulted in a prosecution.) After the RCA he performed in the London Clubs and refined such talents as plucking a tune on the spokes of a penny farthing, and how to play the collapsible piano.

"I found that all the acts I tried to do seriously went terribly wrong, and somehow I triumphed in disasters. Like doing the trapeze with a dummy, I used to get tangled up with the dummy, and tightrope walking – I kept falling off . . . Sawing a woman in half,

with a volunteer from the audience . . . There were terrible times,
like when the saw came out with part of the woman's underwear,
because I'd forgotten to put a piece of metal inside. I did knife
throwing too . . . "[47]

The happening became fashionable, but was also "what I'd been
doing all my life." Lacey speaks of his work at this time as a form of
psychotherapy, as "getting things out of your system". One evening
in the basement of Better Books, a Nuttall-Lacey-Marowitz venture
took the form of psychotherapy for the bomb generation. Lacey
contrived to have the walls run with blood, to create images of
dismemberment, and as a climax to have a solid brick wall demolished by white-clad surgeons, who would pluck a stooge from the
audience whom they would then gut in public, by ripping up the bag
of offal tied to her stomach.

"The feeling at that time was one of anger at all things around us
. . . Macmillan saying you've never had things so good, and we felt
things were awful. A feeling that everybody was complacent. We
wanted to shock them out of their complacency. But we found that
people were immune to it somehow. There might have been people
who were upset, but there were sophisticated people who might say
'Oh it's just another happening'."

Lacey's talent for machines kept him employed by television and
the theatre, working on *The Army Game*, Milligan's *A Show Called
Fred* and Michael Bentine's *It's a Square World* – Lacey was responsible for Bentine's flea circus routine, and helped create some of the
zaniness that made the show work – but he was never happy with
what he thinks of as 'straight' comedy. It was a madness too structured for his taste.

Lacey found kindred spirits in Tony and Douglas Gray, brothers
who performed under the name of The Alberts. They had been
founder members of the trad jazz band the Temperance Seven – of
whom there were nine – queries as to this would be answered with
'We're one over the eight' – but had left to pursue their own brand
of anarchy and music. Together with Bruce Lacey they played the
Establishment Club on Friday nights. Lenny Bruce shared the bill
with them in 1962 and liked them so much he invited them to play in
Los Angeles. The Alberts and Lacey sailed across on the *Queen
Mary*, for a tour they thought would last years, to be met at New
York with a cable from Lenny Bruce – in jail again, no contract, no
job. For two months they played around in New York, a small part
of a larger wave of British comedy.

"While we were in New York, *Beyond the Fringe* opened . . . one
day we sat outside the theatre in a big cage, dressed smartly as

Englishmen taking tea – like a miniature zoo, 'this is how English-men live'."

On getting back to England, they were approached by Donaldson and Codron, to assemble the acts they'd been playing in the clubs for years into *An Evening of British Rubbish*.

"No one had ever had confidence to do a comedy show which was comedy all the way through. The Goons never did that. There was a belief on *The Goon Show* that you couldn't sustain half an hour of mad humour – you had to have Max Geldray or Ray Ellington playing . . . There was a big gulf between the way that I performed and the way that they [the Goons and Bentine] performed. Every-thing had to be scripted and very, very carefully rehearsed. Whereas the Alberts and I used to make it up as we went along. [Someone gave me a stuffed monkey one day] so I turned up at the Estab-lishment with the Alberts and did an act with a stuffed monkey. Sometimes we'd 'phone each other up and sketch out the bare bones of something, and then make up the rest, we improvised it . . . the straight performers were shit-scared of it – they wouldn't dare do that sort of thing without a script – and so we were looked on as sort of rank amateurs . . . When we came to do *British Rubbish* it ran for four months solid – no interludes at all – the only compromise we made was to Michael Codron, who'd promised a spot to Ivor Cutler . . . so we had Ivor doing his weird songs. It worked very well. We would find that in the first ten minutes twenty or thirty people would walk out. Early on there'd be a cooking act from me 'Take two eggs and beat them together' and I'd go like that – Splat! – and the eggs would fly everywhere."

The first people to leave would usually be those at the front.

" It was a packed house on the opening night but there were only half a dozen seats sold for the second night. And it was only because of Bernard Levin's review, that we became packed and stayed packed – and he was closing shows down right, left and centre – and my God to see him in the audience! . . . We peered out from between the curtains and saw him clutch his stomach and fall off his seat like he was being sick or something, we thought he hated it all so much!"

Far from it.

Levin: "There were pillars alongside the stalls, and I being a critic was on the aisle – at one point I was laughing so uncontrollably . . . I hurled myself forward and damn near knocked myself unconscious by my forehead banging into the pillar . . . "[48]

Levin's review for the *Daily Mail* was effusive in its praise, com-paring Lacey and the Alberts to the best: "How could an inventory of the articles on the stage be made, consisting as they do of huge piles, heaps, atticfuls of junk, mostly insane machinery, whose function is to fall to pieces at the appropriate moment? . . . It is like *The Goon Show* . . . it is like the best of Beachcomber . . . it is like the Marx Brothers in their heyday."[49]

Lacey's old colleague Charles Marowitz saw even more significance in the knockabout: " . . . The qualities which make *Rubbish* generally amusing and consistently refreshing are precisely those which, in professionals, have fallen into disuse: i.e. instinctive abandon, a genuine sense of free play, an irreverent attitude to form and method, a freedom from logic and its repugnant concomitant, psychological realism. At its best *Rubbish* resembles a kind of Zen revue . . . Lacey with eyes like poached eggs . . . What he lacks in timing he makes up for in speed. When his gags wilt before his eyes, imperturbably, he turns to assault the next circumstance . . . even when bits misfire or end badly, one is *with* the clowns and the whole anarchic premise of the show. Making love to an embalmed camel; dancing with a bandy-legged mannequin, or demonstrating the virtues of mechanical as opposed to live actors, the show erupts into comic flames that one would not encounter anywhere else."[50]

There is, in Bruce Lacey's own account, a powerful thread running through this mixture of slapstick and mayhem – a critical sensibility at work, a deep seated resentment at the dominance of certain cultural forms, an acute consciousness of human vulnerability. A bomb-age comedy. Destruction is so often the mode of *British Rubbish*, a world in which things fall apart, in which machines are as likely to play you a tune as explode, in which the dancing partner's body will fly apart limb by limb. It was an uproarious, but dark and bloody slapstick.

"In many ways it was a send-up . . . of the establishment theatre. Because I was working under the table, as I was for Michael Bentine, I thought I want to get back at them – so I thought I'll make two robot machines – two robot super-actors. I'll play the part of the actor I hate, big headed, always swaggering about, who forgets his lines and has a heart attack . . . so I began the act as a big-headed, bumptious actor-laddie, then I slumped over a box and with secret switches these two robots came to life – one was clock-face, he had a face like a clock, and he'd do a soliloquy, the other would start singing 'I'm forever blowing bubbles' and bubbles would start coming out of his chest. That was going back to psychodrama, having robots take over from this type of actor that I hated so much.

"I had this penny farthing bicycle and I found that by fitting throat mikes I could throw things at it, and on one wheel I found I could play *Show Me the Way to Go Home* amplified. In tune.

"I think it was Jonathan Miller who said we weren't just making jokes, we were making jokes about jokes about jokes about jokes . . . about the whole business of being a performer. We weren't taking ourselves seriously, we were operating on all these different levels, and I don't think the Alberts appreciated all the levels, and they thought I was very pretentious when I'd talk about these deeper levels. One thing we all had in common was that we'd always collected things, horn gramophones . . . magic lanterns . . . things from Victorian times, but the music was twenties' jazz. The best thing I had was a full-sized stuffed camel. It stood in my hall for months and months and then I had the idea of cutting a trapdoor in it and then I had an African xylophone and painted it white and stuck it inside like the ribs of the camel. I'd come on dressed as an Arab and sing a love song to it, *The Sheik of Araby*, open up the trapdoor and play the middle eight on the ribs of the camel.

"Everything the establishment theatre did had to be so carefully rehearsed . . . If we felt we were getting too slick we'd start to play tricks on each other to mess each other up, so we'd have to find an alternative way of doing it. We didn't want any sets. We were in a theatre . . . you could see the brick wall at the back. All the stage lights were hanging down to be seen, and after all these acts the debris was left on the stage, and at the back we had the chassis of a car, and we built up all the props so it became like a gigantic piece of sculpture. At the end we'd jump on it and drive off . . . smash into the wings."

Junk became fashionable. There's something definitive of the era in Lacey's objects and the clutter of the Steptoe living room. With the paraphernalia of the past, the rubbish of our imperial glory. Lacey and the Alberts somehow managed to turn mayhem into a form of protest – they were simultaneously nostalgic and destructive, loving conservationists and anarchic protesters. Tony Gray touched on a mood of the times that reached to the prime ministerial level when he said of *British Rubbish*, "In our show we use the past – our Victoriana and Edwardiana – to satirise the present."[51] It's hard to see the satire, but it was there, and the subversive in Bruce Lacey is never far from the surface.

"Although the British Empire had largely gone people were still pro Empire. It was a very strong feeling. They hadn't recognised that it was gone . . . the British Empire was a sacred thing . . . still alive in people's minds . . . I felt this was out of touch, very pompous, the old ways of doing things . . . Going into hospital [with all its petty restrictions] with TB pulled me up for the first time in my life, and made me question all the different attitudes, conventions around me . . . I went to art school – everyone thought this was the great liberating experience, and I found that once again there were all these restrictions, so a lot of my extra-curricular activities were fighting restrictions.

"I'd collected things . . . swords, pistols, drums. African idols . . . Japanese armour, then I started collecting shop-window dummies to stand them on. I think it was inevitable that I would somehow bring them all together. I used to feel very sorry for objects, because they'd pass through a period of neglect, they'd be relegated to the loft before being thrown away, and for a long time I felt I was looking after things and helping them through their difficult years – *Monitor* called me the Preservation Man . . . I thought if an object was once useful and once loved, it was terrible if it was discarded only later on to be loved again as an antique – and I felt I wanted to preserve them all. Looking back . . . I'm appalled at some of the things I did to them. I'd buy a lovely old vacuum cleaner, and somehow or other, almost through having hundreds of objects, a head would get stuck on top of it, and I'd think that looks like a pair of shoulders, so arms would get stuck on it and then a motor, so then I'd have to cut a hole in it to fit the motor . . . and these things I'd started out loving I'd end up destroying . . . I'd feel very guilty that I'd actually destroyed things."

Bruce Lacey began a trend that, in the mid-sixties, came to symbolise Swinging London, and to crystallise the marriage of nostalgia to irreverence: he was the first person to adopt the red imperial jacket of the British soldier as part of his own anti-uniform. In the end this irreverence put paid to Rubbish – their poster had always been based on the design of the union jack – the ticket agencies refused to display the poster, and sales went down again – as Lacey says, " . . . We never got the coach tours from the agencies so . . . it seemed that after four months we'd used up all the people and it just tailed off."

On March 19th the Theatre Workshop, under the direction of Joan Littlewood, opened at the Theatre Royal at Stratford in East London, with *Oh, What a Lovely War!* – a play that had been evolved by improvisation. It was Littlewood's first work for the Workshop for two years. Like so many of the plays done by the Workshop, it revolved around the remarkable talents and personality of Joan Littlewood, who had started the company at the end of the war, and settled it in the Theatre Royal in 1953, where its reputation had been made with original works by Brendan Behan and Shelagh Delaney, and with *Fings Ain't Wot They Used To Be* by

Frank Norman. Many actors gifted in song, dance and comedy passed through the company – Barbara Windsor, Roy Kinnear, Murray Melvin, Brian Murphy and Welsh actor Victor Spinetti. Spinetti's recruitment to the company in the late-fifties says something about the idiosyncratic style of Joan Littlewood.

"It was 1959, I was working in London. I'd just done a tour in my first big show – *South Pacific* – I'd shared a dressing room with Sean Connery – I came into London and got a job as a compere in a little revue theatre, the Irving in Irving Street, one of those revues that always had a girl posing in the back. Suddenly I got a marvellous review from Harold Hobson – he did a comparison between Olivier as *The Entertainer* and me as the entertainer in this place. Wolf Mankowitz read the review and came in one Monday. He said, 'Joan Littlewood is directing *Make Me An Offer*.' I thought fucking hell – you work with her, all that dedication! I'd got a job. He said, 'You'll have to go and see her, at Wyndham's.' I went in a twenty minute break. She said 'Have we met?' I said, 'No.' She was terrible at names. 'What would you give me for this set?' she said. I looked around . . . it was the set for *The Hostage*, there was a barrel and half a window. I said, 'Fifty quid'. 'But it's a Sean Kenny set!' She said, 'listen if you owned this theatre and somebody offered you a million quid to pull it down and put up a potato warehouse, would you?' 'Take the money and fuck off,' I said. She said, 'You've got the part love. You can play Charlie.' And a man in the stalls shouted, 'Charlie's the lead, Joan.' She said, 'You've got the lead, love. Where are you working?' 'In a strip,' I said. 'I'll come and see you' . . . She caught the late show, we went out to supper and I've known her ever since."

Oh, What a Lovely War! juxtaposes the slaughter of the First World War with the music hall songs of the day – a company of pierrots, in ruffs and white satin, play all the parts against back projection, slides that build up the images and statistics of mass slaughter. It is one of the most bitter anti-war plays ever seen on the London stage. In its context, it is the age of terror handled by a simple displacement, and that without invalidating the obvious subject of the work. Tynan reviewed it for the *Observer*: "It seems quite likely that when the annals of our theatre in the middle years of the twentieth century come to be written, one name will lead all the rest: that of Joan Littlewood. Others write plays, direct them or act in them: Miss Littlewood alone 'makes theatre' . . . The big, tough, purposeful heart that beats throughout the evening belongs only to Joan. You feel that her actors have a common attitude towards more than acting, a shared vision that extends to life in general; it is thus, rather than by any rehearsal method or technique of staging, that true theatrical style is born . . . and after the final scene, in which a line of reluctant heroes advances on the audience, bleating like sheep in a slaughterhouse, one is ready to storm Buckingham Palace and burn down Knightsbridge barracks. The production brings off a double *coup*: it is revolutionary alike in content and form."[52]

Victor Spinetti describes the working method of *Oh, What a Lovely War!*: "Joan's actual work was unbelievably detailed, the ground plan was amazing, it was balletic work. The critics used to say that everyone up on stage was having a ball, but that was a result of amazing rehearsals, amazingly detailed stuff. Joan is like an Elizabethan scholar, a great love of language. The way we had to work, we had to take a step up. You never improvised by going on stage trying to be funny, you went on stage trying to be real.

"Working with Joan you have to know background, you have to read. We were all given piles of books to read . . . She played the songs from World War One on a tape. I hate those songs – I said, 'I can't bear them, the masochism in the British thumbs-up-as-long-as-we've-got-a-cup-of-tea-we'll-survive. I loathe the First World War. Millions died for fuck all.' Joan said 'You'll never have to sing them, you can be the MC.' She cast the show from our reactions to the songs and the books.

"We never saw a script, it was total improvisation. Joan asked if anyone had been in the army. Me – talking about National Service – I'd tell her some funny stories about the things that went on, and she'd say, 'Right we'll have that.' We were trained to use bayonets – Joan got RSM Brittan in to drill the cast. [She did not attend herself.] When he left she came in and said, 'Sorry darlings but I just can't stand those licensed killers. What did he say?' I said, 'I never knew what they were saying.' 'Don't tell me,' she said, 'Show me' . . . and for the two and a half years I was in that show none of the other actors had a clue what I was on about."

Out of this Spinetti improvised a part he has played on and off ever since – including the Beatles' *Magical Mystery Tour* – the wholly incomprehensible, gibbering RSM.

"Quite a lot of the stuff we improvised was never used. It was a way of working that was tough, interesting, demanding, extending one's awareness of the world . . . it was a university. 'You have to accept the responsibility for having talent – it's up to you, everything is up to us individuals' . . . that's one of the things she told us. Joan's the sort of person that will talk to three in the morning . . . architecture, painting, music . . . she's really a renaissance person . . . If we'd had a government worth its salt they'd have made her Minister for the Arts, something like that. She got her first grant from the Arts Council under Norman St John Stevas. She got nothing from Labour – they were terrified of her."[53]

In June *Oh, What a Lovely War!* transferred to Wyndham's in the West End, and ran and ran. In 1969 it was filmed by Richard Attenborough.

Centre 42 was a much younger organisation than Theatre Workshop – similarly radical it was more precise in its political aim, to bring the trade union movement and the arts together. Arnold Wesker was one of the most successful of the wave of new playwrights in the late fifties – in 1960 he had sent a pamphlet to every trade union secretary in Britain, criticising the Labour movement's indifference to the arts. Of these a mere four responded – Natsopa, the Tobacco Workers' Union, the Society of Technological Civil Servants and ACTT. The ACTT drafted a motion to be put to the 1960 TUC conference to "set up a commission to investigate and discuss what relationship the Trades Union movement should have to the cultural life of the community." Wesker then wrote an open letter to the TUC General Secretary in the *New Statesman* headed "Vision! Vision! Mr Woodcock". He came perilously close to parody in his Hoggartian, earnest vision: " . . . people stopping Auden in the street to thank him for their favourite poem, teenagers around the juke-box arguing about my last play, miners flocking to their own opera house . . . a nation . . . unable to wait for Benjamin Britten's next opera, arguing about Joan Littlewood's latest . . .

" . . . we want a principle established – that art is a common heritage, not the habit of the few. And if the opera house that the miners build, or Joan Littlewood's theatre, or the Liverpool Philharmonic only play to half filled houses in our generation, that doesn't matter either. There are other generations to follow."[54]

The TUC referred the matter to one of its education committees. Centre 42 launched officially in November the following year. By the Autumn of 1962, they had received nothing from the TUC, but were able to undertake a tour of six English towns with poetry, plays, films and folk music after a £10,000 award from the Gulbenkian Foundation. It became a much discussed 'noble' venture, run by an ad hoc body of artists crossing with other radical organisations like CND and the Committee of 100, of which Wesker was a member. In the Summer of 1963 Centre 42 published its first annual report, which Wesker prefaced with a piece in the *Observer*, fending off the criticism that had been levelled at the organisation:

"42 works: this is a fact whatever our inadequacies may be
. . . If I say that we have enemies I am not being wilfully dramatic
. . . the 42 movement touches more than the social issues of
whether art is a minority preoccupation or not . . . it appears also to
affront some basic democratic principle and arouses anger and
hostility."

The attacks were part of the long debate descending from *The
Uses of Literacy* – Centre 42 was accused, wrote Wesker, of "taking
art to the masses", which, if complaint it was, Wesker rebutted by
pointing out that they performed only where they were invited – of
"knowing better and being better", the old problem of patronage –
and, worst of all, of ignoring the profit motive. If Centre 42 held the
danger of educating the working classes, in the drift of the times it
quickly looked too serious in its art and too presumptive of passivity
– how about stopping Auden in the street to read him a poem, or
Wesker listening to what's on the juke-box? There was by 1963 an
air of do-it-yourself entering the arts, perhaps epitomised by Bruce
Lacey, but nurtured by pop music, that by the late sixties made
Centre 42 seem anachronistic. Wesker immersed himself in it – but
that meant that he had no new play performed for six years and one
of the most powerful voices in the theatre was silent throughout
1963, most of which he spent raising money and trying to secure a
permanent home for the Centre in a disused, circular engine shed in
north London, the Camden Roundhouse. Today the Roundhouse,
after several incarnations, stands as idle as it did nearly thirty years
ago.

1963 also saw Joan Littlewood's only venture into making a full
length film – *Sparrows Can't Sing*. Interviewed by Barry Norman in
February, Littlewood reflected on the itinerant life she had been
leading for the two years before *Lovely War*: "I'm not a theatre
person you see . . . What I hate about the theatre is all that *art* . . .
I'm still a bum trying to forget old ideas and think of new ones. I do
this every ten years. It's the only way to stop yourself becoming
stale. But I'm not sure what I'm going to do next. I'd like to make
films, only the way I want to make them I'd probably get into union
trouble."[55]

By March Littlewood was reported to have asked for her name to
be taken off *Sparrows Can't Sing*, after cuts had been made to the
finished film without her consent. Her next film was a short that
seemed to grow directly out of her involvement with the East
Enders. The film was designed to show off some of the local talent,
pub entertainers, even strippers, that Littlewood had come across in
East London, and to promote the idea she had for building a

pleasure park in the declining area of docklands. Walter Lassally, Director of Photography on *A Taste of Honey* and *The Loneliness of the Long-Distance Runner*, shot the film for Joan Littlewood, and recalled in his memoirs that the film was abandoned at the edit stage when it became clear that they had "failed miserably in the film's objective, i.e. to prove the need for a pleasure park, as everybody we filmed was obviously having a great time already."[56]

The discovery of the working class continued. Littlewood had turned eyes towards London's East End. Satire had turned TV towards new comedy. As the BBC began *That Was The Week That Was*, and as Wesker took art to the people, Associated-Rediffusion was looking at the potential of pub entertainment – the art *of* the people? – as a source of the new comedy. Producer/presenter Daniel Farson had settled in a flat over a builder's yard in Limehouse, and had bought a pub on the Isle of Dogs which he rechristened the Waterman's Arms. It became a venue for the talent, some traditional, some tending towards the satirical, that he was finding:

"You'd be amazed at the talent you can find flogging itself to death for a few quid a week in the public bars. Music hall was born in the pubs a hundred years ago. And now the Variety theatres are finished it's returned there. The people I'm using are real professionals. Queenie Watts, for instance, got a part in *Sparrows Can't Sing* after I'd taken Joan Littlewood to see her.

"The West End is dead. A dreary place and the pubs are just beer halls and gin palaces. But in the East End there's a fantastic feeling of energy and community spirit. People get together to enjoy themselves there and the places where they do it are the pubs."[57]

Among the talent that shone were a one-legged pop singer, a taxi driver who sang like Al Jolson, a Country and Western cab driver, and a comedian reputed to be sicker than Lenny Bruce. In March of 1963 this latter was to be found appearing at the Deuragon Arms, Hackney. His name was Ray Martine, and he seemed confident of his talent and cocksure of his material: "I could make the Palladium if I dropped the dirt and kept the camp . . . People like me, despite me. Lenny Bruce came over here and said 'I don't do that. My stuff is more zany than dirty.'"[58]

On the other side of Hackney in the Rising Sun the presence of television interest in a fresher kind of humour was making itself felt, as journalist Michael Wale observed: "The attitude of the barmen is blasé. One produces Elkan Allan's card, he is chief of A-R TV's entertainment. Another murmurs that Dan Farson had been in the night before and that they were going to be on the tele, adding for good measure that the *Observer* had been down too."[59]

Martine replaced Lenny Bruce at Peter Cook's Establishment Club, but cleaned up his act enough to become the host of the pub show A-R eventually mounted on television as *Stars and Garters*. Farson described it as "very much cold tea in tankards which defeated the whole point: of filming the real people in the real places."[60]

§

In December 1962 the BBC appointed a new head of drama, Sydney Newman, the Canadian who thought up *The Avengers* and who had been head of drama at ABC since 1958. In that capacity he had run *Armchair Theatre*. Before Newman the influence of the stage, the three act play and the world of 'french windows', had left TV drama awkward and lacking an identity of its own. Faced with a weekly series of live one hour, one-off plays, he had evolved new production techniques, new relationships between producer, director and writer, and had fostered a commitment to new writers: "I decided right away . . . I'm only going to do the events leading up to and the climax – and that was the essence of a one hour drama. So they were always very fast and compressed and I used to tell writers to tell the story when they're charging towards the goal posts, which is the climax. And that was the form of it – they had to be fast, every second had to count, the opening had to grip the audience within the first thirty seconds otherwise they'd switch off and go somewhere else. That was absolutely cardinal. Of course the shooting had to be very dynamic, the camera had to move, the scenes visually had to have depth."[61]

Newman had defined the vocabulary of television drama for the next ten years, but he'd also defined the subject matter in his sense of purpose – a sense of purpose he now took to the BBC: "I was very concerned about the turning points in British society – the changing relationship between father and son, parish priest and worshipper, union organiser and union members and so on – and changing morality. And these were the things I concentrated on. I never waited for plays to come in from the outside. I had script editors whose job it was to find plays. I used to have a meeting every week with my story editors and talk about what was going on in the news and the subject matter we ought to be doing. We would commission writers to write. We didn't wait for the stuff to come in. We commissioned Harold [Pinter] to write *A Night Out*[62] . . . Alun Owen to write on many subjects . . . of course people like

Alun and Clive [Exton] I had them under exclusive contract . . . I used to joke to my wife 'It's going to be a big job but I'm going to change England.'

"I'm a 'child' of John Grierson's. I worked for him for five years, and I learned that any dramatic or any work of art, I think, had to have relevance to contemporary life. And I also learnt from him the power of film to change minds. I was very concerned that my plays had meat in them . . . whether I was doing a murder mystery, a romance or a hard-edged social drama, kitchen-sink if you like, it had to have some essential meaning and it had to be done in such a fashion that the audience would think about the play and talk about it for two or three or four or five days afterwards. I use the word 'entertain' as meaning entertaining options – a very legitimate use of the word entertain – I was giving my audience options and under-standings of the reality in which they lived . . . [it's been said] I discovered the working class – that is they were not comic foils in my plays. That was unusual in 1958.

"The BBC were doing the occasional very good play on Sunday night opposite *Armchair Theatre* – but the fact is they didn't know how to schedule them . . . I had a precise notion of the audience I was dealing with. I had evolved a whole mystique of how to win audiences on a regular basis of one-off plays, which is now a lost art . . . I was not going to give them a kitchen-sink drama one week, Ibsen the next, because I felt that the cultural spread was too great. I never looked down on my audience and I never thought of my audience's intelligence – I thought of their cultural breadth and I catered to a narrow band of cultural breadth – somebody who didn't know who Picasso was, or who Ibsen was, somebody who never saw Shakespeare, and I rejected many very good plays saying 'it just isn't for my audience, they wouldn't go for it' . . . most of the BBC's productions were good but rather static, safe, and they would give you, say, a play by [a new writer like] Jack Pulman and then the next week, say, Shakespeare – you can't hold an audience for the one-hour play on that basis. *Armchair Theatre* plays were never designed for stupid people. They had real content, but they were layered – so that on the surface they glittered with smart camera work and good costumes, marvellous acting, but underneath, for those who could discern it, there was a relevance to contemporary society . . . If *Armchair Theatre* had a good style . . . it didn't arise out of any notion of style on my part, it arose out of clarity and an immediacy of communication. I wanted the audience to see, to hear and then to understand . . . I wanted social action as a result of my plays. Shelter was formed straight after we put out *Cathy Come*

Home as a Wednesday Play.

"I'm somewhat disillusioned with England today. When people today see a problem that needs a solution they don't take action. Media – to change men's minds – has to do more than simply reveal the truth in the hope that the truth will bestir men into taking action."

There's little doubt that when the Pilkington report criticised an excess of 'sordid domestic dramas', they had the work of Sydney Newman in mind – he doesn't think any play he put out was sordid, but then the Pilkingtonians didn't ask Sydney Newman to give evidence, despite the fact that he had, by the time of their enquiry, established himself as the most influential drama producer in British television.

"He [Sir Robert Fraser of the ITA] used to say to me 'Sydney, why can't you do nice plays for nice people?'"Since ITV had found its feet there had been a steady drift of BBC staff to the other side. With the appointment of Newman, Hugh Greene reversed that drift for the first time. Less than a year after Greene took over as DG, Newman was approached.

"[Greene] didn't poach me personally. He did it through his director of television, Kenneth Adam . . . Adam said, 'Would you like to come to the BBC?' – 'As what,' I said – 'As producer of our Sunday night play' – I laughed. I said, 'You want to buy me to do exactly what I'm doing now.' I said no. Then he said, 'Would you like to be our Head of Drama' – I said, 'That's interesting.' . . . The negotiations were secret, and once we'd come to an agreement on contract I wrote a letter of resignation [to ABC] . . . I was told I couldn't leave. I had a contract . . . I phoned Kenneth Adam and said 'You better forget about me' . . . he [discussed it with Greene] and called me back. 'We'll wait for you,' he said. That knocked me for a loop."

Fourteen months later ABC finally released Newman from his contract. During the interval he made one his most controversial plays, Clive Exton's *The Trial of Dr Fancy*, in which a doctor is on trial for his ethics – he shortens tall men into midgets – a play so argued about that its transmission was held up until December 1963, a year after Newman had left. "I was asked to come to the BBC late at night, when nobody could see me – and we were in Kenneth's office, drinking. I'd never met Hugh Greene, and the door opened and this great big man came in, he was six foot seven. He shook my hand and as he sat down I fell in love with him the very first second because he slumped low so that his head was level with mine, and I thought any man who'd be so considerate is a great guy. And he said, 'I've just come from the board and it's my pleasure to invite you to join us.'"

Newman says it was the range that drew him to the BBC, a chance to move into children's drama, and classics. Part of Greene's brief had been to point out that most of the writers who had worked for Newman at ABC had started out with BBC radio – Newman must get them back for BBC television. One of the problems he faced was that for all Greene's new broomery the BBC was full of "dead wood". How was Newman to get the staff he wanted to make the programmes he'd been hired to make? BBC2 offered the solution – it was taking shape throughout 1963 and provided the mechanism for a rearrangement of staff, thus letting Newman bring in talent from outside. He broke up the script department, replacing it with three departments – series, serials and single plays, and brought the BBC into line with the rest of the industry by distinguishing between producers and directors, and putting script editors and directors at the service of individual producers. By 1964 Newman's most memorable achievement was on the screen – the long running, provocative Wednesday Play. Before that there came a landmark in children's television. Among the newcomers Sydney Newman brought in was the twenty-seven-year-old Verity Lambert, a script editor at ABC. Newman appointed her producer, and between them they brought *Dr Who* to the small screen on November 23rd 1963, with the story 'An Unearthly Child.' The programme was designed to bridge the gap on Saturday evenings between the end of *Grandstand* at 5.15, and *Juke Box Jury* at 5.45.

"I dreamed up the character of a man who is 764 years old; who is senile but with extraordinary flashes of intellectual brilliance. A crotchety old bugger (any kid's grandfather) who had, in a state of terror, escaped in his machine from an advanced civilisation on a distant planet which had been taken over by some unknown enemy. He didn't know who he was anymore, and neither did the earthlings, hence his name, Dr Who; he didn't know precisely where his home was; he did not fully know how to operate the time-space machine."[63]

The title role went to William Hartnell, until then better known as cantankerous sergeant-majors in staple British films, and most recently seen as the weasel-like scout in *This Sporting Life*. He was equipped with a Tardis (Time and Relative Dimension in Space) machine, capable of assuming any form, but jammed in the unlikely guise of a Metropolitan Police box, a granddaughter called Susan, and reluctant passengers – in best avuncular *Blue Peter* vein, two of Susan's schoolteachers. The Tardis could go anywhere, and

257

anywhen, as long as you had no specific preference – and the first four episodes took the four time-travellers to palaeolithic Earth and the discovery of fire. Newman, right from the days when he had worked on the *Pathfinders in Space* series at ABC, had been insistent on scientific and historical accuracy – as he put it to me "no bug-eyed monsters". In episode five, the Tardis visited another time, another planet, and there encountered a one-eyed monster that would clinch the programme's success. Watching at home, shortly before Christmas 1963, unaware of precisely what his producer, writer and designer had done in the second adventure, Newman was horrified at his first sight of a Dalek.

The idea for the Dalek came from writer Terry Nation – the image of the beast came from designer Raymond Cusick, who had joined *Dr Who* when Ridley Scott had to leave at short notice. Terry Nation's notes for the Dalek were brief – indicating that they were inhabited machines rather than robots, but that no sign of human life should be visible from the outside – a single eye on a stalk, mechanical grabs in lieu of arms, and legless gliding movement like the Georgian state dancers. Left to his own devices – in the face of an unofficial boycott of the programme by the visual effects department – Cusick experimented with the basic design of a glass salt cellar, and tried out various methods of propulsion, rejecting a tricycle in favour of castors. If this sounds makeshift, then that's part and parcel of the art of illusion, and despite a low budget each Dalek cost £120 and still managed to have a home-made touch – the mechanical grab was fashioned out of a sink plunger and looked as though it was fashioned out of a sink plunger. This was part of the success of the monsters in *Dr Who* – the Cybermen looked as though they were cobbled together out of bits of vacuum cleaner – and of *Star Trek*. Somehow these programmes invited the nodding consent of the audience to their inventive hamming, both in script and design. Transferred to the big screen neither *Star Trek* nor *Dr Who* benefited from the money spent or the effects achieved. At its best *Dr Who* was always both pioneering and Heath Robinson, and this meant risking things like equipping demonic dustbins with sink plungers for hands.

No monster has ever quite displaced the Daleks in *Dr Who* mythology – and in the first series they saved the programme. Shortly after episode one, Verity Lambert was told that the series would have to end after only thirteen episodes. Long before that the Daleks had captured a large enough audience – children and adults – to guarantee its future. If, in the long run, Sydney Newman's educational impulse towards historical and scientific accuracy has been lost, he has long since relented over his initial hostility to the Daleks. On the shelves in Sydney Newman's flat sit a BAFTA award, an award from the Writers' Guild for 'outstanding services to writers' – and a Dalek.

§

Lindsay Anderson, a man who had been 'on the boil' for ten years according to Ken Tynan, produced the finest British film of 1963 – *This Sporting Life*, adapted by the Yorkshire novelist David Storey from his 1960 novel, and produced by Karel Reisz. It would be a mistake to regard this film as the last in that wave of screen adaptations of northern novels, in much the same way that it seems almost superfluous to term Storey a Yorkshire writer. It's the start of something rather than the ending. It is, in a way, the growing up of English cinema. Anderson was one of the editors of *Sequence* magazine at Oxford in the 1940s, and in the mid-fifties worked in television (directing the *Robin Hood* series on ITV) and in documentary with the Free Cinema Group, picking up an Oscar (not a system he seems to approve of) for Best Short Film. In the late fifties and early sixties he worked with George Devine at the Royal Court Theatre during its most productive period. 1963, in view of Anderson's track record as director and critic, was a late point in such a career to be making a first feature film. In the wake of Jack Clayton's film of *Room at the Top*, it seemed possible that any gritty northern novel could be turned into a film, and most were. After Karel Reisz's *Saturday Night and Sunday Morning* came Tony Richardson's version of Shelagh Delaney's play, *A Taste of Honey*, and his adaptation of another Sillitoe novel, *The Loneliness of the Long Distance Runner* – Bryan Forbes filmed Mary Hayley Bell's *Whistle Down the Wind* and John Schlesinger Stan Barstow's *A Kind of Loving*. I've already indicated that if a new naturalism or a perceptive sociology was the intention of some of these films, then they can't be counted a success. But if that was the intention it met critical challenge. As Penelope Houston wrote in *The Contemporary Cinema*, published in 1963: "Our film-makers travel as mass-observers rather than as artists prepared to turn the landscape upside down if it happens to suit their purposes . . . [they] have decided in advance exactly what they expect to find there . . . Too often in a British film, when the director turns his camera on some picturesque bit of urban squalor, one can almost visualise the mobile canteen and studio cars parked just out of camera range."[64]

This Sporting Life does not pretend to represent the urban

landscape of Yorkshire. Neither Anderson nor Storey had a sociological purpose. There are no dashing feet down cobbled streets, no
good northern bonhomie, no homespun folklore. There is no musical theme by a brass band, but an almost abstract jazz score that sits
deliberately at odds with the images on the screen, reminding the
watcher that the clichés are not going to work here. The wide shots
are few and serve only to establish the context. The film's subject is
the emotional landscape of its leading characters. Much of the film
consists of just these two people arguing in a back kitchen, and was
made in a studio set. That said, the naturalism that mattered was
there. Richard Harris, his fair hair dyed jet black, playing the miner
turned professional rugby player Frank Machin, practised with
Wakefield Rugby Club and the necessary sense of his height and
bulk is suggested by the camera angles, for Harris is not tall.
Anderson applied theatre techniques to making his film. The actors
rehearsed for ten days before shooting began, and the emotional
intensity of the scenes was retained by filming in sequence, and
Richard Harris's mish-mash of Yorkshire with his native Ireland
simply doesn't matter. For the first time in several years a British
film had got beyond obsession with surface, with the mereness of
story-telling. British cinema had surrendered its guilt over the national neglect of the provinces and allowed that human life exists
there outside of the specimen jar, outside of the less than eternal
quest for fish, chips and abortion.

Machin has no vocabulary to express his emotions. For reasons
that are never even hinted at he takes as the target of his frustrated
love, forces himself upon, his landlady, a widow ten years older than
himself, who has, as he says, "put up the shutters" on her life after
the death of her husband in a factory accident. Machin's sole means
of expression, the brutality and determination of the rugby field,
cannot cope with her, cannot persuade her to live again. The violence of the relationship is destructive and compulsive. Only one
scene out of dozens between Harris and Rachel Roberts ends without an argument or a fight, and that when Harris returns home
defeated on the field for the only time, and missing six of his front
teeth. Yet she does not ask him to leave. She is tied to him in her
stubborn silence. It is a meeting of opposites, and, as Penelope
Gilliatt remarked, reviewing the film for the *Observer*, a tragedy on
the heroic scale: "The tension between the two of them is suffocat-
ing . . . Like the classical tragic hero, Frank has no power to change
his life, because he has no insight into it."[65]

In the end Margaret Hammond dies of a brain haemorrhage – it's
possible to believe that this has been brought on by the fights with

Machin, but that physical cause matters less than that she dies of the lack of any will or reason to live, and in death is finally beyond Machin's reach, and silently defiant has cheated him. *This Sporting Life* built upon and moved beyond the emotional and intellectual range of the earlier northern films. It gave Penelope Houston (co-editor of *Sequence* with Anderson and Reisz) hope that the sociological wave of British cinema ("the post-*Room at the Top* era") was over – "the directors who have emerged from it have to find their own way towards a more cinematic cinema . . . "[66] But Lindsay Anderson did not make another feature film for five years, and whatever the cinematic intentions of the directors, the audiences plumped for James Bond and Modesty Blaise – the high hope, the new start of *This Sporting Life* was not fulfilled by the sixties as a whole. There's a chasm between the pain of *This Sporting Life* and the triviality of *Darling*, and for that matter between the sharpness of *The Ipcress File* and the banality of *The Billion Dollar Brain*.

This Sporting Life made a star of Irishman Richard Harris. The early sixties threw up many working-class or non-London actors, almost to the point where received pronunciation became a liability. *Saturday Night and Sunday Morning* made a star out of Manchester-born Albert Finney, *A Kind of Loving* of Derbyshire-born Alan Bates, *Lawrence of Arabia* (released at the end of 1962) of Bradford-born Peter O'Toole, *Zulu* and *Billy Budd* of East Enders Michael Caine and Terence Stamp, *Billy Liar* of Tom Courtenay and *A Taste of Honey* of Rita Tushingham – to which list could be added the name of Julie Christie, as a class exception to the rule, once rumoured to be shortlisted for *Beyond the Fringe*, but established by the BBC's sci-fi series *A for Andromeda*. Names like these dot the show business columns of the papers throughout this period. In September 1963 Barry Norman, in his regular column for the *Daily Mail*, looked to Stratford for the stars of the future. Under the bizarre Beatle-ish headline 'Top of the Longhair Pops',[67] he saw the connection between such as John Lennon, Sean Connery, Albert Finney and David Warner:

"At first sight they might be the Beatles – casual young men in laconically 'with-it' clothes – indeed the resemblance goes deeper than that. For they too have become 'pop' this year. And in that most unlikely of places, the Royal Shakespeare Theatre at Stratford-on-Avon.

"They are the Oliviers, Gielguds and Redgraves of the future. A new kind of star, who unlike Finney and O'Toole will not be lured away by the chance of wider fame, but remain deeply loyal to Peter Hall and the company they call the 'organisation.'"

261

Reflecting upon his choice today, Barry Norman adds: "It had started a while before, with Albert Finney. He'd been a sensation standing in for Olivier as Coriolanus at Stratford. Until Finney very few working-class actors had actually made it in Britain. He'd broken through very young, and doors had opened in the British theatre . . . the Beatles did a hell of a lot towards making everybody youth conscious and introducing a kind of youth culture. I suppose it was part of a world movement. The same kind of thing was happening in America. The people who were getting all the fame and all the attention were getting younger and younger. Peter Hall was very young to be running something like Stratford.

"It was soon after that that David Warner did his Hamlet, and you would have thought that he was going to be the most successful of the three. Holm was the most successful of them at that time, the best established of the three. Warner was the exciting prospect – about to play Hamlet at twenty-four. I picked out those three to interview because it seemed to me that they were the members of the company most likely to go on to some kind of stardom. In varying degrees I suppose they did. But not huge stardom, none of them became Olivier or Gielgud or Schofield."[68]

Ian Richardson, twenty-nine, was in *The Comedy of Errors* and *A Midsummer Night's Dream*. Ian Holm, thirty-three, and David Warner, twenty-four, were appearing in one of the RSC's most ambitious projects – *The Wars of the Roses*, John Barton's reworking of the three parts of *Henry VI* and *Richard III*;[69] the following year it transferred to the RSC's London home at the Aldwych and was aired by the BBC in the Spring as a celebration of the 400th anniversary of Shakespeare's birth. The temptation was, of course, to stage all four plays in a single day – it took seven and a half hours to watch the entire cycle.

Reviewing the first night of *Richard III*, Norman's colleague, Bernard Levin, was more conventional in his praise of a remarkable production: "Amid it all there moves a fine, a memorable cast. Dame Peggy Ashcroft, completing her unique three play role as Margaret, now widow of the saintly Henry VI, is a majestic and heartbreaking ruin; Mr Roy Dotrice a moving Edward IV (his repentant grief at the news of Clarence's death is impeccably done); and it is good to be reminded, in Mr David Warner's momentary appearance as the ghost of Henry VI, of this astonishing young man's performance as the living king.

"And Mr Ian Holm's Richard III fulfils what he promised. His villainy is credible without being psychopathic, for it springs from the savage times in which it is set; his humour is that of a man who knows his own strength and can afford to laugh at others' weakness; his voice is under beautiful and expressive control throughout; and he fights and dies with horrible realism."[70]

The Shakespeare Memorial Theatre might be termed a theatre that begat a company – there had been a theatre at Stratford since 1879, but the Royal Shakespeare Company itself did not take shape until Peter Hall's arrival in 1959. Since 1960 the RSC had also had the use of the Aldwych. The National Theatre, at the start of 1963, had a director in Sir Laurence Olivier, who had left the Chichester Festival Theatre for the National in August 1962, but had neither a venue nor a company – it was a large idea, possessing a foundation stone (laid by the Queen in 1952) and a site, at a changeable spot on the South Bank. In the Autumn of 1963, the National Theatre moved into the Old Vic, while the search for a design for their permanent theatre went ahead, and staged its first production – *Hamlet*, with Peter O'Toole. O'Toole, at this stage, could do little wrong – he had become a superstar at the end of 1962 with only his second film, *Lawrence of Arabia*. The play opened on October 22nd. Kenneth Tynan had left the *Observer* to join the National Theatre as 'dramaturge'. It fell to his successor, Bamber Gascoigne, to review O'Toole's Hamlet:

"This is a Hamlet of action, convincing and at ease when there is something for him to do, whether jesting with the gravedigger, mocking Osric, stage-managing the players, duelling with Laertes or even reacting, against his will, to the charms of Ophelia. The trouble with this is that one begins to feel there is nothing to stop him murdering his uncle, particularly since O'Toole is much less convincing in the dark scenes of quiet and doubt. I never felt the brooding, wounded introvert, even though the outward signs were there. O'Toole seemed to wear his melancholy like a mask, lengthening his face and staring at us with sad unfocused eyes when grief was in the air. Too often this was a clown of sorrow. A huge, blond Marcel Marceau."[71]

Albert Finney, as he remarked himself, could have gone on playing Arthur Seaton for the rest of his life. He didn't. He has moved between theatre and cinema, often seeming to use the former to escape the latter, and, by and large, has chosen his film roles with a care that should embarrass Michael Caine. For his second film he chose the title role in Tony Richardson's *Tom Jones*, as much of a break for Woodfall Films, after three northern films in a row, as it was for Finney. Barry Norman: "This *Tom Jones* is colourful, epic-scaled – thousands of extras and practically every actor who ever trod the boards of the Royal Court – and packed with gimmicks. Too many gimmicks? Well, perhaps. There is the silent movie movie with captions gimmick; the speeding up of film gimmick; the talking and winking at the camera gimmick. Every time invention flagged, if only for a second, somebody flung in another gimmick. Yet the overall effect is splendid. Just as Woodfall's earlier pictures were true to the times and the backgrounds they depicted, so does this capture the feel and the smell of the eighteenth century. And the result is the finest gimmick of all – sheer entertainment."[72]

Tom Jones was shot over ten weeks in the Summer of 1962 in the West of England, on and around Cranborne Manor – for the modest sum of £450,000. Tony Richardson's lighting cameraman was once again Walter Lassally, the writer was John Osborne – besides Finney the film also featured Susannah York, Hugh Griffith, David Warner, Edith Evans and in support two of Britain's most accomplished comic actors, they who 'trod the boards at the Royal Court', Jack MacGowran and Wilfrid Lawson, and the director of the Royal Court, George Devine.

The film opened to great critical acclaim in the Spring of 1963. It broke with the subjects of Woodfall's earlier work, but furthered the technique. *Tom Jones*, unlike any 'costume drama' previously made, and there had been a vogue for studio-made period pieces in the nineteen-forties, was devoid of hokum. This was no attempt to pastiche the eighteenth century – it tackled its subject in modern terms, with modern techniques. Lindsay Anderson had turned the northern film on its head by filming *This Sporting Life* largely in studio – Tony Richardson took location work for *Tom Jones* to new limits. Lassally is particularly proud of the hunt scene: " . . . We staged the meet that precedes the hunt as an event to be covered newsreel fashion by three hand-held cameras, with the sound dubbed on later . . . the dialogue had to be done that way, but as it consisted mainly of little snatches, it was a small sacrifice to make for the greater realism that this method of covering the scene produced . . . The hunt itself became the most commented-on scene in the film, the secret of its success being, I feel, the intercutting of low-angle ground and low-level helicopter shots. Once again hand-held cameras were used for scenes of violent action . . . "[73]

Such methods broke the distancing effect of costume – the authenticity of appearance and location combined with the intimacy of this technique – another example being the scenes shot by candlelight – to create a feeling of immersion – *Tom Jones* had, for the time, an unusual, innovative, un-English feel to it.

If Finney went from strength to strength, Terence Stamp had hit a bad patch without ever seeming to be out of the limelight. At twenty-four he'd been nominated for an Oscar for his portrayal of Billy Budd, and shortly afterwards had turned down the lead in *A Kind of Loving*.

"I thought it would be another *Saturday Night and Sunday Morning*. That was a mistake . . . "

By July 1963 he had not worked for eighteen months, and had, as the *Mail* put it, "a few pounds in the bank, a broken romance and the memory of a duodenal ulcer."

"All they offer me are roles as a cosh boy or a cockney lorry driver . . . I've got to the stage where I need to work, but I don't want to rush into any old rubbish."[74]

That which Sid James – a South African – could play till the cows came home was Stamp's burden, and such easy stereotyping seems to dog British actors. After the immense success of his work with Theatre Workshop Victor Spinetti's first offer of a television play called for him to play an Italian who spoke no English – a role he turned down. Stamp's reaction to being the Cockney breakthrough was to consider leaving England altogether – a common enough reaction at the time – the same thoughts ran through Peter Sellers' mind at the time of *Strangelove*, and Spike Milligan, following the Lord Chamberlain's hatchet job on *The Bed-Sitting Room*, had accepted Irish citizenship, in preference to British, only the year before.

§

Tony Hancock was the most acclaimed British comedian since Stan Laurel or Charlie Chaplin. 1963 was the year in which he fell from grace.

Hancock had worked in radio since the start of the fifties, first with *Workers' Playtime* and *Educating Archie* and then with his own series, *Hancock's Half Hour*, scripted by Ray Galton and Alan Simpson, and supported by a largish cast of Hattie Jacques, Kenneth Williams, Sid James and Bill Kerr. It broke new ground for radio comedy – it was a 'playlet', not a series of sketches, and there was no obligatory musical interlude for such as the Fraser-Hayes Four, who punctuated *Beyond Our Ken*, or the Ray Ellington Band, who did the same for *The Goon Show*. The series relied heavily on the mournful voice and misanthropic nature of Hancock, and when the series moved to television in 1956, to the delight of millions, Hancock was found to have a face and a physique that matched. Overweight and jowly, the Hancock character was pompous, pretentious, more than faintly ridiculous, christened Anthony Aloysius

St John, and wore a black homburg and a black coat with an astrakhan collar, which made him resemble a dodgy theatrical agent rather than the out of work actor he was usually supposed to be. Again the series set new standards. Hancock has rightly been acclaimed as the first comedian to work in close-up and to let a facial tick say more than a string of gags. By 1962 the series had evolved into *Hancock*, and the old image had given way to the beatnik's sloppy-joe sweater, and avant-garde rather than bourgeois pretensions. He was at the top of his trade and had done something that was virtually unthinkable in TV comedy – he had made a programme in which only he appeared, alone in his room talking to himself or to the mirror.[75] It was unexpected, startling and it worked. Hancock played comedy constantly on the brink of tragedy, he stretched its boundaries in a way few other comedians have touched. But he could go no further.

His first feature film, again written by Galton and Simpson, *The Rebel*, did less well than expected – although it did secure a general release – and flopped totally in the USA. He now broke with his writers, moved to ITV and began work on a second film, *The Punch and Judy Man*, which he co-wrote.

Hancock defended his move with reference to his previous break, harking back to what haunted him more than his most recent image, the fictitious Railway Cuttings East Cheam: "The setting began to get restricting, we were getting tangled up in it. That room in East Cheam, with the same old furniture, the same old clock on the mantelpiece – it was beginning to choke us. The thing was getting more difficult to write and to perform."[76]

The ITV series did very badly in the ratings. As it was followed immediately on the BBC by Galton and Simpson's new series, it was easy to see what Hancock had thrown away. In January 1963 his series was attacked in the *Sunday Pictorial* for its excessive artiness: "Has Tony Hancock gone all high hat on his public?" The piece went on to deal with Hancock's abandonment of slang – something which had featured heavily in the banter between him and Sid James, and which had caught on with the public. Hancock had discussed this with no less a figure than Stan Laurel:

"Stan gave me a lot of good advice. Most important of all he told me not to use slang . . . what might get laughs from a British audience might baffle Americans."[77]

Hancock clearly wanted the widest possible audience for his work, he craved international recognition, and there's a note of bitterness in the *Pictorial*'s piece, as though they are reluctant to let a national figure like Hancock 'grow up' or grow out. But he topped any complaint by adding that far from changing the arty style of his present series, he intended to do two shows for it purely in mime. Hubris. By the summer Hancock was saying to the *Daily Mail*'s Barry Norman: "Trouble, of course I'm in trouble."

"'It has been,' said Hancock, a crumpled and impenetrably mournful figure, hunched over a vodka and soda, 'a rotten year, one of the worst I can remember. People don't understand, you see, they don't realise I couldn't go on saying 'Stone me' for laughs. It would have been death. I had to try to develop . . . I know people are fickle, but it surprised and hurt me that they should be so violent about what I'm trying to do. At times it seemed like a plot against me. It was like persecution . . . '"

Barry Norman: "I knew Hancock very well. I interviewed him a number of times over the years. He tended to give interviews to people he knew and trusted, so that he knew that whatever he said the tenor of the interview as written would be pro-Hancock. I think it was his way of pleading with the public not to give up on him, a cry for help. I didn't realise it at the time – one never does – but I'm sure that was what it was. I'm not sure he was a genius, I don't think he was a big head. His trouble was he was racked with self-doubt. I don't think he really believed in himself. Even at the height of his fame. He became a big head briefly when *Hancock's Half Hour* on radio and television became so enormously successful. He did for a while feel that he wasn't getting his due – that Galton and Simpson, Sid James and Hattie Jacques and others around him were getting too much credit. He began to believe that he alone was the reason for the success of the show, and I think that as an interpreter of comedy he was as good as there's ever been. He was brilliant at interpreting other people's words. What he began to believe was that he could write it himself – but he wasn't creative, he was not a creative comedian. And that was where he went totally wrong and that was why he was in trouble. He'd cast off Galton and Simpson and they were basically his life-support system. He worked with Philip Oakes, who was a very good writer, but the combination didn't work. As soon as things weren't absolutely marvellous all that brooding self-doubt came to the fore. I knew Hancock's second wife, Freddie Ross, very well. She was a very good PR agent. I'd known her long before she married Tony. We'd have lunch occasionally or a drink, and by this time, towards the end, he was getting a kind of persecution complex I think. He began to believe that I, and other people, were having an affair with Freddie. She told me once that Tony had accused her of having an affair with me – and at other times with other people. It was all part of this personality breakdown that happened. It was very sad to watch . . . you could see him just crumbling away.

"The last time I saw him personally it was in a hotel in Leeds. He was knocking back the vodka very solidly from about half past ten in the morning onwards. The last time I saw him perform was at the Royal Festival Hall, when he did a one-man show, and it was pathetic – he was reading the whole thing off idiot boards. The booze had really got to him by then."

Hancock's career never recovered. He died by his own hand five years later – five years of little accomplishment and great effort. At no point, when working at his best, was Hancock given less than his due – the finest comedian of his age – and in an age of radio and TV repeats Hancock's work with Galton and Simpson is repeated and celebrated.

Galton and Simpson's break with Hancock has been written up in conflicting ways – most of them centring on the character and ego of Hancock himself. *Private Eye* made him the subject of an Aesop Revisited as Halfcock – everyone who worked well with Halfcock – Kenneth Williams, Sid James, Galton and Simpson and finally the BBC – is dropped, and the concluding moral is 'To thine own self be true.' Peter Black's semi-official history of the BBC's first fifty years – *The Biggest Aspidistra in the World* – refuted this version, seeing it as natural artistic growth, but the writers themselves gave an interview to David Nathan for his 1971 book *The Laughtermakers* indicating their feelings: "The break with Hancock and the manner of it left them hurt and angry. Hancock called them to his flat in London one day and told them that he did not wish to work with them any more. He was under the illusion that his creative talents were as individual as his interpretative genius and had reached a stage where he could no longer share acclaim with anyone else."[78]

Galton and Simpson's new series for 1963 grew out of a one-off written, at the inducement of Tom Sloan, head of Light Entertainment, for the BBC series *Comedy Playhouse* in March 1962. It was called *The Offer* and featured a father and son team of rag and bone men, totting out of Oil Drum Lane, Shepherd's Bush, in a set that, whilst appropriate for a junk yard, looked over the years like the set of every other avant-garde play put on in London, and, needs be, like *An Evening of British Rubbish*. The writers are inclined to see *Steptoe and Son* as being very like *Hancock's Half Hour*, to see Harold and Albert as being extensions of Sid and Hancock, but it's the differences that are more telling. *Hancock's Half Hour*, particularly on wireless, only intermittently sustained drama – half hour scripts such as *The Reunion* and *Sunday Afternoon* are streets ahead of the regular output in their capacity to tip comedy into tragedy and to make the sitcom format into a commentary on the times. It's tempting to think that *The Reunion* could stand on its own as a one-off play without Hancock or James. Too often second-rate *Hancock's Half Hour* could slip into fantasy. From start to finish *Steptoe and Son* was a dramatic vehicle for recording the tensions of, for want of a better phrase, Wilson's Britain. In the very first episode Harold has received an offer of employment somewhere else, and the two main strands of the next ten years are teased out, Harold's legitimate pretensions and his crippling inability to leave his bigoted, wily, Tory father. Legitimate because his pretensions were the nation's pretensions. Hancock adopted a pose of pompous belligerence, seeking a bourgeois dignity where there could be none, and in defeat sank once again into his 'natural' vocabulary of 'stripe me' and 'a punch up the bracket'. Harold Steptoe is seeking something completely different. He is of the burgeoning sixties, he wants to press on rather than restore a lost pre-war world or cling to its vestiges. In lieu of the homburg and the astrakhan collar Galton and Simpson gave him first a pipe and then a Gannex macintosh. Within a year of Wilson's accession to the leadership of the Labour party, Harold is playing at being Wilson. Galton and Simpson have taken on the myth of his New Britain. Harold's pretensions aren't just social, they're intellectual, educational and political. Harold's vocabulary is striving upwards in a very different way from Hancock's – he uses words like 'propitious', 'untenable' and 'sensuous' – there's more to it than class bluff. "Albert: Sitting there reading George Bernard Shaw! He ain't going to pay the bills is he? (reading the title) '*Everybody's Political What's What.*' Who do you think you are, the Prime Minister?"[79] To which Harold, puffing on his pipe, does not need to reply "No, the leader of the Opposition." He could as easily have been reading the *Financial Times* as Shaw, but there's no other politician whose pose he would so readily have assumed.

Sid and Hancock were opposites, by some quirk of post-war bachelorhood living together, and the pretensions that Sid cut down were those of character and class. This was often achieved by comic devices that were crude, a caricature of the wide boy, always one jump ahead of the police, that Sid James had played as far back as *The Lavender Hill Mob*. There was nothing, logically, to keep the two together other than choice, and the improbability of Hancock and Sid ever choosing each other was part of the humour. Steptoe and Son are chained to each other. Whereas Sid and Hancock represent only types, Albert and Harold represent different ages, different ages of the nation, and that almost regardless of their generations. In Harold Steptoe a new Britain is struggling against the odds to throw off the old, but his father is wrapped around him, with all the old ways and old prejudices, more tightly than the old man of the sea.

Late in the Wilson government, *Steptoe and Son* could offer acute comment on the state of the nation with scarcely a political reference, when Leonard Rossiter breaks out of the Scrubs and takes Albert and Harold hostage in Oil Drum Lane. If nothing else he'll have a few fags and a decent meal before they pick him up – by the end of the play he is sharing his last cigarette and offering food to the Steptoes, who are worse off on the outside than he was on the inside. The nearest Hancock, in his last series with Galton and Simpson, got to politics was in his solo performance, daubing his top lip with shaving foam and intoning to the mirror 'You've never had it so good'.

CHAPTER TEN

THE EMPEROR OF ICE CREAM

"His decomposing visage and somehow seedy attire conveyed the impression of an ageing clergyman who had been induced to play the part of a Prime Minister in the dramatised version of a Snow novel put on by a village amateur dramatic society."

Malcolm Muggeridge[1]

"This is the great psychological danger facing the British people today – that we may bury ourselves under the rose-petals of a vast collective nostalgia, lost in a sweet love-affair with our own past."

Michael Shanks[2]

"Alec Douglas-Home I like as a good guy, but I think he should have remained the 14th Earl of Home. But he *is* a nice guy, and politics has so many of the other kind."   George Brown[3]

In February 1963 Harold Macmillan sought to inspire the Young Conservatives, meeting in London, with the Book of Joel – "Your old men shall dream dreams," he told them, "your young men shall see visions." Macmillan himself turned out to be the dreamer, dreaming throughout the Summer and early Autumn that he could lead the Conservative Party into the next election. The young man of vision was *Private Eye* cartoonist Timothy Birdsall. In May, as the Profumo scandal unfolded, he conjured up a vision of London life as drawn by a modern Hogarth – 'Britain Gets Wyth Itte 1963' – in which Trafalgar Square becomes a scene of debauchery unparalleled, where everything and everyone is for sale, where the Coliseum mounts 'TW3 on Ice', where Beaverbrook is trouserless, a duchess topless, where the royal family pose for the tourists, where David Frost provides the running commentary, where Macmillan presides over such 'happinesse' and where the meritocratic society flourishes in terminal binge as the meretricious society.

This was the image from which the Prime Minister was temporarily rescued in July as the Tory shires rallied to the cause: "I have had telegrams, letters, messages etc., on a scale never equalled (I

271

am told) in the history of No. 10 . . . Workmen in the streets call out 'Stick it, Mac!' . . . people of all kinds went out of their way to express their sympathy . . . "[4]

In part it was illusion – he was safe only for the time being, since to drop Macmillan now would be as good as owning up to all that Birdsall implied and hence political suicide for the party and who-ever succeeded Macmillan. In part it was real, and two international events helped lift him further from the depths.

On June 29th the man-god and a vast entourage descended on Macmillan's country house at Birch Grove, en route from sentimen-tal journeys to Ireland, where half the nation rose up to claim kinship, and Derbyshire, where President Kennedy visited the grave of his sister, the Marchioness of Hartington – and an even more sentimental journey to becoming 'ein Berliner'. It was the most publicised tour of Kennedy's short career, a field day for the press of several nations and no bad thing for Macmillan to be sandwiched between two of Kennedy's greatest personal triumphs. Macmillan had never underestimated the appeal of Kennedy's youthfulness and its propaganda value in association. Back in 1960, few things could be guaranteed to make the Prime Minister feel more out of time. Macmillan had been left wondering how he would get on with a man a generation younger than himself, after a good relationship with his own generation in the shape of the outgoing President Eisenhower, who had stepped down at the age of sixty-nine – the age that Macmillan was now. The reach of the old school ties may be limited – not so those of the family. Macmillan was married to a daughter of the late Duke of Devonshire, Kennedy's sister Kathleen had married his grandson the Marquess of Hartington – hence Macmillan was uncle by marriage to the President's sister. Not much, but it would do. Kennedy was an anglophile at heart, re-ferred to Macmillan as Mr Prime, and boastfully confided to him the extent of his marital infidelities with the memorable phrase that he 'got a headache if he didn't have a woman every day'. Against the odds, the ageing PM and the young President had an immediate rapport. In 1961 alone they had met four times. Somewhere in the generation gap the special relationship grew, and grew in spite of the crises of the Kennedy years that seemed at the time tailor-made for the humiliation of a Prime Minister – Cuba, the world on the brink, and a British Prime Minister in no way consulted, and the scrapping of Skybolt, the substitute for the British independent nuclear deterrent, and hence a face saver for the failure of our own contribution to the death race, Blue Streak and Blue Steel. The unimportance of Britain in world affairs, so rudely pointed out by

Suez and by the American role in ending the invasion, was increasingly emphasised in the years of Kennedy's presidency. As with most other things where John F. Kennedy was concerned it was something the British chose to forgive or failed to notice in the first place. The breath of fresh air Kennedy brought to the political scene was so much in contrast to our own flagging not-ancien-enough regime. The myth of the 'brightest and the best', describing the make-up of Kennedy's government, was more potent here than it ever was at home, if only out of envy.

At Birch Grove in that June of 1963, Kennedy was well aware of the Prime Minister's difficulties and had no wish to be seen to bail Macmillan out of a party problem. All the same Macmillan avoided sharing the kudos. There was no meeting between Kennedy and Wilson.

Macmillan's diaries of this period are dotted with references to there being one more 'service' he might perform. Part of the dilemma was a duty to the party – on July 12th he told Henry Fairlie of the *Daily Express* that he had considered "chucking it all in" but had concluded that "there was still one essential duty to perform . . . I was determined that no British Government should be brought down by the action of two tarts." Part of the dilemma was that he felt he might be of some use on the international scene. Macmillan had despatched Hailsham to Moscow[5] as Britain's negotiator in the test ban talks on July 15th, in a fifth attempt to bring the Soviet Union and the United States to agreement on an end to testing. A temporary lay-off had been shattered in 1961 by a series of thirty nuclear explosions by Russia, culminating in the biggest bang the world had ever seen on October 30th with a 57-megaton bomb. In April 1962 the USA had resumed testing after an interval of three years. On July 25th after much haggling over inspection – a pretext for spying as far as Khrushchev was concerned – and underground testing, the Nuclear Test Ban Treaty was initialled, and Hailsham returned triumphant clutching gifts from Khrushchev. In principle it was the single greatest achievement of international policy on nuclear weapons since their inception. Much of the credit was Macmillan's, for sheer persistence – even though his most cherished aim of a nuclear non-proliferation clause had fallen by the wayside – and this was registered in the Commons, where Macmillan indulged in prime ministerial cheek and bowed to his audience as he left:

" . . . The whole of the Conservatives stood up and waved their order papers. Many of the Opposition stood up also . . . "[6]

Labour's commanding 18 point lead was cut to 8 in the *Daily*

Mail's National Opinion Poll.

Better still, only five weeks after his low point in the Profumo debate, Macmillan was able to face his 1922 Committee earlier the same day to a banging of desks and tumultuous applause, and say to them that he had but one purpose "to serve the Party and the Nation and to secure a victory at the next election."

The same diary entry records how much the wear and tear of the last few weeks had affected him: "No doubt, tomorrow, some horrible revelation on security or morals or what-not will threaten to destroy the government, and I shall be down again. However for the moment it's up."[7]

§

Even before the Profumo scandal the press had entertained the idea that Macmillan might retire. It was not entirely a matter of age, nor simply a reaction to the Vassall aftermath.

The *Sunday Pictorial* had tipped Reginald Maudling, Chancellor of the Exchequer, as 'the man to watch' in January: "He is only 45. He is fast talking, amiable, confident, un-pompous. He gets on well with everybody from TUC delegates to Treasury officials. He can stand up to the hottest attack in the House of Commons . . . he is one of the new middle-class conservatives . . . Mr Macwonder has been reduced by time and adversity to Mr Mac-wonder-why-he's-still-there?"[8]

The ultra-chic *Sunday Times* Colour Supplement, now in its second year, profiled Maudling on the eve of his £250 million giveaway budget. Meanwhile the *Daily Sketch* plumped for the decidedly un-middle-class Lord Hailsham: "An influential group of Tories is behind a secret move to bring Lord Hailsham back to the Commons with a bang and establish him as a leading contender to succeed Mr Macmillan."[9]

In July, with the question of the leadership now in the open, both contenders cautiously put a toe in the water. Mr Maudling, in a speech in Sawston, played what might be called the Wilson hand: "Time is no longer on our side . . . We have not been successful in obtaining the allegiance of the younger generation of voters, because we have not yet found a way of talking to them in language they understand or in terms of ideals they cherish."[10]

And Lord Hailsham in the Lords debate on the Peerage Bill said: "I can give no hint on whether I might be leaving . . . if I was ever to visit a constituency in which a selection committee might possibly be sitting the most sinister interpretation might be put upon my action."

There was a case against Macmillan and his government building both in the popular and the party political imagination, of which the most coherent part was the drive towards youth which favoured such as Hailsham (young in Tory terms even at fifty-six) and Maudling. That at least could be understood in terms of the new brooms currently sweeping through the Labour Party. There was more to it than that, but not necessarily more of substance. Truth may not be a vital ingredient in the mixture, but it's still worthwhile weighing the case the nation felt it had against Macmillan at this time.

The Economy – Unemployment was around the 800,000 mark in early 1963. This is a fraction of what it had been in the thirties, but more than double the average for the fifties. There was no march from Jarrow, and the Prince of Wales, being tucked away at Gordonstoun with his bottle of cherry brandy,[11] did not visit the mining villages of South Wales muttering pointlessly that something must be done, but on March 26th five thousand unemployed from unions all over the country marched through London, and then, by design or accident, besieged parliament against the efforts of mounted policemen. In the running battle that ensued MPs were drawn to the windows around the St Stephen's entrance in wonder at the fracas below. The press accounts report that the police were attacked, but then that was the accepted wisdom on the reporting of any demonstration. The unemployed chanted "We want jobs . . . Out with the Tories." As the arrests began cries of "Democracy died today" went up and departing MPs had their cars showered with pennies, like copper confetti.

1962 had seen a round of strikes, particularly in the public sector, such as the railways, the post office and the nurses. Manufacturing industries, notably the motor industry, had been plagued throughout the early sixties with demarcation disputes and a phenomenon known as the 'wildcat' – impromptu, unofficial – strike. With four and a half million workers out at the peak, 1962 was the worst strike year on record since 1926. 1963 opened with the threat of a London bus strike, and it was widely held that British working practices were hopelessly out of date, our unions too strong and too large and our management unimaginative. Much of the resentment at this bubbled up in progressive, right-wing tracts. Michael Shanks produced a much reprinted Penguin Special, *The Stagnant Society*, summing up the management in terms that anticipated Wilson's speech of October 1963: "The model is very much that of the political system, where it is the amateur – the 'all-round man' – who as cabinet minister decides policy, while experts – his civil service advisers – are kept in firmly subordinate position. One of the basic tenets of British society is that no expert or specialist should ever be trusted to take an executive decision. The place for the 'boffin' is in the 'back room'."[12]

Anthony Hartley, deputy editor of the *Spectator*, offered his view, in imagery much in vogue, in *A State of England*: "As for the Trade Unions, it is common knowledge that their antiquated organisation and restrictive practices in industry are archaic and destructive of the very ends they are intended to serve. What were once organisations designed to serve a real need have become the dinosaurs of the economy . . . "[13]

The benchmark of economic health, the balance of payments, showed a modest surplus at £120 million, but there were still strong memories in politics and the press of Selwyn Lloyd's 1961 budget, tackling a deficit of some £250 million and of the sterling crisis that followed.

The culmination of this unbounded criticism from all quarters can be found in the July issue of *Encounter* – subtitled 'Suicide of a Nation?' – which bashed away at the proven scapegoats of poor management, union pettiness, poor standards of product, the perpetuation of the class war and the lack of any role for the nation on the world stage, in essays by Colin MacInnes, Malcolm Muggeridge and Lord Altrincham among others. More positively, if still predictably, it banged the drum of youth and celebrated Europe as mentally and economically modern, whereas Britain, unsurprisingly, dwelt in the past. Given a chance to update his book, Michael Shanks lamented the British gerontocracy, pointed out that the war had done Europe the great service of 'catapulting' younger men to power, attacked the civil service as 'compartmentalised' and the trade unions for their part in 'the cold class war', and with some originality called for the abolition of the distinction between staff and workers in industry.

Out of the economic crisis – to deflate, reflate or whatever – came the second case against.

Loyalty To One's Own – The 'pay pause' had run from July 1961 to April 1962, as a crude attempt at an incomes policy at a time when wages were outstripping production and hence feeding inflation. Such a device could only work in industries controlled by the state, hence the pay pause directly provoked the wave of public sector strikes. With its ending it was thought that innovative, effective new measures would be introduced to deal more fairly with the same problem, yet Selwyn Lloyd's 1962 budget had only one new idea – a tax on sweets and ice cream. (Children wrote to the Chancellor and complained.) It was left to Macmillan, anxious to expand the economy and fearful of the rising unemployment figures, to set up a National Incomes Commission – the Chancellor seemed to be doing nothing constructive, and, in the mind of the Prime Minister, to be irrevocably tagged as the inventor of the nationally loathed pay-pause. On July 12th Macmillan dismissed Lloyd and six other members of his cabinet. It was the biggest purge in sixty odd years, and became known, with dire lack of originality, as the night of the long knives. The sacked were Lord Kilmuir, Lord Chancellor – John Maclay, Minister for Scotland – Harold Watkinson, Defence – Lord Mills, Minister without Portfolio – Charles Hill, Housing – and David Eccles, Education. Eccles on hearing the news had requested the Chancellor's job, but others among the seven had previously indicated to Macmillan that they were willing to retire – nonetheless the suddenness of it brought forth wonderfully arcane Tory responses. One felt like a shopgirl caught with her hand in the till, another had been given 'less notice than a housemaid', and Kilmuir less than his cook, to which a wag replied 'good cooks are harder to find'. Macmillan had contemplated removing the Chancellor in August, but his hand had been forced. One of the few in the know had been the Home Secretary, Rab Butler, who had let the news of Lloyd's imminent sacking leak to the *Daily Mail*, which ran with the story on July 12th. What should have been orderly and considerate became a hasty political bloodbath that sent shock waves through the party, brought forth criticism from Macmillan's own supporters, and damaged the Prime Minister's image for unflappable cool. The Conservative Party has always prided itself on loyalty to its own – Macmillan was now guilty of a bad breach of faith with that whereby men kid themselves they live.

Image was a large part of the problem. The Tories had been in power too long by this time. Whatever his shortcomings, Selwyn Lloyd was sacrificed to modernisation, as Macmillan looked to the next election – the boy-wonder Maudling was appointed in Lloyd's place – and back at the tide of by-election defeats and the new surge of life in the Liberal Party.

The Liberal Bubble – Shortly before Selwyn Lloyd's last budget the Liberals won an astounding by-election victory in Orpington, Kent. It is still the most famous by-election of the century. Labour lost its deposit, the Tories limped home second and Eric Lubbock romped in with a 7,855 majority. In the 1959 general election Orpington had been safely Tory with a majority of 15,000. A month later William Rodgers held Stockton for Labour with an increased majority. This was acutely felt by Macmillan. Stockton had been his seat during the twenties and thirties, and he had taken the unusual step of speaking there during the campaign. At the end of March a *Daily Mail* NOP poll put the Liberals in the lead by 0.1% over Labour, with the Conservatives third. It was such stuff as ministerial nightmares are made of. As things turned out, the Liberals' finest hour was to be their last spurt. They had begun their revival – accompanied by a sharp rise in the membership of the Young Liberals – with Mark Bonham-Carter's win in 1958 in Torrington. Between then and Orpington they had come second in nine by-elections, and the official Opposition had had to go four years without a win. After Orpington the Liberal revival fizzled out. At the time few could have guessed this, and to the Prime Minister, worse still to the party, it looked as though the Liberals were going to split the 'natural' Conservative vote. Macmillan, as he put it himself, seemed to have made the country "safe for Liberalism".

As late as August 1963 the Liberals could still appear to menace a safe Tory seat, to wit Finchley. Anthony Howard wrote in the *New Statesman*:

"What kind of story is it that has transformed this middle class north London suburb from being a bastion of Toryism into becoming perhaps the most exposed flank that the Conservatives will be offering to the Liberal party at the next election?"[14]

The sitting MP, a junior minister in Pensions, by name Thatcher, Margaret Hilda of that ilk, said: "It's the golf club, you know. That's where it all started."

Had the true blue Finchley Golf Club gone soft? No such luck; the leaderene-in-waiting was referring to the accusations of anti-semitism in the golf club that had caused the good citizens of Finchley to seek another club, and another party.

The following year saw an acutely cynical film about social climbing, *Nothing but the Best* – Alan Bates as the working-class boy, murderously making good, and learning the tricks of snobbery from Denholm Elliott whom he passes on the downward journey. Elliott's political lesson for Bates, delivered in a squash court, was . . . loosely:

"What's wrong with the Conservatives?"

"Pink at the edges."

"Labour?"

"Too bloody middle-class by half."

"The Liberals?"

"The who?"

By the Autumn of 1963, that exchange just about summed up the Liberal threat.

A Something for Nothing Society – There are many strands to this, but mostly they concern 'new' money. On July 8th Ben Parkin, the MP for Paddington, who had asked the House for compassion for "the poor little slut" at the end of the Profumo debate, rose to tackle a subject close to his heart: the activities of a slum landlord, the late Peter Rachman, former lover of both Christine and Mandy, in exploiting the poor and the increasing black population of his constituency. He told the House how "dwellings were taken from legitimate working-class people" as property speculators acquired streets wholesale at public auction: " . . . Had those houses been bought individually, it would have meant £1500 for a house with five floors – £300 a floor, £600 for a basic two floor dwelling. That would have helped a property owning democracy . . . A year after that one of the houses . . . by then owned by Mr Rachman, was let . . . at a fantastic rent, all perfectly legal, to a . . . coloured man. He knew how to let the house as seven separate dwellings to seven separate girls at £3 10s per dwelling, per day, payable daily at noon. That was £10,000 a year from one house – enough to pay the interest on the price paid for the whole road."[15]

Parkin ended with a rash assertion: "All Fleet Street is full of the idea that Rachman is not dead." Behind this legend were endless stories of the strong-arm, bully-boy activities by which Rachman was said to rule his slum empire.

The 1957 Rent Act was held to be at the root of the problems on which the likes of Rachman fed. The value of houses, to which their rent was set, had been pegged since the end of the war at the 1939 level. The new act decontrolled some 317,000 houses and flats by lifting controls on property with a rateable value of £30 (£40 in Greater London) and on all new tenancies. What seemed designed to open up more property to profit, and hence to occupation at a time of acute shortage, could also be a spur to exploitation and eviction. A week after Ben Parkin's remarks, the Labour Party tabled a motion of censure . . . "deploring the intolerable extortion, evictions and property profiteering resulting from the 1957 Rent Act". In the debate that followed Wilson made no bones about apportioning blame: "If the Rachman HQ could be found there must be honoured places for portraits of Macmillan, Sandys, Brooke, Hill and Joseph."

Yet the last of the Rowntree reports on poverty, in 1961, had found "no evidence that the Rent Act had reduced 'under-occupation'. It seems clear that comparatively few tenants have been either evicted or driven from their homes as a result of the act."[16] The report pointed out that nearly half a million houses were let out at illegally high rents, and that the incentive to repair that had been included in the act was ineffectual, but this seems more like continuity than consequence. Rachman had acquired his property and largely made his fortune before the 1957 act, and specialised in the cheaper properties not decontrolled by that act. The scam worked by Rachman was roughly this: in the early fifties the Church Commissioners sold off more than 30,000 houses in London. Rachman, and others, would buy cheaply, divide houses into flats, mortgage each flat separately with a conveniently 'bent' building society for many times the value of the house, pay off the original purchase loan, fix rents that would meet all outgoings and pocket the balance – an almost instant profit. Further to this, if a property was already split into flats, controlled tenants could be persuaded to move by the process of 'schwartze and de-stat' – which meant moving in a large number of musical Jamaicans who played until everyone else left, at which point the remaining flats would be re-let to more West Indians, who would pay extortionate rents simply to escape the 'no coloureds' prejudice which denied them accommodation in most of the city. Investigations into Rachman by public health authorities, rent tribunals, the police and Paddington Council had found, surprisingly, no evidence that he was doing anything illegal. Rachman, the high rents apart, was careful enough to operate on the fringe of the law rather than outside it, but the tales of threats and violence persisted. The exposure of his activities, real or imagined, by the Ward connection, produced one of the most powerful symbols of the moral decay of Macmillan's last days.

Rachman's biographer Shirley Green concludes her book thus: "By the 27th of July it no longer mattered what kind of a landlord Rachman had been. He had already served his purpose. He had reinstated the press as crusaders for truth and filled the news-gap leading up to July 22nd when Ward's trial began and pushed Rachman from the front pages. And he had provided the Labour Party with the tools it needed to hammer the last nail in the Tory Government's coffin."[17]

It's only fair to point out that whatever use the Labour Party as a whole made of the connection, Parkin had campaigned for years against the property racket in his Paddington constituency, and could not be expected to miss such an opportunity. Wilson had stopped him from putting any questions on the matter during the Profumo debate, and if he had to cash in on the nonsensical 'Rachman is Alive' story to make his point, so be it. If Rachman was not the villain he was held up to be, 'Rachmanism' beyond a doubt existed, and Mr Rachman has given his name to the language as surely as Captain Boycott or Monsieur Leotard.

But there was more to the popular reception of this bogeyman than the Ward scandal. A long growing symbol of the something-for-nothing society had been the property boom. If in Birdsall's cartoon the buildings around the mayhem in Trafalgar Square look unfamiliar it's because they are his compression of what was happening all over the centre of London. As famous as the property racketeer was the property speculator.

"Anyone who owned land, whether or not it was built on, at the end of the war, and anyone who has bought land since, is likely (though by no means certain) to have gained – to have made money for nothing. While both landlords and owner-occupiers have there-fore gained, the people who have gained most are those who buy and sell land frequently – the property developers, and those who speculate in land without developing it . . . "[18]

London had seen a rapid rise in land prices and a surge in the construction of skyscrapers. In 1962-3 such buildings as the Vickers Building, the Shell Building, the Hilton on Park Lane and Millbank Tower were all built, and mid-1963 the Post Office Tower was rising over Howland Street. Many of them were, and are, derided as monstrosities, but by no means all. This is how Ian Nairn, writing in 1965, described Portland House: " . . . no masterpiece, but it has got a spark, it is a real live idea of a building, where the dead fish all around it are just so many square feet of lettable office space . . . The huge slab with tapered ends rises sheer out of the ground, hoisted up bodily by a granite arcade faced with marble. This is the best part: above there is too much fuss, especially in the vertical strips . . . but enough of someone's vision has got through."[19]

Fortunes were being made out of such buildings and out of the ownership of the land on which they stood. With new fortunes came new reputations – those of such men as Jack Cotton and Charles Clore of City Centre Properties, self-made millionaires who devel-oped new buildings like the Hilton and the Royal Palace Hotel and managed old ones such as the Prince of Wales Theatre and the Royal Exchange in Manchester. In 1959 Jack Cotton put forward a scheme to develop Piccadilly Circus, a plan which seems to surface periodically only to be shelved repeatedly. In the Autumn of 1963 another scheme for a 300-foot tower and a thousand-bed hotel in a pedestrianised Piccadilly Circus was rejected and a compromise suggested – a traffic free zone from the Haymarket to Charing Cross Road, across Leicester Square, and that, more or less, is what we have today. Perhaps the most famous of London's property developers was Harry Hyams, who developed a site at the corner of Charing Cross Road and New Oxford Street with a 385-foot skyscraper that stood empty throughout the Wilson government. Centre Point came to symbolise the development of London for profit rather than people. Not only was it an eyesore, it was an empty eyesore.

As Wilson was stepping lightly rightward, Labour's plans for the public ownership of development land were silently dropped.

The most colourful flower of the Opportunity Society was John Bloom. Bloom was part of the great working-class influx of talent on to the national scene, the popular East Ender, much as Terence Stamp or David Bailey, but he wasn't an actor or a photographer, he was a salesman.

John Bloom owned the Rolls Razor company – once manufacturers of a patent strop razor, under Bloom they became importers and manufacturers of twin tub Rolls Rapide washing machines, which were sold directly from factory to public, by saturation advertising, free gifts and trading stamps, at the astoundingly low price of 39 guineas (half the price of his competitors). At its peak in 1963 the company was valued at £13 million, commanded 30% of the market – even Hoover held less – and sold six thousand machines a week. Bloom became something of a celebrity, featured, if not lauded, in the press and on television. One who did not find Bloom's fame to his liking was Bernard Levin. In November 1963 he interviewed him on *That Was The Week That Was* and said, apropos of Bloom's sales technique and the quality of his product: "It's up to the public to make up their minds whether you ought to be prosecuted or only sued by one and a half million dissatisfied customers."

In December 1961 questions had been asked in the House of Commons about the technique of 'switch selling', whereby a Rolls salesman invited by a housewife to sell her a machine for 39 guineas, would offer instead to sell the de luxe 59-guinea model, and by 'silver tongues', as the *Economist* put it, or by tougher methods, as *Private Eye* had it, often succeeded. Bloom's line was: "We are going to see a revolution in the next year in retailing. Prices will tumble down because this is what the public wants. It'll be survival of the fittest."[20] In answer to Levin he placed advertisements that openly played upon the legend of his youth and wealth – 'Britain's youngest self-made industrialist' – Bloom at thirty-two seemed to revel in both fame and fortune and to believe in his own spurious image, inflating sales figures into a messianic movement – "the Give-The-Housewife-Something-Extra-Movement that has been sweeping the country during the past few months."[21] If ever writing was on the wall this was it. In six months Rolls Razor crashed, and Bloom faced criminal charges. From left and right the analyses hurtled forth. In the *New Statesman*: "Here was an ambitious young man who grew up in the opportunity state and absorbed its atmosphere of unrestrained commercialism almost in the schoolroom . . . " As Bloom would have been at school during the war this seems wildly exaggerated, but: " . . . He has been taught to believe that the best employment for agile brains was to make a million before you were thirty – preferably through tax-free capital gains – and he did it . . . what is required is a far wider examination of the social ethics which created the moral environment in which Bloom flourished and faded."[22]

And in the *Spectator*: "If a very ordinary character is built up by [press and television] into something extraordinary . . . not only will the public begin to believe in financial miracles, but the character himself . . . the god was bound to fall after he had been photographed with his wife in a colossal four poster bed in a *Sunday Times* Colour Supplement."[23]

Had Mr Maudling been privy to such augury he might not have posed so readily for the *Sunday Times* himself. The last line apart, the *Spectator* declined to see a symbol of the Macmillan era in the rise and fall of John Bloom – it was not a matter of easy money, only of money mismanaged and muddled – but they are wrong to see Bloom as ordinary. Years later Bernard Levin returned to the matter of Bloom and summed up his achievement: " . . . Whatever he may or may not have done vis-à-vis the law, he had without question improved the sector of British industry that he had entered, and long after he had disappeared from the business, the prices of washing machines remained where he had forced them."[24]

Where Terence Stamp was merely adored by the housewives, John Bloom was loved and loathed. He struck a resounding note with both materialists and anti-materialists, simply because, as Tony Crosland had lamented in *Encounter* as far back as 1960, the idea of improved conditions was too readily confused with the idea of something-for-nothing – and in the British this could bring forth a tut-tutting puritanism: "Why, the moment that workers acquire the cars, holidays and gadgets which the critics have been enjoying all their lives, should they be condemned as 'fatty and degenerate'?"[25]

Mr Macmillan, as his own people might have put it, had created a fatty, degenerate society.

Mr Marples – If you do not recall the command of the popular press once held by Ernest Marples, Minister of Transport, take Edwina Currie, multiply by Cyril Smith and divide by Cecil Parkinson. Marples was a gift to the papers. The grammar school Tory, northerner, ex-RSM, self-made businessman, with a talent for showmanship, an inordinate number of hobbies and a trendy Moulton mini-bicycle, on which to be photographed riding to the Commons almost in defiance of the motorists who detested him. Marples was a very new kind of Tory, a man who was no part of any of the old circles, whose rise to power seemed to demonstrate the meritocracy. He was close to Macmillan, having been his junior at the Ministry of Housing in the early fifties, and in 1959 was appointed to Transport. Marples did not initiate the parking meter and the traffic warden, but under his rule such scourges of the motorists spread, and they took up Marples as a hate figure. It seemed to a section of the nation that their inalienable right to drive where and as fast as they liked and park where they wanted was being demolished. By 1963 the rear windows of thousands of cars bore stickers reading 'Marples Must Go', and a few of wit simply read 'Why Only Marples?' Marples, playing to the gallery, gave out pink stickers at the 1963 Party Conference – 'Give Ern a Fair Turn'. In July someone expressed an opinion of Mr Marples by throwing a chunk of parking meter through the window of his house in Eccleston Street and in August it was announced that an Independent Motorists' candidate would oppose him at the next election.

The peak of Marples' attempts to come to grips with the growing number of private cars on the roads was the Buchanan report published in November 1963. It called for a new 'executive agency for traffic', the banning of cars from the centres of cities larger than seventy-five thousand people, the construction of pedestrian walkways, multi-level towns and town zoning. It was all but ignored. London, even then, was said to be choking on traffic, but such a drastic, planned alteration of the 'face' of Britain was not something any party would undertake; instead the face of the country continued to alter piecemeal.

Marples' most famous deed was the appointment of ICI executive Dr Richard Beeching to run British Railways in 1961. Dr Beeching's Reshaping Report[26] was published in March 1963 and proposed to axe 5000 miles of track, 2363 stations and 160,000 jobs over the next seven years. No more Lyme Regis, no more Millers Dale, no more Ardleigh or Midsomer Norton. Whole lines would vanish – the old Midland route from Derby to Manchester Central, the Somerset and Dorset Joint from Bath to Bournemouth. If implemented the

Beeching Plan would streamline the system, but in so doing would plunge some parts of rural England, and vast parts of the West Country, Scotland and Wales into a degree of isolation they had not known since before the industrial revolution. The railways had been losing money since before the war, and in 1962 more than £1000 million had been written off. Beeching proposed to make the railways economic, to streamline passenger services and to rationalise the transport of freight by closing large numbers of depots, inherited from the pre-nationalisation companies, and developing containerisation. This was not well received by the public or the railway unions – British Railways mounted a propaganda campaign and throughout the Summer and Autumn Tony Hancock was to be found in the daily papers misanthropically endorsing the scheme in 'The Hancock Report'. More than any other Marples scheme it looked like the dismantling of the structure of the country. It also looked, against the grain of all his other measures, like an attempt to put *more* traffic on the roads. In the days before MPs were obliged to declare their business interests, rumour rippled about the possible benefits to Marples from such a plan. His company, Marples Ridgeway, was said to be involved in the construction of the new motorways, the first of which had been opened by Marples in 1959.

What the Beeching Plan revealed was a problem that persists today. Britain lacked a coherent, co-ordinated transport policy. In the Commons debate that followed, Wilson, squarely on his own turf with this the subject of his research at Oxford, ate Marples for lunch: "Mr Marples says that he will build roads in all possible directions, making us a nation of concrete. And then suddenly, with a stroke of his ministerial biro, he is to rebuild all the cities. How in heaven's name does Mr Marples think that this can be done?"[27]

Bland futurism is one of the most curious characteristics of the years between the war and the late-sixties – that people in power, so often rooted in and defensive of tradition, regarded the bricks and mortar of our towns as transitory. It looked as though not a brick should be saved if there was a buck to be made. We would soon all be living in the glass and concrete bubbles of the twenty-first century, except for those of us in Scotland, Wales and Midsomer Norton who would be living in the eighteenth.

The Mess Of Pottage – Under Macmillan the transition from Empire to Commonwealth accelerated. The Gold Coast, Nigeria, Sierra Leone, Tanganyika, Zanzibar, Jamaica, Trinidad, and Uganda all became independent during his time as Premier, and Kenya, Nyasaland and Northern Rhodesia all followed in the last year of the Conservative government. It was a worldwide trend, as the old empires dissolved, the Belgian Congo, Dahomey, Upper Volta, Chad, Senegal, Mali and Gabon all cast off the yoke of Europe. Only Portugal seemed to want to hold on to an empire – Portugal and a certain kind of Englishman, who had been muttering for fifteen years that we should never have got 'out of India' and looked upon white South Africa as our 'kith and kin'. On a visit to South Africa in 1960, Macmillan made his feelings subtly clear, perhaps too subtly for the South Africans to grasp what he was saying: " . . . it is our earnest desire to give South Africa our support and encouragement, but I hope you won't mind my saying frankly that there are some aspects of your policies which make it impossible to do this without being false to our own deep convictions about the political destinies of free men, to which in our own territories we are trying to give effect."[28]

Southern Rhodesia remained a problem long after South Africa had left the Commonwealth. It had been stitched into a Central African Federation with the North and Nyasaland, under the leadership of Sir Roy Welensky, but as the other two territories approached majority rule, Southern Rhodesia remained white supremacist, and it was impossible either to hold the federation together or to grant the South independence. Macmillan chose instead to break up the federation. When in March 1963 the North was allowed to secede from the federation prior to independence, Welensky vented his fury at the press, saying that "The people of Central Africa – black and white alike – are being betrayed by these men" – by which he meant nationalists like Kaunda, but might just as well have been referring to Macmillan and Butler (Deputy Prime Minister with responsibility for Central Africa). Welensky made a point of refusing to have lunch with them at Admiralty House – a petty gesture, but it's undeniable that Welensky had his 'constituency' among that vociferous section of British society that felt the Empire was being given away 'to a bunch of darkies', and for whom our attempt to join the EEC (bitterly opposed by Labour), which was so firmly vetoed by de Gaulle's 'Non' in January, was a form of betrayal, the surrender of our birthright. Between the views of such cranks and the General is a germ of truth. The attempt at British membership of the EEC was less a quest for belonging than it was a leader looking for the led, the country which had, to quote Acheson again, 'lost an empire but not yet found a role', seeking the world stage once more, in Europe rather than in Empire. A trade-off which could please no one.

The Sins of Henry Brooke – Brooke, the "honest, upright idiot", had succeeded Rab Butler as Home Secretary in the 1962 reshuffle. In a relatively short term of office, he managed to achieve a remarkable reputation for insensitivity and blundering. Brooke was hated, not in the way Marples was by a self-interested group playing back to the performance of a minister, but politically and morally loathed. The list of the sins of Henry Brooke is long, and may appear at times remote from his direct actions but in these matters freedom of speech and the sense of decency and justice of many British people were violated and Brooke, as Home Secretary, was held to be ultimately responsible.

Lenny Bruce, the American satirist, had appeared at the Establishment Club in 1962. Twice in 1963 he had returned for repeat engagements only to be refused admission and deported, on the arbitrary grounds of bad taste. It was censorship – the extension of the role of the Lord Chamberlain by other means. Hal Woolf, a London painter and friend of a friend of Christine Keeler, died in St George's Hospital in November 1962, supposedly of injuries received in a road accident in Park Lane. On enquiry his ex-wife discovered that Woolf had been discharged from St George's after treatment and arrested at once by the police. The next day he was returned to the hospital suffering from the injuries from which he died. *Private Eye* concluded its account with this veiled speculation: " . . . that the entire event took place at the moment when the Profumo case was about to break has excited some observers, but according to our information, may be entirely irrelevant."

It probably was irrelevant, but it was another example of public attention being drawn to police corruption. The most famous case was that of Det Sgt Challenor, the arresting officer in the case of Donald Rooum,[29] who planted a brick on Rooum at Savile Row police station. Challenor and three other policemen were charged with conspiracy the following March – but the most surprising revelation was not conspiracy or corruption, but that Challenor was deemed to be "mentally unbalanced". This fuelled a spreading belief in the unreliability of the police, as more stories of police brutality, of rubber hosepipes and rhino-hide whips, came to light.

Brooke also refused political asylum to Robert Soblen, an American spy who committed suicide while awaiting deportation, and to Chief Enahoro of Nigeria. The Enahoro case became a cause célèbre and resulted in a motion of censure from the Labour Party and a debate in the Commons. The charges against Enahoro in Nigeria were politically inspired and when deported in May 1963 he faced certain imprisonment and a possible death sentence.

The political climate in which all these incidents took place was set by civil disobedience and the repeated manner in which a peaceful protest movement was met with brutality in the streets and the courts. Brooke appeared to be a man with little sense of justice presiding over a judiciary with no sense of proportion and a police force with no respect for the law. In the final series of *That Was The Week That Was* David Frost played Eamonn Andrews to Willie Rushton's Brooke in a parody of *This Is Your Life*. After Frost had listed all his 'crimes', including the hounding of Stephen Ward and the imprisonment of Mandy Rice-Davies, Rushton wound up with: "Just shows. If you're Home Secretary – you can get away with murder."[30]

At the general election in 1964 his 12,000 majority in the safe Conservative seat of Hampstead was dented, and it dawned on the local Labour Party that the seat could be won – in 1966 Brooke lost his seat in a rare display of voting against an individual as much as for a party.

§

Macmillan's official biographer, Alistair Horne, has speculated that Macmillan suffered from trouble with his prostate throughout the Summer and told no one, not even, it seems, his capacious diary.[31] During this time his ideas of staying on or quitting ebbed and flowed, perhaps as a result of private misgivings about his health. There were both hypochondria and melodrama in his character – the chapter of the autobiography that might have been 'And So To Bed' or 'Now we are Seventy' at the pen of another hand was "The Stroke of Fate" to Macmillan, as though Zeus had shot a thunderbolt directly at his ailing organ. There were more public reasons too. Macmillan awaited the publication of Denning's report with some apprehension. While this seems almost unbelievable now – Denning's acquittal of the government has acquired an inevitability in retrospect – Macmillan felt obliged to "stay to deal with Lord Denning's report"[32] in case the report blamed him. But all arguments quickly become circular. Would he have served his party better by taking the burden of guilt upon himself in departing or would the Tories be damned ever after as having been "brought down by the action of two tarts"? He was spared this particular choice, but in his own mind the fundamental problem remained – whenever he went there would be repercussions. It centred so tightly upon himself that at times he seems almost oblivious to the trend of thought among Conservatives, and at others self-pitying and paranoid – referring to himself in the diaries as "the old limpet". Some members of his party – his son Maurice for example – and of his cabinet – Lord Home for example – shared the shall-I-shan't-I? of these weeks, others did not. By Macmillan's own account very little doubt was expressed by the party Chairman Lord Poole, who represented a substantial body of thought in the higher ranks in his conviction that Macmillan should go.

Before the publication of the Denning report Macmillan formulated the sequence of his stepping down. He would announce in his closing speech at the party's October Conference that he would step down before the next election (due at the very latest by October 1964), probably in January or February. This would allow Conference to proceed unhampered, and from January on would allow the new leader a settling-in period of nine months or so. He told the Queen of his decision at the weekly audience on September 20th. By early October Macmillan had begun to have second thoughts and would go on having them even after he had resigned. As his closest supporters urged him to stay he rejigged the logic of his own arguments and became diplomatically deaf to the contrary point of view. By Monday, October 7th he was able to put this case for staying on to Lord Poole:

"1. I should seem to be 'deserting' and this would especially affect the 'marginal' seats. 2. I would seem to have yielded to the group of malcontents, who are swayed either by personal or purely reactionary sentiment. 3. I should leave the party in complete disarray – with some for Butler, some for Hailsham and some for Maudling."[33]

The first two points fail to see much further than the end of his nose. Butler's mid-summer analysis of the tide against the Prime Minister was more acute: " . . . There is a very strong movement in favour of somebody not too closely associated with the Establishment . . . the herd instinct is unleashed . . . they are tending to attack anybody in authority . . . there is not so much positive approval of a younger man as there is a recognition that this may make a clearer picture for the next election."[34] Macmillan's last point proved to be very accurate.

Early in September Macmillan recorded his views on the succession in his diary, a section not quoted in his autobiography: "It needs a man with vision and moral strength – Hailsham, not Maudling. Yet the backbenchers (poor fools) do not seem to have any idea except 'a young man'."[35]

Traditionally leaders of the Conservative Party were chosen, not elected. The choice of the outgoing leader, for obvious reasons, had to be one that commanded the support of the party. Around this arose the idea that new leaders emerged by something akin to natural selection. In the course of the campaign that followed many Conservatives expressed this belief.

Lord Hailsham: "I don't think we should look on this as a contest for the leadership . . . in the Conservative Party the leader just well . . . emerges."[36]

Lord Home: "We have no set processes. We never have. We never believe in choosing a leader by vote and so we have our means which are informal."[37]

Rab Butler: "It is not the British custom to contend or to concede."[38]

And Iain Macleod in almost identical terms on the same day: "It is not the British custom either to contend or to compete."[39]

It's contentious whether anyone really believed this. At the point when Butler and Macleod spoke the party was self-evidently in the throes of contest and competition, which sooner or later would oblige someone to concede. The problem was that there was no single obvious successor, and Macmillan's favouring of Hailsham, which he made known to Hailsham in the Summer, and his careful recording of the support for Hailsham didn't guarantee that he was 'the choice' – nature, for once, had deserted the Conservatives by not evolving a natural successor. All the same the pretence that the new leader would emerge through organic processes was kept up in flagrant defiance of what was happening.

In backing Hailsham, Macmillan had passed over his deputy Rab Butler and an entire generation of new men, some brought up through the party ranks by Butler's patronage – Macleod, Powell, Maudling – others scions of the dynasties – Soames and Sandys, both Churchill's sons-in-law, Amery, Macmillan's son-in-law – and, of no particular faction but Macmillan's own, the grammar school boy Edward Heath. Butler was never seriously considered by Macmillan, yet his claim on the job was strong. He was very much the architect of the post-war Conservative Party, changing it from the party of the great land-owning families into something that could be said to represent a wider field of interest and to share the consensus politics of the forties and fifties – in fact Butler had helped to define the terms of that consensus before Labour came to power with his 1944 Education Act. Butler shifted the party base while Churchill, by then a living anachronism, wrote his histories, painted watercolours and built walls. When Churchill was returned to power, he was often absent or ill and Butler acted as ex-officio Prime Minister for weeks on end, only to lose out to Eden in 1955. He had been number two again when Eden resigned in 1957 and lost out to Macmillan. It had taken that rare creature, the radical Tory intellectual, to modernise the party – this made Butler the object of suspicion among more traditional Tories. In a party that represented itself as being run by 'gifted amateurs' Butler looked too much like a professional. His own verdict was that he had been in office too long and had too many enemies. It was thought that Butler had no heart for yet another struggle to 'emerge'. Anthony Howard said as much in the *New Statesman* in February: "With Mr Butler content to be a king maker rather than a king – Mr Macmillan stands with his breast bared to the younger generation of Tory lions."[40]

Macmillan echoed this six months later: "He doesn't want another unsuccessful bid . . . he is sixty. He likes politics . . . he would prefer to be Warwick (which he could be) and not try to be King (which he can't). On the whole he is for Hailsham."[41]

On the whole for Hailsham . . . but Hailsham sat in the Lords – no Prime Minister had sat in the Lords since the Marquess of Salisbury at the turn of the century, and it had been an unwritten rule since the twenties that none should. That Hailsham could be a contender was due to a change in the law that took place only that summer, almost entirely as a result of the vigorous campaigning of Labour peer Lord Stansgate. There have probably always been reluctant peers. In 1950 MP Quintin Hogg had gone to the Lords as the second Viscount Hailsham, and had appealed unsuccessfully to Attlee for a change in the law. By the time Anthony Wedgwood-Benn MP became the second Viscount Stansgate in 1960 he had been fighting ten years for the right to disclaim. On succession he had declined to take his seat in the Lords and fought his old seat in Bristol in a by-election and won. Barred from taking up his seat in the Commons he again pressed for legislation and in January 1963 a Joint Select Committee of both houses recommended the introduction of a Peerage Bill. Hailsham spoke in the Lords hearings on the bill, and it was assumed that he was one of the few members of the Lords who would consider disclaiming. Two possible catches in the law were eliminated on the way – firstly the idea that the bill should apply only to peers who had not actually taken up their seats, which quickly died (Hailsham wrote a memo to the Joint Committee in the Summer of 1962 objecting to this idea), and secondly the idea that the act would only come into force at the next election. The Lords vote on the bill took place in July – a Tory revolt moved in favour of an amendment, previously rejected by the Commons, and the bill became operative immediately on receiving royal assent at the end of July. By the time of that vote the leadership of the party was an issue and it may be thought that Hailsham's path was being cleared by his colleagues – the amendment being the work of Labour MP Patrick Gordon Walker it may also be thought that Labour too had some interest in seeing Hailsham compete for the Tory leadership. About this time Wilson confided to Richard Crossman that the only Tory he feared as leader was Maudling, the rest he would destroy in debate, the peers among them were political jokes. On July 31st Viscount Stansgate was the first to present his papers at the office of the Clerk of the Crown, closely followed by Lord Altrincham, who emerged as plain John Grigg. Lord Hailsham did not disclaim, but the way was open for him to do so, and for that matter for any other Conservative peer who thought he was in with a chance.

§

During the night of October 7th-8th Macmillan's prostate flared up and he found himself in great pain and unable to pass water. A doctor was called twice in the night, and Macmillan 'limped' through the cabinet meeting the next morning. His press secretary, Harold Evans, watched him walk to the cabinet room: "Maurice was with him . . . he walked slowly and looked tired, but it would not have been apparent to anyone not in the picture that he had just been through a physical ordeal involving great pain . . . I button-holed Maurice when he left his father. He was hailing the night's developments as an opportunity for his father to retire with honour."[42]

Macmillan told the cabinet he would still speak on the 12th, but could no longer be sure what announcement he would make. He did not tell any of them that he was ill, but twice excused himself from the meeting as the pain became intolerable. The race for the leadership began unofficially in one of those brief absences – Dilhorne, the Lord Chancellor, raised the possibility of Macmillan's sudden resignation, and declared that as he was not a runner he was open to consultation. Lord Home, Macmillan's Foreign Secretary since 1960, added that he too was not a runner and hence would assist in any way he could.

Enoch Powell: "He didn't give much evidence of being a man incapable of staying in the room because of pain. He didn't give the impression of a man who was constantly battling with disability. It was in the course of this cabinet meeting that he invited his colleagues in his absence to consult amongst themselves and offer him their opinion whether he ought to carry on. The manner in which he played the cabinet game, as it were, did not seem to me to be strikingly different from that in which he normally played it. After all, [I] had little emotional sympathy with the Prime Minister, whom [I] was disposed to regard as a deft operator."[43]

The cabinet broke up, and most members made their way to Blackpool for the Conference still expecting their leader to speak on the Saturday and wondering what announcement he would make.

Macmillan's moods, which appear to have changed day to day throughout the summer, now swung almost hour to hour. Until he was finally admitted to the King Edward VII Hospital for Officers at 9 p.m., he veered between thinking he could carry on with just a break to recuperate, thinking he could at least go to Blackpool, recognising the truth of his son's notion of an honourable way out, and complete despair. Harold Evans encountered a pathetic figure that evening: "He was in his red dressing gown . . . over pale blue pyjamas . . . the old brown cardigan . . . I posed the critical question I would have to answer, 'Does this mean the Prime Minister will resign?' Was it unfeeling? Walking up and down by the windows, in the half light of the table lamp, he threw his arms up in a dramatic gesture. 'Of course, I am finished. Perhaps I shall die . . . '"[44]

Later the same evening, less than two hours after he had announced to the press that the Prime Minister would speak as usual, Iain Macleod was called out of the agents' annual dinner to be told that Macmillan would not be coming to Blackpool. By nine thirty television and radio news carried the story.

The next day Lord Home called on Macmillan at the hospital. Here he received a letter of resignation that Macmillan asked him to read out to Conference. The immediate accounts do not agree on the willingness with which the letter was offered – Butler's memoir suggests that the letter was all but screwed out of the ailing PM, while Harold Evans writes that it was ready and waiting when Home arrived. It was this moment that Macmillan chose to put the cat among the pigeons by asking Home whether he too had not thought of running for the leadership.

In Blackpool the starters began to line up at the gate. Hailsham received a huge cheer from the assembled Conservatives (can one call them delegates?) as he took the platform in the Winter Gardens. Butler, now acting as caretaker Prime Minister, took over the suite allocated to Macmillan and fought a skirmish in cabinet to retain the right to give the leader's closing speech in his place. Maudling made a sensible suggestion that was disregarded almost as flippant – no one should make the speech, Conference should have a 'half-holiday'. Maudling was, predictably, thinking of himself as a candidate[45] – against the earlier speculation of the press and the Prime Minister, so was Butler, but neither so precipitate as Hailsham.

That evening, Wednesday, October 9th, Lord Hailsham spoke at a meeting in Morecambe. He made a strong speech attacking the Labour Party in terms so broad that it is difficult not to see it as an electoral, rallying speech, whatever Hailsham's modesty had been about his own chances and intentions. Such modesty was by now wearing thin. After the speech Lord Lonsdale, former MP for Morecambe and Lonsdale, "wondered aloud whether 'a constituency with a good Conservative majority' was in a position to invite Lord Hailsham to be its candidate?"[46] Lord Hailsham replied: "I cannot in these bitter circumstances of the present moment even contemplate what my own future will be . . . sometimes one has to say to oneself that one must not think of oneself at all and this is one of those moments."[47] A position he emphasised on television later that night when questioned as to his intentions by Robin Day: "I am not thinking about myself at the moment." Hailsham had remarked months before if he were ever to visit a constituency in which a selection committee might possibly be sitting the most sinister interpretation might be put upon his action – it's possible such a committee was sitting at Morecambe. The MP Basil de Ferranti had already made it known that he would not seek re-election. Lonsdale had put the proper interpretation on Hailsham's action; whether it was sinister is another matter. Nor was he the first to discern Lord Hailsham's intent – the *Daily Sketch* had carried a story in March, claiming that Sir Wavell Wakefield, MP for St Marylebone, had offered to step down for Hailsham. Wakefield wanted to retire, and there was speculation that he was only staying on in order to save the seat for Hailsham. In the meantime did Lord Hailsham go about London scrupulously avoiding the borough of St Marylebone? Butler records a tone of some surprise when he was told by Lord Poole in early October that St Marylebone was being "kept on ice" for Hailsham. On hearing the news of Macmillan's illness Wakefield said: "Quite clearly some decision will be forced upon the party as to the leadership"[48] – which sounds like relief that at last he could get off the ice.

Meanwhile in Bolton Sir Gerald Nabarro bade farewell to Macmillan, and uttered what must have been thought by the great majority of his party: "He has been a great Prime Minister for seven years. But Britain cannot be governed and led by a sick septuagenarian. The Prime Minister may hand over in the next few weeks. The mantle of the premiership should fall on Hailsham." So far so good, but Nabarro, a betting man, stuck his neck out too far and added . . . "Any erratic tendencies he has recently displayed on television would surely melt away."[49]

On the Thursday Lord Home arrived at the Winter Gardens with Macmillan's letter. Butler had spoken in the afternoon session and had been cheered even more loudly than Hailsham. As the crowd began to drift off thinking that was all, Mrs Peggy Shepherd, Chairman of the National Union, said that Home, the Conference President, had a special announcement. In "the flat matter of fact voice he would employ for dictating a stern note to Patagonia"[50] Lord Home read out the letter Macmillan had given him the day before: "It is now clear that, whatever might have been my previous feelings, it will not be possible for me to carry the physical burden of leading the Party at the next general election . . . In these circumstances I hope that it will soon be possible for the customary processes of consultation to be carried on within the party about its future leadership."[51]

Hankies came out in the stalls and a woman wept openly at the news that Macmillan had finally quit.

In the *Daily Mirror*, Cassandra remarked on the fortuitous timing of the Prime Minister's illness and hinted strongly that he did not believe it.

§

Hailsham's supporters – Julian Amery and Maurice Macmillan – now urged him to disclaim his peerage, with, as Randolph Churchill wrote, "what Hailsham regarded as the authority of the Prime Minister".[52] None of them knew of the question Macmillan had put to Home, or of the continuing vacillation as Macmillan's feelings turned and turned again. At the meeting of the Conservative Political Centre in the Pavilion Cinema, Hailsham spoke on the non-subject of national excellence. At the end of the speech he embarked on a rambling statement leading via his father's ennoblement, his own love of the Lords and his responsibilities to Macmillan to: "I shall continue to try and serve my country honourably as a friend to my colleagues, but I ought to say tonight that my intention is, after deep thought, to disclaim my peerage."[53]

The cheers drowned out his closing words. One John Eden, a nephew of Sir Anthony, leapt on to the platform and danced a jig, wildly waving his arms in the air. Cooler observers remarked that the scene resembled a Nuremberg Rally or a Chicago Convention – it was, whatever else it was, decidedly un-Tory. Above the hubbub

Hailsham added: "If I can find anyone to receive me as a candidate at an early moment to stand for the lower house I shall accept."

As his supporters tramped the streets of Blackpool chanting, 'We want Hailsham' and 'For he's a jolly good fellow', the object of their fanaticism went on digging his own grave. Back at the Imperial Hotel, he mixed up baby food in front of the television cameras and fed his one-year-old daughter. If Wilson had tried to turn televised politics into cinema verité with *World in Action*, Hailsham turned it into an advertisement and sold himself like Omo or Oxydol or Philip and Katie the Oxo couple. At the young Conservatives Ball, by tradition an upper-crust version of a Club 18-30 holiday, Lord and Lady Hailsham danced the twist.

"They say it's slimming," trilled Lady Hailsham, "which pleases me and certainly won't do my husband any harm."[54]

Somewhere in all this ballyhoo there lurked a suspicion that Hailsham knew what he had done. He was overheard saying to Edward Boyle, the Education Minister: "A very distinctive step has just been taken by a very frightened old Hogg."[55] Boyle had no time for him. Nor did most of the hierarchy. Lord Home later remarked that people felt bounced by Hailsham, and they didn't like being bounced. As A. A. Milne might have said, 'but that's what Tiggers do, they bounce people.' John Guest, chairman of St Marylebone Conservatives, was to be seen talking to Lord Home's people, and on Home's arrival offered him the seat. Before the day was over, Selwyn Lloyd, one of Hailsham's supporters, was making his way to Lord Home's suite to put the same question Macmillan had put. Out in the corridors of the Winter Gardens and the Imperial Hotel, such phrases as "It's Alec's for the asking" and "If Home stands there is no contest" could be heard. All this for a man who had not declared himself a candidate.

Up to this time Lord Home's position was pro-Hailsham, but he records in his memoirs that had he known in advance the immediate course that Hailsham's candidacy would take, he would have advised him against it.[56]

Again Robin Day interviewed Lord Hailsham, and put to him a question suggested by Wedgwood-Benn: "It is a sad comment on Lord Hailsham's respect for the House of Commons that he is only prepared to give up his hereditary privileges when he stands to gain something from it personally."[57] To which Hailsham replied: "I felt very strongly that unless I was prepared to make an unconditional sacrifice of my own, nobody could take seriously the possibility that I was worth that kind of position."[58]

In his memoirs Lord Hailsham recalls that the Prime Minister sent for him on the eve of Conference and "told me that he wished me to succeed him if he retired".[59] Macmillan's memoirs make no mention of this meeting, although it's clear that at some point Macmillan had let it be known that Hailsham was favoured[60] – it all depends on the weight given to words like 'wish' and 'if', for that evening the Prime Minister had gone to bed convinced that he would stay and lead the party into the next election, and two days later was sounding Home on his willingness to stand. Macmillan took the unusual step of announcing his departure at the start of the conference, rather than waiting until Saturday, as an act of support for Hailsham.[61] Yet, if Macmillan had already switched to Home and wished to destroy Hailsham he could not have done so more effectively, along the lines of those whom the gods wish to destroy they first make silly. In the *New Statesman* Anthony Howard put the bleakest possible interpretation on Macmillan's action: " . . . for the moment only one objective interpretation seems possible – that, like some latter day Samson Agonistes, Macmillan was prepared to bring the whole temple of Toryism down with him."[62]

Perhaps not – there's no hint of such a motive in his published diaries – but he had turned the tame Conservative Party Conference into an unprecedented theatrical event. What was said in the speeches scarcely counted with the press. No speech by a Conservative minister received headline coverage – all were eclipsed by the noises off. Where Labour had been able to present their arguments in an atmosphere of unity, the Conservatives lost the national audience for their arguments and presented a house in disarray.

Throughout this disarray Lord Dilhorne continued with the first stage in 'the soundings' and privately polled the cabinet on their preferences. By Friday evening, according to reports in the *Observer*, he had the result.

§

On the Friday Lord Hailsham seemed chastened, calmed his supporters and sat quietly in the stalls rather than on the platform. The day was not his but Home's. Maudling spoke on Wilson-ish lines about "youth" and "challenge" and was received modestly, with no standing ovation. Home opened his Foreign Office speech with a joke – "I am offering a prize to any newspaperman who can find a clue in my speech that this is Lord Home's bid for the leadership"[63] – and was received with overwhelming applause.

"At the end of his speech the delegates clapped. Then they cheered. Then they stood and cheered their heads off. Home smiled and waved like royalty. This had never happened to him before. The man who was the laughing stock of England the day he was appointed Foreign Secretary suddenly found himself the potential leader of Britain. He knew it. He knew at that moment that the 'crown' was his . . . "[64]

Despite Home's intentions, a 'draft Home' movement was under way that was rapidly realigning the factions. 'Draft Home' was the compromise that could 'Stop Quintin' and 'Stop Rab' and, in line with the doctrine of emergence, present the candidate acceptable to both camps. That morning Macmillan's most feared critic, the former Treasury minister Nigel Birch, arrived and openly pushed out the bandwagon for Home. Randolph Churchill, in the first book on the subject, *The Fight for the Tory Leadership*, wrote that Birch had heard before the Pavilion speech that Macmillan had acknowledged that Hailsham would prove unacceptable to the party, even that Duncan Sandys had reported this opinion to Macmillan as early as Wednesday – the day Macmillan chose to sound out Home for the first time.

The feet of the Conservative silent majority, in the shape of such figures as ex-Chancellor Selwyn Lloyd, shuffled down the carpeted corridor to Lord Home's suite. Lord Home agreed that he would consult his doctor – as a preliminary measure – but indicated that he did not wish to run against Hailsham.

On evening television, Robin Day made little headway with the 14th Earl of Home:

RD: " . . . Lord Home, is it possible in the Conservative Party, of which you have great knowledge, that, given strong enough support, a reluctant individual could be drafted to serve as leader of the party?"

AH: "It would depend on the individual and how reluctant he was. And I don't know who you have in mind . . . "

§

On Saturday a *Daily Mail* NOP poll showed a significant lead for Butler over Hailsham, with Maudling a poor third and Home not even in double figures. The *Mirror* offered bookies' odds – Butler 6 to 4 on, Hailsham 7 to 4, Maudling 6 to 1, Home 10 to 1. Lord Dilhorne's poll of the cabinet also became known to the cabinet that day, and seemed to show a preference for Home. If accurate this was the first real evidence of the disruption of the received wisdom on the voter appeal of the candidates, whereby Butler held the cabinet, Hailsham the constituencies and Maudling the Commons.

So much depends on the questions asked.

Home chose to be candid with his colleagues. He told Butler that he had been approached and of his idea that he must consult his doctor. Together he and Hailsham walked from the hotel to the Winter Gardens. Home admitted that he could now see circumstances in which he might agree to be drafted. Hailsham told him he did not have the necessary domestic experience for the job.

As Chairman it fell to Home to introduce the 'leader's' speech and he used the chance to put a perspective on a week of self-destructive madness: "I hope you will discount what people do at Blackpool – whether on land or in the sea." He looked at Hailsham, known for his seaside dips, as he spoke. Hailsham grinned sheepishly and twiddled his thumbs. "We choose our leader not for what he does at Blackpool but because he is in every sense a full man, fit to lead the nation. Everyone knows that no one has given more loyal or more unselfish service to the party than Mr Butler."

Butler, by insisting on his prerogative to make this speech, had lumbered himself. The speech was a dreadful combination of his words and Macmillan's. To be in Macmillan's shoes at this moment was to have traded opportunity for status, a status which provided little scope for Butler to shine. He rose to "tepid applause and a standing ovation of four", Churchill wrote,[65] and he meant four people not four minutes. Butler made his part of the address an ambiguous response to Wilson's White Heat, picking up several of his points, loosely endorsing them with the Conservative emphasis on individualism, still after twenty years furthering consensus – it sounded neither new nor inspiring and rather like a parody on a *Private Eye* giveaway floppy disc. In Tory terms it was pink at the middle let alone the edges. It was impossible for him after twenty years a radical to make his radicalism fresh – it now seemed merely to be Wilson's old coat with a Tory buttonhole. Nevertheless the assembly rose to its feet as one after his fifty-three minutes. Butler complained in his memoirs about "democracy by decibels", as Home was generally agreed to have received louder applause and to have stolen the day from him.

Lord Home went home for the weekend and talked to his family. On the Sunday he made a telephone call to Redmayne.

Few newspapers grasped the fall of Hailsham. Saturday's *Daily Telegraph* was the most acute and noted the 'Stop Quintin' movement, offering odds of 1000 to 1 on his winning. Sunday's *Observer* acknowledged Home's leap into the lead, but speculated idly that Macmillan himself might serve in the new government under him. Randolph Churchill, who had turned up at Blackpool almost at the last minute to hand out Q for Quintin badges, still backed his choice in his *News of the World* column: "It would be pathetic if Lord Home were to come downstairs and be elected to the House of Commons . . . Hailsham . . . is a patriot, a Christian, a man of honour, a poet and a lord of language."[66] He did not point out that the lord of language had secured the services of a professional, if unpaid, publicist for his campaign staff. If paid he would surely have been fired and asked for a refund by now. Monday's *Express* headlined "BUTLER'S THE MAN" – and stated that over the weekend Home had decided on the role of power broker not candidate, even though he would have been "swept into office" at the nod of his head. Over the weekend Lord Home had decided just the opposite. He would run, and told Macmillan so on the Monday.[67]

§

On Monday the Conservative factions reassembled in London. Lord Hailsham did not disclaim. By now he had been offered at least three seats – Morecambe, Hexham and Wimbledon (in the last two, sitting MPs had offered to step down for him), in addition to whatever arrangement might obtain in St Marylebone. In August Stratford-on-Avon had offered him a seat. Benn had telegraphed, urging, if not daring, him to disclaim. The offer had been withdrawn when no decision had been forthcoming.

Macmillan set up soundings of the party. Dilhorne would sound out the cabinet (but in fact had already done so), Lord St Aldwyn the Lords, Redmayne the junior ministers and the Commons, Lord Poole, Lord Chelmer and Mrs Shepherd the constituencies.

On Tuesday Lord Hailsham did not disclaim. The *Daily Express* offered him a "do-it-yourself-disclaimer" – all he had to do, they wisecracked, was cut it out, sign it and post it. Lord Home, as promised, spent an hour with his doctor, and was found to be, as he himself expressed it, "unfortunately fit". One by one Macmillan's inner cabinet came to his bedside – Butler, Home, Hailsham, Maudling, Macleod and Heath. He formed the same opinion Dilhorne had at Blackpool, that Home led, albeit by adding up the second choices. Dilhorne described the method of sounding on the Third Programme in December: "The Whips were each given a bunch of names. They were told not simply to get votes but full views on the leadership . . . there were three basic questions. 1. Who would you like to see in office? 2. Do you want to choose possible runners-up? 3. Is there anybody you would rather not see in office?"[68]

Home's name was in the 'bunch' – Butler's account gives the impression that he was kept in the dark, that he was surprised when he discovered that the whips "stressed that Alec was standing".[69] (Hailsham, according to Richard West and Anthony Howard's account, was told by Randolph Churchill only on Wednesday that Home was definitely running.)[70] Did Macmillan use the soundings as active canvassing for Home? Was the third of Dilhorne's questions designed to favour Home, by eliciting the blackballing of other candidates? More than this, was he actually rigging it from his sickbed?

On Wednesday Lord Hailsham did not disclaim. Macmillan saw the rest of his cabinet – Thorneycroft, Boyle, Soames, Hare, Brooke, Joseph, Sandys and Selwyn Lloyd, who, though still out of office, had played the Warwick role that had been expected of Butler.

On Thursday Lord Hailsham did not disclaim. Macmillan met with his fact-finders, first one by one and then all together so that each should know what the others had reported once Macmillan had been able to digest the information, and deduce a result. Thirty minutes after the pollsters assembled a man was seen to approach the hospital with a large tombola drum. A wag in the street cried out, "Surely they're not deciding it that way?"[71]

The precise breakdown of these soundings was not divulged in Macmillan's lifetime. Once Redmayne had informed Home and Butler, the news was out – Home was the next Prime Minister. The only area in which he had not led was the constituencies, where, it was argued, it hadn't yet filtered down that he was actually a candidate.

That evening the cabinet dissidents gathered at the Belgravia home of Enoch Powell: "It is necessary to understand what had happened before on that day, and that was that Reggie Maudling, having picked up authoritatively that the Prime Minister was going to recommend Alec Home to the Queen, informed Iain Macleod, and Iain Macleod informed me, and we decided that as soon as all three of us could meet we would meet. I'm sketchy about the hour but I believe the general order of events is correct. We were, all three of us, horrified at the idea of Alec Home being Prime Minister. And all three of us, in varying degrees of intensity, believed by then – and I'm putting in 'by then' for the sake of Reggie Maudling – that Rab was the right person, at that time, and in those circumstances, to become Prime Minister. We couldn't believe that there was substantial support amongst the members of the cabinet for Alec Home. So our first object was to ascertain what degree of support existed for Rab Butler and by that time, by midnight or thereabouts, we were all satisfied either by direct personal statement or by communication at a distance, that there was a majority of cabinet members who were in favour of Rab Butler becoming the Prime Minister. I myself obtained from Hailsham the assurance, which was the same as the assurance I had directly from Reggie Maudling, that he, Hailsham, no more than Maudling, would not accept office under Home if the premiership had been declined by Rab. It was our next step, to inform the chief whip, who came here at our request, that support in the cabinet was for Rab Butler – and that neither Maudling nor Hailsham would take office unless Rab did; that is to say, if Rab could be Prime Minister they would join his cabinet, but they would not join a cabinet under a Prime Minister that Rab declined to serve. That conclusion I personally conveyed to Rab Butler himself over the telephone. By the way, I'm sure that I had already said to Alec Home, 'I have to tell you straight away, that I don't think you ought to be Prime Minister.' At what stage I had that conversation I can't remember, in so far as my recollection is any good at all; I would have done it before I had the conversation with Hailsham. Hailsham wasn't here, I spoke to him on the phone from here.

"Well, one of Rab's remarkable characteristics was his unfailing ability to behave like Rab Butler. Butler was not by temperament, any more than the very differently temperamented Reggie Maudling, an individual who rose beyond himself in response to a challenge or opportunity. In fact, one of the outstanding characteristics of Butler which made me, which still makes me, confident that he would have been a success as a Prime Minister, if he'd ever become one, is that he had to become one first, he had to be put there, and then he would exercise all that was germane to that position. But to step out of himself in order to get there, to wade through blood to that position, was not in his nature."[72]

On Friday events moved at speed. Early in the morning Redmayne brought Macmillan up to date on the night's developments. Home telephoned Macmillan and talked of withdrawing – he had only agreed to be drafted in the interests of unity, now there was no unity. Macmillan would not hear of it and had sent his resignation to the Queen by half past nine. At eleven-thirty the Queen heard Macmillan's recommendation, and at twelve-fifteen sent for Home. Home answered the summons provisionally and modestly by saying that he would try to form a government.

Over the next twenty-four hours, Home saw the cabinet rebels one by one, and put the same question to them all: "Are you willing to serve? Will you help to save the government and the Conservative Party from catastrophe?"[73] Hailsham accepted almost at once, Butler and Maudling held out till the Saturday. Powell and Macleod stuck to their guns, and declined to serve.

Enoch Powell: "The decisive act was Rab Butler's. From the moment that Rab Butler had agreed to serve under Alec Home, it was arguably Quixotic for anyone who thought Rab ought to be Prime Minister to say 'Well I'm not going to join the cabinet, because I thought Rab ought to be Prime Minister.' Now, I'm not in a position to say why Iain stayed out. It's probable that his reason for staying out was not quite as 'deadpan' as mine.

"I was one of those, of course, whom Alec Home invited to come and see him to ask them to continue to serve. This was before he went back to the Queen and accepted office. I said, 'No, I won't because I don't think you ought to be Prime Minister and I think there is only one person who ought to be at this stage. This is the only moment I can influence this decision, and I influence it by saying I won't serve under you.' When he sent for me again on the Saturday when he was Prime Minister he said, 'I put to you the same question again,' and I said, 'Well, you know well enough that if I gave a different answer from what I gave you yesterday, I should have to go home and turn round all the mirrors.' And we laughed and I went out.

"I admit that it seemed grotesque to fetch a peer to be Prime Minister, but that was subordinate to my conviction that the right person to be Prime Minister was there staring you in the face all the time."

By Saturday lunchtime Home was standing outside No. 10 as the new PM, before a cheering crowd of seven hundred. He had kissed hands at the Palace. He had been serenaded with *Oh, What a Beautiful Morning* by the Irish Guards in St James' Park.

"I hope everyone on this fine Saturday morning can forget about politics, except me."[74]

A subdued Hailsham had little to say to the press, but said it acutely:

"There are times in a man's life when he would rather say nothing. This is one of those times. There are those who say that Lord Hailsham has talked too much in the past and that is why I cannot talk to you now."[75]

On the Sunday Home was adopted as candidate for the Kinross and West Perthshire by-election. Lord Hailsham reiterated that he would disclaim his peerage. On the Wednesday Lord Home did, and surrendered the titles of 14th Earl of Home, 4th Baron Douglas and even older Baron Dunglass, to become, as he was also a Knight of the Thistle, plain Sir Alec Douglas-Home. For three days a British Prime Minister had 'sat' in the Lords rather than the Commons. For the next three weeks he sat in neither.

§

Throughout the contest voices in the press and in all the political parties had said that 'the people' would never accept a 14th Earl as Prime Minister. This was guesswork, rather than polling. If what the Conservatives needed was the ordinary, youthful image Labour had, of a stout middle-aged-man-with-a-mortgage as leader, they did not get it by picking the tall, gaunt, filthy-rich sixty-year-old Earl of Home, owner of two country houses in Scotland, a London house in Carlton Terrace, 56 farms, 300 acres of forest and 53,000 acres of hill farm, whose pedigree filled three columns in *Burke*'s. In Manchester on the Saturday Wilson lined up his soft target: "In this ruthlessly competitive, scientific, technical, industrial age, a week of intrigues has produced a result based on family and hereditary connections. The leader has emerged, an elegant anachronism . . . of three hundred and fifty MPs, we are told, there is not one fitted to lead them."[76]

Home struck back on television the next day with a most effective remark: "I suppose Mr Wilson when you come to think of it is the 14th Mr Wilson" – and asked if all men were to be equal except peers. In the first of his New Britain speeches Wilson hit out at the prevailing "Edwardian Establishment mentality". Home replied with a more exact but less remembered jibe, that Wilson was "a slick salesman of synthetic science".

Neither the choice of Home nor the method by which he was chosen were subjects readily abandoned in the weeks and months that led up to the 1964 election. The party of gifted amateurism had thrown up one gifted amateur too many. The attacks on Home were immediate and unrelenting. The *Sunday Times* was typical of the quality press in its welcoming of Home: "If personal rectitude, combined with a gentle manner and a total absence of opportunism were the qualities which make a great Prime Minister, then Sir Alexander Douglas-Home KT would prove as illustrious an occupant of one side of Downing Street as he has been of the other. But whether these are the qualities of a leader of a party already bruised by the weight of long years in office is another story."[77]

On *That Was The Week That Was*, Bernard Levin dismissed Home as "a cretin", and left those without dictionaries wondering what a cretin was.

In the popular press Cassandra pointed out that Home had never done a day's work in his life, while John Beavan wrote that Home had been accustomed to wielding power all his life.

The attacks on the soundings were many. In the course of the campaign Tony Benn had written to *The Times*, taking issue with a nonsensical bluff to which almost every leading Tory, but most especially Macmillan, had resorted – the Queen's prerogative. By invoking this constantly the Conservatives disguised the true course and nature of power within their own party, and glossed over the fact that Macmillan could make whatever recommendation he liked to the Queen, and for all the nation knew he had done. But, there is another side to the argument. Enoch Powell was, and is, a firm believer in the idea of the royal prerogative:

"The proposition that no Prime Minister advises on his successor is a logical and sound proposition. You are Prime Minister because you enjoy the monarch's confidence. You cannot use that confidence in order to advise the monarch on what to do in the event of your *not* being Prime Minister. The thing is contradictory, you are thereby pre-empting the advice which will be offered to the sovereign in other circumstances. It is unthinkable, though the thing that is unthinkable could nevertheless be performed, it is unthinkable for the same man simultaneously to say to the sovereign, 'Next week I'm going to decline to advise you any further but before I decline to advise you any further I shall put myself in the position to advise you on what to do afterwards.' So Harold Macmillan, not untypically, was a destroyer of that piece of royal prerogative. Of course in this case, it was done publicly, it was done as a public act and thereby the advice improperly tendered to the sovereign was loaded. It might be one thing for an outgoing Prime Minister to stumble into the impropriety of saying 'In case you were to ask me after I've gone out of this room, I would mention so and so.' I dare say that's happened; but it is quite different for a Prime Minister while still Prime Minister, when he hasn't resigned, to conduct a public and publicised operation, for discovering for whom the Queen ought, after his resignation, to send.

"It's been my belief, in retrospect, that not later than the day before the Conference Macmillan had settled both upon Home as his successor and upon the manner by which the thing would be organised. I happen to believe that Harold Macmillan lied to his Sovereign, I happen to believe that the count which he purported to have taken was a fudged count, because I cannot reconcile it with what I knew as a member of the cabinet. I cannot reconcile it with what happened in my house on the

Thursday night."

In the *Sunday Express* A. J. P. Taylor scored a bullseye with: " . . . the only question that mattered was . . . how many blackballs has he received? The question perhaps does in a club. It was a poor question to ask concerning a Prime Minister . . . "[78]

Interviewed in the *Listener* of December 19th, Redmayne re-asserted the organic principle, but in his efforts to describe it he demonstrated just how vague and absurd the soundings had been: "When one came to assess this mass of opinion one had to start off by getting what I would call a numerical guide about what the situation was" – did he mean adding up? Curious – "One then had to consider carefully the shade of opinions expressed in various letters and reports" – and curiouser. A numerical guide plus a shade or two of opinion equals a mess.

A month or so later Macleod responded to this and to Churchill's book with a long piece in the *Spectator*. He stated plainly that Macmillan's object throughout had been to stop Butler, and challenged Redmayne's numerical guide in terms of simple Dilhorne addition. "From my personal knowledge . . . there were 11 [cabinet ministers] for candidates other than Home"[79] . . . although he did not call either Dilhorne or Macmillan a liar. Macleod attributed the outcome to the operation of the old Tory magic circle, the Etonian, Brigade of Guards clique – Home was the third Old Etonian PM in a row.

In contrast, Churchill, a Hailsham supporter who accepted that Home had 'emerged', had offered an analysis of the soundings that no one inside the party hierarchy could even pretend to have believed: "Never in the history of the Tory Party . . . have such full and diligent enquiries been made in the selection of a new leader. This was no decision made in a smoke filled room. Everyone in the party had an opportunity to make his or her views felt and the result of the canvass had been decisive. It was Tory democracy in action." Macmillan had " . . . at the risk of his life . . . contrived out of chaos that the Queen was spared embarrassment, that the nation should have strong government . . . "[80] – and so had rendered a service to the nation – which says nothing of Macmillan's role in fostering that chaos.

§

It is, given such a poor start – damned as a toff, bedevilled by the lack of democracy that had brought him to power, destroyed by the satirists – remarkable how well Alec Douglas-Home fared. That he held Kinross with 75% of its previous majority was no surprise. That over the year he was in power he cut Labour's potential one hundred-seat majority to a real result of only four was. Never good on television, tight-lipped, clenching his teeth, and looking, as a TV make-up girl told him, as though he had a head like a skull ("Doesn't everyone?" he replied), he fought the last old-fashioned campaign, redolent of the way things had been done when he last sat in the Commons in 1951, stamping the country in the pouring rain and talking to people in market squares and village halls. It was more effective than he could have hoped. Wilson, by comparison, seemed a media figure and, as Tony Benn said many years later, "sat in Transport House giving WEA lectures".[81] "Home had a certain quality about him – it was easy for Wilson to make fun of him, but he had a certain straightness about him – 'good Old Alec Home'. That's why the Tories picked him, they wanted a straight man after a fixer. And he campaigned very powerfully. I think he's a much underestimated figure. He was very competent and hard working."[82]

Straight, and consistent. Home was out of keeping with the mood of the times less by being titled than by being on the right of the party on almost every issue on which he had had a say, from Munich, when he was PPS to Chamberlain, via Suez where a 'Russian-Egyptian plot to dominate the Middle East' had been stopped, and African independence, where as Commonwealth Secretary he defended the imprisonment of Hastings Banda, to the Cold War, where he was thoroughly anti-communist, as he had been ever since Hitler had struck him as less of a menace than Stalin. His appointment as Foreign Secretary in 1960 had been greeted by critics as a piece of whimsy on Macmillan's part, or worse as his gimmick. Yet, by the standards of his party, he had proved a good Foreign Secretary. Surely by now he was immune to the personal attacks?

On November 8th, the day the Kinross result was announced, Lord Hailsham was adopted for St Marylebone. At last on November 20th he disclaimed his title, six weeks after he had thrown his hat into the ring, saying: "Lord Hailsham is dead. Long live Quintin Hogg."

Hailsham has pointed out that he disclaimed after he had anything to gain by doing so – he implies purity of motive. On the other hand, it could be argued that Hailsham had cornered himself. Having made a fool of himself by offering to disclaim, he could only make a bigger fool of himself by not disclaiming.

§

Mr Macmillan remained Mr Macmillan. He dashed off a flurry of baronetcies and peerages for his personal staff at No. 10, and cocked a snook at the Lords by declining the usual offer of an earldom – one role he did not wish to play, at least until the age of ninety when he went to the Lords as the Earl of Stockton, sans eyes but hardly sans teeth, to be a thorn in the side of his former junior Pensions Minister. One man in his time plays many parts, but, as every writer on Macmillan has commented, few play as many as Macmillan. Fewer still play them as repertory. Somewhere in the strontium mist of post-war history Enoch Powell is said to have dubbed him the 'old actor-manager', but the nickname that stuck was the one given to him by the cartoonist Vicky in the London *Evening Standard* in 1958 – Supermac.

Macmillan described his own political skill as like juggling five balls, and with each zenith he presented a different image. The truth of Enoch Powell's label was in Macmillan as a shy person reinventing his public persona as a constant disguise, never entirely surrendering any part he had once played in case he needed it again. The danger of this particular psychological tool of survival is that it's impossible to stop. His fondness for play-acting and music hall – he visited Russia flamboyantly wearing a white fur hat, not, as I used to think, a gift from Khrushchev but something he had dug out of his own bottom drawer – he donned a leopard-skin in Nigeria – he delighted an audience with a rendition of "She wouldn't say yes, she wouldn't say no" – was frequently put to use. By the time he became Prime Minister in 1957, he had a bewildering repertoire. Arguably it took such a man to preside over the age in transition that was the first five years of his premiership.

As is often said, he flew the flag of empire whilst walking steadily away from it. He presented a comforting old world image while foisting the new upon party and country. He parodied himself and his generation, and in the parody divorced image from reality – that which he was changing, the Britain that had been, was the more easily surrendered. When it returned it was as a pure image, the mock-Edwardian chic of Swinging London, the imperial army coats of Lord Kitchener's Valet, the Union Jack waistcoat, the red, white and blue Minis of *The Italian Job*, the pop celebration of a style that only ten years before had seemed to cramp the country oppressively.

From shortly after the July purge of 1962, a date I've set at the arrest of William Vassall, the nation changed faster than the old conjurer could pull something new from one of his many hats. He was caught wearing the image of an unworldly Old Edwardian in the Profumo fiasco, and went down wearing it – lost in a world whose morals he could not begin to fathom, racked with self-pity, feeling betrayed and confused, and as a last act reviving a Victorian practice, perpetrating an Edwardian jape in his choice of successor.

Against expectation Mr Macmillan did not immediately retire. He saw out the term of the parliament, and then retreated to write a huge and, the first volume apart, almost unreadably detailed autobiography. He did not have to preside over the cultural acceleration of the next few years. He was spared its excesses; he did not have to give the Beatles the MBE; he did not have to reopen the Cavern.

CHAPTER ELEVEN

MISCHIEF

"But what I feel we do need is more engagement in the outer world. And daring. And wit. And, finally, satirists, who are needed as truth is needed – for is not satire, simply, truth grinning in a solemn canting world?"

Gore Vidal[1]

"It was in my capacity as a subversive anarchist that I yielded to the enormous pressure from my fellow subversives and put TW3 on the air; and it was as a pillar of the Establishment that I yielded to the fascist hyena-like howls to take it off again." Hugh Greene[2]

"'There can only,' [Greene] said ominously, 'be one reason why a writer like you could possibly be interested in that subject; to make mischief.' At once he broke into the broadest smile and rubbed his hands together. I have never seen a man so delighted by a single word."

David Hare[3]

" . . . We are all of us piss-takers."

Joan Littlewood[4]

In 1959 a young man came down from Cambridge with a couple of good ideas – to open London's first satirical nightclub and to start a satirical magazine. He had already written two London revues for Kenneth Williams while still a student, and had been 'working' at comedy since he first sent cartoons in to *Punch* as a child. By the spring of 1962 both those ideas were in practice and no less a figure than Peter Ustinov had dubbed him the funniest man alive. His name was Peter Cook: "I had this notion – I was certain somebody else would do it first, it just seemed such an obvious idea – to do, for want of a better word, political cabaret. Before I went to Cambridge I'd been in Berlin and Paris and I'd seen political cabaret there, and I thought it was pretty dreadful.

"Nick [Luard] was treasurer of Footlights. I don't think he was personally wealthy, but he looked as if he might know about money or people with money. We were looking for premises in our last year at Cambridge. Originally I wanted it to be in Covent Garden, because there were a lot of buildings there which were perfect, those long empty warehouses, but you couldn't get a change of usage in those days."[5]

In October 1961 Cook-Luard Productions opened the Establishment Club, billboarded as 'London's First Satirical Nightclub', at 18 Greek Street, a stone's throw from Shaftesbury Avenue, in the heart of Soho, the traditional home in the capital of striptease and prostitution.

"I was not initially that keen on Soho, but we couldn't get [any other] premises where we could get a liquor licence or a theatre licence, so we wound up in Greek Street, negotiating with Mr Lubowski, freeholder of the Tropicana Strip Club. Neither one of us knew anything about business. I assumed Nick knew about business, as a performer I could be expected not to know, indeed the salaries in *Beyond the Fringe* proved that none of us knew about business. Management made a fortune, and we were very pleased to be earning . . . about a hundred pounds a week."

Peter Cook had performed in *Beyond the Fringe* on and off since 1960, and stayed with the show until 1964. Originally put together by William Donaldson and John Bassett to showcase the writing and performing talents of Cook, Dudley Moore, Alan Bennett and Jonathan Miller, it had been, despite the name, part of the official 1960 Edinburgh Festival. It had been well received out of London and when it entered the West End at the Fortune Theatre on May 10th, 1961 it took London by storm. Whether or not it was 'satire' has been argued endlessly, but it produced sketches which still surface from time to time in Amnesty shows and in Cook's E. L. Wisty, a durable comic character. Nothing quite like it had ever been seen before.

"Revue had more or less strangled itself in its own clichés," wrote Michael Frayn. "The *Fringe* people were the first in this country with the genuine originality to hack their way back to first principles and start all over again . . . the show made its audience laugh at the unthinking attitudes of respect which up till then the audience themselves had shared."[6]

Kenneth Tynan reviewed *Beyond the Fringe* for the *Observer*:

"Mr Cook qualifies . . . at least thrice for the revue anthologies: once as a Beaverbrook journalist, nervously protesting that he has not ditched his liberal principles and proudly declaring that he still dares, when drunk, to snigger at his employer: again as the Prime Minister, casually tearing up a letter from an old age pensioner: and again as a Pinteresque outcast who would have liked to be a judge, if he had only had enough Latin."[7]

311

Beyond the Fringe had no songs, other than Dudley Moore's parodies, no set to speak of, and affected a stark monochrome, the cast assembled in what looked like plain black Marks & Spencer's lambswool pullovers. It sent up the sacred – class, politics, the church, the law, royalty, race – and, hooking the pullover over the head for moments of cod-melodrama – the unmentionable . . .

"Prepare for the end of the world. Fifteen seconds . . . "

"Have we got the tinned food?"

"Yes . . . ten seconds . . . "

"And the tin opener?"[8]

And was Peter Cook the first man to impersonate a Prime Minister on the London stage? *Beyond the Fringe* became one of the first cracks in the breaking of the old Britain – Tynan summed it up as "the moment when English comedy took its first decisive step into the second half of the twentieth century"[9] – but it didn't make them rich. Neither Peter Cook nor Nick Luard was looking for a way to burn up money.

" . . . I put some money in, Nick put some money in, but the club was largely paid for by people joining before it was opened. We had a lot of publicity, and sent out a lot of leaflets. People either joined for a year or became life members. I think we raised about ten thousand quid through people joining a club that didn't yet exist. Downstairs there was the long, thin ex-striptease room, two floors upstairs and a basement, but Mr Lubowski kept discovering subleases of which he claimed to be unaware – Maltese prostitutes, I don't know what – so the lease cost us a great deal more than it should have done.

"I persuaded Sean Kenny to design the club, partly on the promise that he could have the first floor as his studio. In the meantime *Beyond the Fringe* had opened in the West End which undoubtedly helped the membership drive. I was just so pleased that nobody else had done it. There were rumours of places starting but none of them had actually started. I'm not particularly good at titles, but the Establishment is the best title I've ever come up with. It came in the middle of the night and I knew it was absolutely right. *Beyond the Fringe* was a ghastly title, but we couldn't think of anything else."

Within a very short time The Establishment built up a membership of eleven thousand. Muggeridge wrote in the *New Statesman* that "One is struck by the general air of affluence. One looks around instinctively for Princess Margaret, or at any rate the Duke of Bedford." Had he visited the New York Establishment he might have looked round for a glimpse of the First Lady. Despite this the club's attendance wasn't always high. Ned Sherrin, then a *Tonight* producer with an eye on bigger things, frequented The Establishment as part of his job:

"Attendance at The Establishment varied between the very full and the very empty but the nucleus resident cast always played to capacity when I was there in the early months. Often they were augmented by Peter Cook, who as co-owner made frequent guest appearances,[10] usually performing scatological solos which were drastically amended when his parents paid visits from the West Country. On other occasions guests took the floor, and the club suddenly assumed the aspect of a deserted soup kitchen."[11]

Peter Cook: "It was a topical show which changed a bit from week to week, and there was a new show every three months I think. The regular company was John Bird, John Fortune, Eleanor Bron, Jeremy Geidt and Carol Simpson, singing. They were a wonderful group, all of whom wrote, and it was a shortish show, rather like *Beyond the Fringe* had been in Edinburgh – we only did about an hour. The main thing was the regular cast. We did little film bits too. There was one which was very good. It looked like a lung operation. Jonathan played the surgeon. There was this bom-bom music – everything depends on the surgeon's skill – and you see the surgeon's smoking through his mask, severing a thread with the tip, dropping ash in the open wound – and the punchline was 'to help him concentrate Dr So-and-so smokes blah-blah's cigarettes'. I've forgotten who made the film – it may have been Dick Lester – but it was really horrible to look at. There was still the Lord Chamberlain in those days – if you were a club you got round that – you could be a little bit dirtier . . . or a lot . . . you could do what the hell you wanted. Apart from being hugely enjoyable, it was a very good commercial idea. It was a huge success, for very good reasons. Altruistically we made the food as cheap as possible, we didn't charge much, you got a three course dinner and a show for really very little. Downstairs there was Dudley and his trio pounding away with some really good jazz. There was a bar which was open late. And it was great value for money."

In the Autumn of 1962 one sketch produced a flurry in the press. The *Sunday Pictorial* referred to the club as "serving some of the highest meaty jokes in the business" and described how Matthew, Mark, Luke and John were portrayed as reporters covering the crucifixion. The twist being that the thieves start complaining that Christ is getting the VIP treatment, even to having a higher cross than them.

Covering drama occasionally for the *Daily Mail*, standing in for Bernard Levin's stand-in Peter Lewis – rather like a character from an early Stoppard play – Barry Norman caught some of The Establishment's cabaret in 1963 – Agnes Bernelle, Irwin Corey, Annie Ross and the unknowns:

" . . . Miss Ross singing at her deliberate worst is still about twice as good as most women singing at their best . . . [and] . . . deserves praise for her courage in sharing the bill with Roddy Maude-Roxby. He is a splendidly zany and off-beat droll of whom I hope we shall be hearing considerably more in the future."[12]

Barry Norman adds today: "It made you uneasy. It was very anarchic stuff. I'm quite sure if you saw the acts now you'd think this is tame, but at that time it wasn't. It was very irreverent. The language on stage was extremely blue – that was unusual. And, again, they tended to be very young performers. It was called the Establishment . . . because it was anti-Establishment. I suppose that was probably what was happening all the time. And that was what was exciting about it all – The Establishment Club was taking the established way of doing things and shaking it all up."[13]

Irwin Corey was one of several American acts brought over by Peter Cook, as a result of the long New York run of *Beyond the Fringe* and the opening of a New York Establishment Club, who played alongside the residents and more familiar faces.

Peter Cook: "I was in England when Irwin Corey, who's one of my favourite comedians, came over, and he mystified London audiences. I seemed to spend a lot of time bringing over people I liked, who had a terrible time because nobody else liked them. Irwin Corey played 'the world's leading authority' . . . and of course [we put on] Francis Howerd . . . to me he was a huge star. We were at the *Evening Standard* Drama Awards, we'd won something and Frankie was compering the evening, and I thought he was marvellous. I approached him with great trepidation thinking why on earth would a great star like him want to do a little club – in terms of show business – and said is there any chance you'd do a few weeks? He said yes, and he's always claimed that he said yes when he was drunk and then panicked and said no, and then got persuaded to do it. I think Keith Waterhouse and Willis Hall wrote the material, and he was wonderful, using all this stuff about Nick and I being 'upstairs' these 'upper class boys asking him to do satire' – and he then did that on *That Was The Week That Was*. But it never occurred to me that his career was in the doldrums, to me he was a gigantic star – I was amazed that he agreed.

"Of the guest people we had over the most celebrated and notorious was Lenny Bruce, who was fabulous for four weeks. He did a swap with Second City and came over from Chicago . . . he only

314

played the club once. The second time we tried to smuggle him in through Ireland and failed. He was sensational – I'd only heard him on record, and he was very funny – not as obviously funny as Mort Sahl, where it was all very clear, good, funny one-liners.

"He got thrown out of his hotel immediately for having hookers in his room, and syringes down the toilet – so he came to stay with me in Battersea. I knew he was a junkie – about two in the morning he decided he wanted some Dilaudin – I think that's artificial heroin – I had this vision of junkies who didn't get their fix, they climbed up the wall, they tore things apart, they hurled themselves off buildings and so on. He had this bit of paper from his doctor saying something about the war injury he had from serving in the Marines – could I get him some Dilaudin? I said OK I'll try. I think drugs? Jazz? So I ring up Dudley who doesn't even take junior aspirin without being at death's door. He put me on the trail of various jazz musicians, who put me on the trail of various bogus doctors . . . anyway I came back at four in the morning completely unsuccessful, and I expect to find this gibbering wreck and there he is sitting quite contentedly in the bedroom. I said I'm sorry Lenny, I couldn't find any Dilaudin. He says never mind – how about some chocolate cake? And I got very cross then. I said heroin might have been possible, but chocolate cake at four in the morning in London is just not on – go to bed!"

Cook denies that The Establishment set out simply or deliberately to shock. It's just as well for what was shocking was unpredictable. Even Lenny Bruce – known as the sickest comic alive – turned over the audience at an unexpected moment.

"He'd been through shit, fuck, cunt – the lot – and the word cancer was mentioned, and this man leapt from his table: 'Come on, Cynthia, Fiona. Cancer – out!'"

Willie Rushton recalls seeing Bruce at less than his best: "I went to see Lenny Bruce on a bad night. Ingrams, Booker and I were taken by Nancy Spain . . . I think she wanted to write something . . . and took us to see what our reactions would be. It was a bit unfair on Lenny Bruce really. He darted off at one stage for 'medication' – but it wasn't on, something wasn't happening . . . if he got his scrapbook out then you knew you were in for a very rough four hours, when he'd read out all his court cases and get very upset about his treatment – rightly so, but it did make for a boring evening, the jokes weren't coming thick and fast. It was just this long litany of appalling disasters at the hand of various police forces all over America."[14]

From Australia came a young man of confusing gender and

identity, whose 'day job' was playing the undertaker in Lionel Bart's *Oliver*. He received this review from *Plays and Players*: " . . . One always thinks of the Establishment as being beyond the conventional nightclub fringe and one tends to take a late night dinner there in the confident expectation that somewhere between the first sip of coffee and the last gulp of liqueur the sacred cows of the English way of life will be neatly demolished . . . [but] . . . Barry Humphries, from Australia . . . offers an entertainment that one could safely take Aunt Edna to if she felt like living it up in Soho."[15]

Could this – great powers! – be the first manifestation, the humble beginning of Mrs Edna Everage, later DBE? Yes, it could.

Peter Cook: "I only knew Barry Humphries' work through a series of LPs – there were a few fans over here who had Barry's LPs. He did a character I liked called Sandy Stone who lived in Moonie Ponds – he's still my favourite character, I'm not sure he's not Barry's favourite character. I didn't see the show, but I understand from Barry that his time at The Establishment was a complete disaster. Everybody hated it. Edna, if indeed he called her Edna then, was a much more subdued character. She was just an ordinary housewife, who came on rather shyly, who'd never been on stage before . . . "

Ned Sherrin also recorded Mrs Everage's debut, an act he caught on one of the deserted soup-kitchen nights: "A well-observed and slightly pathetic matron, clad in a homespun brown dress. She had not, as I remember, yet invented the gladiolus."[16]

With *That Was The Week That Was*, The Establishment and *Private Eye* all active satire became the rage of 1963, a year Peter Cook spent mostly abroad in the Broadway version of *Beyond the Fringe*. Back in London Cook-Luard Productions ran into money trouble – since 1962 they had run not only The Establishment, but also the magazine *Scene*. They also owned a shareholding in *Private Eye*. By the September of 1963 a creditor's meeting estimated the company's losses at £65,000. The winding-up was unavoidable.

"The thing that brought it down was the magazine. *Scene* was wholly Nick – but I was too greedy. Just as I was going off to the States I saw these very flashy dummy issues – well-designed, colour photographs, it all looked quite nifty – and instead of saying I don't want anything to do with that, because I wasn't anything to do with it, I went along with it and I was fed what turned out to be absolutely inaccurate reports of its fortunes while I was in America. It had pretensions to be the sort of smart magazine you'd be well advised to leave hanging around on your coffee table, but we'd have been better off selling coffee tables I think . . . again it shows how naïve we were financially, the same limited company ran both *Scene* and The Establishment, so when *Scene* went down the tube it dragged The Establishment down with it. The Establishment never lost money."

At the creditors' meeting Cook and Luard's solicitor described his clients as "utter fools . . . it is quite obvious from the figures that the club has been very badly managed, but the directors are young and inexperienced", and a chartered accountant added, "The directors have acted in a stupid foolhardy way. In fact, just think of any similar adjectives and they will apply to them."[17] Nick Luard commented at length on running The Establishment, on being a victim of success:

"People think that if you open a nightclub you have only to sell food and drink to make thousands in profit. It's not so, as I have found to my cost. The overheads are tremendous. Ironically, the satire started to hit the club. Satire is supposed to be golden, but only big record companies and TV can now exploit it properly. The publicity has made satirists too expensive for small operators to hire."[18]

He added that the banning of Lenny Bruce by the Home Secretary had cost the club a lot of money.

But, the situation was more serious, as Peter Cook recalls, than any of these comments suggest: "Along came a gangster – he's still alive and living in Marbella I think – Lebanese, karate expert, very good-looking, drank only milk, always carried five grand around in a briefcase, I think he was a sort of Rachman enforcer, great personal charm. He flew out to see me in New York, said he'd take over all the debts, when I got back from the States I could take over my 50% again. And it was the usual spiel 'you mustn't believe my reputation, when you're in the nightclub business in the West End you have to have a certain reputation, don't believe all that stuff.' I got back, took one look at the place and the situation was just irreversible. It was filled with heavy men. And the atmosphere was completely gone . . . "

Peter Rachman visited The Establishment some time in 1962, at the invitation of the 'gangster', to sit in the audience and watch, just like anyone else. Some time in 1963 Det Sgt Challenor visited to say that any trouble could always be brought straight to him – it's hard to know whose visit was the more sinister.

"The only thing I retrieved from the whole thing was that Nick and I had put money into *Private Eye*. I suppose I was quite cross with Nick at the time, and I got hold of his half of it, of our mutual shareholding in *Private Eye*. As a financial proposition the *Eye* wasn't particularly good, but it was something I wanted to stay involved with. I wanted to salvage something from this chaotic collapse.

"The club in the USA did very well. We had it in the former premises of the El Morocco on 52nd Street. It was much plusher than The Establishment in London, it had been a beautiful, plush nightclub. The policy was exactly the same – an hour-long show, dinner and jazz. Ran there for two or three years, had a touring company – one of whose members was John Cleese if I remember right. We built a theatre with Joe Levine's money upstairs – we put on a dreadful play called *The Knack* which did very well, directed by Mike Nichols – it was his directorial debut. When the base of The Establishment went in London I suppose we could have gone on, but I came back to London."

§

In the summer of 1964 Peter Cook came home to take charge of his last asset, *Private Eye*. By then it too was in trouble.

Private Eye published its first issue in the same month that The Establishment opened. Despite the 'good idea' there was no connection between this venture and Peter Cook's.

"I knew none of the people involved in it. When *Private Eye* started it annoyed me because I, in those vaulting years of ambition, had the intention of starting a magazine not exactly like it, but similar to it."

The first issue was largely the work of Willie Rushton and Christopher Booker, and was printed on yellow paper – they had rejected titles such as 'The Bladder' or 'The Yellow Press'. Rushton and Booker had been at school with later contributors Richard Ingrams and Paul Foot. Booker was a contemporary of Cook's at Cambridge, and Foot, Ingrams and John Wells had been at Oxford together, where they had worked on prototype satirical magazines *Parson's Pleasure* and *Mesopotamia*. The original backer of *Private Eye* was another Oxford colleague Andrew Osmond. By February 1962 the magazine was appearing fortnightly.

Willie Rushton: "*Private Eye* was a sort of exercise really. We never actually thought it would take off. The idea we had about it hasn't changed to this day. Sitting around in the King's Head and Eight Bells, we came up with this notion of a sort of topical magazine . . . the brilliant idea was to make it a fortnightly. I don't know where that came from. I think that was laziness. The thought of a weekly was too much. A fortnightly was absolutely brilliant. It's saved them to this day. It does allow you much more room, and it recognises the fact that if you do a weekly people miss the jokes – it takes about a fortnight for a good joke to really sink in."[19]

Peter Cook was interested from the start and chipped in ideas – suggesting for their third issue the bubble and photo cover which is still in use. With issue 4 Lord Gnome made his appearance, and *Private Eye* grew as quickly as The Establishment. The original yellow issue had a print run of only three hundred copies – most of which were given away. By issue 5 they were aiming at five thousand copies, and were getting money directly from selling advertising. By May 1962 the circulation was eighteen thousand. In that month Osmond decided to join the Foreign Office. *Private Eye* being strapped for cash, and Cook-Luard at this point not so strapped, he sold most of his majority shareholding to Cook and Luard for £1500. For seventeen months Cook was the proprietor of London's first satirical nightclub and its first satirical magazine. He had at last, if so briefly, achieved both of his ambitions.

What *Private Eye* needed first of all were premises. They had operated out of Neal Street, Covent Garden for six months and now found themselves sharing a waiters' changing room in The Establishment – Rushton's recollection is of "the crackle of hypodermics underfoot as you went into the gentlemen's lavatory". And of an unfortunate accident that befell John Fortune "when he offered to help the Alberts down the stairs with a double bass which exploded. I think he's still slightly deaf to this day." A permanent office was found only two doors away at 22 Greek Street, where *Private Eye* remained for many years.

Peter Cook tried to bring the two halves of his empire together: "There was meant to be this sort of satirical interchange between The Establishment and *Private Eye* which never really worked." For a brief interlude The Establishment met the *Eye* in what seem to have been fairly humourless, mutually suspicious encounters.

Willie Rushton: "When Cook took us over, he thought it would be good if the Birds and Fortunes met the Ingrams, Bookers and Rushtons. And we used to sit, discussing satire in general and the world, and see if jokes erupted. Naturally all the parties looked at each other in complete silence, we finished a quite nice buffet lunch, then Cook would go off into extraordinary things about the great bee of Ephesus or some fantasy of his own devising which had nothing to do with anything and then we'd all go back to the office again."

Ever willing to bite the hand that feeds it, the *Eye* made Cook an

319

early target. The first Aesop Revisited told the tale of Jonathan
Crake, Satirist who, after a successful revue and running his own
nightclub, finds that he " . . . cannot open his mouth without
everyone collapsing at brilliant satirical comment" such as "where's
the gents?" An angry, dispirited Crake is shown in the last frame
leafing through ancient volumes of *Punch* in search of jokes –
"Moral: Humour is a serious business."

The method of production at *Private Eye* was simple and has
remained basically unchanged. Rushton describes it as being based
on the principle of a betting-shop floor:

"All the jokes have mostly been team stuff. That started very
early. Booker would invariably have the piece of paper, then
Ingrams took it over . . . you could sometimes see Cook do about
fifteen minutes of very good stuff, and Ingrams would write down
about four sentences. Sort of editing-on-the-trot. It worked very
well."

The entire magazine was produced on an ancient manual typewriter, the pages cut and pasted up on the floor with Cow gum, and
then printed by the relatively new, relatively cheap offset litho
process. Although *Private Eye* had some trouble keeping a printer,
as their reputation for trouble grew, the technology was of great
importance. Given the costs of conventional typesetting and printing it was unlikely that voices like *Private Eye*'s would have broken
into print or stayed in print without new technology. To this day
they've never bothered with typesetting, and much of it, whatever
the reality, still looks as though it was typed on an old typewriter.

By 1963 regular features had evolved – Logue's True Stories,
usually the bizarre and the whimsical, Booker and Rushton's upper-
crust nonentity Chatto, who always managed to blurt out in a quick
four lines what his 'people' were thinking but not saying, Lunchtime
O'Booze the Fleet Street hack, Eric Buttock (after Eric Lubbock,
Liberal victor in the Orpington by-election), the new boy in the
Commons who wrote in the style of Nigel Molesworth, and Romantic England, a mock anthropology of the ailing nation – as well as
the long-serving bubble covers and Bores of the Week. That said, it
was a markedly different magazine from the one it is now. The
parodies seem more literary – there was no Murdoch press crying
out for an easy spoof – and, recognising the contributions of Trog,
Steadman, Rushton, Tidy et al, it was a wordy, narrative-based
journal. What it didn't have was the now familiar back pages, what
Rushton refers to as 'the serious bits' – but at this stage it lacked the
contribution of Paul Foot (still on the *Scottish Daily Record* in
Glasgow). The editorial list for the Spring of 1963 listed Booker,

Rushton and Ingrams, with 'contributors' including Barry Fantoni, Alan Brien, Gerald Scarfe and J. Campbell Murdoch – an obscure pseudonym for John Wells, then still a schoolmaster at Eton.

Two of *Private Eye*'s 'principles' are apparent even in issue 1. They set out to knock the stuffing out of the complacency of the recent past, in the shape of the tired old man of humour Mr Punch, whilst simultaneously admiring those of the older generations who lived up to their own standards of irreverence and dissent. *Private Eye*'s reputation for lashing out at everything was wholly compatible with its admiration for the traditions of campaigning, muckraking journalism. Muggeridge, who as editor of *Punch* had made efforts to put some teeth back in the old man, was one of Ingrams' heroes. Without Muggeridge *Punch* slipped back into boredom. Mr Punch himself was interviewed on the back page as the first Bore of the Week.

"*Punch* is nothing if it's not up to date. Rock'n'roll, expense accounts, teddy boys, hula hoops, – there's nothing we don't take a good laugh at."[20]

On the front page Sir Winston Churchill was implicitly compared to Stalin, under the banner headline 'Churchill Cult Next For Party Axe?' in a piece accredited to one Edouvard Khrankschov. Another go at Churchill led the *Eye* to its first crisis of 1963 and to no less than thirteen writs. In the issue of February 8th, Aesop Revisited (drawn by Rushton, written by Booker) took as the subject of its fable the Greatest Dying Englishman, Churchill. His son Rudolph Rednose is hard at work in his Suffolk factory rewriting history for volume one of his Life of Dad. Among the items Aesop felt sure to be fudged were "wild futile military gestures, regardless of cost . . . shooting Welsh miners . . . opposing every manifestation of the 20th Century . . . "

Willie Rushton: "Booker had a thing about Churchill. He didn't like him because of the way he treated the Welsh in 1911, Tonypandy and all that stuff. That was really what he was getting off his chest. And we threw in incidentally pictures of dear old Randolph sitting there with his hacks reading off lecterns and writing his books for him, which transpired later to be totally true. There was no fighting the old bastard. He rang up his lawyers in the middle of the night, immediately briefed the four top libel men in the country."

Everyone at *Private Eye* received a writ – from editor to typist. There'd been occasional writs before, but never in such number or from a foe so formidable.

Willie Rushton: "Luard and I went to see him – Luard in his suit –

I not in mine, I was along as light relief. Luard reckoned I was probably the one – with my easy charm – he thought Randolph Churchill might like me. I wasn't quite sure this was sound. I was in no position whatsoever to do jokes. It was about ten o'clock in the morning, he sat us down and immediately handed us this apology, said 'This is what I want.' We wrung a few concessions, but he wanted us to put an ad in *The Times* which would have cost a lot of money – it ended up in the *Evening Standard* and we managed to get a few names lopped off the list of those he wanted to apologise. We said OK. We'd had enough trouble. There's been some nice scraps along the way. We'd had this picture I'd drawn up in the window downstairs – the Great Boar of East Bergholt – a Randolph-like pig taking a crap – very subtle – and within about an hour of it going up more writs arrived. The moment we said OK suddenly large whiskies arrived. He had the largest whisky I'd ever seen, must have had a tumblerful, half a pint. Then he introduced us to the lectern – the one I'd drawn with remarkable accuracy, since I'd never actually seen it. Alan Brien had actually worked for him, done this for him, written out large chunks for him, gone in, slapped his bits of paper on the lectern and read 'em to him."

The apology was duly printed in the London *Evening Standard*, although several of the signatories would appear to be fictitious. Ingrams has written that but for this incident he feels sure Randolph Churchill would have joined the old blood that occasionally coursed into *Private Eye*. Luard opined that the clash with Churchill had really put them on their feet, whether for nerve or originality isn't clear, but the fortnightly print run was raised in anticipation. That Summer circulation peaked at an incredible eighty thousand. This was largely due to the national mood, confusion, prurience, enquiry, and that was largely due to the Profumo affair. What the *Eye* knew was what most journalists knew, but people expected more from *Private Eye*. Even after a close brush with a major libel suit, they suggested more than most papers would allow. As early as March top *Eye* journalist Lunchtime O'Booze wrote, or 'revealed', the story of Miss Gaye Funloving and friends: "Dr Spook is believed to have 'more than half the cabinet on his list of patients.' He also has a weekend cottage on the Berkshire estate of Lord *, and is believed to have attended many parties in the neighbourhood. Among those it is believed also attended 'parties' of this type are Mr Vladimir Bolokhov, the well known Soviet spy attached to the Russian Embassy, and a well known Cabinet Minister. Mr James Montesi, a well known Cabinet Minister, was reported last night to have proffered his resignation to the Prime Minister on personal grounds. It is alleged that the Prime Minister refused to accept his alleged resignation."[21]

The evening of the day that piece appeared George Wigg got to his feet in the Commons to raise the issue of 'rumour upon rumour'. When Stephen Ward came round to see Rushton and Ingrams, it was not as a result of this almost direct revelation, but after seeing a cryptic corner in a piece by Booker and Timothy Birdsall, The Last Days of Macmilian, in the next issue.

Willie Rushton: "Ingrams and I were there – and my version of this is quite different to his. In my version Ward said, 'I knew you knew everything as soon as I saw the Per Wardua Ad Astor in the Timothy Birdsall cartoon.' My theory is then we said, 'Well, carry on as though we didn't, just refresh our memories . . . you'll probably find it easier to get it all out, good for your soul' . . . Ingrams gives the impression he didn't tell us anything, but mine is that he told us everything."

The Last Days of Macmilian is a spoof of Gibbon, of a nation in decline under a corrupt emperor: "All these happenings brought the capital into a frenzy of speculation that was far from healthy for the continued reign of Macmilian, and the scribes and pamphleteers were only the leaders and articulators of the widespread hostility and contempt aroused by the government in the hearts of the people."[22]

Several years later, Ingrams, whilst clearly proud of the Macmilian piece, reflected sadly upon the imperviousness of politicians to even the sharpest journalistic barbs:

"To us in late 1963 it seemed almost incredible that Harold Macmillan should still be Prime Minister. We had done everything short of assassinating him. We had called him mad, senile, mangy, buck-toothed – and we had accused him of lying, of megalomania, of treason. And none of it seemed to have had the slightest effect. The old fellow continued on his way as bland and unflappable as ever."[23]

Whatever the indestructibility, Macmillan's ailing government provided constant raw material for *Private Eye*. At times it must have seemed like shooting fish in a barrel – the image and actions of Brooke, Butler and Hogg all lent themselves to caricature. In May, by simple juxtaposition, they managed to print a list of those rumoured to have been the lovers of the Duchess of Argyll, on which list appeared the name of another of Macmillan's cabinet, Duncan Sandys.

Willie Rushton: "The other notion was that there'd also be the serious stuff. We were never certain how to do it. There was a little thing in one of the first ones – 'black borders will surround all the serious bits,' and a little woman appearing saying 'we don't take black boarders' . . . but we always had this feeling, and it became absolutely true, that journalists would turn up with stories that had been spiked or turned down on the grounds of bad taste or libel by other newspapers, and they'd see us as an outlet for them . . . "

An object lesson in how to do the serious stuff was provided when, in August, Ingrams handed over editorship of an issue to another of his heroes, Claud Cockburn. According to Peter Cook, the young faithful gathered at the master's feet as he called his first editorial meeting. Cockburn asked: "'Is there anyone you think is thoroughly admirable, pukka person, good chap?'

"We thought about it. Richard said, 'Albert Schweitzer.'

"'Obvious shit,' says Cockburn, 'let's attack him . . . '"[24]

As Peter Cook remarked years ago: "That's been our policy ever since."

No attack on Schweitzer appeared in Cockburn's *Eye* of August 9th – a notably different issue entitled Everything's All Right, that was even wordier than the regular edition, as though Cockburn, out in the wilds of Ireland, had been saving it all up for one splurge. He savaged Beaverbrook at great length, uncovered the affair of the mysterious death of Hal Woolf, and doled out good cheer to the youngsters.

"Looking fixedly on the brighter side, as I always sought to do . . . I used to point out that at the peak of its influence during the last century, the purchasers of *The Times* formed scarcely a larger percentage of the literate and mentally active population than ours did today."[25]

His editorial began on the cover and spread over three pages, as he gently but relentlessly went to the heart of the summer of scandal, to matters of freedom and legality more than sexual morality: "Foreigners have asked the question why Lord Astor was not requested to appear at the Ward trial. There were even nine or ten million humble British who, between one pull and another of the forelock, asked the same question . . . the Prosecution thought of calling him but were advised that another spate of lies would not advance their cause."

He threw in along the way such minor details as the real name of the head of the Secret Service.

" . . . We are a democracy, so that we have two departments of political police instead of one, and how they hate one another. This means freedom . . . You think that a man called Menzies is head of what you so romantically term the British Secret Service [there followed Menzies' *Who's Who* entry]. As you will see the fellow is 73 and does not want to be bothered with a lot of telephone calls asking which Ministers of the Crown are Scottish agents and were they instructed to go to bed with the Duchess of Argyll? The man you should ring is [there followed the *Who's Who* entry of Sir Dick White]."

After this helpful tip, according to Peter Cook, Cockburn returned to Ireland, Cook himself to America, leaving the rest to face the curious, but less than wrathful response of MI5. The secretary of the D notices committee paid a call, and then asked the editors to see him at the MoD.

Willie Rushton: "His name was Colonel Lohan. I lived in the same street as him, but I'd never really spoken to him. He was a redfaced man with a moustache, I've drawn him dozens of times. We – Ingrams, Booker and me I think – were all ushered in. Lohan was very good natured, offered us all a cup of tea or a whisky . . . deeply affable, and then men would keep sticking their heads around the door, as though they didn't know he was occupied – Oh sorry Sammy, didn't realise you were talking to these chaps from *Private Eye* about the D notices – Oh come in. Have some more whisky . . . and the room filled up very slowly with these surprised looking individuals who seemed to get more and more senior . . . I think they offered us D notices and we turned them down."[26]

Ingrams concluded his account of this incident with "This was the only occasion on which the government made any attempt to interfere with *Private Eye*." Would that the BBC could say the same.

In November Lord Home, having disclaimed his peerage, chose Kinross and West Perthshire as the site of his re-entry into the Commons. Home had figured regularly in the *Eye* as one of Macmillan's more outrageous aristocratic indulgences, though he was not dubbed the Baillie Vass until the summer of 1964. There's a sense of outrage in the Romantic England episode (most of which tackled archaisms anyway) on 'The Taking of the Soundings'.

"Although Britain is a 'democratic' country, many traditional procedures of government are not accompanied by the more vulgar 'manifestations' of democracy, such as 'voting', which flourish in other countries.

"This is especially true of the traditional 'Conservative Party', an age-old body of men who govern England. These men in the light of hallowed custom conduct their affairs according to 'gentleman's agreements' and such is their great mutual loyalty and respect that all decisions are assumed to be 'unanimous' and traditionally 'democratic.'

"None more so than at 'The Taking of the Soundings' . . . "[27]

The conclusion of this mysterious process is the passing over of "the traditional Mr Butler". It's worth adding that the article was published many months before the traditional Mr Butler was indeed passed over and before the controversy over Macmillan's methods had arisen, but when the new leader had appeared out of 'the traditional Mists of History', *Private Eye* decided to contest him. Rushton drew the short straw, and disappeared into the mists of Perthshire.

Willie Rushton: "This is roughly how it happened. We were sitting in the Coach and Horses. The Baillie had won, and this man in Scotland had stood down. And we thought we ought to do something about it. We ought to go in there. All eyes turned to me. Because of *That Was The Week That Was* I was the best known face, and it was very much the sort of notion you have at lunch after three or four pints. When we got back to the office the *Evening Standard* was on the phone asking, 'Is it true you're doing this?' It was one of those moments like turning right instead of left at the gate and changing the course of your whole life. I could have said no and that would have been the end of it . . . but I said yes, and all hell broke loose. It was viewed as absolutely tremendous, but this sort of thing goes sour very quickly . . . because I was a 'telly comic' my red nose got larger and larger and my pants baggier every time they described me. And it didn't really work. It was the wrong place. If we were going to do anything it should have been St Marylebone where Hogg was also casting off his Hailsham. It would have been in London, everyone could have joined in, we could have had a wonderful time. As it was we set off for Perthshire, it might as well have been Persia. The lads came up for about two days but the magazine had to carry on, so I was left virtually on me tod with a lot of people I didn't know. The only real enjoyment I ever found was driving very, very late through small villages with a megaphone on the roof, bleating like sheep and seeing the lights popping on – 'This is your Tory candidate, baaaaa!'

"Levin wrote a very good election pamphlet. We got class around us. Foot and I wrote a very good speech. The only time we ever worked on anything together. I put the jokes in and he did the serious stuff. It broke down into two points. The way Home was doing it was wrong, and even if it was right he was the wrong person because etc . . . a nice ordered thing, a constituency having this bloke foisted on them . . . and then Home's life and times . . . He'd already said this thing about the matchsticks and the economy.

"I know exactly who voted for me. Forty-nine people. I gave most of my votes away. The Liberal got fifteen hundred more than the polls said he would. The night before the poll I said that all my lot should vote Liberal . . . the only people who did vote for me were some dustmen in Crieff who all promised loudly as they whizzed past on their cart . . . probably the ten [sponsors] if they'd got over their celebrations by the time they got to the polling booth . . . and their friends who seemed equally unreliable . . . We should have done St Marylebone."

By 1964 the *Eye*'s fortunes were flagging. The high circulation of the Profumo boom could not be sustained, sales fell by nearly half.

Cook's return in June 1964 brought money and ideas. He put in another £2000 of his own money, set about raising more via £100 donations in exchange for £1 share holdings, and brought in Barry Humphries to do the Barry McKenzie cartoon strip, with cartoonist Nicholas Garland – now to be found in the pages of the *Independent*. Claud Cockburn made a return visit – and once again the capacity of *Private Eye* to break the politics of Fleet Street innuendo and silence was demonstrated. Cook approved the naming of a pair of London gangsters in the issue of June 14th: "Whole areas of London East and West are being terrorised . . . the *Sunday Mirror* . . . and the *Daily Express* . . . still unable to take the fluff out of its mouth and name plainly the men they are talking about. They, of course know the names. So, of course, do the police . . . the men referred to have for a week been discussed and denounced in every bar in Fleet Street. *Private Eye* considers this situation both farcical and intolerable . . . the two people being written and talked about are the twin brothers, Ronald and Reginald Kray."

The circulation slide was reversed. *Private Eye* survived from enfant terrible to middle-aged terrible.

Peter Cook: "Of all the things in the sixties *Private Eye* was regarded as the one which would never last – that was the most ephemeral – part of the satire boom – but it's been the one thing which has continued."

§

The word 'satire' is more likely than not to bring forth a guarded disclaimer from its practitioners. Bernard Levin, for example: "I never liked the word from the start for what we were doing. But it stuck, of course. It narrows things – 'we know what satire is so that's what this is.' It was, but it was much more."[28]

Ned Sherrin goes so far as to quote Gilbert Highet's definition from *The Anatomy of Satire* in his autobiography, while Richard

Ingrams writes, "Everyone was suffering from the consequences of being fashionable. While it was nice to be successful, there was also a feeling that it was not quite right for satirists to inspire such general acclaim."[29] Their caution is understandable – as long as it was called satire anyone who didn't like it was free to write to *The Times* or the *British Christian and Church Weekly* or whatever and protest that of course this wasn't really satire because satire was Juvenal (Latin masters were overfond of instructing us on the paucity of *That Was The Week That Was* with such comparisons) or Swift or anybody but Frost, Booker, Ingrams et al. Thirty years on Peter Cook sticks by the word: "We had 'Satire' on the outside of the club – London's First Satirical Nightclub. It was satire at The Establishment I think – current events, political stuff, social behaviour – satire was a perfectly good word for it. It was when satire became an all-purpose description for anybody whom nobody had ever seen before on television that people withdrew from the term."

In the Autumn of 1962 a lot of people nobody had ever seen before, but scarcely those to whom Cook refers, took over the television screens on Saturday nights. Ned Sherrin had returned to *Tonight* after an unhappy spell in 'Light Ent'. By this time *Tonight* was ready to expand again. Donald Baverstock (Blatherstick to *Private Eye*), Deputy Controller of Programmes by the Summer of 1962, had been discussing a new late night Saturday show with Alasdair Milne, editor of *Tonight*. His memo to Stuart Hood, Controller of Programmes, summed up the freedom he wanted to exercise under the Greene regime:

"This programme . . . must be more vigorous than the common run of communication offers. Another and most important key to its success will be the humour and wit with which opinions and observations are expressed. We are contemplating the world not our navel . . . "[30]

Producing this unnamed programme fell to Ned Sherrin – Sherrin was well aware of the growth of satire, and frequently visited The Establishment and New York clubs looking for potential performers for *Tonight*. He was helped in launching the new programme by the implicit backing of senior BBC men like Hugh Greene and Kenneth Adam, and by the atmosphere of freedom and innovation that Greene had created, but also by the sheer vagueness of the idea and their perception of it as the series was developed.

Ned Sherrin: "I think it might not have happened with Hugh Greene if they'd known more what it was about. Because he had that very clear picture of Berlin cabaret in the thirties, and Kenneth Adam . . . had a very clear idea of Notting Hill Gate late night

revue in the late thirties and forties. And the fact that we were able
to do something quite different was because they had their own idea
of what it was going to be like. The [programme] grew through the
two pilots. It was originally supposed to be sort of an anthology of
the best film items from *Tonight* and a bit of late night conversation,
perhaps a song, and then the moment we started thinking about
being in front of an audience and having a band it automatically
changed the texture of the piece – and it slipped away from Alasdair
and Donald in terms of their doing anything to shape it . . . Donald
was always talking about 'language, boy, language', so eloquence
had to be a part of it – but . . . they did very little to shape it apart
from being useful and acute in criticising after each event."

Sherrin's idea for an aggressive mixture of improvisation, satire,
songs, sketches and talks drew him once more to The Establishment
regulars. He chose John Bird as his anchorman: "I was trying to
explain the idea of the programme to John Bird, in Bertorelli's, how
we would wrap up the week and shrug it off and think about a new
one. Oh, he said, a sort of That Was The Week That Was, echoing
the Shell ad . . . and it seemed too good not to be a title . . . "

But Bird, like Eleanor Bron and John Fortune, both of whom
Sherrin says he would have hired, chose to go to New York to Peter
Cook's other Establishment. In the Blue Angel Club, in Berkeley
Square, he had seen David Frost, another contemporary of Cook's
from Cambridge, another impersonator of Mr Macmillan, and had
hired him as a supporting performer. Frost now got the front seat.
The rest of the team came together – an ad hoc mixture of professional and not-so-professional performers. Roy Kinnear had
been seen in the Theatre Workshop – a fine comic actor with a sad,
umistakably working-class face. Willie Rushton was seen in a rare
theatrical performance: "Ingrams, Wells, Barbara Windsor and I
had done this extraordinary show at the Room at the Top in Ilford.
William Donaldson was looking for a successor to the *Fringe* and we
looked a likely lot, and he put Barbara Windsor in it – she was
supposed to be Alan Bennett. The four of us did a month there.
One of the things I did was Harold Macmillan – it was an old *Private
Eye* joke, talking to Kennedy 'Macmillan – that's M-A-C . . . ' And
Ned saw that, and he wanted Harold Macmillan. Another little
blank to fill in, here was somebody who could do Macmillan. My
Macmillan was quite an affable impersonation. All I was doing was
slightly exaggerating the act that he did himself. I did that in the
pilot. The first pilot was extraordinary – went on for about four
hours. Extraordinary people – Norman St John Stevas. Brian Red-
head was up for the job – he and Frost did this dual hosting. I

somehow stayed there. Don't know quite how. And then we did another pilot which was a bit more like the show itself. And I ended up on it. I can remember feeling wonderfully unnervous, standing in the scene dock or somewhere like that, having a last cigarette before the show, and poor old Roy Kinnear shaking like an aspen leaf. He thought it was terrifying – live television, and all these bloody amateurs. His agent had told him the whole thing was going to be total disaster and he shouldn't have done it anyway. I was thinking what a wonderful thing to tell the grandchildren – very, very briefly I enjoyed this moment of television fame . . . I didn't know any better, I thought this is how it is, what it's always like on television. They who knew better were terrified.

"I was lucky. I didn't have the pressure on me. I didn't mind whether I carried on or not. I was quite happy at *Private Eye*."

Lance Percival, who acted and could improvise songs to the guitar, was also seen in the Blue Angel, cartoonist Timothy Birdsall came from *Private Eye*, Kenneth Cope, actor and *Coronation Street* regular, came in at the suggestion of Sherrin's assistant John Bassett, one of the originators of *Beyond the Fringe*, and David Kernan, Millicent Martin and Bernard Levin had all worked on *Tonight*.

Ned Sherrin: "We felt we had to have an area that was conversation. There were the three people Ken Tynan had talked about as the wittiest conversationalists in London, George Melly, Seth Holt the film director and Harold Lang the actor. We thought we were being very clever. We knew that to get these very amusing people to talk about something funny . . . usually kills the laugh. So we got them to talk about human unhappiness, because that would allow them to be terribly funny. In fact they went on for twenty minutes burrowing into a deeper and deeper gloom. That had to be excised after we'd shown it to Grace. And the other spot was the idea to have a confrontation between Bernard and a group of people. So the first lot we chose were Mrs Peggy Shepherd and the Conservative ladies. Which was lucky. They then protested so much, that after the pilot had been rejected and gone into oblivion it had to be seen by other people to meet the protests of the Conservative Party, and the other people thought it was rather good and that's why it got on the air."

It's worth noting that Ned Sherrin records that Hugh Greene, for all that he supported 'the idea', saw neither of the two pilots. Grace Wyndham Goldie as Head of Talks did. Mrs Goldie was one of those in the chain of BBC command – Milne was by this time her deputy – a chain of command that seemed to give *That Was The*

Week That Was an excess of supervision which should have rendered the arguments over responsibility that followed almost meaningless. If anything, Sherrin, as producer, had too many bosses. Mrs Goldie's initial response to the first, over-long pilot was that it was: "Amateurish in its endeavours to seem casual, and politically both tendentious and dangerous."[31]

But she praised it for its 'audience awareness' and Sherrin took as a rule of thumb her dictum for *Tonight*, that it should be on the side of 'the powerless against power'.

The first show went out live on Saturday, November 24th, 1962. What was startling was that it respected no reputations. It might have been predictable after a year or more of *Private Eye* that the leading politicians of all parties would take a drubbing, but it attacked the new as well as the old and established, the church and the arts as well as politics. It brought the irreverence of *Private Eye* to the screen, and drew upon a large pool of writers, including David Nathan and Dennis Potter, Peter Lewis and Peter Dobereiner, Caryl Brahms, Waterhouse and Hall, Joe Haines and Andrew Roth, Christopher Booker, briefly Richard Ingrams, once Kenneth Tynan, occasionally Peter Shaffer, and songwriters Steven Vinaver and Herbert Kretzmer.

Ned Sherrin: "Tuesday was too early to be making up one's mind about doing things, because the week is like a baby who hasn't developed its character . . . You begin to see what might be happening on Wednesday. Occasionally people would ring up with universal or eternal ideas which weren't particularly topical. And you could say we'll commission that because if we can't use it this week we'll use it next week. And then as the news of the week built up one began to see what it would be, and there were people one didn't know who would send material in out of the blue, there were people one had a nodding acquaintance with, who, if they rang up with an idea, one would certainly commission it, and there were the people who were on regular things – Kretzmer and Lee did a number a week, Waterhouse and Hall did a number a week. They wouldn't usually make up their minds until sometimes as late as Friday morning . . . Quite often you'd find that they couldn't write the sketch that we'd discussed and they'd come up with some alternative. Then there was Booker . . . Caryl Brahms doing the opening number. It was probably Thursday before you got an idea of what was going to be happening, and then the scripts would be either picked up by taxi or brought round on Thursday or Friday. I'd do the shooting script on Friday afternoon, and it was typed up and put onto the teleprompter . . . if we had acting sketches the actors would come in and rehearse on the Friday. We'd meet in the studio on Saturday morning and go through it. I think we used to stagger through it slowly and then have a sort of run through and then do it . . . We started about ten-thirty or eleven, we could get through it once. They could have a run at it, and we'd stop once to record Millie's number before we did the run. [It was] exhilarating. It's never exhausting if you're on a roll. If it had been disastrous from the start . . . but we saw ourselves as young turks and we were getting a lot of adrenalin going.

"There was a crock of gold there to be explored. In retrospect one feels very sympathetic towards these poor guys on, say, *Spitting Image* who've had nothing but Mrs Thatcher for ten years. We had thirteen years of Macmillan which we could raid as treasure trove for scriptwriters. They've been at it since she came to power . . . and they have to go at it week in week out. There's no residual grab-bag of subjects to which they can go in the same way that we could."

The small, sophisticated, late night audience that most of the programme makers were expecting topped three and a half million.

Ned Sherrin: "I don't think it could possibly have worked if it hadn't been live, at that time. We were lucky that the first one went out and was a smash . . . Frostie and I [were in] the Kenya coffee bar in the King's Road on the Sunday morning just to post-mort and not really expecting any notices, and suddenly one of us turned over the back page of the *Sunday Telegraph* and someone called Pat Williams had written this enormous great paean of praise in the last place where we expected to find it . . . we couldn't have written it more attractively ourselves . . . "

The audience for the programme rose rapidly to six and a half million by the new year, and, at its peak, twelve million. Across the Atlantic Peter Cook observed the hysteria that greeted the birth of *That Was The Week That Was*, and summed up Britain as " . . . Sinking giggling into the sea. I was very pissed off at the end of that awful, ludicrous government of Macmillan's. I got a perspective from New York . . . you read about sketches and think I know that one, we're doing that one – I think all of us felt that *TW3* was a bit of a rip-off, which if course it had to be in a way. I think I'd originally approached the BBC with an idea of doing a *That Was The Week* – not called that – from The Establishment. Their reason for not doing it was that they'd be seen to be endorsing a commercial project."

The *Sunday Telegraph* was soon joined by almost every other paper. Derided or praised *That Was The Week That Was* was news. In January the *Sunday Pictorial* ran the headline "Clever or Sick. Disgusting or Brilliant?" and took on 'the rage of '63' in a piece that dealt with sketches performed not only on *That Was The Week That Was*, but at The Establishment and on *Tonight*. By this time the instant nature of a sketch had altered – there was no question of performance, reaction and then forget it as the next week's sketches came up – the argument could run and run. Two sketches in particular attracted long term attention – the Thirteen Silent Men of Westminster, by Gerald Kaufman, was raised in the House of Commons, as Sir Norman Hulbert, one of the thirteen who had made no speech within recent memory, accused the programme of breaching parliamentary privilege. This sketch, he claimed, had resulted in five hundred protests to the BBC. He was particularly irked by the fact that no mention had been made of his chairmanship of thirty-three sittings of standing committees or the eighteen occasions when he had taken the chair of the house. He threatened the BBC with a suit for libel. Higher up, Postmaster General Reginald Bevins told the House on December 19th that he had 'no intention of censuring' the programme – a statement that must have stuck in his throat, for when he had unwisely let it be known that he would censure the BBC over *That Was The Week That Was*, a note appeared on his desk from Macmillan worded simply "Oh no you're not". The other sketch was The Consumer Guide to Religion, by Robert Gillespie and Charles Lewson, which weighed up the value of the main religions in the simple terms of "a) What do you put into it? b) What do you get out of it? c) How much does it cost?" The conclusion favoured the Church of England: "All in all we think you get a jolly good little faith for a very moderate outlay and we have no hesitation in proclaiming it the Best Buy."[32] The complaints flooded in.

Ned Sherrin: "Alasdair had made the decision that it could go out and there was no problem, but Kenneth Adam was coming down to hospitality to watch the programme that night. I vividly remember Alasdair handing him the script, saying I'm putting this out so you don't have to make a decision, but I thought you ought to see it, but I have made the decision and it will go out. And Kenneth hummed and haaed and would certainly have taken it out if he were not being dealt with so firmly."

Willie Rushton: "[That] caused tremendous uproar – always from different religions. Jews ringing up saying we don't think this is anti-semitic at all, but by God you were rough on the Catholics. Catholics ringing up saying we don't mind what you say about us but it was very anti-semitic."

The publication of the number of complaints about the programme became a regular feature of the Monday morning papers.

After its long article the *Pictorial* received letters too, supporting the programme four to one. From the pros: "If *TWTWTW* succeeded in making pompous, overblown officialdom take another look at itself and make itself less pompous, it is doing a great service to the country."

From the cons: "It is not cricket to hit a man when he's down and by the same token baiting royalty and the church is not only in bad taste but cowardly."[33]

The church agreed. Eric Treacy, the steaming Bishop of Pontefract, referred to Millie Martin's rendition of Herbert Kretzmer's Lullaby for an Illegitimate Child ("Conceived you may have been in sordid passion; But baby, you've arrived, and you're in fashion!")[34] as "a cruel misuse" of the producer's freedom at the BBC. The Rev. John Culey, a parish priest from Cheshire described – in his parish magazine – Millie as "a repulsive woman with a grating voice", the audience as "rabble," and Levin as "a thick-lipped Jew-boy". (Levin: "An ordained clergyman, not some wild sect but a Church of England vicar – dear me!") While to the *British Weekly and Christian World* wrote a woman who was: " . . . Incensed by the lack of reverence (bordering on blasphemy) and the indecency of the wit and humour (parading under the guise of satire)." But then she let the cat out of the bag and admitted that she, like so many of its critics, had seen very little of the programme, but it was, all the same . . . "Blatant sin . . . the brainchild of someone singularly immature in spirit . . . why has the BBC no censors?"[35]

If no censors, the BBC did have its layers of management, its chain of command. In January, after the Consumer Guide to Religion, Baverstock, less than happy with the course the series had taken, wrote to Hugh Greene and to Alasdair Milne that the last programme had been "the worst yet"[36] and had contained obscene gestures. The series was walloping the politicians, much as *Private Eye* had, and such obvious comic targets as Hailsham and Brown were getting pasted. Greene's response was, "Tell them I take my hat off to them", but at the same time Sherrin was told to ease up on George Brown. Two weeks later Greene spoke publicly on the matter, albeit in Germany: "I think I can safely say that this policy is a responsible one and that it is helping our country adjust itself honestly and without illusion to the facts of its position in the world today . . . get the best people and give them the chance and don't be afraid to make mistakes because if you make no mistakes you will be dull and that is the worst sin of all." [37]

That first sentence must have seemed like the unconscious of the

PM himself. Did the politicians mind? There was, about this time, a cartoon depicting the home life of the leader, wrapped up with a plaid blanket and a mug of cocoa in front of the telly on Saturday as the dot disappears down the tube – Lady Dorothy has turned to him and says "Don't be so silly. If they do you you're furious and if they don't you sulk." Many a true word et cetera. Rushton says, "Macmillan never complained. When he was asked if he'd ever seen it he came out with a classic – 'No, I haven't got a gramophone.' Not bad – kept him out of trouble."

Visiting the BBC Macmillan played just as coyly.

Ned Sherrin: "[He] came down to do a party political – 'I hear you have some sort of saturnalia here on Saturdays.' I remember Ted Heath coming down to do a party political, and standing at the back during rehearsals because he was fascinated by it. There was the wonderful case when George [Brown] came down and was photographed laughing in the audience. So the very next week Conservative Central Office wanted the right of reply and we had to have Reggie Maudling sitting in the audience. I think it was Kenneth Adam who made the mistake of saying 'of course you mustn't put the camera on him,' and of course Maudling was furious because he'd only come all that way to be seen being a good sport."

§

One of *That Was The Week That Was*'s most original ideas was one of the simplest and toughest – and it wasn't satire by any stretch. Each week Bernard Levin sat on a stool in front of the studio audience and was agin it, whatever it was.

Bernard Levin: "Ned's idea was that there should be something solid in the middle. Lots of skit, obviously, and taking the mickey out of absolutely everything and everybody, but he wanted this to be a complete item – and that was me. I'd done a good deal of work in television all ad hoc, but this was my first big exposure on television.

"There were serious things. Occasionally I would do a piece to camera. When Gaitskell died, for instance, I did a tribute, and the famous one [the whole team did] on the Kennedy assassination . . . [but] . . . the idea that we settled on was there would be a group of people with some common theme or trade or position and I would argue with it. The idea being that I would take up the opposite position to whatever it was they represented . . .

"In that form I was probably the first person to do what we called in shorthand – not unreasonably – the punch-up. The whole point of it was that I disagreed with whoever it was, there was always a lot of back and forth, but it was always very friendly and calm. The Tory women piece never went out – it was part of the second dry run – which was a great pity. It was one of the most hilarious episodes we could have had. I don't remember now what I did to upset them, but they got very hysterical. I was baiting them, obviously. They were Tory women in the sense of the caricature that we think about – the hangers and floggers . . . that wasn't the core of it but that was the attitude – I was attacking attitudes like that. The more hysterical they got the more I baited them. And then there was the great cry which David Frost frequently greets me with . . . one of them screeched – and I'll never forget this – 'How would you like your daughter to be walking down a dark lane Mr Levin and nothing done about it?' And those were her exact words. I suppose when they got home and thought about what they'd actually said rather than what they'd felt, they then got very shirty and the item never went out. Ned, of course, invited them to come back and do it on a real programme, but even they had enough sense not to.

"There were also individual ones. We moved from groups to the one on one. It was improvised . . . I stated a theme and we were off, and I had nothing thereafter but my wits. When there was a group – and idiotically nobody spotted this – you think we're an army he's one footsoldier we'll beat him to death – of course it doesn't work like that. The group tangle each others' arguments, fall over each others' feet – and the solo man has the advantage. The thing that amazed me most was why they came on. Some were just exhibitionists, wanted to get on the telly, advertising themselves – but they were only a few. The whole point of it was a punch-up and even if they won with a knock-out it didn't do them or their trade or whatever any good. Charlie Forte is the perfect example. He never spoke to me for twenty years after [he'd debated with me on the programme], but the thing I could never understand was why he'd done it in the first place . . . there were plenty of them . . . if they got something out of beating me and making me look a fool well and good. But in ninety-nine cases out of a hundred it didn't do them any good anyway."

Such was the foundation of Levin's notoriety, but it did not provide his most memorable confrontation. That moment came not from the likes of John Bloom or Charles Forte. On April 20th Levin was debating with a group of nuclear disarmers, when out of the audience stepped one Desmond Leslie, husband of the singer Agnes Bernelle. Bernelle's *Evening of Savagery and Delight* had begun at The Establishment in January, when Barry Norman reviewed it for the *Mail*. On its transfer to the Duchess Theatre Levin reviewed it himself for the same paper: "She does not talk well, walk well or stand well, overlays everything with a horrid archness that makes one squirm."

Leslie advanced with obvious intent to redress a bad review, and the phrase punch-up achieved a new accuracy.

Bernard Levin: "I'm not a boxing fan, but I'd heard the phrase 'the boxer was signalling his punches' – as he came towards me I could see the angle at which his fist was approaching me – in slow motion – and I decided that when the fist arrived my head had better not be where it was . . . I moved the angle of my head, and he . . . struck me a glancing blow on the shoulder which spun me round – he was a big fellow, there was weight behind the fist – it didn't hurt, it just pushed me . . . except that my glasses fell off and I knocked over the stool . . . on playback it looked as though I'd been very badly hit. Not so. The scene froze. Ned said two things [via the earpiece] . . . 'Who the fuck is that?' and 'Go in close in case there's blood.' In that order. Ned's a professional . . . then everybody . . . the stage people leapt and trapped him and bundled him off. He didn't fight or struggle.

"I looked at the nuclear disarmers and they were absolutely stunned. When I saw him come at me I had thought this was some kind of stunt they had cooked up. It wasn't. With a presence of mind I'm not sure I would have today my first words were 'Now ladies and gentlemen, can we get on with this discussion of non-violence.' There was a tremendous hand from the audience as you may imagine."

Picking up his cue Frost turned to the camera, saying he'd no idea who that was, but hoped he was 'being safely set in concrete'. In the next day's papers Leslie was quoted as uttering the wonderful archaism: "In my father's day he would have got a horsewhipping."[38] But there the story does not end.

"Many, many years later I was in Dublin, and . . . I wandered into the Shelbourne for tea. And there was a man sitting alone at a table. And I thought 'I know that man'. And I suddenly realised it was Desmond Leslie. I thought it's been several years – he can't be holding a grudge that long can he? So I somewhat gingerly approached the table, put out my hand. And he shook it and motioned me to sit down. And we had tea. And didn't discuss the event at all."[39]

§

That Was The Week That Was made stars of three of its performers –

David Frost, Millicent Martin and to a lesser extent Willie Rushton. Every newspaper at some point in 1963 ran its 'Millie' story. *Time and Tide* called her 'The Girl Everyone's Talking About' – and asked her about the religion sketch.

"[It] was more an attack on consumer guide methods – you know where they go around asking everybody do you prefer things in a tin or a bag . . . we just wanted to show how ridiculous this method could look if you took it to extremes."[40]

Yes, Millie.

The egregious Donald Zec, for the *Sunday Pictorial*, produced prose as ghastly as his Beatles coverage: "She is a gorgeous tease. She is gently outrageous. And though she emits a sound like a circular saw gnashing through tree trunks she is as devastating as Cleopatra, without problems . . . There may not be much meat on the bone (5'1" tall by 34, 24, 36) but what there is is prime choice . . . red hair, smoky blue eyes, soft peachy lips . . . "

Millie's self-assessment had more wit in it. She told Zec: "There's a sort of brittle, bitchy, cyanide-wouldn't-melt-in-my-mouth look which must work pretty well."[41]

For the *Mail*, Barry Norman sought the opinions of Ned Sherrin, and addressed the altogether more serious question of why there weren't more women on television. Sherrin replied: "TV is basically a dreary medium. Most of it is nonsense and most of the programmes which aren't nonsense are documentaries.

"Women don't fit easily into such shows. At the same time it's difficult for a woman to be good at comedy because most of them, Millie Martin excepted, are funny at the expense of their dignity and femininity.

"As things stand now, girls are used on TV merely as foils to the men. It's deplorable, but a fact."[42]

The men of *TW3* was really only one man – David Frost. His rise to fame was nothing less than 'meteoric'. Frost had been one of Cambridge's lesser comedians – so much so that Peter Cook says there was some surprise among the cast of *Beyond the Fringe*, in New York, when it was heard that Frost had landed the job of hosting television's first late night satire show. But Frost proved exceptional. Before the cliché of 'Hello, good evening and welcome' there was the cliché of 'but seriously though', and people who worked with Frost pay tribute to his skill at moving so quickly, effortlessly and convincingly between the light and the serious spots in the programme. As far as the press were concerned Frost was a star – and they were much concerned with the only physical oddity that could be played up. Frost, it was said so often, had innovated the 'combing of his hair forward' – in some way this was different from a plain fringe, and served to excite the tabloids almost as much as a mop top. Prince Charles once made the papers for, supposedly, adopting a David Frost hairstyle. But there was, as the years revealed, much more to David Frost than a gimmick.

Ned Sherrin: "David Frost is simple and uncomplicated, and a tremendous impresario and organiser. An enormous amount of script gathering, especially among the young Cambridge people, was done by David. Also he was immediately aware, in a way that nobody else in England was, although Americans always have been, of the value of being able to use your television face as a visiting card to boardrooms and banks. Since he likes business as much as he likes performing it's an unstoppable combination."

The flicker of fame passed also over Roy Kinnear – not that he noticed. The actor/director Stanley Baker decided that what his film *Zulu* needed was 'one of the satire boys'. He asked for 'K . . . K . . . K . . .'

'Kernan?' said a helpful assistant.

'That's the one. Get him!'

On the plane, flying out to the location, Baker noticed a thin, blond young man and asked who he was.

'That's David Kernan,' came the reply, 'the satire boy.'

'I meant the fat one!'

Some of the limelight spilled onto the BBC's young turks. Milne, Baverstock, Michael Peacock and Paul Fox all found themselves mentioned in the press. It must have been the first time since the abdication of Sir John Reith that a BBC executive was thought newsworthy. In January *Time and Tide* reported that the variety guidelines – the producers' guide to lodgers, fig leaves and commercial travellers etc. – were being dropped, at precisely the moment when their spirit was receiving new life, and pointed out somewhat belatedly the rise of new blood at the BBC, with Baverstock at thirty-eight, Milne thirty-two, Fox thirty-seven and Peacock thirty-three. The following week they were interviewed, and it's inescapable that their views mattered at this time largely, if not only, because of *That Was The Week That Was*, as the latest manifestation of Hugh Greene's changes. Peacock summed the changes up succinctly: "We have lost our Aunty BBC image – and a jolly good thing too . . . I have never known a case where a producer's political judgment has influenced the slant of a programme. Protests from viewers are roughly split down the middle, half from the left half from the right."

This was less than a fortnight after the BBC Secretariat reported on the reaction of the Conservative Party to the series – "general bias . . . extremely left-wing, socialist and pacifist."

Baverstock was quoted as saying: "I don't consider myself left-wing. But in a job like mine you have to keep asking questions and that's considered radical, which to a certain type of person means left-wing."

There is about this defensiveness an air of a crisis brewing. Alasdair Milne echoed the common line of professionalism before politics: "We all of us hold fierce political views. Certain things move in me a ferocious indignation, but when you actually get down to producing a programme, you are detached."[43]

§

In March 1964 Greene gave a lengthy interview to Kenneth Harris of the *Observer*. Harris asked what he might make of reports of "rows between the Director-General and the Governors", to which Greene replied: "Complete nonsense. If there was an honest to goodness row and a real breach between the Director-General and the board of Governors, the Director-General would have either resigned or been sacked before you read about the row in the newspapers."[44]

This is an honest statement that still manages to conceal the truth. Greene had spent the Summer and Autumn of the previous year heading off just such a breach. He had already remarked in September 1963, when the row over *TW3* was at its most turbulent, that "No government can sack me. Only the board of Governors can."[45] Which seems to be a cryptic explanation to the effect that, whatever political grumblings made the papers, the Board was his problem, not the politicians. During *That Was The Week That Was*'s Summer lay-off, Sir Arthur fforde, the chairman of the Governors, remarked in praise of the programme that "it would be a pity to spoil the ship for a ha'porth of dirt". From this appears to stem the pervasive issue of 'smut'.

I saw most of *That Was The Week That Was*. I've no recollection of anything that could have turned fforde's remark into a make or break issue – but then it wasn't the issue so much as the excuse for the issue. In June, in *Encounter*, the American-backed cold war organ of the Congress for Cultural Freedom, Alfred Sherman wrote: "*TWTWTW*, *Private Eye* and 'The Establishment' have all followed the tradition of the popular Sunday newspapers in giving the public the opportunity to enjoy their weekly moral indignation and sexual titillation scrambled. *TWTWTW* has succeeded in combining censoriousness and salaciousness – in sketches ostensibly satirising strip-tease and Sunday journalism – with a touch which the *News of the World* could be proud of (plus the added advantage of live chorus girls). They really manage to eat their cheesecake and have it too.

"If nothing is to be sacred, then even sacred monkeys can scarcely hope to retain their immunity for very long."

The gist of Sherman's argument was yet another discrimination between many generations of real satirists and these 'pseudo-satirists', who, he suggested, were getting away with their juvenilia by hiding behind Auntie's skirts, the Reithian immunity of the unassailable, trustworthy BBC that they were claiming to have swept away.

On July 4th the Board asked Kenneth Adam and Stuart Hood to appear before them. The subject under discussion was the editorial control of *That Was The Week That Was* – with reference to 'smut'. Sherman's views considered, it's still hard to know what this meant. The Kinnear-Martin sketch 'Your flies are undone'? Or the same pair reflecting on a late night satire programme: "You're allowed to do it. You can say 'bum', you can say 'po', you can say anything"? Following this Stuart Hood addressed a press conference to launch the new series in September and said that the issue of 'smut' would be monitored, and that the programme would no longer be open ended – nor would it be the last programme on Saturday night. The relationship between the first matter and the last two is nebulous, unless you presume that, as Greene would put it, there was some row brewing behind the scenes that wasn't being even hinted at.

The new series opened on September 28th for a six-month run. Sherrin admits that the first three programmes were less than their best – but they had set themselves a high standard; even their fans would be exacting. At the board meeting of October 10th the new series' 'dullness' was used as an argument against it – for the first time it was asked whether the programme would be allowed to complete its run. With the programme of October 19th *That Was The Week That Was* found its stride once more, in Booker's Disraeli sketch – an open letter from one Prime Minister to another, Sir Alec Douglas-Home, which Frost concluded with his own line comparing Home to Wilson as 'Dull Alec versus Smart Alec'. Again the complaints flooded in – some nine hundred by letter and telephone. It was, as Sherrin wrote, the most savage attack on a politician ever delivered on the BBC. Four days later another set of BBC initials convened, the GAC – General Advisory Committee, in some way meant to be representative of the viewing public, the licence payers

– at which both the smut and the political content of the programme were raised. By now the chain of command was in force to its full extent – from bottom to top it ran Sherrin (producer) – Milne (assistant Head of Talks) – Goldie (Head of Talks) – Baverstock (Deputy Controller of Programmes) – Hood (Controller) – Adam (Director of Television) – Greene (DG) – fforde (Chairman of Governors). No longer could Greene take a back seat and be content with the remote congratulatory memo. Milne reported to him on a regular basis, and one or the other of them attended rehearsals on Saturdays. Further behind the scenes, Grace Wyndham Goldie arranged lunches for herself, Sherrin, Milne and Frost to discuss future plans for the programme. "Almost any item," she wrote, "could be cut on the grounds that the programme was overrunning." This in itself explains why Stuart Hood's press launch had emphasised that the programme would not be open ended.

Sherrin still praises Greene's role: "He was a wonderful umbrella over it all." And describes another incident which brought him and Greene into conflict. "I desperately wanted to do something about Lord Dilhorne – the dreaded Bullying-Manner – and I think we had it direct from Hugh Greene that we couldn't do anything about Lord Dilhorne, and I thought perhaps we could do something about Lord Devlin and compare the good judge and the bad judge – drag Dilhorne in by the back door. I got Booker to write such a piece – which was wild beyond belief . . . and I got Gerald Kaufman to rewrite it. Gerald was a notorious fact checker and wouldn't have allowed anything to get through. So we eventually put it out one weekend when all those who knew about Dilhorne not being a suitable target were away, and Grace Wyndham Goldie was chaperoning us that weekend and she didn't know about and thought it was rather a good strong sketch . . . so we put it out and apparently Carleton-Greene got a phone call from Bullying-Manner's brother. He was absolutely livid on Sunday night, and I got hauled over the coals on Tuesday morning with a great fuss . . . I'd been told not to, there were three clear factual inaccuracies – and if it had been Booker's script I'd have been terribly worried about this, so I rang Gerald Kaufman . . . one of [the inaccuracies] was a suggestion of nepotism, because he'd been related to Macmillan. Gerald was able to prove through family trees that he knew the connections between the Devonshires and the Manningham-Bullers far better than the old boy himself . . . in fact all three of the reputed inaccuracies fell down and Carleton-Greene was a great deal more civil once we'd found that the three unstoppable things were stoppable. I think that's the only case where I played foul – because I did feel rather strongly about that and I wanted to get it out."

With the programme of November 9th a new issue arose, neither smut nor bias, but accuracy. Frost read out details of the application form for people wanting to join the Scarborough branch of the Labour Party: "Are you willing to assist in running bingo sessions? . . . Are you or have you ever been a member of CND? Have you ever been mentioned in legal proceedings?"[46]

Completed forms, it was said, were to be sent to a Mrs J. Long-bottom. There was indeed such a lady, but she denied any knowledge of the application form. The General Secretary of the Labour Party lodged a formal complaint. The document was, he said, a forgery. *That Was The Week That Was* replied that the form had been received from five different sources in Scarborough. But it was a forgery. *That Was The Week That Was* had been set up. Kenneth Adam was reported as asking to know how such an item could have got on to the programme without its authenticity being checked. A stupid mistake at this point in their fortunes was the last thing they needed.

On November 17th Greene announced that rather than continuing until April, *That Was The Week That Was* would come off the air for good on December 28th. 1964 would inevitably be an election year and it was felt that " . . . the political content of the programme, which has been one of its principal and successful constituents, will clearly be more difficult to maintain."[47] Few people chose to believe this. Nine hundred letters 'poured, flooded, gushed' in, opposing the decision three to one.

Ned Sherrin: "There's no question that there was a lot of pressure. It was getting too hot a potato. They really didn't know quite how to get us, because we were so popular it wasn't a good idea to be seen to be knocking us. When we came back the second time, Stuart Hood had already said in a speech at Blackpool that we would be coming back, but we would be cutting out the silly school-boy smut – and [from that] moment they had an easy handle, because they hadn't really homed in on that before. And we came back trying too hard with three of our less-than-best episodes and so the combination of that and 'smut' made us more vulnerable and gave the dissident Governors the chance to launch a harder attack. I think Hugh just decided it was too much trouble."[48]

On November 7th Greene had recommended to the Governors that the programme should be axed – a decision neither he nor fforde had wanted to take, but the programme "had assumed an exaggerated importance."[49] The deciding factor was that fforde's deputy, Sir James Duff, had threatened to resign unless *That Was The Week That Was* was dropped. Such disunity would have done considerable damage to Greene's stewardship of the BBC. Mrs Goldie wrote in her memoirs that Greene saw the necessity of taking control of *TW3* and that rather than restrict it he preferred to kill it. Her own opinion was that the programme died not from "excessive censorship but from confusion of purpose". This remark seems to contradict her account of the ease with which control had been gained once the excuse of programme length had been duly set up.

Harold Wilson did not accept Greene's explanation, but by then it was perfectly safe not to: "We would very much deplore it if a popular programme were taken off as a result of political pressure . . ."

For the Conservatives Sir Cyril Osborne revelled: "I'm damn well pleased. It wasn't English at all. There are some things that English men and women hold sacred and they are against these clever dicks and their filth."[50]

Logically, all that was required was that *TW3* should be off the air from the dissolution of parliament until the day after the General Election, which at its latest had to be the end of September 1964. As *Private Eye* pointed out, a reason for suspending the series had been blown up into an excuse to abandon it. As far as Greene's account is concerned, he never deviated from the reasons publicly given, and any elaboration he offered was couched in vague terms: "*TW3* became the symbol for the BBC's new look, It was frank, close to life, analytical, impatient of taboos and cant and often very funny . . . the BBC had always been a target for those who could not bear to hear the expression of their opponents' views in a controversy. Now it was also a target for the defenders of taboos, especially those which surrounded public discussion of sexual matters."[51]

TW3 was nobbled, but it would be distortion to suggest that it was nobbled by the politicians – that phrase of Tom Mangold's, the 'non-conspiracy', needs to be invoked again. What did various bishops, crazed clergymen and Sir James Duff represent? Not the Conservative Party – but more that nebulous, loose coalition of opinions, the Establishment. On the matter of sex, Greene, perhaps thinking that a characteristic of Establishment is its self-satisfying assumption that it is representative, that there is someone beyond itself for whom it speaks, declined in the July of 1963 to see a member of the Moral Rearmament movement – a Birmingham schoolteacher named Mary Whitehouse. Mrs Whitehouse had been roused to anger by an edition of the programme *Meeting Point* on March 8th, which had dealt with the issue of pre-marital sex. It was, she wrote, "a classic example of the way in which the BBC was then allowing itself to be used as a launching platform for the so-called 'new morality'." The refusal irked. Mrs Whitehouse came to see Greene as a symbol of all that was wrong with Britain: "Throughout 1963 the whole country was in an uproar, Women's organisations, magistrates, church leaders, feature writers, public and private figures joined in the clamours of protest which the Director-General was to dismiss as the voice of the 'lunatic fringe'."[52]

Mrs Whitehouse sees this disparate body of people, this lunatic fringe, as succeeding in getting *TW3* axed. She may be right. But Sir Cyril Osborne also wanted the credit, in that he had publicised the hundreds of letters he had received about *TW3*; and ITV, in the shape of Brian Tester, programme controller at ABC, also claimed the kill, saying, "We have killed it off with *The Avengers*."

There is distortion on both sides. Neither the support nor the complaints from politicians seem free from self-serving. The claims of 'we slew the beast' are fatuous. What matters is the nature of the beast. And in this Greene's last remark needs a closer look. What was the 'new look' at the BBC at this time? Greene's biographer Michael Tracey suggests that the issue of revamping of the BBC and the 'death of Auntie' really only meant *That Was The Week That Was*. I've already said that I think Greene practised a sleight of hand in his representation of the BBC to the Pilkington Committee, and passed off the same old programmes as being better than the output of ITV. But by the end of 1963, with Pilkington safely behind him, there was evidence of a new look – not necessarily the abandonment of old favourites or even the introduction of more earth-shaking or at least Portland Place-shaking programmes like *TW3*, but in the space being given to imagination and confrontation, be it *Monitor*, approaching its peak in the films of Ken Russell and Melvyn Bragg, *Dr Who* or Sydney Newman's planned *Wednesday Play*. But then it could also be argued that *That Was The Week That Was* shook Portland Place less than has been claimed.

Bernard Levin: "I've always been sceptical about the effects of *TW3* on the BBC hierarchy. I'm not all sure that it did more than ripple the surface, that the battles – there've always been battles in an organisation like that, naturally – were really not to do with *TW3*, and the decision to take it off was a kind of weary acceptance that all the flak was getting too tedious. My feeling is that it was much smaller than it was being portrayed . . . I ceased to believe in great conspiracies many years ago."

§

Sometime afterwards Millie Martin is reputed to have said, "If I'd known I was a piece of history I'd have taken more notice at the time." Peter Cook did take more notice. It was, I put to him, no time for false modesty. How does he see his role in the creation of the 'rage of '63'?: "*That Was The Week* wouldn't have happened without The Establishment. The Establishment wouldn't have happened without me."

CHAPTER TWELVE

ALL ALONG THE WATCHTOWER

"You can't be idealistic all your life, Jim." "Except to yourself."
Exchange between Jim Backus and James Dean in
Rebel Without A Cause, 1954

John F. Kennedy had a speech ready for the Dallas Citizens Council on the afternoon of November 22nd, 1963. It was released to the press only half an hour before he was assassinated. His 'last words' as President are the same deceitful, cold war bombast with which he opened a thousand days before:

"We in this country, in this generation, are by destiny rather than choice, the watchmen on the walls of world freedom. We ask, therefore, that we may be worthy of our power and responsibility, that we may exercise our strength with wisdom and restraint, and that we may achieve in our time and for all time the ancient vision of 'peace on earth, goodwill toward men.' That must always be our goal – and the righteousness of our cause must always underlie our strength. For as was written long ago: 'Except the Lord keep the city, the watchman waketh but in vain.'"

A depressing mixture of Polk, Isaiah, the Book of Psalms, and a little Christmas carol thrown in for good measure – the overall effect amounting to 'who writes this rubbish?' When Kennedy took office there were nine hundred American 'military advisers' in South Vietnam. At the time of his death there were nearer sixteen thousand. Such was his restraint, such was his vision of peace on earth. Only three weeks before he had connived at, encouraged, vacillated over, discouraged and finally lamented the assassination of the President of South Vietnam, Ngo Dinh Diem and his brother Ngo Dinh Nhu. Such was his wisdom. He had in two and a half years succeeded in involving the United States in a war which would last another ten, the resistance to which would become the defining action and provide the abiding images of the nineteen-sixties.

§

347

In Diem the United States had nurtured a monster. A monster they saw as necessary to the independence of South Vietnam, which in turn they saw as necessary to halting the rapid extension of communism in South East Asia – a boundary that, depending on the degree of judicious paranoia being evoked, could be extended across the Pacific to the point where the sails of a Chinese junk could be sighted through the Golden Gate.

After the Geneva Accord of 1954, marking the end of the French-Viet Minh colonial war, the United States, not a signatory to the accord, set up the Republic of South Vietnam. Even before the final declaration of the Geneva Conference in July 1954, and a month before the French surrender at Dien Bien Phu, Eisenhower, in a homespun style they'd understand back in Kansas, had speculated on the subject of an independent South Vietnam – Nixon had checkers, Ike had his dominoes:

"You have a row of dominoes set up, you knock over the first one, and what will happen to the last one is the certainty that it will go over very quickly. So you have a beginning of a disintegration that would have the most profound influences . . . the loss of Indochina, of Burma, of Thailand, of the Peninsula, of Indonesia . . ."[1]

Ike's Secretary of State, John Foster Dulles, when asked what his attitude would be to a Viet Minh victory or a coalition as a result of free election, replied: "I don't think present conditions are conducive to a free election there and I don't care now to answer the hypothetical situation of what might result if they did have elections . . ."[2]

The 'hypothetical situation' was that the Geneva Accord laid down that all-Vietnam elections should be held by July 1956. Eisenhower himself is on record as saying that he was frequently advised that the Viet Minh would win an 80% majority. The United States had, as Dulles implies, no intention of ever submitting the South to those elections. A year later Dulles had advanced to the position that successive US governments stuck to as the right illusion to be offering: "The only government that can succeed there [South Vietnam] is a government which is independent of foreign controls and which is really operating on a national basis."[3]

The outward face of this national basis was Ngo Dinh Diem. With a rigged election, and with the covert blessing of the CIA, in October 1955, he rapidly reduced South Vietnam to a one party state, run by one family. His brother Ngo Dinh Nhu became chief adviser and head of special army units, his sister-in-law, Madame Nhu, became 'official hostess' and government spokesman, and her father became Ambassador to the USA; brother Ngo Dinh Can headed the police; another of Diem's brothers became Archbishop of Hué – they were Catholics in a largely Buddhist country – with the extended family filling regional and cabinet positions. With such personalised control Diem was able to suppress all opposition, using anti-communism as a front. McCarthyism's legacy still scarred America, but the real consequences of institutionalised paranoia were playing out in the new American dependency. Under Diem's regime local democracy disappeared, the press was censored, and the notorious law 10/59 allowed judicial murder – trial by a military tribunal, with the power to impose death sentences against which no appeal was allowed. Simply to write an article favouring communism could carry a five-year jail sentence. While estimates vary, figures as high as 75,000 killed and 50,000 imprisoned, in conditions several commentators have termed 'concentration camps', have been offered. Such tactics, surprisingly, did not immediately turn the population against Diem. The drift into the arms of his enemies was gradual.

In the USA Diem began an unusual course of self-promotion. If the US was willing to believe that he was all that kept the dominoes upright, he was willing to encourage them for all it was worth. He made contact with Senator Mansfield (who would replace Lyndon Johnson as Senate Majority leader in 1961) and with Senator Kennedy, and was much favoured by Cardinal Spellman, through whom he was brought to the attention of *Life*, *Time*, the *New York Herald Tribune* and former Ambassador and king-maker Joseph Kennedy. Through the CIA, since its head, Allen Dulles, was the brother of John Foster Dulles, it could also be argued that he had a good, if not direct, line to the State Department. In 1955, the American Friends of Vietnam was founded and Diem opened a $30,000 a month account with the public relations firm of Newcomb-Oram. This is probably the first time in history that a government recognised the value of this tactic – some twenty-five years before it became prevalent in Britain to treat politics as advertising. A boom time for journalism on Vietnam was engineered – Diem was dubbed 'the Biggest Little Man in Asia' in the pages of *Readers' Digest* the following year.

By Clause 4 of the 1954 Geneva Accord, the introduction of foreign troops, personnel and munitions into Vietnam was prohibited – the American mission, according to I. F. Stone, fixed at 648 men – but there were ways round this – using advisers and civilians. For example, the training of Ngo Dinh Nhu's secret police was carried out by people who were, nominally, at least, academics. The

National Security Council asked Michigan State University, which ran a course in police administration, to train the secret police and to set up a civil service – a bureaucracy to cope with the burgeoning social problems of South Vietnam, which the Ngos were actively fostering by their regime of repression, the chief instrument of which was the secret police, which those same academics – some fifty-four in all – were training. All this was passed off as 'aid to an underdeveloped country'. At the same time the pervasive legend that South Vietnam had undergone an economic miracle became widespread. True, the aid from America poured in – the cost in 1961, for example, was $300 million – yet conditions in South Vietnam got worse, not better.

In 1959, with Diem repeatedly refusing to discuss the matter of reunification, North Vietnam instructed its supporters south of the seventeenth parallel to defend themselves. This was interpreted by those supporters as a move to the offensive, and the illusion of the communist threat, so often exploited by Diem, became a reality. By the end of the Eisenhower era there were some nine hundred United States 'military advisers' training Diem's native army. Reports of his alienation of the population were becoming so frequent as to be impossible to ignore, and in November 1960 his own paratroop battalions staged an unsuccessful coup against him. Diem, in contrast to his early phase of self-promotion, was now a virtual recluse, and was, if not yet a monster, a problem – the problem for the USA was whether to back him, meeting his repeated calls for increased aid with demands that he reform his domestic policy and win over the local population, or to reduce his role by taking over and controlling the war from Washington. Getting rid of Diem does not seem to have been an issue at this time, but the usurpation of his war by his backers was something Diem, taking Dulles' line on independence literally, would not accept.

During the late fifties the more urgent matter for Ike had been the war in Laos. On January 19th, 1961, the day before the inauguration, he met with President-elect Kennedy at the White House, to show him the homestead – how to summon a presidential helicopter by the press of a button – and drop a few words about South East Asia – a beginner's course with the dominoes. "If Laos should fall to the communists, then it would be just a question of time until South Vietnam, Cambodia, Thailand and Burma would collapse."[4] What was new was the prospect of unilateral American military action: "You might have to go in there and fight it out."[5]

By most accounts Kennedy took Ike very seriously, listening quietly and then asking a lot of questions – how long, for example, would it take to get a division into Laos? Was the situation in South East Asia approaching a climax? Ike's best, in answer to this, was that the situation was "extremely confused".[6] At some point in the interregnum Kennedy remarked to Sorensen that he wished that "Whatever's going to happen in Laos, an American invasion, a communist victory or whatever . . . would happen before we take over and get blamed for it."[7]

The next day, at the inauguration, Ike took his successor aside and repeated his point: "I think you are going to have to send in troops and if you do I will come up from Gettysburg and stand beside you and support you."[8]

The domino theory was passed on – along with the torch. Kennedy's ebullient stand on anti-communism did not dispose him to question the historical basis of this theory, to distinguish between external subversion and genuine nationalism, to see countries as distinct as his own instead of an undifferentiated bloc of like-looking, and therefore like-minded people.

§

Rigged elections and coups mark turning points in America's involvement in South East Asia. Eisenhower's concern over Laos was prompted by the turnabout in the Laotian civil war that the CIA had inadvertently achieved in the Autumn of 1960 – following a rigged election, paratroop captain Kong Le, ostensibly friendly to the USA, had staged a coup in favour of Prince Souvannaphouma. The US backed the Prince's chief rival, and, against the odds, he had sought aid from the Soviet Union, who had kept his army supplied with a food airlift. The lesson in this was not wasted. Kennedy came to office well aware that the wrong action or the wrong policy could drive more and more Vietnamese into supporting the Viet Cong (as the Viet Minh were now called) instead of the increasingly unsupportable Ngo Dinh Diem. One of his first moves was to convene a joint task force, a rolling seminar, on Vietnam, with the Defense and State Departments, the joint chiefs of staff, and the CIA. He also brought General Maxwell Taylor out of retirement, and within days of taking office approved an Eisenhower scheme to fund a 50,000 man increase in the South Vietnam army to the cost of $40 million. But he was a President committed by his inaugural speech to an active, confrontational foreign policy. As yet no-one could know how far the new administration would go in its confrontation with Russia – only, with cold-war consciousness, that Russia's leader Nikita Khrushchev had promised, in a remark he said was quoted always out of context – "We will bury you".[9]

In April another part of Ike's legacy played out to its grisly conclusion, in the defeat of the US-backed Cuban landing at the Bay of Pigs. The following month the prospect of a settlement in Laos arose, and the war was referred to its own Geneva conference. With these two problems 'solved' in failure and negotiation South Vietnam moved silently up to the front line. Up to this point the USA had lost only two lives in the Vietnam War. After the farce of the Bay of Pigs it might seem wilful in the extreme to want any further involvement in Vietnam – if a war could be neither won, nor win home approval, some ninety miles off the southern coast of America, what chance in a climate akin to hell, ten thousand miles away? Kennedy was fearful of the charge that could so often be levelled against any Democrat, that they were soft on communism – more than that he was acutely conscious of his own position – as with so much in his thousand days he looked too much to re-election. His ambassador to India, J. K. Galbraith, told him that Vietnam was relatively unimportant.

"Yes," said Kennedy, "I agree with you. There is the political problem. I can only have so many political defeats in one year."[10]

Publicly he said: "The complacent, the self-indulgent, the soft societies are about to be swept away with the debris of history . . . our security may be lost piece by piece, country by country, without the firing of a single missile or the crossing of a single border . . . I am determined on our system's survival and success, regardless of the cost and regardless of the peril."[11]

The White House task force, with the President as a dissenting voice, became increasingly hawkish – the number of troops they favoured deploying rose with the political temperature, shooting up from a few thousand to around 120,000, with at least one suggestion that Hanoi should be nuked. Diem had to be made to put his house in order – or the war would be lost. If he could not do this, the US must take greater control of the conduct of the war. In May Kennedy sent Vice-President Johnson on the first of a bewildering number of visits made by members of his government to South Vietnam. Johnson had two tasks – to increase the pressure on Diem to reform, and to get him to ask for US combat troops, thereby creating the loophole that might allow the USA to break the Geneva Accord.

Johnson was a superb politician, travelling with crates of Vice-Presidential bourbon and initialled ball-point pens to hand out by the thousand – and flattering a petty tyrant with 'You are the George Washington of Vietnam' or 'the Winston Churchill of South

East Asia'. But he was not the man for such a mission. So long the Senate's wheeler and dealer, he was accustomed to horse trading and compromise – this situation was couched in absolutes.

Johnson's report was a mixture of honest appraisal and a fantastic reworking of Monroe. "Battle must be joined in South East Asia," but "Asian leaders – at this time – do not want American troops . . . combat troop involvement is not only not required, it is not desirable . . ." So . . . "We must decide whether to help these countries or . . . pull back our defenses to San Francisco and a 'Fortress America.'"[12] The gist of his argument was 'support Diem or let Vietnam go'. Almost lost in this is a warning that the greater danger was not 'the momentary threat of communism' but hunger, ignorance, poverty and disease.

In November Kennedy sent General Maxwell Taylor and White House aide Walt Rostow to Saigon. They reported back what must already have been known, that the US representatives in South Vietnam, CIA included, recommended that troops be sent in. Some nine or ten thousand might do the trick – they could be passed off as 'a flood control mission'. By now the President was being bombarded with suggestions, as various government groupings and military factions came up with their own figures, their own combinations of aid, pressure and action, and their own hypothetical date by which the war might be won. In November the definitive version, prepared by Secretary of State Rusk and Secretary of Defense McNamara, was drawn up. It marked an end to fudging, and called for the use of Category B (combat) troops, around six divisions, some 205,000 men, if that was the only way to win, and warned of the international diplomatic consequences. With this in mind they suggested the cooking up of letters between the President and Diem, whereby Diem would state the extent of communist infiltration, set out his own attempts at reform – the USA could not be seen to give open support to an unmitigated tyrant – and then call for American assistance.

This tissue of lies was duly concocted.

Diem to Kennedy. 7.12.61: "We must have further assistance from the United States if we are to win the war now being waged against us.

"We can certainly assure mankind that our action is purely defensive. Much as we regret the subjugation of more than half our people in North Vietnam, we have no intention, and indeed no means, to free them by use of force."

Kennedy to Diem. 14.12.61: "The authorities in Hanoi . . . have thus violated the Geneva Accords designed to ensure peace in

353

Vietnam . . . In accordance with that declaration, and in response to your request, we are prepared to help the Republic of Vietnam to protect its people and to preserve its independence. We shall promptly increase our assistance to your defense effort as well as help relieve the destruction of the floods which you describe."[13]

In view of Diem's repeated assertion that he did not want colonisation by the back door, nor to lose control of the war by accepting advisers, who, in reality, could be nothing but combat troops, it's tempting to ask what pressure was brought to bear on Diem behind the scenes. The logical bluff, if it was made, being the withdrawal of all aid, military and economic.

Even before Kennedy had replied to Diem a 15,000-ton aircraft ferry arrived at Saigon. Within days American troops were on their way to Vietnam. At first a mere five hundred – helicopter pilots and Special Forces, but by early 1962 the number of American 'advisers' had reached four thousand, and by the end of that year twelve thousand.

The deception involved in this covert invasion – in passing off combat troops as advisers – was also self-deception. Throughout 1961 Kennedy had resisted the weight of advice which called for thousands of US troops to be sent into Vietnam, but by committing himself to that first five hundred he had set America on the course to twelve thousand troops, and eventually to the presence, at peak in 1969, of more than half a million. The problem of Vietnam had passed beyond paper and argument into committed action, the line between peace and war had been quietly, perhaps imperceptibly, crossed. Kennedy was, as John Ranelagh succinctly put it in his history of the CIA, "choosing somebody else's anvil on which to crush somebody else's enemies."[14] He had also, yet again, accepted assurances from a proven dictator that he would institute economic and political reform at home as the price of US intervention which he didn't want in the first place. The likelihood that Diem would use the dubious power the US conferred on him at the end of 1961 for such reform was slim – starve a cold, but feed a tyrant. In February 1962, as US War Headquarters, known as the Military Assistance Command Vietnam, was set up in Saigon, Kennedy remarked privately to Ben Bradlee, editor of the *Washington Post*, "Diem is Diem and he's the best we've got."[15]

§

1963 opened with five US helicopters shot down and three dead. Senator Mike Mansfield returned from Vietnam and uttered the unpalatable truth that the war was turning into an American war that could not be justified in the national interest. Shortly afterwards State Department assistant Michael Forrestal returned saying, "We are probably winning." So often, one mission would simply contradict the one before. Opinion was everything.

In May the Hué incident took place, precipitating the Buddhist crisis, the handling of which spelt out finally to the Kennedy administration just how little Diem's promises of reform meant. In a country where political protest was ineffective by being, in many forms, illegal, religious dissent became the focus and form of all protest. On May 8th the popular suspicion and resentment of the increasing power of the Nhus showed itself when thousands of demonstrators turned out for the raising of a traditional Buddhist flag in celebration of the Buddha's 2587th birthday, in the city of Hué, of which Diem's brother Ngo Dinh Thuc was Archbishop. The easy course would have been for the government to do nothing – instead they invoked a regulation which forbade any flag but the government flag. Troops fired on the crowd and nine demonstrators were killed. The government lamely blamed the Vietcong. In the *New York Times* David Halberstam quoted an anonymous State Department official as saying: "The thing that bothers me about this government is that the only people who are for it are Americans." And added in his own words, "Most observers believe that if the government had moved quickly, acknowledging responsibility . . . and paying reparations, the entire issue would have ended there. Had President Ngo Dinh Diem made a dramatic gesture at the pagoda, they say, or delivered a few warm and magnanimous words, he could have emerged stronger than ever."[16]

Whatever Diem felt, the Nhus and the Archbishop opposed any reconciliation with the Buddhists. In June the protests spread. In Hué, again, some sixty-seven people were hit by gas grenades. As United States pressure mounted on Diem to end the crisis, the priests learnt the American way and became skilled at working press and publicity, ensuring that their demonstrations were seen and heard – never more effectively than on June 11th, the same day President Kennedy addressed America on the matter of race.

At a crossroads in Saigon an old Buddhist priest, Thich Quang Duc, sat down in the lotus position. Two other priests doused him in petrol, then he struck a match. As he sat and burned alive, he neither spoke nor moved, while all around him the flashbulbs popped. Halberstam described the scene: " . . . His body was slowly withering and shrivelling up, his head blackening and charring. In the air was the smell of burning flesh: human beings burn surprisingly quickly. Behind me I could hear the sobbing of the Vietnamese who were now gathering. I was too shocked to cry, too confused to take notes or ask questions, too bewildered to even think."[17]

Afterwards, it was claimed, Thich Quang Duc's heart, like that of St Joan, was found unburnt.

"The Buddhist leaders . . . took Quang Duc's heart to the pagoda and placed it in a jar, claiming that since the heart did not burn, Quang Duc left this world unsatisfied. This simply added to the legend: Quang Duc became a martyr for the people in many parts of Vietnam."[18]

Madame Nhu, playing Marie Antoinette, dismissed it as a 'barbecue', but the pictures were seen around the world. The slow, painful death of Thich Quang Duc became, more than anything thrown up by the frenzy in Britain or the turmoil in the USA, the most memorable image of 1963. It's probable that few of the many millions who saw that photograph over the next few days knew the priest's name, just as probable that few who saw it will ever forget it. Madame Nhu's father, Ambassador to Washington, resigned his post, shaved his head and declared for the priests. Kennedy was described as being deeply disturbed by it – even the CIA admitted that it contributed strongly to the downfall of Diem. Over the next ten weeks another five priests died in this way.

This led to a rapid and temporary truce, with the signing of a five point settlement on June 16th – but the government still accepted no responsibility for the Hué incident. There's a sense at this time that Diem was trapped between his family and his 'friends', between American pressure and the combativeness of the Nhus – his sister-in-law is reputed to have called him a coward.

There appears to have been a shift too in the leadership of the priests – part of the worldwide pattern – towards younger, more forceful people with more overt political and social aims. Halberstam wrote in the *New York Times*: "They represented a new force in Vietnamese politics, for by now they were deep in politics. These priests are in their thirties and early forties, men clearly affected by thirty years of political revolution and political war in Vietnam . . . they became increasingly open in their attacks on the government and the leading family. Soon they were clearly trying to create an atmosphere in which the government would fall."[19]

Halberstam speculated that a vital tactic was to goad the government into stupid acts of repression in order that the world, or at least the new US ambassador, might see them as they really were.

In June Kennedy had changed ambassadors, replacing Frederick Nolting with Henry Cabot Lodge – another of his surprising cross-party choices, Lodge had been Nixon's running mate in 1960 and Kennedy's own opponent for the Senate in 1952, and was a strong, politically independent man. Lodge went out with few doubts – the problem of Vietnam was the problem of Diem. Kennedy gave him complete control over the flow and apportionment of aid to Vietnam, as near as dammit control over Diem.

As though sensing his enemy Diem struck first, stormed pagodas across the country on the day Lodge was due to arrive, and imprisoned some fourteen hundred Buddhist priests. An unmistakable demonstration of power, an attempt to confront the new ambassador, charged with getting Diem to solve the crisis, with a fait accompli. Privately, General Ton That Dinh, who had led the raids, remarked, without illusions, that he had defeated Lodge: "He came here to hold a coup, but I . . . have conquered him and saved the country!"[20] Arriving on August 21st, Lodge instantly froze out Diem. He visited the Xa Loi pagoda the following day, and put off presenting his credentials to the President for five days. Robert Kennedy went as far as to say, and he was exaggerating, that Lodge hardly spoke either to Diem or to the head of the MACV, General Harkins, for the next two months, but the independence of thought in Lodge and his willingness to turn it into action are clear.

The CIA in Saigon had been contacted by dissatisfied Vietnamese generals towards the start of the Buddhist crisis. As Lodge arrived in Saigon they, in the person of General Tran Van Don, made contact again through CIA agent Lucien Conein. As Conein briefed his station head John Richardson, Lodge came in and heard from Conein the outline of a proposed coup. According to Conein, Lodge dismissed Richardson and instructed Conein to report directly to him.

"I didn't want to get my ass in a sling, so I did what Cabbage Head told me."[21]

Conein continued to deal with the generals, describing them as 'corporals with stars on their shoulders'. Richardson reported the plan to CIA head John McCone, and Lodge immediately cabled Washington with news of the planned coup. At the same time rumours came through that Ngo Dinh Nhu was secretly dealing with the Viet Cong.

When Lodge's cable reached Assistant Secretary of State Roger Hilsman, the President was at one of the Kennedy family homes in Hyannisport on Cape Cod. Neither Rusk nor McNamara was in Washington. The answer to Lodge was drafted at non-executive level by Hilsman, Averell Harriman and White House aide Mike Forrestal.

It gave 'the green light' to the coup by saying that the USA required the removal of Nhu, and that if this was not done it should be made clear to the generals that aid would cease – the cable further said that the US would recognise and support a new government formed by the army, but made no direct mention of a coup:

"US Government cannot tolerate situation in which power lies in Nhu's hands. Diem must be given chance to rid himself of Nhu and his coterie and replace them with best military and political personalities available.

"If, in spite of all your efforts, Diem remains obdurate and refuses then we must face the possibility that Diem himself cannot be preserved."[22]

This hedged bets. It set out the preference for keeping Diem but getting rid of Nhu, and then dealt with the probable consequence of almost certain refusal. This cable of August 24th is a much argued turning point in America's commitment to Vietnam. According to Robert Kennedy, his brother was not given the opportunity to clear the cable, and when they all returned to Washington on the 26th the government split in two over the rights and wrongs of the decision.[23] One of the more recent historians of America's involvement, Anthony Short, disagrees, writing that Kennedy sounded out all his advisers and found that Hilsman's cable was unanimously endorsed.[24] It was not retracted – it was supplemented. On August 26th Voice of America in Vietnam broadcast that Nhu's secret police were behind the pagoda raids, and suggested that US aid might be cut off – thus attempting to drive a wedge between the generals and Diem and between Diem and Nhu. On the 29th Kennedy sent a personal message to Lodge saying, "We will do all we can to help you conclude this operation successfully. Until the very moment of the go signal for the operation by the generals I must reserve a contingent right to change course and reverse previous instructions . . . I know from experience that failure is more destructive than an appearance of indecision." Even as this was being sent the coup was fizzling out – the generals did not feel that US support was clear enough and that they might have shown their hand too soon.

At a State Department meeting on the 31st there was some plain speaking on the mess that American involvement had become – Hilsman informed the committee that a Korean study was under way with the damning thesis "how much repression will the United

States tolerate before pulling out her aid?" State Department official Paul Kattenburg said, "If we undertake to live with this repressive regime, with its bayonets at every street corner and its transparent negotiations with puppet bonzes, we are going to be thrown out of country in six months." And with cowboy simplicity Johnson, heading the committee, wound up with "We should stop playing cops and robbers."[25]

On CBS a couple of days later Kennedy, in need of some reassuring hokum, invoked Dulles once more: "In the final analysis it's their war". Walter Cronkite asked if the Diem government had time to regain the support of the people. Kennedy replied, "With changes in policy and perhaps with changes in personnel, I think it can. If it doesn't make those changes, I would think the chances of winning it would not be very good."[26] This might have been cryptic to most people, but not to Lodge or Diem – it was a clear statement that Diem was dispensable.

The USA and Vietnam exchanged visitors. Madame Nhu,[27] thought by many to be worse than her husband and brother-in-law, toured the USA speaking against the new policy on Vietnam, and Kennedy dispatched General Krulak and White House aide Joseph Mendenhall. When their reports contradicted each other, Maxwell Taylor and Robert McNamara rapidly followed, on what I. F. Stone called "Another Fact-Evading Mission – you can't go on pouring napalm on villages and poisons on crops, uprooting people and putting them in prison-like compounds, and expect to be liked."[28] Again this visit produced contradiction. Lodge had cabled: "The ship of state is slowly sinking". McNamara and Taylor claimed the war was being won and the US could seriously think of pulling out troops. Kennedy had also said on CBS that he thought to pull out would be wrong and mentioned the forty-seven American lives lost thus far in the war – yet he was contemplating just that, cutting his, and America's, losses and pulling out – not for the reasons asserted by this latest report but because it was the only sanction left. On October 2nd Voice of America announced a selective cut-back of aid – so selective, says Arthur Schlesinger, as to do little harm to the war effort[29] – and Kennedy took the decision to withdraw a thousand men by the end of the year.

The next day General Duong Van Minh made contact with Colonel Conein. The coup was on again. Plans were outlined – this time Diem and Nhu were to be assassinated. This reached Kennedy via another cable from Lodge to the State Department,[30] and via John Richardson and the CIA. The President had a personal meeting with John McCone. McCone stated the agency's view – they did not favour assassination, one coup would simply beget a wave of coups. Richardson, following his dismissal by Lodge, was recalled.

Tran Van Don asked to meet Lodge. Lodge assured him that the USA was ready to help, that Conein acted with his authority. Washington divided over the coup – those in favour, those against and those in favour so long as it was a success and no one could ever point the finger at US involvement, which was the view that prevailed. At the last minute, on October 30th, a cable was sent by McGeorge Bundy, the President's Special Assistant on Security, making these points clear to Lodge – a Marine battalion was put on alert at Okinawa. What was also clear from the cable was that they had no contact with Conein, and hence none with the generals, except through Lodge. In firing Richardson Lodge had effectively taken over the American involvement with the coup.

The next day, Friday, November 1st, Lodge paid a rare visit to Diem. They talked till past noon. By that time three task forces of rebel troops had begun to take over key points in the city – with four howitzers and forty tanks and armoured cars. By 1.30 p.m. they had occupied the Post Office, the radio station and the Central Police HQ. Tran Van Don stood up from his lunch at the Officers' Club, announced the coup, invited his fellow diners to join him and arrested those who did not. By this time Lodge was back at the embassy and heard the sound of machine-gun fire. The siege of Gia Long Palace had begun. The generals had cut off Diem from any provincial support and almost any means of escape. An hour and a half later Tran Van Don called the embassy and asked if they had made any plans for the evacuation of Diem in the event that he surrendered. He was told that a plane was standing by. At 4 p.m. a scene that could have have been clipped from *The Conformist* or *The Godfather* took place. Diem phoned Lodge. Lodge dodged the questions:

Diem: "I want to know what is the attitude of the US?"

Lodge: "I do not feel well enough informed to be able to tell you. I have heard the shooting, but am not acquainted with all the facts. Also it is 4.30 a.m. in Washington and the US government cannot possibly have a view."[31]

It is curious how in an age of telecommunications when, for example, an Argentine warship is sunk by the Royal Navy or an urgent telegram is sent in the name of the President of the United States or a coup takes place in a global trouble spot, the leaders of the world somehow manage to be unattainable, asleep or on holiday. Diem and Lodge concluded like theatrical agents trying a brush-off: " . . . you have my number?" "If I can do anything . . .

360

please call me." The plane standing by does not seem to have been mentioned.

At midnight after heavy bombardment, the barracks of the Presidential Guard surrendered. Throughout the evening the rebels had called upon Diem and Nhu to surrender and had guaranteed their safety. The staff of the US embassy watched from the roof. At 6 a.m. the President's remaining forces surrendered. Marines stormed and seized the palace. Diem and Nhu had escaped by a tunnel, but not long afterwards they were found in a French church in the suburb of Cholon.

Lucien Conein had been with the generals throughout the coup – uniformed and armed. He had delivered $40,000 of 'death money', with which the families of rebel soldiers killed in the coup were to be compensated. Lodge's lack of acquaintance with 'the facts' was at odds with the technology at hand. Conein had both radio contact and a telephone hotline with the US embassy. When the ceasefire occurred the generals called in the press. Under orders to keep America out of it, Conein returned to the embassy. By the time he got back to the palace Diem and Nhu were dead. General Minh, the man who had first informed the CIA that Diem and Nhu were to be killed, told Conein that they had committed suicide. Conein found this hard to believe of two Catholics. He declined to view the bodies, but it soon emerged that Diem and Nhu had been murdered.

William Colby, head of the CIA's Far Eastern operation in 1963, who was in Washington throughout the coup, wrote this account in 1989 of the death of Diem:

"The generals sent an armoured column to take them into custody, an aide of General 'Big' Minh joining the unit at the last minute. When the Ngo brothers were picked up at the appointed place, they were placed in an armoured personnel carrier for the ride to general Staff Headquarters near the airport. The route crossed a rail line, and a passing train forced the column to stop. Minh's aide entered the carrier, shot both brothers with a submachine gun, and stabbed them repeatedly. The column then proceeded to the headquarters . . . Clearly the decision to murder the two was made by the coup's titular leader, General 'Big' Minh, and by him alone."[32]

For the *New York Times* David Halberstam wrote the epitaph for Diem's regime: "The government had fallen, the Ngos were dead, and the military leaders had won all they sought.

"The war with the Vietcong, the questions of subversion, loyalty, poverty, and religious conflict at this point became

361

theirs to deal with."[33]

Over the next twenty months ten different governments tried their hand at dealing with all those problems.

§

By all accounts the news of Diem's death distressed Kennedy greatly. Schlesinger wrote: "He was sombre and shaken. I had not seen him so depressed since the Bay of Pigs. No doubt he realised that Vietnam was his great failure in foreign policy and that he had never really given it his full attention."[34]

Maxwell Taylor recalled seeing Kennedy receive the news – he jumped up and left the room in silence, and stayed out for several minutes. Also present was William Colby. He said that Kennedy was 'distraught' and thought that he took the responsibility personally. But Kennedy's most recent biographer, Herbert Parmet, quotes Senator Smathers of Florida, who recalled Kennedy saying, "I've got to do something about those bastards" – meaning the CIA? For whose benefit he uttered this isn't clear, and presumably Colby had left the room by this point. It prompts questions. Who's blaming who, who's passing the buck? The CIA blame Minh, Kennedy blames the CIA?

If the reports in the *New York Times* of September 9th are to be believed, the CIA had played it both ways, backing the worst excesses of Nhu and then collaborating in the coup. A reported $250,000 a month had been channelled to Nhu's pagoda raiders by the CIA. The US government was recorded as declining to comment, but "officials" in Washington refused even to stand by their own denials, "because they simply do not know what is being done by the CIA in Saigon."[35] The same day, interviewed live on NBC, Kennedy was asked about this report. Could the President shed any light on the story?: "No." Does the CIA make its own policy?: "No, that is the frequent charge, but that isn't so. Mr McCone, head of the CIA, sits in the National Security Council. We have had a number of meetings in the past few days about events in South Vietnam. Mr McCone participated in every one and the CIA coordinates its efforts with the State Department and the Defense Department." More than ten years after, Colby, a later Director of the CIA, loosely confirmed the *New York Times* report saying of that interim between the pagoda raids and the coup – during which time Diem had arrested thousands of students – that "We cut off the support the CIA was giving to a particular unit of the Vietnamese army."[36] The President's confidence does not tally with the casual element in Robert Kennedy's remarks the following Spring:

"Oh, they [the US Embassy] had been talking to some fellow who in turn talked to the generals. It was rather nebulous."[37]

The interviewer, unprepared for this answer, said simply, "Jesus!" Such 'nebulous' involvement by the CIA seemed less than credible, less than exact, less than accountable. There is a sense throughout Robert Kennedy's interview on Vietnam that he is, unlike his Civil Rights interviews, fudging and lying. 'Some fellow' was Lucien Conein. The removal of the link in Richardson, and the exclusivity of Conein's contact with the generals and Lodge may well have struck the Attorney-General as making things nebulous, but his answer may also be a way of dodging the issue and shifting the responsibility. What, after all, was wanted: the impression that the CIA was accountable or that it was not?[38] The CIA's own staff are consistent in their statements that they favoured neither the continuation of the war nor the removal of Diem – they cast themselves repeatedly as the bearers of bad news to successive presidents, who chose not to accept their information. But, among the information supplied was the news that Diem was a target for assassination. Was this too ignored? Parmet, for Volume 2 of his life of Kennedy, interviewed the widow of Congressman Torby Mac-Donald. MacDonald, it was said, had undertaken a secret mission to Diem at Kennedy's behest, without the knowledge of the CIA, to warn Diem that he might be killed.

None of this quite adds up. Why did Kennedy replace Nolting with Lodge at that precise moment, knowing Lodge was in no way disposed towards Diem? What did the administration expect of Lodge? What did Lodge feel the administration expected of him? Is it a convenient coincidence that news of a planned coup came in twenty-four hours after Lodge arrived in Saigon? A fortuitous piece of bad luck that his cable to Hilsman came in while the President was out at Cape Cod, a believable notion that this somehow sundered Kennedy from a precise grasp of what was happening? Why did Lodge whittle down the channel of communication to himself and Conein? Why, since he must have known that Conein's part in the coup was only that of bagman, did Kennedy blame the CIA?

Colby, in a much quoted remark, said: "This was a Vietnamese generals' coup . . . But I think the fundamentals of it were decided in our White House . . ."

If this was the CIA's way of acquitting itself – it wasn't good enough. In December I. F. Stone warned of the consequences of the CIA's activities: " . . . The very existence of a secret agency which boasts of 'cloak and dagger' activities in countries with which we are

at peace creates suspicions which poison our foreign relations . . .
no one can be sure that the right hand of our government really
knows what its left hand is doing . . . Again I ask – in the wake of
our own President's assassination – how long are we going to maintain what other nations consider an assassination agency of our
own?"[39]

Asking anyone of the right age where they were on the day of
Jack Kennedy's death has become a macabre party game. One
answer to the trite question pointed up the contrast between the
legend of universal grief and the reality, as experienced in parts of
the USA that were less than sympathetic to the President's aims.
Joe Keegan, a native of Brooklyn, was twenty-three at the time:
"I'd been out of the army about eighteen months and I was major-
ing in photography at Sam Houston State in Huntsville, Texas
during the fall of 1963. Several weeks before President Kennedy was
due to come to Texas I kept hearing students say 'If that nigger-
lover comes down hear we'll shoot his ass.' I really didn't think that
they meant it, but I remember back to a month and a half before
when a black man in Livingston, Texas had supposedly raped a
white woman. He had been arrested and thrown into the local jail.
The afternoon that he was arrested many of the students were
talking about going over to Livingston to watch the lynching and
they invited me to come along. Horrified, I looked at them and said,
'You better be kidding. This is 1963, they don't lynch people anymore.' And I went off and did my own thing. When I awoke the
next day, around the school I heard the story about what had
happened over in Livingston the night before. The Sheriff had gone
out to someone's ranch outside of town and the deputy who was in
charge was down at the coffee shop and had conveniently left the
keys hanging on the hook behind the Sheriff's desk. A mob of
people broke into the jail, released and set the black man free, but
not before dousing him in gasoline and torching him as he ran down
the street. Because of this incident I really feared for Kennedy's life
when he came to visit Texas. As the time grew closer and closer the
students kept referring to 'that nigger-lover'. They kept talking
about the violence they were going to do to the President. That
eventful afternoon when we heard over the radio that President
Kennedy was dead I went downstairs and lowered the American
flag to half mast. Some of the students said I shouldn't be doing
that. I reminded them our President was dead and they just
laughed. That night when I went out to dinner, I sat down in the
restaurant, the waitress came up, put down the menu and said 'Isn't
it great?' The whole world stopped that night, but there in

Huntsville, Texas the local High School had its football game as usual."[40]

I have no theory as to who assassinated Kennedy. The only suggestion worth making is about the motive for a cover-up, if there was one, of God-knows-what. What would it take to achieve the cooperation, in conspiracy to conceal the facts of the assassination of John F. Kennedy, of J. Edgar Hoover, head of the FBI, Lyndon Baines Johnson, the accidental President, and Robert F. Kennedy the Attorney-General? Three men, who, by most accounts, probably loathed each other. Whatever it was, it must have been something of such magnitude that its revelation would have wrecked the Kennedy legend and damaged the office of President. Was Kennedy up to his neck in plots for the assassination of foreign heads of state? How many exploding whoopee cushions had Castro received? Did JFK pay the price of failure at the hands of some gruesome anti-Castro/Cosa Nostra coalition? To return to the issue, why was Henry Cabot Lodge sent to Vietnam?

With Kennedy's death the move to begin the withdrawal became instantly problematic. It was in the first place geared to the problem of Diem. Diem was no more, but the approval for withdrawal had already been signed. Among Johnson's first meetings as President were sessions with Kennedy advisers urging that the plan should be dropped. Johnson picked up the torch and with it Ike's dominoes: "I am not going to be the President who saw South East Asia go the way China went."

If this was the opportunity for the US to get out, the reasons why they stayed, why they conducted a war that was, for much of its course, disguised from both Congress and the American people, are complex. General Maxwell Taylor recorded in his memoirs the consequences of the responsibility that Diem's death left to them: "In the post-Diem period when the political turbulence in South Vietnam offered the United States an excuse to withdraw from its involvement, the realisation of our role in creating the Vietnamese predicament was a strong deterrent to anyone inclined to make such a proposal."

In 1963 US planes flown by US advisers staged 6,929 air raids over Vietnam. The United States was, in a much used image, sucked in. The inadvertent war became, in 1963, a turning point in the history of the decade, the act that points out of the year of change and into the notion of the Sixties.

§

A couple of years before his death Abbie Hoffman said in an interview: "I accept American culture, its demand for entertainment. Europeans who observed the period of the sixties tell me that my contribution to revolutionary theory was to come up with the idea that revolution could be fun. Only an American could have done that."[41]

There's a long-running television programme that gives the impression that most of the events of the mid and late sixties took place to the accompaniment of rock'n'roll. Neither that nor Hoffman is really inaccurate, but the combination that strikes me in hindsight is that the British invasion, as America terms the wave of British rock that hit the USA on February 7th, 1964, revitalised what was moribund in their own youth culture, and, allied to the organisational ability worked up through the Civil Rights protests, gave the Sixties its force and its movement – music, politics, protest and the vast numbers of people in their teens and twenties begat the 'revolution' Hoffman referred to. It's fashionable now to decry the 'excesses of the Sixties' – when I talked to Jerry Rubin in 1988 he used that term more meaningfully, and also defined it – and part of the definition of 'excess' was identification with guerilla movements of foreign countries. Perhaps the most obvious example is Vietnam – Rubin himself is on record as saying. "If there hadn't been a Vietnam War, we would have had to invent one. It was a way to talk about America, about the racism in America, the militarism in America, the mindless anti-communism . . . Vietnam was the lightning rod that changed American society."[42]

During the course of that war some 2.2 million young men – no, children – wars are fought by children – were conscripted. Ten thousand or so dodged the draft. Fifty-eight thousand died. And that's just the Americans.

Over the next twelve years the images of protest dominated the headlines, and crossed international frontiers and cultures – the burning draft cards – the march on the Pentagon, joining hands in a huge circle to levitate the building, with McNamara watching from the top floor, standing next to an unknown Pentagon official called Daniel Ellsberg[43] – the sit-down protests in Grosvenor Square – the siege of Chicago – the Washington Moratorium. Many of the movers behind these protests had begun in the Civil Rights movement. Abbie Hoffman and Tom Hayden, both tried as Chicago conspirators, were active in the movement in 1963. Julian Bond, who had run SNCC's information office, was by 1966 an elected Georgia Assemblyman, but was refused his seat because he had endorsed SNCC's policy statement on Vietnam:

"We ourselves have often been victims of violence and confinement executed by US government officials . . . We know for the most part that elections in this country, in the North as well as the South are not free . . . We question then the ability and even the desire of the US government to guarantee free elections abroad."[44]

At the Chicago Democratic Convention in 1968 Bond's name was put forward as a candidate for Vice-President: the youngest person ever to be nominated. But that too, as Bond was under the constitutional age for the office, was a protest. Outside in Grant and Lincoln Parks Mayor Daley's Police turned protest into battle – even that served a purpose, as Jerry Rubin said, if the police at home could behave with such violence what could we believe our boys were doing in Vietnam? I. F. Stone wrote that the country owed "a debt of gratitude to the tatterdemalion army of yippies, hippies and peaceniks . . . they made opposition to the war visible." But he added, "the best of a generation was being lost – some among the hippies to drugs, some among the radicals to an almost hysterical frenzy of alienation."[45] This line would not have been lost on the outgoing President, Lyndon Baines Johnson.

§

"I knew from the start that I was bound to be crucified either way I moved. If I left the woman I really loved – the Great Society – in order to get involved with that bitch of a war on the other side of the world, then I would lose everything at home . . . Losing the Great Society was a terrible thought, but not so terrible as the thought of being responsible for America's losing a war to the communists. Nothing could possibly be worse than that."[46]

Johnson's programme of social action, his war on poverty, was hinted at in the first speech he made after Kennedy's death – at once and for the duration of his office it was bound up with the mantle of Vietnam:

"Three times in my lifetime, in two World Wars and Korea, Americans have gone to far lands to fight for freedom. We have learned at a terrible and a brutal cost that retreat does not bring safety and weakness does not bring peace."

On May 22nd, 1964, speaking at Ann Arbor, University of Michigan, Johnson formally announced the social programme:

"The Great Society rests on abundance and liberty for all. It demands an end to poverty and racial injustice, to which we are totally committed in our time. But that is just the beginning.

"The Great Society is a place where every child can find knowledge to enrich his mind and to enlarge his talents. It is a place where leisure is a welcome chance to build and reflect, not a feared cause of boredom and restlessness. It is a place where the city of man serves not only the needs of the body and the demands of commerce, but the desire for beauty and the hunger for community."

At this point there's a consonance between Johnson's thinking and the pre-protest thinking of the youth movement – in the recognition of the restriction on human potential in America. At that same university, Ann Arbor, grew the largest of the student movements, Students for a Democratic Society (SDS). Their first convention in Port Huron in June of 1962 produced a radical manifesto, the 'Port Huron Statement':

"We are of this generation, bred in at least modest comfort, housed now in universities, looking uncomfortably to the world we inherit . . . Men have unrealised potential for self-cultivation, self-direction, and creativity. It is this potential that we regard as crucial and to which we appeal, not to the human potentiality for violence, unreason and submission to authority . . . we seek the establishment of a democracy of individual participation, governed by two central aims: that the individual share in those social decisions determining the quality and direction of his life; that society be organised to encourage independence in men and provide the media for their common participation."[47]

It would be nigh outrageous to suggest that LBJ knew or cared what SDS thought and wrote (the statement was the work of Tom Hayden) but both were influenced by the work and activity of Michael Harrington – author of *The Other America*, a book which burst upon America in 1963 and which both Kennedy and Johnson were said to have read. When Johnson set up the War on Poverty Programme, under Sargent Shriver, Harrington was recruited to the team. For a short time, a period of less than a year, there seemed to be a prospect of a common aim, of co-operation across the generations.

Johnson's administration set up seventeen different task forces to draw up the legislation of the Great Society, on Medicare, education, minimum wages, farming subsidies, housing projects, hunger projects, vocational training, civil rights, schools for Indians, unemployment benefits, pensions, conservation and so on: the things America needed but by and large does without. His own verdict was that the Vietnam war gave the conservatives in American politics the perfect excuse not to support the Great Society programme – too costly, inappropriate in time of war. But it was the youth revolt that became the most visible protest against Johnson, that made him the most opposed and resisted President since his namesake a hundred years before. From the opposite perspective, the youth movements grew to see the Great Society as a sham. From the start they'd recognised the connection between oppression at home, at its most fundamental in the denial of black civil rights, and the latent imperialism of cold war foreign policy. When an organisation like SDS, with its social and democratic programmes,[48] turned its attention to Vietnam the rift in American society, between American generations, between the society LBJ was trying to make and the one the youth movement was trying to make, became a chasm.

In the middle of July 1964, only two weeks after the passing of the Civil Rights Act, LBJ called a White House meeting on the matter of the Harlem riots – Whitney Young, Roy Wilkins and Martin Luther King all attended, and a joint statement was agreed:

" . . . The greatest need now is for political action . . . we call on our members voluntarily to observe a broad curtailment if not total moratorium of all mass marches, picketing and demonstrations until after election day, November 3rd."

Johnson's biographer, Doris Kearns, commented shrewdly that this statement "assumed a sharing of interests between officials in government and rioting youth in the streets, an assumption that, within two years, would become untenable."[49]

SDS organised the first teach-in on the Vietnam war in March 1965 at Ann Arbor. Three thousand people came. The teach-in spread. On April 17th SDS organised an anti-war rally in Washington – I. F. Stone addressed twenty thousand marchers. The protests spread. Over October 15th and 16th eighty thousand people in fifteen cities took part in the first mass protests against the war, and then the first backlash came. Nick Katzenbach, by then Attorney-General, announced that SDS would be investigated by the Justice Department.[50] The FBI took an interest. The Kennedy dream was over. To answer the wave of criticism SDS secretary Paul Booth held a press conference in Washington:

"The commitment of SDS, and of the whole generation we represent, is clear: we are anxious to build villages; we refuse to burn them. We are anxious to help and change our country; we refuse to destroy someone else's country. We are anxious to advance the cause of democracy; we do not believe that cause can be advanced by torture and terror . . . we propose to the President that all those Americans who seek so vigorously to build instead of burn be given their chance to do so. We propose that he test the young people of America . . . "[51]

After this there was always the danger that the war would dominate every aspect of youth politics, as it finally dominated and destroyed the presidency of Johnson.

Interviewed shortly before his death Michael Harrington still managed a few words of praise for LBJ: " . . . I'm convinced Johnson was honestly concerned on the basis of having been a young New Dealer. He was also concerned to have a programme that was a Lyndon Johnson programme by 1964, and this was perfect, it was a Kennedy programme but had not been named a Kennedy programme.[52] It could be his . . . When Shriver took our original proposal to Johnson – which was much more radical than anything that was ever acted on – in late February or March of 1964 – Johnson's response in the Oval Office was 'pretty radical stuff Sarge, but if it takes that to complete what Mr Roosevelt began I'll do it' . . . I have always thought that Lyndon Johnson was a tragedy, that it was not so much that he malevolently got involved in Vietnam. I think that Johnson simply got in over his head . . . got sucked in and sucked under . . . Even at the height of the anti-war movement I felt the stuff about 'Hey, hey LBJ how many kids did you kill today?' was unfair."[53]

Long before, Harrington had commented that "eventually the New Left is going to have to radicalise the mainstream of society and take over the often unprophetic burdens of adult leadership."[54] But they didn't. On both sides of the Atlantic the baby-boom generation opposed the generation that bred it into 'modest comfort', challenged and rejected 'the world we inherit' and any position that might be called adult leadership.

There's an accidental symbolism in the words with which I prefaced this chapter, an illustrative confrontation between father and son in *Rebel Without A Cause*. The great fifties archetype of articulate, coherent rebellion and youthful burnout warned of the perils of adult life by the actor who played Mr Magoo – the man who could see no further than the end of his nose, blundering through life without being able to tell a bull moose from a fire hydrant. "Except to yourself!" Dean yells back at Magoo, "Except to yourself!" Most of the young who emerged in 1963 and 'made' the Sixties are still under fifty. It's probably too early to say what finally becomes of such idealism, except to state the almost-obvious, that in being idealistic to themselves, the generation that iconised James Dean side-stepped power politics. After protest no participation. The Magoos inherit. Blundering, as MagooNamara puts it these days, into disaster.

ACKNOWLEDGMENTS

There are certain debts.

To those people who were kind enough to let themselves be interviewed, who are named in the text, and to . . .
Jerry Booth, Bernard Clark and Fay Weldon (for the title), Elizabeth Cook, Cosima Dannoritzer, Kirin Davids, Anthony Johnson, Pat Knopf, Spencer Leigh, Diana Norman, Barty Phillips, Mary Poole, John Ranelagh, Hannah Scott-Joynt, John Taft, Ion Trewin and Gore Vidal.

. . . and to the staff of . . .
The British Library, Bloomsbury and Colindale
The Martin Luther King Library, Washington DC
The John F. Kennedy Library, Columbia Point, Massachusetts
The Old Homestead Bookshop, Marlborough, New Hampshire.

NOTES

Chapter One: Cat Among the Pygmies (pp. 3–13)

1 John Vassall, *Vassall: The Autobiography of a Spy*, Sidgwick & Jackson 1975, p. 66.
2 *Ibid.*, p. 67.
3 Draper, Mulholland and Newthwaite, *Daily Mail*, October 23rd, 1962.
4 *Ibid.*
5 Now known as the *Sunday Mirror*.
6 The Radcliffe Report was published on April 5th, 1962.
7 Harold Macmillan, *At the End of the Day*, Macmillan 1973 p. 431.
8 Unsigned article, *New Statesman*, November 16th, 1962.
9 Macmillan, *op. cit.* p. 431.
10 Bernard Levin, *The Pendulum Years*, Jonathan Cape 1970, p. 60.
11 Interestingly, while such lines were being written, the ITA had seen fit to ban a *World in Action* programme on defence as being biased against the government. Paul Fox of *Panorama* came to the rescue. Granada sold the programme for a nominal £100 to the BBC who broadcast it on March 11th.
12 Christopher Booker, *The Neophiliacs*, Collins 1969, p. 188.
13 Brown won by 133 votes to 103. He does not mention the Vassall case in his all too brief memoir *In My Way*, Penguin 1972.
14 Vassall served ten years of his sentence and was released in 1972 at the age of forty-eight.
15 *News of the World*, November 11th, 1962.
16 Macmillan, *op. cit.*, p. 431.

Chapter Two: That Cripps Feeling (pp. 14–40)

1 'Forget *that Cripps Feeling . . .*' placard displayed in the film *Passport to Pimlico*, Ealing 1949.
2 Macmillan records his words as 'most of our people'. Too many other sources quote him as saying '*some* of our people', and I find his memoirs unreliable on the exactitude of things said. Hence I use both versions.
3 The balance of payments under Cripps rose from a deficit of over £300 million to a surplus of over £300 million in 1947–50.
4 The origin of the phrase is credited to American Trades Union leader George Meany of the AFL–CIO. Macmillan's own verdict on his use of the phrase was 'notorious'.
5 Christopher Booker, *The Neophiliacs*, Collins 1969, pp. 130, 132.
6 Anthony Sampson, *Macmillan: A Study in Ambiguity*, Penguin 1968, p. 164.
7 Harold Macmillan, *Riding the Storm*, Macmillan 1971, p. 350.
8 Penguin 1964.
9 In support of this case I'd cite Brittan, but the opposite view is forcefully and

eloquently put by Rex Mallik: 'It is currently axiomatic that, given more capital investment by industry, output would increase. This is the view that Mr Macmillan evidently shares. It can be described simply as rubbish, for our investment is already higher than most countries. I write this during the farce that is national productivity year.' In *What's Wrong with British Industry*, Penguin 1964.

10 Dennis Johnson in R. Fraser (ed.), *Work*, Penguin 1965.

11 Alan Sked and Chris Cook, *Post War Britain*, Penguin 1979.

12 'The exercise of power in Britain (more specifically in England) cannot be understood unless it is recognised that it is exercised socially.' *Spectator*, September 1955.

13 Hugh Thomas (ed.), *The Establishment*, Blond 1958, p. 14.

14 *Ibid*.

15 *Ibid*., p. 203.

16 Sampson, *op. cit*., p. 329.

17 Heinemann 1978, p. 158.

18 Stan Barstow, *The Desperadoes*, Michael Joseph 1961, p. 21.

19 Alan Sillitoe, *Saturday Night and Sunday Morning*, Pan 1960, p. 20.

20 *Ibid*., p. 191.

21 Geoffrey Moorhouse, *The Other England*, Penguin 1964, p. 107.

22 *Ibid*., p. 108.

23 Britain built only two hospitals between 1945 and 1960.

24 I interviewed two Americans who had been teenagers in the mid-fifties and who saw Elvis perform live in his home state of Mississippi before he became famous. The man said he was most struck by the reaction of the group of upper-class college girls he was with – they had screamed and writhed in a way he didn't think girls of their class would have been able to imagine. The woman, from the same social rung as Elvis himself, remarked that she had not realised until she saw him live 'what a clean-cut, good lookin', Christian boy he was – he sure din't sound that way' – which might be a polite way of saying that she had presumed Elvis was black.

25 The word itself was probably new to Britain. 'I can't remember the first time I heard the word "teenager" . . . I doubt that many other people can either.' George Melly, *Owning Up*, Penguin 1970, p. 163. In the USA it goes back at least as far as the war.

26 'Rock Takes Over', *The History of Rock*, part-work, Orbis 1982, p. 83.

27 'The Dilemma of Sex and Romance in Fifties Rock', *ibid*., p. 238.

28 *Ibid*.

29 Richard Hoggart, *The Uses of Literacy*, Penguin 1958, p. 204.

30 T. R. Fyvel, *The Insecure Offenders*, Revised edn Penguin 1963, pp. 70–1.

31 Billy Morton interview, Harrogate, January 20th, 1990.

32 Melly, *op. cit*., Penguin 1977.

33 Doris Lessing, *In Pursuit of the English*, Panther 1980 (first pub. 1960), pp. 189, 218.

34 That said, the toughest opposition came from the Parliamentary Labour Party.

35 See Chapter 9.

36 Grace Wyndham Goldie, *Facing the Nation*, Bodley Head 1977.

37 Julian Pettifer interview, July 12th,1988.

38 *Picture Post* was soon followed by the *Empire News*, *News Chronicle*, *Sunday Despatch*, *Sunday Graphic* and the *Star*, all of which folded between 1960 and 1963. The impact of television must have been a factor, nevertheless the *Sunday*

Graphic was still selling over a million at the time.
39 Pettifer interview, July 12th, 1988.
40 Goldie, *op. cit.*

Chapter Three: The Fourteenth Mr Wilson (pp. 41–64)
 1 Richard Crossman, *Diaries*, Hamish Hamilton and Cape 1981.
 2 Daniel Boorstin, *The Image*, Penguin 1963, p. 55.
 3 *Daily Mail*, January 19th, 1963.
 4 A phrase originally coined by Nye Bevan and aimed at both Attlee and Gaitskell, frequently applied to Wilson about this time.
 5 *Daily Mail*, January 24th 1963.
 6 e.g. Anthony Sampson, *Anatomy of Britain*, Hodder & Stoughton 1962.
 7 Leslie Smith, *Harold Wilson*, Fontana 1964, p. 138.
 8 *Ibid.*, p. 52.
 9 *Ibid.*, p. 70.
10 *Ibid.*, p. 210.
11 *Ibid.*, p. 157.
12 *Ibid.*, p. 191.
13 *Daily Express*, February 15th, 1963.
14 From a speech made in his constituency, Huyton, February 16th, 1963.
15 Crossman, *op. cit.*, p. 981.
16 Andrew Roth, *Sir Harold Wilson: Yorkshire Walter Mitty*, Macdonald & Janes 1977, p. 271.
17 Crossman, *op. cit.*, p. 982.
18 'I think it has arisen because I am one of George's close friends. I did not tell Harold Wilson that George wanted the Shadow Foreign Secretary's job.' *Evening Standard* Diary, February 21st, 1963.
19 Crossman, *op. cit.*, p. 983.
20 *Daily Express*, February 21st, 1963.
21 Anthony Howard and Richard West, *The Making of a Prime Minister*, Cape 1965, p. 26.
22 The Labour Party's 1918 Constitution. Clause 4, subsection 4: 'To secure for the workers by hand or brain the full fruits of their industry and the most equitable distribution thereof that may be possible, upon the basis of common ownership of the means of production, distribution and exchange and the best alternative system of popular administration and control of each industry or service.'
23 George Brown, *In My Way*, Penguin 1972, p. 74.
24 Paul Foot, *The Politics of Harold Wilson*, Penguin Special 1968, p. 123.
25 Press conference, February 10th, 1960.
26 Dudley Smith, *Harold Wilson*, Hale 1964, p. 208.
27 *Daily Express*, January 14th, 1963.
28 Jeff Nuttall, *Bomb Culture*, Paladin 1970, p. 51.
29 Bertrand Russell, *Autobiography*, Unwin 1978, p. 619.
30 See Chapter 10.
31 Peggy Duff, *Left, Left, Left*, Allison & Busby 1971, p. 144.
32 Howard and West, *op. cit.*, p. 39.
33 *New York Times*, April 2nd, 1963.
34 *New York Times*, April 1st, 1963.
35 Dr John Poole interview, April 1989.
36 John Poole, unpublished paper.
37 *Daily Mail*, October 2nd, 1963.

38 Faber & Faber 1963.

39 *Times* leader, October 2nd, 1963.

40 *Guardian*, October 1st, 1963.

41 Crossman, *op. cit.*, p. 829.

42 Labour Party Research Department, *12 Wasted Years*, September 1963, p. 423. The issue of nuclear disarmament is wonderfully fudged. You'd never know from reading this book that unilateralism had ever been an issue. See p. 362.

43 The Ministry of Disarmament went to *Times* defence correspondent Alun Gwynne-Jones, given a life peerage as Lord Chalfont.

44 Geoffrey Goodman, *The Awkward Warrior: Frank Cousins: His Life and Times*, Spokesman 1979, p. 374.

45 Crossman, *op. cit.*, pp. 1012, 987, 978, 976, 978, 1014.

46 Ted Eldred interview, March 1989.

47 *Daily Mail*, December 2nd, 1963.

48 Crossman, *op. cit.*, pp. 1042–3.

49 In July 1963: see Chapter 9.

50 Michael Foot interview, June 1st, 1989.

51 Tony Benn interview, February 27th, 1989.

Chapter Four: Self-Evident Truths (pp. 65–86)

1 'Still' needs qualifying. The Civil War successfully abolished slavery and for fifteen or twenty years afterwards the Reconstruction took place. During the 1880s it collapsed under white political power and the South retrenched under the 'separate but equal' ruling as handed down in the Plessy v. Ferguson decision of the Supreme Court in 1896 – the last word of that famous phrase being virtually ignored for over fifty years.

2 James Baldwin, *Nobody Knows My Name*, Dell 1963, p. 89.

3 John Howard Griffin, *Black Like Me*, Signet 1960, p. 101.

4 Brink and Harris (eds), *The Negro Revolution in America*, Simon & Schuster 1964, p. 25.

5 John Lewis to Howell Raines in *My Soul Is Rested*, Penguin 1983, p. 99 (first pub. Putnam 1977).

6 Howard Zinn, *SNCC – The New Abolitionists*, Beacon 1964, p. 29.

7 Arthur Schlesinger, *Robert Kennedy – His Life and Times*, Houghton Mifflin 1978, p. 224.

8 This is RFK's own version as given in an interview in 1964. Harris Wofford wrote in his 1980 book (*Of Kennedys and Kings*, Farrar, Straus & Giroux 1980) that RFK called Mitchell direct, out of anger and at the prompting of another Kennedy aide, Byron White.

9 Harry Golden, *Mr Kennedy and the Negroes*, World Publishing 1964, pp. 136, 170.

10 Burke Marshall interview, New York, May 1988.

11 *Ibid*.

12 A constitution which had as its main purpose the effective separation of power and the securing of the rights of individual states within the union, to which, it might seem, the Bill of Rights and most of the succeeding dozen amendments were added as valuable, if unworkable, afterthoughts on the civil liberties of the individual. For example, the XIVth amendment of 1866, 'nor shall any state deprive any person of life, liberty or property without due process of law; nor deny to any person within its jurisdiction the equal protection of the laws,' would render the discriminatory practices of the South illegal; or the XVth of 1869,

'The right of Citizens of the United States to vote shall not be denied or abridged by the United States or by any State on account of race, color or previous condition of servitude,' which was openly flouted in every Southern state.

13 In March 1961 Kennedy signed Executive Order 10925, establishing a Committee on Equal Employment Opportunity, but thereafter no further order on Civil Rights would be signed until November the following year, when the much vaunted Executive Order ending discrimination in federal aided housing finally surfaced. Several times during the campaign Kennedy had promised to end such discrimination 'at the stroke of a pen'. As he delayed the order, Civil Rights activists posted pens to the White House, which piled up on Wofford's desk.

14 Quoted in Schlesinger, *op. cit.*, p. 308.

15 RFK to *NYT* correspondent Anthony Lewis in 1964 interview for oral history program of John F. Kennedy Library, Boston. Transcribed and pub. as *Robert Kennedy In His Own Words*, Bantam 1988, p. 83.

16 Whatever image we in Britain may have of the FBI, this is not their role. The FBI at this time had only 6000 agents nationwide. Even had Hoover not been extremely hostile to the notion of using them (preferring to rule America with the word rather than the sword) it was hardly a function he could have asked them to carry out, and who in their right mind would have wanted a national force run by him?

17 Article in the *Nation*, 1964.

18 The limitations and desirability of this system are the subject of Burke Marshall's book *Federalism and Civil Rights*, Columbia 1964.

19 Raines, *op. cit.*, p. 310.

20 Nick Katzenbach interview, Princeton NJ. March 26th, 1988.

21 Lewis interview in *RFK In His Own Words*, *op. cit.*, p. 101. David J. Garrow in *Bearing The Cross* quotes JFK more specifically as saying some two years later 'SNCC – those sons of bitches'. Cape 1988, p. 296.

22 Mary King, *Freedom Song*, Morrow 1988, p. 141.

23 Victor Navasky, *Kennedy Justice*, Atheneum 1971, p. 250.

Chapter Five: Grinning at Nothing (pp. 87–125)

1 Geoffrey Moorhouse, *The Other England*, Penguin 1964, p. 140.

2 Quoted in Michael Braun, *Love Me Do*, Penguin 1964, p. 52.

3 *Melody Maker*, February 23rd, 1963.

4 George Martin, *All You Need Is Ears*, St Martin's Press 1979, p. 128.

5 *Melody Maker*, February 9th, 1963.

6 Martin, *op. cit.*, p. 129.

7 I say dutifully. It's not bad. It just doesn't bubble in the way the Pacemakers' version does, and bubble seems to be what the song required.

8 John Lennon, *New Musical Express*, March 8th, 1963.

9 Martin, *op. cit.*, p. 130.

10 Martin, *op. cit.*, p. 124.

11 Paramor was sent up by *That Was The Week That Was* for the number of times and ways he managed to get his name onto records.

12 Hank, like the Beatles, had learnt much from imported American records, studying the work of James Burton on Rick Nelson records, and, if memory serves, Jet Harris was the first bass player in Britain to use an electric bass rather than an acoustic double bass, and Hank was among the first to own a Fender electric guitar, brought back from the USA by Cliff. It was with the

Shadows that the classic line-up first took shape – lead, rhythm and bass guitars fronting a drummer. In Tommy Steele's act, at least as represented in his 'Story', Tommy played an acoustic six string, backed by a sax, drums and a double bass. Even Buddy Holly's band featured a double bass.

13 Bob Wooler, *Merseybeat*, no. 5, September 14th, 1961.
14 Quoted in Philip Norman, *Shout*, Corgi 1982, p. 180.
15 Spencer Leigh lists most of them in his Vermilion 1984 book *Let's Go Down the Cavern* – from The Aarons to The Zephyrs, via Faron's Flamingoes and Pete Picasso and the Rock Sculptors.
16 John Lennon interview, after Hollywood Bowl concert, for local radio in Los Angeles, August 24th or 25th, 1964.
17 John Lennon, *Melody Maker*, February 9th, 1963.
18 Holly was killed in February 1959. Original records by him, not reissues, continued to make the British charts for another six years.
19 Gillian Reynolds interview, London, November 7th 1989. Lennon, for example, didn't take a Saturday job to pay for his first guitar – for all her arguments about teddy boys his Aunt Mimi bought it for him.
20 *New Society*, February 20th, 1964.
21 Stanley Reynolds interview, London, November 25th, 1989.
22 Gillian Reynolds interview, London, November 7th, 1989.
23 Allan Williams, *The Man Who Gave the Beatles Away*, Elm Tree 1975, p. 129.
24 Paul McCartney, undated interview circa 1964.
25 John Lennon, quoted in Hunter Davies, *The Beatles: The Authorised Biography*, Mayflower 1968, pp. 96, 105.
26 Bob Wooler, interview given to Stanley Reynolds, *Guardian*, October 8th, 1963.
27 Billy Morton interview, Harrogate, January 20th, 1990.
28 Billy Kinsley still plays today, with Liverpool Express. Tony Crane still performs as one of the Merseybeats. David Bowie paid them the tribute of covering *Sorrow* on his LP *Pinups*, George Harrison listed it as one of his favourite records, and it's regarded as one of the best singles of the sixties.
29 Billy Kinsley interview, Liverpool, January 21st, 1990.
30 These two songs later made the charts recorded by the Fourmost and Cilla Black.
31 Brian Epstein, BBC interview, 1964.
32 *Merseybeat*, no. 15,February 22nd, 1962.
33 Er, Shome mishtake shurely? The Beatles were very proud of their 'drainies'.
34 *Evening Standard*, January 26th, 1963.
35 Martin, *op. cit.*, p. 131.
36 John Lennon, *Melody Maker*, February 9th, 1963.
37 e.g. Lee Curtis and the All Stars on Decca, the Swingin' Blue Jeans on HMV, the Dennisons on Decca, Faron's Flamingoes on Oriole, the Undertakers – who wore frock-coats and had speakers shaped like coffins – on Pye. In July the Oriole label spent two days in Liverpool taping ten unsigned acts.
38 The Fourmost, Tommy Quickly, Billy J. Kramer and Cilla Black all had debut singles written by the Beatles. Billy Kinsley adds that there was an emergent pecking order in the Epstein stable. Given the chance the Merseybeats would have liked to record *Hello Little Girl*, which went to the Fourmost.
39 Cilla Black was signed in September 1963, at Lennon's suggestion. She'd worked with the Big Three and King Size Taylor and the Dominoes. What's surprising is that she wasn't snapped up sooner. After the Beatles, Cilla is

Epstein's most enduring performer.

40 Johnny Gustafson interview, London, December 14th, 1989.

41 Billy Kinsley interview, Liverpool, January 21st, 1990.

42 *The Lennon Tapes*, BBC 1981, p. 56.

43 John Ford's Western, *The Man Who Shot Liberty Vallance*, made the previous year and on general release throughout 1963.

44 *Daily Mirror*, September 10th, 1963.

45 *Daily Mail*, October 21st, 1963.

46 Barry Norman interview, August 10th, 1990.

47 George had unwisely admitted to liking them. On their 1963 Christmas record, made for the fan club, the Beatles backtracked and offered suggestions for anything but jelly babies. In the USA, the following year, the fans, jelly babies being a British institution, pelted them with jelly beans.

48 Barry Norman: 'I was never aware of any conspiracy to hide the fact that the Beatles swore, got drunk and fucked . . . I was aware that they did all these things. I think one of the reasons these things never got explored in the newspapers was that newspapers were different in those days. They were much more conscious of the libel laws for one thing. And in a curious way there was far less intrusion into privacy and far less interest in absolute trivia than there is now. The *Mail* would not have been interested in that sort of thing. It might have been different on the tabloids, but I didn't work for a tabloid.'

49 The *Mirror*'s advertising showed the cost of the hi-fi hardware. A small tape recorder cost 33 gns, a record player with auto-changer 15 gns.

50 *Daily Mirror*, October 2nd, 1963.

51 Abrams was the author of the 1959 pamphlet *The Teenage Consumer*. The *Mirror*'s economic analysis seems only to be an updating of his original paper, which, for example, set teen spending power at £900 million.

52 *Daily Mirror*, October 9th, 1963.

53 *Daily Telegraph* leader, November 2nd, 1963.

54 *News of the World*, November 17th, 1963.

55 Lizzie Bawden interview, London, November 27th, 1989.

56 *Daily Telegraph* leader, November 2nd, 1963.

57 *New Statesman*, February 28th, 1964.

58 *Guardian*, October 8th, 1963.

59 EMI sales figures for 1963: sales £84,357,000; pretax profit £5,058,000. *Times*, December 6th, 1963. It's worth noting the Beatles–Epstein–Liverpool achievement in figures. Epstein's acts topped the charts for thirty-seven weeks in 1963. In the twelve months from the Beatles' first No. 1 Liverpool acts topped the charts thirteen times. The *Melody Maker* top twenty for December 7th recorded eleven entries for Lennon and McCartney:

   1 *I Want To Hold Your Hand*

   2 *She Loves You*

   6 *I'll Keep You Satisfied* – rec. Billy J. Kramer

  11 *Twist and Shout* (EP)

  17 *Beatles' Hits* (EP

  19 *Beatles' No. 1* (EP)

  21 *I Wanna Be Your Man* – rec. the Rolling Stones

  43 *Hello Little Girl* – rec. the Fourmost

  49 *Love of the Loved* – rec. Cilla Black

  No. 1 LP: *With the Beatles*

  No. 2 LP: *Please Please Me*

60 *Times*, February 17th, 1964.

61 *Daily Mirror*, December 9th, 1963.

62 *Observer*, November 10th, 1963.

63 *Daily Mirror*, November 19th and 20th, 1963.

64 *Times*, November 18th, 1963.

65 *Times*, December 27th, 1963.

66 *Daily Mirror*, January 8th, 1964.

67 *Daily Mirror*, November 2nd, 1963.

68 *Daily Mirror*, February 7th, 1964.

69 *Daily Miror*, October 7th, 1963.

70 *Daily Mirror*, September 19th, 1963.

71 Josie Neap interview, London, December 3rd, 1990.

72 That said, it was 1965 before they put out one of their own songs as a single. 'The Last Time' went to No. 1 in March of that year.

73 Lennon's home with Aunt Mimi was in Menlove Avenue, one of the most well-to-do streets in Liverpool.

74 Asked why he wore so many rings on his fingers, Ringo replied that he couldn't get them all through his nose.

75 On their 1963 Christmas record, Lennon said it had been 'a really gear year'. Twelve months earlier the phrase would have meant nothing.

76 *Today*, June 22nd, 1963.

77 Stanley Reynolds interview, London, November 25th, 1989.

78 Later the Earl of Harlech.

79 Michael Braun, *Love Me Do*, Penguin 1964, pp. 120–1.

80 Questions about this were later raised in the Commons.

81 *Melody Maker*, November 9th, 1963.

82 *Daily Express*, January 10th, 1964.

83 Asked too often if he wore a wig, Lennon said if he did it was the only wig with real dandruff.

84 'Meet the Beatles', their first American LP, sold four and a half million copies.

85 Jan Wenner, *Lennon Remembers*, Penguin 1970, pp. 45–6.

Chapter Six: Unholy Joy (pp. 126–175)

1 Bernard Levin, *The Pendulum Years*, Cape 1970, p. 62.

2 Diary for July 7th, 1963 in Harold Macmillan, *At the End of the Day*, Macmillan 1973.

3 *Hansard* for March 21st, 1963.

4 Andrew Roth interview, London, August 9th, 1988.

5 Mandy Rice-Davies interview, London, December 5th, 1988.

6 Mandy Rice-Davies (with Shirley Flack), *Mandy*, Michael Joseph 1980, p. 120.

7 115,000 immigrants entered Britain in 1961.

8 Macmillan, *op. cit.*, p. 437.

9 On the other hand there are rumours that the CIA 'lifted' Ivanov.

10 See *Hansard* for June 17th, 1963.

11 Tom Mangold interview, London, August 8th, 1988.

12 *Westminster Confidential*, March 1963, reprinted in the Denning Report, September 1963.

13 March 15th, 1963.

14 *Sunday Pictorial*, March 17th, 1963.

15 *Hansard* for March 21st, 1963.

16 See Macmillan's speech, June 17th, 1963.

17 *Hansard* for March 22nd, 1963.

18 Diary for March 22nd, 1963, in Macmillan, *op. cit.*, p. 439. If this seems quaint and unworldly, gullible even, it is at least preferable to the knowing priggishness of Crossman's 'Keeler and her Negro friends' and 'I can't think of a more humiliating and discrediting story than that of the Secretary of State for War being involved with *people of this kind.*' Crossman, *Diaries*, Hamish Hamilton and Cape, 1981.

19 *Hansard* for March 22nd, 1963.

20 Macleod, quoted in Anthony Howard and Richard West, *The Making of the Prime Minister*, Cape 1965.

21 Levin. *op. cit.*, p. 61.

22 Wayland Young, *The Profumo Affair: Aspects of Conservatism*, Penguin 1963, p. 33.

23 *Times*, June 11th, 1963.

24 Wayland Young, *op. cit.*, pp. 20, 39.

25 *Hansard* for June 17th, 1963.

26 Enoch Powell interview, London, October 18th, 1989.

27 Norman Shrapnel, *The Performers*, Constable 1978, p. 30.

28 Crossman, *op. cit.*, p. 992.

29 *Hansard* for June 17th, 1963.

30 George Wigg, *George Wigg*, Michael Joseph 1972, p. 285.

31 Tony Benn, *Out of the Wilderness*, Hutchinson 1987, p. 37.

32 Ludovic Kennedy, *The Trial of Stephen Ward*, Penguin 1965, p. 25.

33 *Ibid.*, p. 22.

34 *Ibid.*, p. 210.

35 'Vicissitudes of Adolescence', broadcast November 1962, pub. in G. M. Carstairs, *This Island Now*, Penguin 1963, p. 49.

36 Kennedy, *op. cit.*, p. 59.

37 Macmillan, *op. cit.*, pp. 450–1.

38 Tom Mangold interview, London, August 8th, 1988.

39 In many ways this excellent book, by a Labour peer, reads like the manifesto for the vision of the sixties yet to be. Lord Kennet attacks the 'vacuous, aimless' upper class who lived off others. He also called for the legalisation of marijuana.

Chapter Seven: Bishops in Outer Space (pp. 176–187)

1 The Rev. Shergold reappeared in 1991, still astride his motorbike, to advertise Wrangler Jeans on ITV.

2 David Boulton, *Tribune*, April 12th, 1963.

3 C. H. Rolph (ed.), *The Trial of Lady Chatterley*, Penguin 1961, pp. 70–1.

4 Bernard Levin, *The Pendulum Years*, Cape 1970, p. 105.

5 John Robinson, *Honest To God*, SCM 1963, pp. 7–8.

6 The idea of the new university was the subject of Prof. Albert Sloman's 1963 Reith lectures. In 1964 Sloman got his new university at Essex.

7 Robinson, *op. cit.*, pp. 13–19.

8 *Time & Tide*, April 4th–10th, 1963.

9 Eric James, *A Life of John Robinson*, Collins 1987, pp. 120–1.

10 *Sunday Telegraph*, March 24th, 1963.

11 *Observer*, March 24th, 1963.

12 Eric James interview, Southwark, December 12th, 1990.

13 Dr Robinson's biographer, Eric James, offers another perspective on this: 'John was the most traditional believer there ever was. He was trying to

reinterpret it – a deeply, deeply believing man . . . It's usually people who don't understand the subject who think that numbers in church are really very significant . . . John certainly never thought that: T. S. Eliot's "Take no thought for the harvest but only for proper sowing" is very important.' Interview, Southwark, December 12th, 1990.

14 Robinson, *op. cit.*, p. 87.

15 *Ibid.*, p. 102.

16 *Ibid.*, p. 119.

17 *The Times*, April 4th, 1963.

18 The phrase is slightly older than the issue. It is held to have originated in the Catholic church in 1956. It was not meant positively.

19 Kenneth Tynan, *A View of the English Stage*, Paladin 1975, p. 366.

20 Quoted in Ned Sherrin and David Frost (eds), *That Was The Week That Was*, W. H. Allen. 1963, p. 156.

21 *Daily Mail*, February 2nd, 1962.

22 *Observer*, November 1963, reprinted in Cyril Dunn (ed.), *The Observer Revisited 1963–4*, Hodder & Stoughton 1964, p. 212.

23 *Observer*, March 24th, 1963.

24 *Daily Mail*, April 17th, 1964.

25 *Daily Mirror*, April 17th, 1964.

Chapter Eight: In the Middle of the Beast (pp. 188–218)

1 James Baldwin, *The Fire Next Time*, Dell 1988, p. 83.

2 *Nation*, July 19th, 1965, pp. 38–9.

3 Mary King, *Freedom Song*, Morrow 1988, pp. 222–3.

4 John Lewis interview, Washington DC, October 5th, 1988.

5 Presidential Tape 86.2, John F. Kennedy Library, Boston.

6 Little Rock, Arkansas, August 1957. The troops were there for weeks, and the National Guard on duty for two years, guarding Black high school children.

7 Nick Katzenbach interview, Princeton NJ, March 26th, 1988.

8 Burke Marshall interview, New York, May 2nd, 1988.

9 White House meeting, June 10th, 1963.

10 Television interview, June 10th, 1963.

11 Katzenbach interview, Princeton NJ, March 26th, 1988.

12 Victor Navasky, *Kennedy Justice*, Atheneum 1971.

13 Howell Raines, *My Soul Is Rested*, Penguin 1983, p. 330.

14 Theodore C. Sorensen, *Kennedy*, Bantam 1966, p. 556.

15 *I.F.'s Weekly*, October 8th, 1962.

16 The bill never passed committee stage.

17 Herbert Parmet, *JFK: The Presidency of John F. Kennedy*, Penguin 1984, p. 270.

18 Katzenbach: 'The problem with the Vice-Presidency is that people are inclined to overlook it . . . I can remember occasions when Kennedy would say, "Where's the Vice-President? Didn't someone invite the Vice-President to this meeting?" Then he'd say, "Oh damn. We messed it up again."'

19 *I.F.'s Weekly*, February 6th, 1961.

20 Anyone who doubts this, I would refer to the Boston PBS series *Eyes On the Prize*, made in 1986.

21 *New York Times*, July 7th, 1963.

22 *Washington Post*, June 13th, 1963.

23 Lewis interview, 1964, in Edwin O. Guthman and Jeffrey Schulman (eds), *RFK*

In His Own Words, Bantam 1988, p. 182.

24 Baldwin, *op. cit.*, p. 141.

25 It's been said that RFK asked Baldwin et al., as he and his brother were wont to ask all who saw them on Civil Rights issues, 'What can you do to help us?' much as JFK had said in his inaugural address 'Ask not what your country can do for you, but what you can do for your country.' This question, if put to America's blacks, makes no sense at all after one hundred years of bad faith on the part of 'your country'.

26 Lena Horne and Richard Schickel, *Lena*, André Deutsch 1966, p. 280.

27 Preface to Burke Marshall, *Federalism and Civil Rights*, Columbia 1964.

28 Navasky, *op. cit.*, p. 148.

29 *New Statesman*, June 7th, 1963.

30 John Lewis interview, Washington DC, October 5th, 1988.

31 Arthur Schlesinger, *A Thousand Days*, Mayflower/Dell 1967, p. 744.

32 Malcolm X (with Alex Haley), *Autobiography*, Grove 1965, p. 280.

33 *Washington Post*, August 19th, 1963.

34 On September 9th, the *New York Times* revealed that $250,000 a month had been channelled to Diem's raiders by the CIA. The US government declined to comment, but 'officials' in Washington refused even to stand by their own denials, 'because they simply do not know what is being done by the CIA in Saigon.' See chapter 12.

35 Dick Gregory (with Richard Lipsyte), *Nigger*, Unwin 1965, p. 211.

36 Civil Rights workers had picketed a store belonging to a white man who had served on an all white jury, which had dismissed charges against a Sherriff accused of shooting a black prisoner in his custody. The federal government prosecuted the demonstrators. The contrast between this and the government's inactivity on so many cases of white brutality enraged many Civil Rights activists.

37 Reuther had raised $160,000 in bail money for the jailed Birmingham protesters in May.

38 Stephen B. Oates, *Let the Trumpet Sound*, Mentor 1982, p. 254; John A. Williams, *This is My Country Too*, Signet 1966, p. 149, quoted in Schlesinger, *Robert Kennedy: His Life and Times*, Houghton Mifflin 1978, p. 366. Schlesinger also quotes the first report in his *A Thousand Days*.

39 Interview with Lee C. White, White House aide, pub. in Charles and Barbara Whalen, *The Longest Debate*, Mentor 1986, p. 27.

40 Audio log tape no. 108.2, John F.Kennedy Library, Boston.

41 *Ibid*.

42 *New York Times*, August 29th, 1963.

43 David Garrow, *Bearing the Cross*, Cape 1989, p. 285.

44 Katzenbach interview, Princéton NJ, March 26th, 1988.

45 Howard Zinn, *SNCC: The New Abolitionists*, Beacon 1964, pp. 230, 239.

46 Harry Golden, *Mr Kennedy and the Negroes*, World Publishing 1964, p. 125.

47 *Washington Post*, June 13th, 1963.

48 Robert Penn Warren, *Segregation*, Vintage 1961, p. 115. Orig. 1956.

49 *Ibid*., p. 109.

50 Interview pub. in Raines, *op. cit.*, p. 461.

51 More likely to be 1964.

Chapter Nine: Cloth Capocalypse (pp. 219–270)

1 Raymond Williams, *The Long Revolution*, Penguin 1965, p. 361. Orig. 1961.

2 Marshall McLuhan, *Understanding Media*, Sphere 1967, p. 355. Orig. 1964.

3 Brian Jackson, *Working Class Community*, Penguin 1972, p. 168.

4 Richard Hoggart, *The Uses of Literacy*, Penguin 1958, pp. 281–2.

5 *Encounter*, January 1960, pp. 42–5.

6 America's broadcast of the Coronation bore out the worst fears of advertising in 1953. Not only was the programme interrupted to allow J. Fred Muggs, a chimpanzee, to plug a product, but just before the moment of crowning the programme broke to advertise deodorant.

7 Raymond Williams, *Communications*, Penguin 1962, pp. 73, 129.

8 Asa Briggs, *The BBC: The First Fifty Years*, Oxford 1985.

9 Three members resigned before the report was completed, including Peter Hall.

10 Pilkington report, Cmnd. 1753, June 1962, ch. VII.

11 *Ibid.*, paper 236.

12 *Ibid.*, papers 29 and 31.

13 'While there are no grounds for complacency, there is no reason to feel apologetic, or ashamed of TV. Television companies feel very anxious of their responsibility.' Kirkpatrick, 1959, quoted in Clive Jenkins, *Power Behind the Screen*, MacGibbon & Kee 1961, p. 256.

14 *Ibid.*, ch. VII.

15 *Ibid.*, ch. V.

16 *Ibid.*, ch. V.

17 *Ibid.*, ch. VI.

18 Sir Hugh Greene, *The Third Floor Front*, Bodley Head 1969, pp. 58–9.

19 *Encounter*, August 1962.

20 Pilkington report, paper 232.

21 Philip Abrams, 'Radio and Television' in Denys Thompson (ed.), *Discrimination and Popular Culture*, Penguin 1964, p. 58.

22 McLuhan, *op. cit.*, Sphere 1967, pp. 343, 354. Orig. 1964.

23 First episode, Troy Kennedy Martin, 'Four of a Kind'.

24 Alan Plater, 'A Quiet Night' in Michael Marland (ed.), *Z Cars*, Longmans 1968, pp. 59–60.

25 Peter Black, *The Biggest Aspidistra in the World*, BBC 1972, p. 214.

26 Sydney Newman interview, London, April 4th, 1990.

27 Ian Fleming, *Casino Royale*, Pan 1961, p. 47.

28 Ian Fleming, *From Russia With Love*, Pan 1963, p. 45.

29 'I write for warm-blooded people . . . I aim for total stimulation of the reader all the way through, even to his taste buds.' Ian Fleming, quoted in *Sphere History of Literature in the English Language* vol.7, 1970.

30 Fleming, *Casino Royale*, p. 31.

31 Ian Fleming, *Thunderball*, Pan 1961, pp. 67–8.

32 *New Statesman*, April 5th, 1958.

33 *Today*, April 21st, 1962.

34 Fleming, *Casino Royale*, p. 102.

35 *Today* folded in the summer of 1964.

36 Politics frequently came to the aid of Fleming. Gaitskell and Kennedy were both known as fans of the James Bond books. When Kennedy's top ten books were listed in *Life*, with *From Russia With Love* at no. 9, sales of Bond in the USA began to rise.

37 Barry Norman interview, Datchworth, August 10th, 1990.

38 Quoted in Richard Gant, *Sean Connery: Gilt Edged Bond*, Mayflower 1967, p. 44.

39 Ian Fleming, *The Man with the Golden Gun*, Cape 1965.
40 Jack Trevor Story, *Live Now Pay Later*, Savoy 1980, p. 17. Orig. 1963.
41 *Ibid.*, p. 22.
42 One of Heath's better jokes was to point out that he was neither a Lord nor a privy nor a seal.
43 Story, *op. cit.*, p. 40.
44 Dave Wallis, *Only Lovers Left Alive*, Blond 1964, pp. 47–8.
45 *Ibid.*, p. 182.
46 *Ibid.*, pp. 50–1.
47 Bruce Lacey interview, Norfolk, November 27th, 1990.
48 Bernard Levin interview, London, July 31st, 1990.
49 *Daily Mail*, January 25th, 1963.
50 Charles Marowitz, *Plays and Players*, March 1963.
51 *Daily Mail*, January 30th, 1963.
52 Reprinted in Cyril Dunn (ed.), *The Observer Revisited*, Hodder & Stoughton 1964, pp. 204–5.
53 Victor Spinetti interview, August 8th, 1990.
54 *New Statesman*, July 30th, 1963.
55 *Daily Mail*, February 1st, 1963.
56 Walter Lassally. *Itinerant Cameraman*, John Murray 1987, p. 136.
57 Daniel Farson interview with Barry Norman, *Daily Mail*, October 26th, 1962.
58 Quoted in Michael Wale, 'Sex and Sympathy', *Plays and Players*, March 1963.
59 *Ibid*.
60 *The Daniel Farson Black and White Picture Show*, Lemon Tree 1976, p. 83.
61 Sydney Newman interview, London, April 4th, 1990.
62 *A Night Out* was broadcast in 1960. It topped the TAM ratings, beating even *Sunday Night at the London Palladium*, which preceded *Armchair Theatre*.
63 Sydney Newman, quoted in Jeremy Bentham, *Dr Who: The Early Years*, W. H. Allen 1986, p. 39.
64 Penelope Houston, *The Contemporary Cinema*, Penguin 1963, pp. 123–4.
65 *Observer*, November 1963, reprinted in *Observer Revisited*, *op. cit.*, p. 196.
66 Penelope Houston, *op. cit.*, p. 124.
67 *Daily Mail*, September 14th, 1963.
68 Barry Norman interview, Datchworth, August 10th, 1990.
69 *The Times* referred to Barton's text as being 'unearthed out of a great deal of old iron . . . what emerges is a view of history that restores the connexion between political tactics and the basic human passions.' August 14th, 1963.
70 *Daily Mail*, August 21st, 1963.
71 Reprinted in *Observer Revisited*, *op. cit.*, pp. 202–3.
72 *Daily Mail*, June 26th, 1963.
73 Walter Lassally, *Itinerant Cameraman*, John Murray 1987, pp. 76–7.
74 Barry Norman column, *Daily Mail*, July 29th, 1963.
75 'The Bedsitter', broadcast May 26th, 1961.
76 *Time and Tide*, January 24th–30th, 1963.
77 *Sunday Pictorial*, January 6th, 1963.
78 David Nathan, *The Laughtermakers*, Peter Owen 1971, p. 134.
79 'The Lodger', recorded January 24th, 1964, published in Ray Galton and Alan Simpson, *Steptoe and Son*, Longman 1971, p. 48.

Chapter Ten: The Emperor of Ice Cream (pp. 271–309)

1 *Encounter*, July 1963.

2 Michael Shanks, *The Stagnant Society*, Penguin 1961, p. 29.
3 George Brown, *In My Way*, Penguin 1972, p. 55.
4 Diary, July 7th, 1963, in Harold Macmillan, *At the End of the Day*, Macmillan 1973, p. 44.
5 Macmillan would later say that he sent Hailsham as a way of bolstering his reputation in the leadership contest.
6 Diary for July 25th, 1963, in Macmillan, *op. cit.*, p. 484.
7 *Ibid.*
8 *Sunday Pictorial*, January 6th, 1963.
9 *Daily Sketch*, March 11th, 1963.
10 *Daily Mail*, July 8th, 1963.
11 Prince Charles had been discovered in a local pub drinking cherry brandy in June. He was fourteen years old.
12 Shanks, *op. cit.*, pp. 212–13.
13 Anthony Hartley, *A State of England*, Hutchinson 1963, p. 228.
14 Anthony Howard, *New Statesman*, August 16th, 1963.
15 *Hansard*, July 8th, 1963.
16 Stanley Alderson, *Housing*, Penguin 1962, p. 87.
17 Shirley Green, *Rachman*, Hamlyn 1981, p. 225.
18 Alderson, *op. cit.*, p. 125.
19 Ian Nairn, *Nairn's London*, Penguin 1966, p. 61.
20 *New Statesman*, December 6th, 1963.
21 *Daily Mail*, November 25th, 1963.
22 *New Statesman*, July 24th, 1964.
23 *Spectator*, July 31st, 1964.
24 Bernard Levin, *The Pendulum Years*, Cape 1970, p. 155.
25 *Encounter*, October 1960.
26 1963 was a year of government reports – the Pilkington, the Trend, the Beeching and the Buchanan, already mentioned, as well as the Robbins report on higher education and the Plowden report on primary education.
27 *Hansard*, April 30th, 1963.
28 Harold Macmillan, *Pointing the Way*, Macmillan 1972, p. 158.
29 See Chapter 3.
30 Ned Sherrin and David Frost (eds), *That Was The Week That Was*, W. H. Allen, 1963, p. 114.
31 Alistair Horne, *Macmillan: The Official Biography, II, 1957–86*, Macmillan 1989, p. 529.
32 Diary, September 5th, 1963, in *At The End of the Day*, p. 492.
33 Diary, October 7th, 1963, *ibid.*, p. 499.
34 R. A. Butler, *The Art of the Possible*, Penguin 1973, p. 237.
35 Diary for September 5th, 1963, in Horne, *op. cit.*, p. 531.
36 *Daily Mail*, October 14th, 1963.
37 *Daily Express*, October 11th, 1963.
38 *Daily Mail*, October 11th, 1963. In *The Art of the Possible* (p. 238), Butler has a diary entry for July 1963, 'I think a leader in the Conservative party should *emerge* and that is the only lasting way of achieving a result.
39 *Guardian*, October 11th, 1963.
40 *New Statesman*, February 22nd, 1963.
41 Diary, September 11th, 1963, in Horne, *op. cit.*, p. 532.
42 Harold Evans, *Downing Street Diary*, Hodder & Stoughton 1981, p. 296.
43 Enoch Powell interview, London, October 18th, 1989.

44 Evans, *op. cit.*, p. 297.
45 The most common argument as to why Maudling alone of the younger men was a candidate is that Macleod had been present at the meeting of the 'Famous Five' and Heath was unmarried – hence both were disqualified in the prevailing 'safe' climate.
46 *Guardian*, October 10th, 1963.
47 *Daily Mail*, October 10th, 1963.
48 *Daily Mail*, October 9th, 1963.
49 *Daily Mail*, October 10th, 1963.
50 *Sunday Express*, October 13th, 1963.
51 *Daily Mail*, October 11th, 1963.
52 Randolph Churchill, *The Fight for the Tory Leadership*, Heinemann 1964, p. 108.
53 *Times*, October 11th, 1963.
54 *Daily Express*, October 11th, 1963.
55 *New Statesman*, October 18th, 1963.
56 Lord Home, *The Way the Wind Blows*, Collins 1976, p. 182.
57 Tony Benn, *Out of the Wilderness*, Hutchinson 1988, p. 68.
58 *Daily Mail*, October 11th, 1963.
59 Lord Hailsham, *The Door Wherein I Went*, Collins 1975, p. 223.
60 Macmillan merely records that he told Hailsham that he *hoped* he would be a candidate. Hailsham's most recent memoir, *A Sparrow's Flight* – not so much a sequel more a remake – modifies the account of his conversation with Macmillan slightly, in that Macmillan drops the 'if'. Hailsham terms the conversation a 'direct intimation' of the PM's wish that Hailsham succeed him. The first tip-off Hailsham receives is from Lord Poole, circa June 1963. In Michael Cockerell's BBC documentary, aired as Hailsham's book was published, Hailsham says of his entering the contest 'I was only doing what Harold had told me to.' Of his photo-opportunism he adds, 'Some odious people subsequently tried to make out that I did this only to advertise my candidature, and I am sorry to say that this abominable calumny was fed by my detractors to Harold in the nursing home and was subsequently swallowed hook, line and sinker by Alistair Horne.' *A Sparrow's Flight*, Collins 1990, p. 354.
61 Evans, *op. cit.*, p. 298.
62 *New Statesman*, October 18th, 1963.
63 Quoted in Kenneth Young, *Sir Alec Douglas-Home*, Dent 1970, p. 164.
64 John Beavan, *Daily Mirror*, October 19th, 1963.
65 *News of the World*, October 13th, 1963.
66 *News of the World*, October 13th, 1963.
67 Whilst perfectly plausible, probable even, I cannot find that Lord Home makes mention of this. The source for this, and for Home's call to Redmayne, is John Dickie's *The Uncommon Commoner*, Pall Mall 1964.
68 *Listener*, December 19th, 1963.
69 Butler, *op. cit.*, p. 246.
70 Neither Hailsham nor Churchill mentions this in their books.
71 *Daily Mail*, October 18th, 1963.
72 Enoch Powell interview, London, October 18th, 1989.
73 *Daily Mail*, October 19th, 1963.
74 *Sunday Express*, October 20th, 1963.
75 *Daily Mail*, October 19th, 1963.
76 *Sunday Express*, October 20th, 1963.

77 *Sunday Times*, October 20th, 1963.

78 *Sunday Express*, October 20th, 1963.

79 Since Macmillan kept the written results of the soundings, and none of the pollsters chose to gainsay him in his lifetime, the fact that Dilhorne had recorded Macleod as voting for Home did not emerge until Alistair Horne gained access to the Macmillan archives for the official biography. Since the cabinet had nineteen members, eleven votes cast for others would have tipped the balance against Home.

80 Churchill, *op. cit.*, pp. 134, 154.

81 Tony Benn interview with John Mortimer, pub. in *In Character*, Penguin 1984, p. 41.

82 Tony Benn interview, Notting Hill, February 27th, 1989.

Chapter Eleven: Mischief (pp. 310–346)

1 *Nation*, April 26th, 1958.

2 Uttered towards the end of 1963: Hugh Greene, *The Third Floor Front*, Bodley Head 1969, p. 135.

3 Pike (ed.), *Ah Mischief*, Faber 1983.

4 At Edinburgh Drama Festival 1963, quoted in *Plays and Players*, November 1963. p. 32.

5 Peter Cook interview, Hampstead, August 13th, 1990. All quotations are from this, unless otherwise indicated.

6 Introduction to Alan Bennett, Peter Cook, Jonathan Miller and Dudley Moore, ed. Wilmut, *The Complete Beyond the Fringe*, Methuen 1987, pp. 8–9.

7 Kenneth Tynan, *A View of the English Stage*, Paladin 1976, p. 311.

8 *Complete Beyond the Fringe*, *op. cit.*, pp. 112–13.

9 Tynan, *op. cit.*, p. 310.

10 Peter Cook disagrees with the 'often', adding that he was usually to be seen in *Beyond the Fringe* in London or New York.

11 Ned Sherrin, *A Small Thing Like An Earthquake*, Weidenfeld 1983, p. 60.

12 *Daily Mail*, March 20th, 1963.

13 Barry Norman interview, Datchworth, August 10th, 1990.

14 Willie Rushton interview, London, August 15th, 1990.

15 Peter Roberts, *Plays and Players*, July 1963.

16 Sherrin, *op. cit.*, p. 60.

17 *Daily Mail*, September 24th, 1963.

18 *Ibid*.

19 Willie Rushton interview, London, August 15th, 1990.

20 *Private Eye*, October 25th, 1961.

21 *Private Eye*, March 22nd, 1963. Montesi was the subject of an Italian political scandal in the fifties.

22 *Private Eye*, April 5th, 1963.

23 Richard Ingrams (ed.), *The Life and Times of Private Eye*, Penguin 1971, p. 15.

24 Rushton adds that the deciding factor was Ingrams' assertion that Schweitzer was 'a rotten organist'.

25 Claud Cockburn, *I Claud . . .* , Penguin 1967, p. 432.

26 Richard Ingrams' account in *The Life and Times of Private Eye* says the D notices were accepted but none ever arrived.

27 *Private Eye*, July 12th, 1963.

28 Bernard Levin interview, London, July 31st, 1990.

29 Ingrams, *op. cit.*, p. 9.

30 Quoted in Alasdair Milne, *DG: The Memoirs of a British Broadcaster*, Hodder & Stoughton 1988, p. 32.
31 Grace Wyndham Goldie, *Facing the Nation*, Bodley Head 1977, ch. 13.
32 Ned Sherrin and David Frost, *That Was The Week That Was*, W. H. Allen 1963, p. 81.
33 *Sunday Pictorial*, February 3rd, 1963.
34 Sherrin and Frost, *op. cit.*, p. 128.
35 *British Weekly and Christian World*, May 30th, 1963.
36 Michael Tracey, *A Variety of Lives: A Biography of Sir Hugh Greene*, Bodley Head 1983, p. 208 and Milne, *op. cit.*, p. 38.
37 Quoted in Tracey, *op. cit.*, pp. 210–11. Not, surprisingly, to be found in Greene's own pocket memoir.
38 *Sunday Express*, April 21st, 1963.
39 Bernard Levin interview, London, July 31st, 1990.
40 *Time and Tide*, January 23rd, 1963.
41 *Sunday Pictorial*, February 10th, 1963.
42 *Daily Mail*, January 25th, 1963.
43 *Time and Tide*, January 30th, 1963.
44 Greene, *op. cit.*, p. 85.
45 *Ibid.*, p. 82
46 *Sunday Mirror*, November 12th, 1963.
47 Quoted in Milne, *op. cit.*, ch. 3 and Goldie, *op. cit.*, ch. 13.
48 Ned Sherrin interview, August 1st, 1990.
49 Quoted in Goldie, *op. cit.*, ch. 13.
50 *Sunday Mirror*, November 14th, 1963.
51 Greene, *op. cit.*, pp. 134–5.
52 Mary Whitehouse, *A Most Dangerous Woman*, Lion 1982, p. 13.

Chapter Twelve: All Along the Watchtower (pp. 347–370)
1 Press Conference, April 7th, 1954.
2 Press Conference, May 11th, 1954.
3 Press Conference, May 12th, 1955.
4 Pentagon Papers, vol II, reprinted in Williams, McCormick, Gardner and LaFeber, *America in Vietnam: A Documentary History*, Norton 1989, p. 186.
5 Theodore C. Sorensen, *Kennedy*, Bantam 1966, p. 722.
6 Pentagon Papers, in *America in Vietnam*, *op. cit.*, p. 188.
7 Sorensen, *op. cit.*, p. 722.
8 Quoted in Michael Maclear, *Vietnam: The Ten Thousand Day War*, Methuen 1981, pp. 78–9.
9 Very recently Khrushchev's son Sergei has suggested that his father may well have been drunk when he said this. London *Evening Standard*, November 27th, 1990.
10 Quoted in Maclear, *op. cit.*, p. 81.
11 Speech to the American Society of Newspaper Editors, April 20th, 1961.
12 Department of Defense papers, in *America in Vietnam*, *op. cit.*, pp. 191–3.
13 Department of State Bulletin, January 1st, 1962, reproduced in Marvin E. Gettleman (ed.), *Vietnam: History, Documents and Opinions on a Major World Crisis*, Penguin Special 1966, pp. 216–19.
14 John Ranelagh, *The Agency: The Rise and Fall of the CIA*, Simon & Schuster 1986, p. 466.
15 Ben Bradlee, *Conversations with Kennedy*, Pocket Books, 1976, p. 59.

16 *New York Times*, September 11th, 1963.

17 David Halberstam, *The Making of a Quagmire*, Bantam 1964, pp. 223–4.
Robert Kennedy, interviewed a few months later, credited Halberstam's
reporting with significantly shaping public opinion in the USA.

18 *Ibid*.

19 *New York Times*, September 11th, 1963.

20 Quoted by David Halberstam, *New York Times*, November 6th, 1963.

21 Interview given by Conein to John Ranelagh, December 1989. Made available
by Ranelagh.

22 Senator Gravel (ed.), *Pentagon Papers*, Beacon 1971, vol II, p. 734. Lodge's
reply to this set the tone for all his dealings with Washington over the next few
weeks: ' . . . propose we go straight to Generals with our demands, without
informing Diem . . . [tell them] . . . it is in effect up to them whether to keep
him.' August 25th, 1963. Persuading Diem had ' . . . no chance of achieving
desired result', August 29th, 1963 ' . . . Whatever sanctions we may discern
should be directly tied to a promising coup d'état . . . in this connection I
believe we should contact [General] Big Minh and urge him along if he looks
like acting', September 19th, 1963. There is throughout a reluctance on the
part of the ambassador to offer Diem any chance to compromise.

23 In Edwin O. Guthman and Jeffrey Shulman (eds), *Robert Kennedy In His
Own Words* (1964 interview, John Bartlow Martin, p. 397) RFK says 'The
President was up at the Cape and they gave him a telegram. He thought it had
been approved by McNamara and Maxwell Taylor and everybody else. It had
not.' Yet in his 1967 book, *To Move a Nation*, Roger Hilsman states that JFK
actually participated in revisions. David Halberstam, in *The Best and the
Brightest*, Penguin 1983, writes that JFK was angry that the cable had been
composed and cleared in such a way as to 'leave an emergency exit for dissent'
(p. 323). What this confusion seems to have generated – fostered by RFK's
remark – is the implausible idea that the President was less than fully informed
and hence less than fully responsible.

24 Anthony Short, *The Origins of the Vietnam War*, Longman 1989, p. 266.

25 Pentagon Papers, reprinted in *America in Vietnam*, *op. cit.*, pp. 203–4.

26 CBS TV, September 2nd, 1963, reprinted in *America in Vietnam*, *op. cit.*,
p. 197.

27 If anyone was born to be one of history's footnotes it was Mme Nhu, the
Imelda Marcos of her day. Several years younger than Nhu, she was the 'face'
of the regime – slim, good-looking, vitriolic and renowned for her
outspokenness. She adopted Catholicism on her marriage and brought the
usual convert's zealotry to the faith – she succeeded in banning not only
prostitution, but also dancing and divorce, the latter to prevent her own
sister-in-law from getting one. She was widely held to be responsible for the
pettiness of the regime's repressions. At the time of Nhu's death she was in
Los Angeles – she might otherwise have been a victim of the crowd rather than
the conspirators – and skipped out of the Beverley Wilshire leaving a $1200 bill
unpaid. The *New York Times*, in 1963, ran with a headline 'NO NHUS IS
GOOD NEWS.'

28 *I.F.'s Weekly*, September 30th, 1963.

29 Hilsman details the cutbacks as being 'tobacco, condensed milk and so
on . . . ' in *To Move A Nation*, Doubleday, 1967, p. 500.

30 Gravel (ed.), *Pentagon Papers*, Document 144, of October 5th, 1963, outlined
three plans put forward by Minh. It's complicated stuff. The first of the plans

calls for the assassination of Nhu and Can, but not Diem – he is to stay in office. The other two schemes do not spell out Nhu's or Diem's fate. Reading between the lines, plan one sounds like a red herring, an unworkable plan to save Diem, that is bound to fail, thus leaving the fate of Diem in either of the other two plans open. Open, since he is to be removed by force, to assassination.

31 Pentagon Papers, reprinted in *America In Vietnam, op. cit.*, p. 207. Johnson repeats in his memoirs a prevalent myth, that Lodge offered 'assistance to ensure the President's personal safety.' (*The Vantage Point*, Weidenfeld 1971, p. 62). According to the Pentagon Papers, Lodge merely asked if Diem had heard that the plotters might be offering it. Even before the leaking of the Pentagon Papers, Hilsman had published an accurate account of this conversation in *To   Move a Nation*, 1967, p. 520.

32 William Colby, *Lost Victory*, Contemporary 1989, p. 154.

33 *New York Times*, November 6th, 1963.

34 Arthur Schlesinger, *A Thousand Days*, Mayflower/Dell 1967, p. 764.

35 *New York Times*, September 9th, 1963.

36 Interview given to Michael Maclear, quoted in Maclear, *op. cit.*, p. 101.

37 Interview with John Bartlow Martin, 1964, reprinted in *Robert Kennedy In His Own Words, op. cit.*, p. 397.

38 Just looking in the English press at this time reveals a virtual consensus on the American role in the killing of Diem. This, Karl E. Meyer writing in the *New Statesman*, November 8th, 1963, would not have been out of place in the *Sunday Telegraph*: 'Yet if the CIA was not responsible, surely the United States was? By its calculated rebuffs of the Diem regime, the US had all but explicitly invited a change.'

39 *I.F.'s Weekly*, December 23rd, 1963.

40 Joe Keegan interview, New York, March 12th, 1991.

41 Joan and Robert Morrison (eds), *From Camelot to Kent State*, Times 1987, p. 294.

42 *Ibid.*, p. 284.

43 In 1971 Daniel Ellsberg leaked the Pentagon Papers, which revealed much of the bloody story of US involvement in Vietnam. His prosecution was abandoned during the Watergate crisis, when it emerged that the 'plumbers' – so-called because they stopped leaks – had burgled the office of his psychoanalyst.

44 Policy Statement, January 1966, reprinted in Gettleman, *op. cit.*, p. 429.

45 *I.F.'s Weekly*, September 9th, 1968.

46 Quoted in Doris Kearns, *Lyndon Johnson and the American Dream*, Deutsch 1976, pp. 251, 260.

47 Paul Jacobs and Saul Landau, *The New Radicals*, Vintage 1966, pp. 150–5.

48 It can be argued that SDS was way ahead of Johnson. In April 1963 Hayden received $5000 from Walter Reuther of UAW to set up the Economic Research and Action Project (ERAP), which took students into the slum neighbourhoods in programmes to combat poverty and inculcate democratic participation. This too has been ascribed to the influence of both Harrington and the Civil Rights movement. 'By 1964 many students had already been South, and they returned North to perceive more clearly the same problems in their own backyard', Jack Newfield, *A Prophetic Minority*, Blond 1967, p. 137. Berkeley's Free Speech Movement [FSM] seems to me to represent one stage further on the road to the Yippies and Chicago '68, in that it began as a protest movement first and foremost, when Berkeley denied students the right to collect funds on campus

for the Civil Rights movement.

49 Kearns, *op. cit.*, p. 193.

50 Katzenbach's own position and perspective were well illustrated in an American documentary on LBJ in 1990. Katzenbach remarked that in the late Sixties Johnson would have been astounded to learn that anti-Vietnam protestors were sleeping at his house and at McNamara's as guests of their teenage children, and that the President would never have understood how the young felt about the war.

51 Newfield, *op. cit.*, pp. 144–5.

52 Kennedy had issued instructions to draw up a programme for a war on poverty three days before his death.

53 *Radical America*, Spring issue, April 1990, p. 50.

54 Preface to Jack Newfield, *op. cit.*, p. 18.

SELECT BIBLIOGRAPHY

Alderson, Stanley, *Housing*, Penguin 1962.
Amis, Kingsley, *The James Bond Dossier*, Cape 1965.
Baldwin, James, *Nobody Knows My Name*, Dell 1961.
Baldwin, James, *The Fire Next Time*, Dell 1988.
Barnet, Richard J., *Intervention and Revolution: America in the Third World*, Paladin 1970.
Barstow, Stan, *A Kind Of Loving*, Penguin 1962.
Barstow, Stan, *The Desperadoes*, Michael Joseph 1961.
Benn, Tony, *Out of the Wilderness*, Hutchinson 1987.
Bennett, Alan, Cook, Peter, Miller, Jonathan, and Moore, Dudley, ed.
Wilmut, *The Complete Beyond the Fringe*, Methuen 1987.
Bentham, Jeremy, *Dr Who: The Early Years*, W. H. Allen 1986.
Black, Peter, *The Biggest Aspidistra in the World*, BBC 1972.
Black, Peter, *The Mirror in the Corner*, Hutchinson 1972.
Bogdanor, V. and Skidelsky, R. (eds), *The Age Of Affluence*, Macmillan 1970.
Booker, Christopher, *The Neophiliacs*, Collins 1969.
Boorstin, Daniel, *The Image*, Penguin 1963.
Booth, Jerry and Lewis, Peter M., *The Invisible Medium*, Macmillan 1989.
Braun, Michael, *Love Me Do*, Penguin 1964.
Briggs, Asa, *The BBC The First Fifty Years*, Oxford 1985.
Brink, William and Harris, Louis (eds), *The Negro Revolution in America*, Simon & Schuster 1964.
Brittan, Samuel, *The Treasury under the Tories*, Penguin 1964.
Brown, George, *In My Way*, Penguin 1972.
Brown, Peter and Gaines, Stephen, *The Love You Make*, Pan 1984.
Butler, R. A., *The Art of the Possible*, Penguin 1973.
Carstairs, G. M., *This Island Now*, Penguin 1964.
Churchill, Randolph, *The Fight for the Tory Leadership*, Heinemann 1964.
Cockburn, Claud, *I, Claud . . .* , Penguin 1967.
Colby, William, *Lost Victory*, Contemporary 1989.
Coleman, Ray, *Brian Epstein*, Viking 1989.
Coleman, Ray, *John Lennon*, Futura 1985.
Crosland Susan, *Tony Crosland*, Coronet 1983.
Crossman, Richard, *Diaries*, (ed. Morgan), Hamish Hamilton/Cape 1976 and 1981.
Curran, James and Seaton, Jean, *Power Without Resonsibility: The Press and Broadcasting in Britain*, Fontana 1981.
Davies, Hunter, *The Beatles: The Authorised Biography*, Mayflower 1968.
Deacon, Richard with West, Nigel, *Spy!*, Grafton 1980.
Dickie, John, *The Uncommon Commoner*, Pall Mall 1964.
Duff, Peggy, *Left, Left, Left*, Allison and Busby 1971.
Evans, Harold, *Downing Street Diary*, Hodder & Stoughton 1981.

Fleming, Ian, *Casino Royale*, Pan 1961.

Fleming, Ian, *From Russia With Love*, Pan 1963.

Fleming, Ian, *The Man With The Golden Gun*, Cape 1965.

Fleming, Ian, *Thunderball*, Pan 1961.

Foot, Michael, *Aneurin Bevan vol. 2, 1945-60*, Paladin 1975.

Foot, Paul, *The Politics of Harold Wilson*, Penguin 1968.

Forman, James, *The Making of Black Revolutionaries*, Open Hand 1985.

Frady, Marshall, *Wallace*, NAL 1968.

Fraser, Ronald (ed.), *Work*, Penguin 1965.

Fyvel, T. R., *The Insecure Offenders*, Penguin 1963.

Galton, Ray and Simpson, Alan, *Steptoe and Son*, Longman 1971.

Gant, Richard, *Sean Connery: Gilt Edged Bond*, Mayflower 1967.

Garrow, David, *Bearing the Cross*, Cape 1989.

Gettleman, Marvin E. (ed.), *Vietnam*, Penguin 1966.

Golden, Harry, *Mr Kennedy and the Negroes*, World Publishing 1964.

Goldie, Grace Wyndham, *Facing the Nation*, Bodley Head 1977.

Goodman, Geoffrey, *The Awkward Warrior: Frank Cousins: His Life and Times*, Spokesman (1979) 1984.

Grant, Joanne (ed.), *Black Protest*, Fawcett 1983.

Gravel, Senator (ed.), *Pentagon Papers, vols 2, 3, and 5*, Beacon 1971.

Green, Shirley, *Rachman*, Hamlyn 1981.

Greene, Hugh, *The Third Floor Front*, Bodley Head 1969.

Gregory, Dick (with Lipsyte, Richard), *Nigger*, Unwin 1965.

Griffin, John Howard, *Black Like Me*, Signet 1960.

Guthman, Edwin O., and Shulman, Jeffrey (eds), *RFK In His Own Words*, Bantam 1988.

Hailsham, Lord, *A Sparrow's Flight*, Collins 1990.

Hailsham, Lord, *Science and Politics*, Faber & Faber 1963.

Hailsham, Lord, *The Door Wherein I Went*, Collins 1975.

Halberstam, David, *The Making of a Quagmire*, Ballantine 1989.

Halberstam, David, *The Best and the Brightest*, Penguin 1983.

Harrington, Michael, *The Other America*, Penguin 1963.

Hartley, Anthony, *A State of England*, Hutchinson 1963.

Hilsman, Roger, *To Move a Nation*, Doubleday 1967.

Hoggart, Richard, *The Uses of Literacy*, Penguin 1958.

Home, Lord, *The Way the Wind Blows*, Collins 1976.

Horne, Alistair, *Macmillan: The Official Biography, II, 1957–86*, Macmillan 1989.

Horne, Lena and Schickel, Richard, *Lena*, André Deutsch 1966.

Houston, Penelope, *The Contemporary Cinema*, Penguin 1963.

Howard, Anthony and West, Richard, *The Making of the Prime Minister*, Cape 1965.

Hughes, Emrys, *Sir Alec Douglas-Home: A Modern Conservative*, Housman 1964.

Hutchinson, George, *The Last Edwardian at No. Ten*, Quartet 1980.

Ingrams, Richard (ed.), *The Life and Times of Private Eye*, Penguin 1971.

Irving, Clive, Hall, Ron and Wallington, Jeremy, *Scandal '63*, Heinemann 1963.

Jackson, Brian, *Working Class Community*, Penguin 1972.

Jacobs, Paul and Landau, Saul, *The New Radicals*, Vintage 1966.

Kearns, Doris, *Lyndon Johnson and the American Dream*, Deutsch 1976.

Kennedy, Caroline and Knightley, Philip, *An Affair of State*, Cape 1987.

Kennedy, John F., *The Burden and the Glory*, Harper & Row 1964.

Kennedy, Ludovic, *The Trial of Stephen Ward*, Penguin 1965.

King, Martin Luther, *Why We Can't Wait*, Mentor 1964.
King, Mary, *Freedom Song*, Morrow 1988.
Lahr, John, *Prick Up Your Ears*, Penguin 1988.
Lassally, Walter, *Itinerant Cameraman*, John Murray 1987.
Leigh, Spencer, *Let's Go Down the Cavern*, Vermilion 1984.
Lennon, John, *The Lennon Tapes*, BBC 1981.
Lessing, Doris, *In Pursuit of the English*, Panther 1980.
Levin, Bernard, *The Pendulum Years*, Cape 1970.
Lewis, Peter, *The Fifties*, Heinemann 1978.
Maclear, Michael, *Vietnam: The Ten Thousand Day War*, Methuen 1981.
Macmillan, Harold, *At the End of the Day*, Macmillan 1973.
Macmillan, Harold, *Pointing the Way*, Macmillan 1972.
Macmillan, Harold, *Riding the Storm*, Macmillan 1971.
Marland, Michael (ed.), *Z Cars*, Longman 1968.
Marshall, Burke, *Federalism and Civil Rights*, Columbia 1964.
Martin, George, *All You Need Is Ears*, St Martin's Press 1979.
McKie, David and Cook, Chris, *The Decade of Disillusion*, Macmillan 1972.
McLuhan, Marshall, *The Gutenberg Galaxy*, Routledge 1962.
McLuhan, Marshall, *Understanding Media*, Sphere 1967.
Melly, George, *Owning Up*, Penguin 1970.
Melly, George, *Revolt into Style*, Oxford 1989.
Milne, Alasdair, *DG*, Hodder & Stoughton 1988.
Moorhouse, Geoffrey, *The Other England*, Penguin 1964.
Morrison, Joan and Robert K. (eds), *From Camelot to Kent State*, Times 1987.
Mortimer, John, *In Character*, Penguin 1984.
Nairn, Ian, *Nairn's London*, Penguin 1966.
Nathan, David, *The Laughtermakers*, Peter Owen 1971.
Nathan, David and Hancock, Freddie, *Hancock*, Coronet 1975.
Navasky, Victor, *Kennedy Justice*, Atheneum 1971.
Newfield, Jack, *Robert Kennedy: A Memoir*, Cape 1970.
Newfield, Jack, *A Prophetic Minority: The American New Left*, Blond 1967.
Norman, Philip, *Shout*, Corgi 1982.
Norman, Philip, *The Stones*, Elm Tree 1984.
Northcott, Jim, *Why Labour?*, Penguin 1964.
Nuttall, Jeff, *Bomb Culture*, Paladin 1970.
Oates, Stephen B., *Let the Trumpet Sound*, Mentor 1982.
Parmet, Herbert, *JFK: The Presidency of John F, Kennedy*, Penguin 1984.
Pearson, John, *The Life of Ian Fleming*, Cape 1966.
Pinter, Harold, *Plays Two*, Methuen 1988.
Raines, Howell, *My Soul Is Rested*, Penguin 1983.
Ranelagh, John, *The Agency: The Rise and Fall of the CIA*, Simon & Schuster 1986.
Rice-Davies, Mandy (with Flack, Shirley), *Mandy*, Michael Joseph 1980.
Riley, Tim, *Tell Me Why*, Bodley Head 1988.
Robinson, John, *Honest to God*, SCM 1963.
Robinson, John and Edwards, David, *The Honest to God Debate*, SCM 1963.
Rolph, C. H., *The Trial of Lady Chatterley*, Penguin 1961.
Roth, Andrew, *Sir Harold Wilson: Yorkshire Walter Mitty*, Macdonald &Janes 1977.
Rubin, Jerry, *Do It! Scenarios of the Revolution*, Cape 1970.
Russell, Bertrand, *Autobiography*, Unwin 1978.
Sampson, Anthony, *Anatomy of Britain*, Hodder & Stoughton 1962.

Sampson, Anthony, *Macmillan: A Study in Ambiguity*, Penguin 1967.

Schlesinger, Arthur, *A Thousand Days*, Mayflower/Dell 1967.

Schlesinger, Arthur, *Robert Kennedy, His Life and Times*, Houghton Mifflin 1978.

Schultheiss, Tom, *A Day In The Life*, Omnibus 1980.

Shanks, Michael, *The Stagnant Society*, Penguin 1961.

Short, Anthony, *The Origins of the Vietnam War*, Longman 1989.

Sherrin, Ned, *A Small Thing Like An Earthquake*, Weidenfeld 1983.

Sherrin, Ned and Frost, David (eds), *That Was The Week That Was*, W. H. Allen 1963.

Shrapnel, Norman, *The Performers*, Constable 1978.

Shulman, Milton, *The Least Worst Television in the World*, Barrie & Jenkins 1973.

Sillitoe, Alan, *Saturday Night and Sunday Morning*, Pan 1960.

Sillitoe, Alan F., *Britain in Figures*, Penguin 1973.

Sked, Alan and Cook, Chris, *Post War Britain*, Penguin 1979.

Smith, Dudley, *Harold Wilson*, Hale 1964.

Smith, Leslie, *Harold Wilson*, Fontana 1964.

Sorensen, Theodore C., *Kennedy*, Bantam 1966.

Stewart, Margaret, *Frank Cousins*, Hutchinson 1968.

Storey, David, *This Sporting Life*, Penguin 1963.

Story, Jack Trevor, *Live Now Pay Later*, Savoy 1980.

Summers, Anthony and Dorril, Stephen, *Honeytrap*, Coronet 1987.

Taft, John, *American Power*, Harper 1990.

The History of Rock, Orbis 1982.

Theatre Workshop, *Oh, What A Lovely War!*, Methuen 1967.

Thomas, Hugh (ed.), *The Establishment*, Blond 1958.

Thompson, Alan, *The Day Before Yesterday*, Panther 1971.

Thompson, Denys (ed.), *Discrimination and Popular Culture*, Penguin 1964.

Tynan, Kenneth, *A View of the English Stage*, Paladin 1976.

Tynan, Kenneth, *Tynan on Theatre*, Penguin 1964.

Vassall, John, *Vassall: The Autobiography of a Spy*, Sidgwick & Jackson 1975.

Vidal, Gore, *An Evening with Richard Nixon*, Random House 1972.

Vidal, Gore, *Homage to Daniel Shays: Collected Essays 1952–72*, Random House 1972.

Wallis, Dave, *Only Lovers Left Alive*, Blond 1964.

Warren, Robert Penn, *Segregation*, Vintage 1961.

Wenner, Jan, *Lennon Remembers*, Penguin 1973.

Whalen, Charles and Whalen, Barbara, *The Longest Debate*, Mentor 1986.

Widgery, David, *The Left in Britain*, Penguin 1976.

Wigg, George, *George Wigg*, Michael Joseph 1972.

Williams, Allan, *The Man Who Gave the Beatles Away*, Elm Tree 1975.

Williams, McCormick, Gardner and LaFeber (eds), *America In Vietnam: A Documentary History*, Norton 1989.

Williams, Raymond, *Communications*, Penguin 1962.

Williams, Raymond, *The Long Revolution*, Penguin 1965.

Wilson, Harold, *Purpose in Politics*, Weidenfeld 1964.

Wilson, Harold, *The New Britain*, Penguin 1964.

Wofford, Harris, *Of Kennedys and Kings*, Farrar Strauss & Giroux 1980.

X, Malcolm (with Haley, Alex), *Autobiography*, Grove 1965.

Young, Kenneth, *Sir Alec Douglas-Home*, Dent 1970.

Young, Wayland, *The Profumo Affair: Aspects of Conservatism*, Penguin 1963.

Zinn, Howard, *SNCC: The New Abolitionists*, Beacon 1964.

INDEX

396